A NOVEL ABOUT TARAS SHEVCHENKO

THE EXILE

TULUB ZINAIDA

GLAGOSLAV PUBLICATIONS

THE EXILE
A NOVEL ABOUT TARAS SHEVCHENKO

by Zinaida Tulub

English translation by Anatole Bilenko

Book created by Max Mendor

© 2015, Glagoslav Publications, United Kingdom

Glagoslav Publications Ltd
88-90 Hatton Garden
EC1N 8PN London
United Kingdom

www.glagoslav.com

ISBN: 978-1-78437-961-2

This book is in copyright. No part of this publication
may be reproduced, stored in a retrieval system or transmitted
in any form or by any means without the prior permission
in writing of the publisher, nor be otherwise circulated
in any form of binding or cover other than that in which
it is published without a similar condition,
including this condition, being imposed
on the subsequent purchaser.

CONTENTS

PART I

1. In the Black Yurt 5
2. Arrival in Orenburg 23
3. To the Jailiaou! 39
4. The First Friends 42
5. Kuljan 57
6. The Visit to The Gerns 73
7. On the Way to Orsk 81
8. Barimta 86
9. Private 3rd Company 91
10. Where the Alatau Sleeps Under the Ice 101
11. The Consolation 107
12. The Taming 128
13. Days and Thoughts 140
14. A Visit to the Bai 145
15. The Soul of the Steppe 157
16. The Ups and Downs of Life 163
17. Kozlovsky's Advice 182
18. The Battue 192

PART II

1. To the Blue Sea 203
2. From Orsk to Raïm 218
3. The Schooner Constantine 237
4. Lieutenant Butakov 246
5. On Kosaral 261
6. The Winterers 281
7. Two Schemes 286
8. The Raffle 292
9. The Big Toi 308
10. Thoughts, Conversations and Arguments 320
11. An Unexpected Role 330
12. Kuljan's Wedding 343
13. The Sailors' Song 351
14. Among Friends 364
15. An Artist From the Capital 377
16. The Polish Circle 389
17. At the Turn of Two Years 393
18. On the Outskirts of Orenburg 412
19. The "Showdown" 422
    Glossary Of Kazakh Words
    Used In The Book 439

PART I

1. IN THE BLACK YURT

Djantemir *Bai* had pitched the yurts of his *aul* in a valley several *versts* from the town of Orsk. It was a fine place for wintering, and it was not the first time Djaniemir had come here. A dense growth of reeds stretched along he banks of the river Or. The herds grazed on a rolling plain nearby, where the obliging wind swept away any extra snow so that the sheep and horses could help themselves to forage in winter. And when a snowstorm broke, they could hide in the valley where, apart from the yurts, stood Djantemir's house and a number of sheds for his goods.

When the frosts grew severe, Djantemir moved from his yurt into the house for three or four months, but as soon as the thaw set in he returned to his white yurt. The black yurts of his kith and kin, servants and *tyulenguts* were scattered along the slope of the valley in strict compliance with seniority and dependence on the *bai*: the newer the yurt was, the nearer it stood to the *bai*'s white yurts; while farther away, on the very edge of the *aul*, huddled the old, black yurts of the poor, the *jataks*, who for offal from his board and for old rags slaved for him from dawn to dusk. In the farthest corner, almost on the pasture ground, stood the black yurt of the herder Shakir, who was as old as his home, which barely withstood the thrust of the steppe winds assailing it on all sides through the threadbare felt, *tunduk*, and the poorly fitting entrance flap.

Shakir was well over seventy years old. Nobody in the *aul*, however, knew his exact age. He was an outlander to them. For thirty years he had been grazing the *bai*'s sheep and horses, and now for the first time he had been visited by a prolonged illness.

Just before the Russian Christmas, a snowstorm had suddenly broken out. The shepherds were late in driving the flock to the refuge of the valley. The frightened sheep burst headlong into the steppe, while the confused shepherds, pressed in between the animals, rushed about helplessly.

When the flock stampeded past the herd of the white-bearded Shakir, the old herder immediately sized up the situation. Whistling to his dogs, he overtook the flock on horseback and met it with loud shouts, whiplashes and a vicious attack from his trained dogs. The flock was forced to a halt, turned in the right direction and headed away toward the valley with no losses.

Old Shakir paid dearly for rescuing the flock. An acute attack of pneumonia brought him down three days later. His wife, Kumish, gave him hot tea with milk to drink, rubbed him with sheep fat, and put little bundles with hot sand all round him. Shakir pulled through, but he was not his healthy self anymore. He was so weak that he lay still for hours or was shaken by a hacking cough. And in the night he was drenched with a wearying, slimy sweat.

On learning about the rescue of his flock, the delighted Djantemir became generous and gave Shakir, apart from two sheep, a thin-legged colt from one of the herd's best mares. The colt was pathetically weak, because Djantemir's son Iskhak had been riding the pregnant mare so hard the previous year that her newborn could not get on its feet for three days and was already marked for the butcher's knife, when the children tearfully begged to have it spared.

Shakir was not a fine herdsman for nothing. He realized at once that a handsome horse would grow out of this little weak colt, and when the *bai* sent him the present, the old man's heart missed a beat for joy; he ordered his wife to crush two handfuls of millet and cook porridge for the colt every day.

"Shakir, my dear, you would have been better off if you cared more for yourself," old Kumish pleaded with him. "There's only the skin and bones left of you, while you refuse to eat horse meat! You're sick. You must get well. Nobody is going to work for us, and without work we'll die of hunger."

"Never mind! I'll be all right. Mark my words — he'll grow up into a horse that'll win any *baiga*," Shakir persisted, breathless for his shattering cough. "We won't have to feed him long; the snow is melting already — and that means spring is on its way. We'll go to the *jailiaou*, and there he'll fend for himself."

Kumish, swallowing her tears, meekly crushed the millet in a large wooden mortar, and added dung to the fire to keep it going.

While Shakir was ill, his son, Jaisak, tended the *bai*'s herd. The first few days the old man explained lengthily to his son what to do under this or that circumstance, but eventually he realized that Jaisak understood everything quite well himself and there was no need to worry about him.

With the advent of spring, the wolf packs became aggressive and sneaked up closer and closer to human dwellings. From his herders Djantemir started receiving ever increasing reports of a couple of fat-tailed rams or sheep having disappeared in the night, and at times a baby camel or colt was missing. Djantemir left for the Orsk Fortress to ask its commandant, General Isaiev, to stage a grand wolf hunt. But the general replied that a part of his garrison had marched off to fight the bands of the rebel Kenessary Kasimov, while the remaining troops had never hunted for wolves. But taking to heart the *bai*'s predicament, the general presented him a fine hunting rifle and two pistols. Back home, Djantemir gave the rifle to his son Iskhak, who was always sent to lend a hand to the herders when the wolves' howls were heard too close to the pastures.

Iskhak was still a youth and a general favorite of the entire family. He complied with Djantemir's orders reluctantly, holding that his father had enough of his own herders and shepherds. Once he got the rifle, however, he was eager to become a good marksman as fast as possible so he could distinguish himself at some great *toi*. On learning that his friend, also a *bai*'s son, was getting married in the neighboring *aul*, Iskhak diligently practiced shooting for several days, after which he mounted his horse, and without so much as saying a word to anyone, galloped off to the wedding, leaving Jaisak alone to look after the herd.

That night a pack of wolves sneaked up to the herd much closer than it had at any other time before. The frightened horses nervously pricked their ears, listening intently to the wolves' howls. And when the green dots of wolf eyes glittered in the dark, the horses stopped grazing altogether and gathered in a huddle: the colts and mares in the middle, the stallions in a tight circle around them to hoof off the attacking beasts.

The sky was curtained with heavy, black clouds hiding the moon. Everything around was gloomy, the color of lead-gray. Six dogs growled furiously and tore at their leashes. Jaisak felt his mount tremble as it tried to move to one side, while the wolves leaped about quite near, their glittering eyes flashing against the rippling snow here and there. They looked like weightless and silent apparitions flitting amid the snowdrifts. Suddenly a huge wolf the size of a six-month-old calf came over the nearest snowdrift in a high bound and landed right in front of Jaisak. The young man did not lose his wits: his sling went into a whining whirl over his head, and the heavy stone hit the wolf's ribs with a crunch. The animal jumped into the air, yelped from pain, and then melted into the murk like a lifeless shadow.

That instant, at the other end of the herd, a piercing scream of agony rent the air. Jaisak unleashed the wolfhounds and rushed in the direction of the scream.

"*Ait! Ait!*" he shouted to the dogs, spurring his horse and reaching for his *soyil*.

One of the wolves had crept up to the herd very close, and the moment a barely perceptible chink appeared between the cruppers of two stallions, he jumped through it and sank his fangs into the side of one stallion. Seized with unbearable pain, the stallion reared and froze for an instant like a motionless statue, the wolf still hanging on to the horse's side and tearing pieces of blood-dripping flesh out of the defenseless belly.

"*Ait! Ait!*" Jaisak shouted, rushing to the rescue.

But the stallion had dropped to the ground by then and was writhing in the throes of death. Half a dozen wolves attacked him at once, the wolfhounds pounced on them, and seconds later everything turned into a confused, blood-mad, viciously growling and teeth-snapping mass. Chunks of hair and flesh, splashes of blood flew on all sides, more and more wolves leaped from behind the snowdrifts and pounced on the scuffling heap or on the herd which instantly backed away and gathered in a tight huddle again. The horses neighed, snorted, kicked furiously and trampled the wolves. The vapor hovering over the fighting animals reeked of blood.

Jaisak killed two wolves with powerful blows of his *soyil*. One of the wolfhounds was lying with a ripped throat in a puddle of blood, and two wolves finished him off in a flash. Jaisak kept twisting on his horse like a gudgeon, dealing mortal blows to the wolves when suddenly the shaft of his *soyil* cracked and broke to pieces. Jaisak threw it away and swiftly grabbed his heavy *shakpar*, although it was not set with steel spikes like the ancient Russian bludgeons, its heavy blows cracked the wolves' ribs and skulls. Jaisak felt that victory was already close at hand when a young wolf suddenly jumped onto his back and started to tear at his sheepskin coat furiously. Casting aside the *shakpar*, Jaisak drew his knife and hit the wolf's throat, chest, and any other place he could reach. The wolf's fangs snapped by his ear like scissors. At last the fangs reached Jaisak's flesh. Blood streamed down his shoulder and side. His eyes went dim from pain, but he kept hitting the wolf with the knife until the animal dropped into the snow. Mad with fright and free of the restraint of the bridle, Jaisak's horse carried him at a gallop to the *aul*.

Jaisak was more dead than alive when he was taken out of the saddle. The *aul's* young men rode to the rescue of the herd which, unresponsive to the human voices, beat off the attacks of the depleted wolf pack together with the wolfhounds. On the snow lay six dead wolves and two hounds, and a third hound was at the point of death as he frantically pawed the snow. Two she-wolves were also bleeding profusely and crawling behind the snowdrifts when the *jigits* arrived from the *ail* and killed them; the rest of the wolves growled and snarled at people as they finished eating the dead horse and tore at the flesh of a still living mare, as its agonized neighing carried through the night.

It was only before dawn that the *jigits* brought together the whole herd, in which one more horse and colt were missing. On learning that Iskhak had gone to the *toi* with the rifle and left the herd in charge of Jaisak only, Djantemir flew into a rage and sent two *axakals* to Iskhak with strict orders that he return to the *aul* at once. He then took away the rifle, and personally gave his son a whipping, as though Iskhak were only a small boy. Djantemir had old Abdullah sent to Jaisak to have a look at his wounds and heal them, and he ordered that his daughter Kuljan take food to Jaisak and Shakir every day.

Time dragged. Shakir and Jaisak were lying side by side, covered with all the rugs and worn clothes that could be found in their black yurt. The first days Jaisak felt so bad he could neither speak nor think, and Shakir only sighed sadly, listening to him moaning, while old Kumish started to moan to herself against her will as she swayed from side to side, tears of pity and fear for her only son trickling down her swarthy age-furrowed cheeks.

As the sun climbed higher and higher over the steppe, the snow melted and turned gray. The mounds of snow, thawed as they were on the southern side, took on the peculiar shapes of white wolves sitting on their haunches. At midday their pointed muzzles dwindled as water dripped from them onto the ground. On one slope of the valley the earth had pushed out of the snow, and the first snowdrop burst into bloom. On her way from the river with a full water skin, Kuljan plucked the snowdrop and took it to the black yurt of old Shakir as she carried food there.

"That's for you, Shakir *Ata*, the first flower. See how warm it is outdoors: snowdrops are blooming in the steppe," she said, smiling kindly at the old herder. "Soon we'll move to the *jailiaou*, but this year it'll be a long trek, right to the river Illi where the mountains rise over the clouds and there are lots of berries and nuts and the grass is green and fresh the whole summer long."

The girl wanted to cheer up the old man, but unwittingly she touched upon a secret and painful thought that had been troubling Shakir for a long time now. Since Shakir was not working, Djantemir would not give him either a horse, camel or even a scrawny gray donkey. Shakir's old camel could barely carry the yurt, while his two-year-old colt had not been broken in yet, and there was no one to do it now. Traveling on foot was now out of the question for Shakir. How then would he get to the *jailiaou*? His strength was waning drop by drop every day. Besides, Jaisak was still bad. A month and a half he had been lying motionless, the wound would not heal, although old Abdullah had set the bones pretty well and frequently rubbed the wound with a rust-red concoction of algae taken from the Aral Sea to disinfect it and make it heal faster. So where would he and his family go during the long and blistering hot summer in the steppe? Shakir thought with despair. Would they have to stay behind at the *kistau* as *jataks* to watch over Djantemir's house and sheds and sow millet on the virgin lands?

Shakir fell to brooding as his toothless gums slowly chewed the mutton the girl had brought, and a heavy gloom gripped his heart. He realized that he was dying: not without reason had his mouth been suddenly filled with salty blood several times already, without him coughing or feeling any pain. At first he spat it out and covered the little red blotch with earth, but then he started swallowing the blood. Kumish, however, saw quite well that her husband was wasting away, and whenever the *aul* women inquired about his health she only sighed sadly.

After eating the last piece of mutton, Shakir wiped the bowl clean with his fingers, licked each finger, and gave the empty bowl back to Kuljan.

"Thank you, girl. Let your life be as bright and sunny as this first day of spring. Give my thanks to the *bai* for not forgetting an old man."

Kuljan smiled in response, and taking the other bowl from Jaisak, slipped out of the yurt.

"A fine girl," Shakir said musingly. "I wish you had such a wife, Jaisak. But the *bai* would hardly marry her to a beggar."

"She is already engaged, *ata*. Soon her wedding will be held, I suppose. To tell you the truth, though, nothing's been heard of her betrothed, as if he didn't exist at all."

The old man did not say anything in reply. He lay there and listened intently to the wheezing of his disease-ravaged chest, and recalled the years of long ago.

"You know, Jaisak," he spoke suddenly, "there was a time when we were not that poor. I was born here, in the Great Steppe, and then moved to the Bukei's Horde beyond the Urals. Djantemir would not have dared make me work for him then. I had a white yurt, big and fine. And I had two thousand sheep, a whole herd of camels, and two wives, older than your mother. It was a big family I had…"

"Yes, I know," Jaisak remarked. "*Apa* told me about it. I even remember how we crossed a big, big river on sheaves of reed one dark night. And then," Jaisak added uncertainly, "I seem to have had brothers. Yes, two brothers and a little sister with red ribbons in her plaits." He looked inquiringly at his father.

Shakir kept silent.

"Yes, you had," he said in a dull voice, at length, and propped himself up on his elbows with an effort, fastening the ragged robe at his chest. "I'll tell you everything. You must know the truth."

"In this steppe," he began, frequently falling silent to regain his breath, "the pastures are poorer and drier than on the right bank of the Ural. The wet meadows there are quite rich, the grass juicy and dense, and along the Ahtub and the Caspian Sea there are boundless expanses of reed. Just the land to enjoy living in and growing prosperous. But wherever there is grass and reeds in plenty there are a lot of rich men with hordes of servants and *tyulenguts,* and even more cattle. They seize the best lands and pastures by force. When I was as young as you, we freely crossed the Ural to winter on the far bank, and came back here in spring. But with time the Russian czar prohibited the *auls* from the Great Steppe from moving to the right bank of the Ural.

"We were under the rule of Sultan Bukei then. He pleaded with the czar to permit us to settle for good on the lands between the Ural and the Volga. The czar agreed, and we were happy at the news. Five thousand yurts moved across the Ural 'to the rich lands.' But our joy did not last long. As we learned, the shores of the Caspian with their fishing grounds and reeds had long belonged to Prince Yusupov and Count Bezborodko, and the lands between the Uzen and the Ural was the domain of the Yayïk Cassacks. Bukei died then, but his son Jangoz and his father-in-law Karaul Hodja were people without either a sense of honesty or honor, or a heart. Apart from the czar's usual taxes and *zakat,* he burdened us with a heap of other taxes. But we never had money, and traded just like we do now — for sheep, but not for money. Karaul Hodja came to an agreement with Yusupov, by which we were permitted to graze our herds on his lands for money. Whereas Yusupov's price was two rubles, Karaul Hodja demanded that we pay five. We suffered from hunger, while he grew rich on our tears. Besides, *aul* after *aul* came pushing from the Great Steppe across the Ural to winter in our parts. There came a terrible winter when snowstorms raged without end, followed by such glazed frost that no horse could smash the ice crust with its hoof. Day and night we were breaking the crust with *ketmens* and shovels, but half of our sheep flock still died. The rest could have been saved it we had been allowed to graze in the reeds, but the Yayïk Cossacks refused flatly. And we had no money to pay them…"

Shakir broke into a heavy cough and could not regain his breath for a long time. Then he continued his story, trying to vent his grief, which had been such a heavy burden for him to bear all his life.

"Our animals perished to the last lamb. Death from hunger stared us in the face. My older wives died that winter. Only Kumish, your mother, stayed alive. Just then a caravan arrived from Bukhara, with rice and flour for which we had neither sheep nor money to pay. Seeing our woe, the Bukharans started selling flour in return for children. Kumish and I went and did a horrible thing: we sold the elder children to save them from starvation and preserve the youngest child. They traded three bowlfuls of flour for a child. So we got nine bowlfuls. The boys survived, but your sister died a day after she was sold. The Bukharans visited us with abuse, demanding that we give you away in her place. And so we decided to flee to our homeland — here, to the Great Steppe. The Russians did not let anyone across the Ural at that time. We had to cross it in the dead of night. But we had neither boat nor raft to do so. We cut dried reeds, covered our heads with hay, and waded into the water. You were put on a sheaf of reeds and covered with hay, too. In this way we were not spotted, because a lot of hay and brushwood washed off the wet meadows by the flood was drifting down the river then. We came to this place, to Djantemir's *aul*. His father Undasin had once been a friend of mine, but he was dead by then. Djantemir received us well, like friends: he had a ram butchered, treated us to a meal, but when he learned that we were beggars... Oh well, you know yourself how we have been faring here —" Shakir stopped short.

Jaisak kept silent, but his tightly compressed lips showed clearly enough what intense bitterness and irrepressible hatred blazed in his heart.

"Listen to me, son," Shakir spoke again, spitting a clot of blood out of his mouth. "If you ever come across a Bukharan caravan or get to Margelan, look for the merchant Habibula

Omer there. He bought your brothers Kasim and Tyulenbai. And if fortune ever smiles on you, redeem them."

"All right, *ata*, I will. I swear I will," Jaisak said quietly, but firmly. "I'll get myself a royal eagle for hunting. They say the Russians pay big money for furs. I'll work hard. Don't you worry, *ata*. I won't let you die of hunger."

"There is one more thing I want to tell you, son," Shakir said quietly after a while. "Take care of our colt as you would of the apple of your eye. He's born of Karligach, the light-footed mare, and" — he dropped his voice to a barely audible whisper — "of Blizzard, the very same Blizzard that wins every *baiga*. The colt is priceless, but he has to be fed better, brought up and broken in really well. You know how to handle a horse and teach it so it responds to your voice and understands you without a whip. A horse, mind you, is a reliable, trusty friend: both in trouble and at a *baiga* it'll come to the help of its master. In it you will find your luck. I called the colt Abkozad, because when he's grown up he'll turn white as *airan*, and will be prized more than pure gold."

Jaisak listened, without saying a word.

"Do you hear me, son? Will you do what I ask you?" Shakir said and feebly lowered himself onto the piece of felt.

"I hear you, *ata*! I'll do everything you say, and my word is firm as an inscription on rock," Jaisak replied.

The old man sighed with relief, as if he had thrown an overheavy burden off his chest, but then he recalled something else and raised his head again.

"Djantemir, as you know, gives me ten sheep for a year's work. In thirty years that could have made a whole flock, but he deducts from my earnings for every sheep and ewe lamb a wolf pack tears down. Now I've got forty-five sheep and seventy ewe lambs. Remember that and don't let your memory grow rusty when he's paying off the poor," he finished, smiling with bitter irony.

Both lapsed into silence — Shakir, because the long talk had made him tired, Jaisak, because just then he was trying to stir his maimed fingers, and he sensed with joy that they were bending slightly, although a sharp pain stabbed him above the elbow or somewhere near the shoulder blades.

"Allah be praised, I can stir my fingers a bit now," he said to comfort his father.

A wane smile lit up Shakir's face, but his eyes, gazing into emptiness, were illuminated by an inward light that appears with people after some terrible suffering or when they approach the threshold of oblivion.

Kumish entered with a sack of dung, raked aside the ashes in the fire, and was about to lower the flap of the yurt when Shakir stopped her.

"Please don't! I want to breathe some fresh air. It makes me feel better."

"But the sun is setting, Shakir dear," she remarked timidly. "There's still snow in the steppe; you'll get cold."

"I'll die tomorrow," the old man said in a stern and matter-of-fact manner. "Let me admire the sun for the last time... and the land... It's so beautiful," he added quietly. "Tell the people to come and bid me farewell."

Kumish glanced at him with pain and horror, hung down her head, and started to move something by the fire with trembling fingers.

"I want to see everyone and bid them farewell," Shakir repeated with effort.

Suddenly both Jaisak and Kumish realized what a horrible truth stood behind these words. Wincing with pain, Jaisak made an attempt to rise.

"*Apa*, help me! I shall go," he said, but could not check the moan escaping his lips.

Frightened, Kumish rushed to her son.

"Lie down! I'll go myself! At once!" she mumbled, and quickly putting on a kerchief, slipped out of the yurt.

When she was back, a few men were already sitting in the yurt. White-bearded old men wearing soft boots, felt stockings, and warm *chapans*, made their salaams before the sick man on entering, then they nodded to Jaisak in a friendly way, and unhurriedly, as was proper for the occasion, settled solemnly around Shakir.

"How do you do, Shakir *Ata*," they said, calling him respectfully as they had never done before. "What is the matter with you? You must fight death like your *batyr* fought the wolves, but not yield to it. It is still early for you to say farewell to life."

"It has got the better of me, *axakals*," Shakir breathed out with effort, and a fit of coughing attacked him.

"*Axakals*, be like fathers to my son. He still needs advice from wise people at an evil hour. Good advice is dearer than a fat ram."

"Rightly so! We shall advise and help him!" the *axakals* responded, interrupting one another.

Jaisak's friend, the sinewy tanner Taijan, rumbled in his low voice:

"Neither his father nor mother have done him out of his share of a good mind. He himself can give good advice to others."

On saying that, he slapped Jaisak's shoulder in a friendly manner, making the latter wince with pain.

"*Oi boi*! I forgot about your wounds!" Taijan said. "Forgive me! How's your arm?"

"It feels a bit better," Jaisak replied. "I could stir my fingers today."

Shakir lay silent for a while, his eyes shut tight against the glittering snow. Then he raised his head again with an effort and looked around. "Where is Djantemir? What did he say?"

The drinking bowl slipped out of Kumish's hand. "But how can you trouble the *bai*! I just didn't dare to..." Suddenly Shakir said severely and loudly, with an unexpected force:

"Go and tell him: I want to see the son of my friend Undasin, and Rahmatulli's grandson. Tell him that Shakir is dying."

Kumish was so confused that neither her feet nor tongue would obey her.

Then Jaisak extended his sound hand to Taijan, and said:

"Help me get up; I will go to see him myself."

Clenching his teeth in pain, he got on his weak feet. Somebody threw a sheepskin coat on his shoulders, girded it with a belt, and helped him walk out of the yurt. The sun was already rolling along the distant horizon, slowly slipping down the other, unseen side of the earth. Cold air wafted from the steppe. Kumish lowered the flap of the yurt silently, raked the ashes aside, picked up some embers to light an earthenware wick lamp with sheep fat, and hung it by the *shangarak*. Then she put dry dung onto the embers, puffed at it, and a thin wisp of smoke curled up to the *tunduk*. That instant somebody obligingly threw hack the flap, and Djantemir entered.

"Salaam to you, Shakir, and to you, *axakals*," he said and settled in the place of honor where Kumish had hurriedly put the family's only piece of white felt with trembling hands. "What did you want to tell me?"

Shakir raised his fading eyes, and suddenly the glow of life was in them again.

"I want you to confirm the truth of what I shall say now," he said, gasping. "I am dying, Djantemir. To lie before death means to condemn my soul to eternal torment. Tell me, have I worked well throughout all these years since I returned lo my native steppe from beyond the Ural?"

Djantemir kept silent for a minute, thinking over whether an answer in the negative would bring him any loss or harm, but unable to hold the fixed gaze of the old herder, he nodded reluctantly.

"That I confirm. You have worked honestly and well. Kumish, too, has worked well, and your son has done a good job and fought the wolves like a real *jigit*."

"Yes, like a *batyr*," the *axakals*, silent until then, said of one accord. "He hacked to death six wolves — and that is no joke."

"He also wounded two she-wolves so badly they were breathing their last when our *jigits* arrived."

"Whenever a snowstorm broke, I rescued your flock as if it

were my own property," Shakir went on in a barely audible voice. "And now I'll explain why all of us have worked like we did. Our honor did not allow us to work badly. So confirm now Djantemir, what kin we come from, and that your father Undasin was my best friend and you visited our *aul* as a boy and were a guest in our yurt — in a white yurt like yours."

"Well, I did visit your home," Djantemir confirmed, this time irritated. "But you, too, Shakir *Ata*, had been my father's guest for weeks. We're quits on that point and nobody owes anybody anything."

"And nobody is asking anything," Jaisak flared up.

Djantemir only shot him a sidelong glance with the narrow slits of his eyes, and turned to Shakir.

"So what can I do for you, Shakir? I have a guest, the *akyn* Abdrahman, waiting for me now. I want to hear his songs. You're holding me up."

"I don't need anything," Shakir said hoarsely. "But Jaisak was mauled by wolves, because your son ran away to a *toi* with his friends and left my son alone. To award him — that is the debt of honor you owe me," he concluded, touching the most sensitive point of the *bai*'s code of honor.

Blood rushed to Djantemir's head. He was about to let bad language escape his lips, but his ear caught a whisper of indignation and a stir among the *axakals*. To make things worse, here were the elders of the entire kin with whom he had to reckon. The words of Shakir, who had never told anyone in the *aul* about his past, had produced a tremendous impression on them. So restraining his tongue which was ready to roll off abuse, Djantemir managed a forced smile and spoke out, lending his voice unusual warmth.

"I have not forgotten anything, Shakir *Ata*. I remember how you taught me to ride on horseback and told me old tales about Koblanda *Batyr*. I know very well the meaning of honor and I shall reward Jaisak. You, too, I shall not forget. So do not worry and get well."

Picking up the ends of his sheepskin coat, the heavy-set and haughty *bai* went out of the yurt, without granting anyone a parting look.

The men listened intently as the slightly frozen snow crunched under his receding tread. After his footfalls had died away, everyone started to speak at once.

"But why have you kept silent?" old Faizullah said, slapping one palm against the other. "We didn't have the slightest idea of what he had done to you!"

The tanner Taijan grated his teeth and spit out angrily.

"What a tight-fisted sort our *bai* is! He'll think ten times before he makes up his mind whether to give you two sheep."

"Two sheep won't save him," the thick-set Baimagambet threw in. "That scum's turned his father's friend into a servant."

"He's disgraced our entire kin," the bone-setter Abdullah droned away. "I wouldn't keep silent; I'd tell the people the whole truth. We'd force him to be human!"

A warm wave of sympathy seemed to have made the yurt a warmer, cozier and dearer place to live in. Kumish looked at the people and did not recognize them. It seemed that suddenly some secret recess of goodness had opened in their souls which she had not suspected before. In the meantime, the angered and excited men kept on talking, interrupting one another, and no one noticed that Shakir's head had fallen back and a heavy rattle came from his chest.

"Tea! Give him hot tea!" Jaisak suddenly cried out, rushing to his father's side. "He's dying!"

The next instant everyone went into a sudden bustle, trying to allay the suffering of the dying man in whatever way they could. Someone ran to a neighboring yurt where a samovar was aboil, and instead of a bowl of tea brought the samovar for the dying Shakir. Someone else produced drinking bowls from a trunk, filled them with fresh tea leaves, and moments later Kumish, swallowing her tears, was giving Shakir hot tea with camel's milk which Kuljan had brought promptly. Faizullah fed the fire with some additional dung which sent a sharp smell throughout the yurt and made the dying man cough heavily.

Taijan rushed out of the yurt and returned with some blazing hot bricks on a shovel; he put them on the fire and threw the smoking dung out of the yurt.

When the blue cloud of smoke dispersed, he went outside and carefully closed the *tunduk*. It became warmer in the yurt immediately.

But Shakir could not recover consciousness any more. He had spent all his effort for the last talk with Djantemir and was drained of strength now, his hair, grown longer throughout his illness, sticking to his sweaty forehead. His chest rose and fell heavily and spasmodically. The *axakals* were leaving the yurt one by one, after having said to Shakir warm words of parting. Only Taijan stayed behind to help the utterly exhausted Kumish and Jaisak who was still bedridden, his teeth firmly clenched lest he moan for the pain his wounds caused.

Shakir gasped for breath and thrashed the whole night through; one hour before dawn his last breath gave way to the serenity of death.

When the sun rose, eight old men came to the black yurt to wash and prepare the deceased for his last road in accordance with ancient custom, while Taijan and two *jigits* galloped off to the cemetery to dig a grave.

Kumish, as a woman, could not be present during the washing of the deceased. She did not leave his side to the last moment, because once he was covered with a shroud, she would never see his face again.

Shortly after, several women came for her and took her to one of the neighboring yurts where she was settled on a piece of felt, surrounded in a tight circle, and made to join a mournful *joktau*, a dirge with which every Kazakh woman accompanied her husband to the grave.

While the women sang the *joktau*, intoxicated by its somber beauty, the *axakals* washed Shakir, shaved his head, trimmed his beard and mustache, and dressed him in a shroud — a long piece of white cloth sewn together only on two sides, with an opening for the head. Then they wrapped him up in three long pieces of thin white cloth from head to toe, and tied his feet, hips, and body below the shoulders with three white kerchiefs. After that he was put down on his right side in the place of honor facing the entrance, and curtained off with a clean cloth screen.

Shakir's words must have hit Djantemir's pride painfully, because this time he did not sting himself and had sent the broad long pieces of cloth, kerchiefs and a luxurious Persian rug in which Shakir was wrapped before being carried out of the yurt, and had three fattened sheep slaughtered for the funeral repast.

The mullah intoned the prayers long and solemnly in the yurt, while Kumish, not daring to break the law, stayed outside, her face buried in the snow she was lying on. When at last the body of Shakir was put on a camel and the sick Jaisak placed in Djantemir's sleigh and almost all the men of the *aul* left to see Shakir off on his last journey, she got to her feet submissively and returned into the yurt where the women were already preparing the funeral repast.

Taijan and his friends had dug a deep grave in the rocky, frost-bound ground which had to be hacked with a crowbar, *ketmen*, and at times with an ax. By tradition, the grave was quadrangular. In the depth of it, Taijan had dug a lateral niche. The deceased was taken off the camel, unwrapped out of the rug, all the three kerchiefs were untied, the pieces of cloth taken off to become, by custom, the property of the mullah, and Shakir was lowered into the grave to the accompaniment of a prayer. He was put in the niche to lie on his right side, covered with the rug, the niche was boarded, the grave filled with earth, on which stones were placed lest wolves and jackals dig it open, and then a tombstone was put up at the head. Later on the name of the deceased, his years of birth and death would be engraved on the stone.

Everyone kept silent on the way back. Even the young *jigits* did not urge on their horses nor rush around the sleigh, trying to outrace one another as they usually did. Djantemir *Bai* sat silently in the sleigh beside the taciturn Jaisak, and when they approached the yurts, he muttered haltingly:

"Since a wolf tore your sheepskin coat and robe, I'll have everything new sent to you, and for your wound you'll get a camel, ten sheep and a horse. You can pick the best you see in the herd."

Jaisak gave a nod, having nothing to say to Djantemir in response.

2. ARRIVAL IN ORENBURG

The sun was slowly setting over the horizon that was as flat as the surface of a calm sea. The boundless steppe was spread out under the sun. The feather grass, still silky in its vernal attire, stood motionless and showed up white in the distance just like the evening mists in the lowlands of Russia's North. But it was parchedly dry in the steppe, without any dewdrops or other traces of humidity.

A tarantass sped down the road with a clang and rattle, leaving a comet-like trail of whirling dust stretching out far behind it.

"They must be needing me very much in Orenburg, if you're in such a hot hurry," one of the occupants of the carriage said with undisguised irony. He wore a round felt hat and was dressed in an old soldier's greatcoat over a crumpled tailcoat and a dirty shirt with starched dicky and collar, but without any tie around his neck.

"You'd have been better off if you swallowed your tongue and wrote less of those squibs, you *khokhol** versifier," the courier ensign sitting at his side snapped back. "It would have been

---

* *Khokhol* — derogatory name of a Ukrainian in czarist Russia

better for you and me: then we wouldn't have had to go to the other end of the world."

Shevchenko shrugged his shoulders.

The dust had made his throat sore and irritated his eyes. His whole body ached from the eight-day jolting without any sleep and rest, with only half-hour halts at the post stations to have the horses changed.

Dusk was falling. The sun declined slowly far behind them, and the blue air of the summer night, so unexpected and beautiful after the "white nights" of St. Petersburg, was approaching from the east.

"Thank God, there is a town over there!" the coachman suddenly roused himself, pointing his whip into the distance.

But because of the gathering night neither the passengers nor the gendarme sitting on the box beside the coachman saw anything, except for a huge solitary building with blank stone walls, the dome of a Muslim mosque, and a tall slender minaret at its side standing far out in the steppe.

A caravanserai, Shevchenko guessed, and even rose slightly from his seat as the *tarantass* drove nearer. He had talked about it with Brüllow the year before last: the mosque was built to the design of the painter's brother, the architect Alexandr Brüllow, but mentioning to the gendarme and courier the name of the teacher he loved so much would have been shrill blasphemy, so the poet only looked silently at the slender minaret which seemed to be soaring toward the first stars.

It was well into the night when the *tarantass* rumbled through a vaulted gateway and the exhausted horses stopped in front of an ordnance house.

The coachman had to knock on the oak window frames, the gate and the door with both whip and fist for a long time before a sleepy watchman reeking of raw vodka and sweat opened the door to let the arrivals enter the office.

"Where is the officer of the day?" the courier asked sternly.

"His Excellency has gone, and left orders not to be disturbed," the watchman answered hoarsely, and fussily went about lighting a candle from an icon lamp in the corner of the anteroom.

"I have brought a convict, a state criminal. Let him stay here, while I'm away at the commandant's office," the courier continued, pointing at Taras Shevchenko. "You shall be responsible for him. And you, sir, don't contrive any tricks during my absence. It'll only make matters worse for you," he added as he was leaving the room. "Let's go, Tishchenko!"

The heavy front door shut with a bang, and the courier and gendarme's footfalls resounded with a crunch under the windows outside.

Shevchenko was silent. The journey had exhausted him utterly. On his way he had seen the marshy lowlands of Ingermanlandia, the dense forests of the Kostroma and Vladimir provinces, towns and their suburbs, villages and fields, the imposing might of the Volga at flood time in spring, the black lands beyond the Volga, and the drearily desolate expanses of the steppe — all of this had merged into a motley jumble of impressions. "Sleep. Sleep only!" his weary body pleaded.

"Do you want anything to eat?" the watchman asked with a yawn. "I'll find a slice of bread and some water to drink. As for cooked food… if you'd come a bit earlier…"

"Give me some water; I don't want anything to eat," Shevchenko said and sat down on a bench.

The watchman brought a big bottle with water and, while Shevchenko drank long and greedily and could not drink his fill, the watchman said, scratching his hairy chest:

"Well, you'll have to sleep in the entrance hall. Just lie down on the floor there, brother, and don't worry, because it's clean: it was scrubbed with a knife today. Don't you worry; we don't have anything like fleas around this place. How come you didnt take any suitcase along?"

"Sleep. The only thing I want is sleep," Shevchenko repeated mechanically, handing back the bottle at long last. "I'll do without a suitcase somehow."

The watchman barred the front door with a heavy iron bolt on which hung a huge padlock, pocketed the key, let Shevchenko into the entrance hall, locked him up in the office, and added didactically through the door:

"Mind you don't smoke in there... or else you'll get chased down 'the green street' to the roll of drums."

Shevchenko took a look at his new surroundings. The only entrance hall window, grated with ordinary prison bars just like the window in the office, barely let in the wan light of a full moon rising leisurely from behind the distant horizon. There was no bench in the room. He chose himself a place by a wall and stretched himself out on the unpainted resinous floor planks, lay there for a while, without thinking about anything, unconsciously delighting in the silence, and then sunk into a deep, dreamless sleep.

It was unbearably hot in the office of the provincial border commission. The bright June sun pouring in through the windows had made the room so stuffy that the luxuriant fair hair of Fedir Lazarevsky had stuck to his forehead, and rivulets of sweat rolled down his face and dripped on an opened Personal File lying in front of him on the desk. It was horribly difficult to sit in the uniform of a civil servant with a tight, starched collar, but since this was a workday and office hours, he had to be dressed in uniform while performing his official duties. Lazarevsky sincerely envied the junior clerk who wore a printed cotton shirt and sat in a draft near the door where he heaved sighs now and then. The other tables on either side of Lazarevsky were empty. His friend, countryman and colleague Serhiy Levitsky had left for the post office to collect a parcel from his mother and old aunt, and Lazarevsky relished in advance the delightful moments in the evenings, when they would be looking through the new journals and books and regaling themselves on the tasty sausages, fruit liqueurs and other goodies which, along with the food for the mind, was sent to them by loving parents and relatives in Chernihiv Province. His other colleague Galevinsky, a secretary, or rather senior clerk, had left to get some blank forms they had ordered a long time ago.

Summoning his will, Lazarevsky forced himself to buckle down to work: he had to write an account on the results of an investigation into an intricate complaint, the disentanglement of which would have made even the devil go up in smoke in cool weather, let alone in a torrid blaze of forty degrees centigrade. Three times he started to write, and every time he had to throw it into the paper basket.

"On the grounds of Instruction No. 179 from the manager of the office of your Excellency, the Military Governor, of May eleventh of the current year, and on the grounds of my personal investigation of File No. 842, I have the honor to..."

Lazarevsky fell to thinking whether it would be better to write "to report" or "to inform"? What should his missive be called anyway: account or report? Of all the papers to write! Besides, the quills were soft that day as if they were not a goose's but a duck's or a hen's. And the inkwell was full of flies Every time the quill picked up a drowned fly there appeared a black blot on the paper. The words came out so clumsy, the work was so boring. Why did it have to be him doing it?

"Stepan, old chap!" he cried out in despair. "Bring me a bottle of kvass."

No sooner had Stepan's blue shirt flashed behind the door than the clerk Galevinsky rushed into the office, threw the bundles of freshly printed blank forms on the desk and exclaimed excitedly:

"They've brought in the Kobzar tonight!"

"Why make so much noise about it? I have a *Kobzar*," Lazarevsky restrained the clerk's outburst.

"But it's not the book I have in mind. The author, Shevchenko, has been brought here! The one who wrote the *Kobzar*," Galevinsky said. "I met the officer of the day who took him over from a St. Petersburg courier in the morning. He's at the fortress now, in the transit barracks."

Impossible! In the barracks! Lazarevsky thought. *So he was made a soldier? Or was he banished into exile? Just like the Decembrists, like Pushkin, Lermontov and Odoievsky for having dared to speak the truth out loud!*

Galevinsky was carrying on about the blank forms and the print shop, but Lazarevsky was not listening. He had to find Shevchenko at once and tell him everything that had accumulated in his heart throughout the lonely winter evenings and nights when his mind had dwelled upon the dear verses of the Kobzar! He had to help him. Immediately, then and there!

He swept the papers off the desk into a drawer, snatched his cap from a hook, rushed out of the office, and made for the fortress almost at a run.

He kept asking around for a long time until an officer told him where to look for the poet. With quivering heart he went past the guard, shoved a crumpled pass into his hand, and crossed the threshold of the partly empty barracks.

By the farthest window four half-dressed men were playing cards, accompanying the game with vile curses. Another pair was squatting before an oven, roasting something skew-red on a rusty bayonet. Yet another two were just loafing around, their eyes probing everyone alertly like some market crooks seeking an easy gain. On a bunk by the nearest window lay a portly man of about thirty-five years, reading a thick, tattered book.

It's him, Lazarevsky thought and went to the bunk with quaking heart.

In the morning, the courier Widler had indeed handed the poet over to the officer of the day, who in turn had the convict sent to General Liefland, the commandant of the fortress.

The general looked quickly through the file of the arrival and raised his eyes to him with curiosity.

The poet returned the look in a calm and intelligent manner. He gave brief and proper answers to the questions and did it with such a degree of dignity that the general found it difficult not to talk to him as an equal, contrary to regulations.

But the verdict was explicit enough in stating that this blue-eyed artist and poet was incredibly dangerous to the state. That was something the general's mind could not grasp, so he thought better of going into the details of the case, and he explained to the poet — just as laconically and formally as he would have done to an officer reduced in rank after a duel — that he would he assigned to the Fifth Line Battalion and sent to his place of service in a couple of days. Then the general ordered that Shevchenko be shown to the bathhouse, issued a new set of underwear, and put on the allowance list.

In the bathhouse Shevchenko was delighted to get rid of the dust and dirt of the road, after which he went to the barber. The latter made the poet sit on a stool, and then a pair of sharp scissors snapped and chirred long over his ears, snipping the thick hair off his nape and head and off his two-month-old beard.

Then the barber took an open razor.

"Give it to me! I'll shave myself," Shevchenko said, reaching for the razor.

"That's against the rules," the barber said sternly. "We've got such rakes around this place that if you give one of them a razor — slash! — he'll cut somebody's throat, yours or his own. A penal battalion is a penal battalion."

A chill crept involuntarily down the poet's spine. That's where he was ordered to be sent away by the obtuse and cruel Holsteinian, the "powerful Orthodox Czar of the State," as the recently approved national anthem, "God Save the Czar," went. Throughout the entire Christ-loving Russian army, German rods, drill, fist law, and stupid discipline held sway, but here, in these line battalions, it was carried to the point of being absurd.

"Don't be afraid; I won't cut you," the barber said, honing the razor rhythmically against a strop. "Every day I shave not only soldiers but the officers and the general himself," he continued, interpreting in his own way the shade of alarm that had passed across the lively face of the new arrival.

"Leave my side whiskers at least," Shevchenko asked.

"That's against the rules," the barber retorted categorically and snipped away at the remainder of the beard and the whiskers which Shevchenko had grown when he received the letter of enfranchisement and enrolled in the Academy of Fine Arts.

"But soldiers are permitted to have a mustache, and in the cavalry it is even a must. This gives them a dashing look," the barber said, lathering Shevchenko's cheek. "Want me to leave you a mustache? You *khokhol* chaps always wear mustaches."

"All right, leave it then," Shevchenko said with a sudden smile. "I'll have a mustache like a Zaporozhian Cossack."

The barber loved his trade and fussed around the poet for a long time, trimming and clipping his hair here and there. At last, satisfied with his work, he clicked his tongue with satisfaction:

"Everything's ship-shape! You are a picture of a lady's man!"

The barber produced a cheap little mirror from behind the cuff of his uniform and handed it to Shevchenko.

The last time he looked at himself in a mirror was on the fifth of May at a coaching inn at Brovary near Kiev, when he wore a tailcoat and had a nosegay of orange blossoms pinned to a lapel as the best man at Professor Kostomarov's wedding. Just over two months had passed since then — only sixty-five days, but looking out of the mirror now was a strange old man in whose eyes was such deep sorrow that it made Shevchenko shrink back involuntarily.

He had grown ten years older within these two months: deep wrinkles of sorrow creased his face from the nose to the corners of his lips. Without the groomed whiskers he was accustomed to, his immature mustache stuck clumsily over the drooping corners of his mouth like the bristling brush of a walrus. The curly dark-copper tuft on his crown was gone as well, and the close-cropped hair lay flat, making his bulging forehead look all the more disproportionately large.

"Just like a fine lady's man," the barber repeated, waiting to be complimented on his work.

I'm more of a horror, Shevchenko wanted to say, but remained silent and gave the barber a ruble.

Overjoyed to have been given an unexpected tip, the barber shot a surprised look at what he took for a peculiar customer, snapped smartly to attention, and shot out like he would have done in front of an appreciative general:

"Thank you very much indeed! I'll have a nip to your health."

In the barracks, Shevchenko lay down on his bunk, oppressed and shocked by the striking change in his appearance. But it was not the lack of his luxuriant hair and smart side whiskers that distressed him: in the cheap mirror he had seen the reflection of his inner torment and realized that he could not hide it behind a sham front of contempt or indifference.

He bit into his lip and turned away to the wall, but several minutes later he sat up and brought his fist down on the bunk.

"Enough! I'll have to learn to keep in check not only my nerves. I'll have to learn to control my facial expression and fashion myself a mask lest my eyes, lips or the line of the eyebrows betray my inner pain. And I'll make it a purpose. Yes, I will, whatever it may take me!"

That moment a man of about thirty with shining pitch-black eyes and a mop of curly disheveled hair of the same color came up with a peculiarly swaggering gait.

"May I introduce myself?" he said. "Kozlovsky, Andrei Kozlovsky! A nobleman."

"Shevchenko," the poet replied dryly with a slight bow, but did not extend his hand.

Kozlovsky did not bat an eyelid at such a greeting, and sat down at Shevchenko's side without any invitation.

"Mon cher, we've landed at the end of the world, as it were. Why did they pack you off here, if it's no secret?"

Kozlovsky's manners and free and easy tone irritated and jarred upon Shevchenko, and so he answered evasively:

"Well, you know how it happens. I wrote something, and some people didn't exactly like it."

"A promissory note, I suppose?" Kozlovsky understood it in his own way and seemed to be glad. "I autographed a couple of them myself. Papa and me, we've got similar handwriting; you might even say it's identical. Both of us are Kozlovsky, and both Andrei. Well, when the time came to pay my debt, my devil of an old man got wildly mad. 'I've earned all that by working my fingers to the bone,' he said, 'and you think you're just going to gamble it away?' Well, my mama saved me a couple of times, but then he went and put me away. The damned old gizzard! He'll croak one day, and you can be sure he won't take his filthy lucre down into his grave. But I'll pay him back yet!" He flashed his eyes angrily. "I'll settle accounts with him one of these days!"

"Please, excuse me," Shevchenko interrupted him. "All this is very sad, even tragic, I would say, but I haven't had a wink of sleep for eight days. My whole body aches from the jolting. I want to rest. Let's have a talk another time."

"I understand! *Comprene* and *pardon*," Kozlovsky said, jumping to his feet. "I'll be going! But... could I have *quelque chose* on credit... Well, at least for a quarter of a bottle of vodka or for a nip."

His brazen face abruptly took on a humble and cringingly pathetic look like that of a hungry dog at the sight of food.

Shevchenko searched in his pockets and gave him some coppers.

"Thank you ever so much!" Kozlovsky said. "Have a good rest!"

He made for the door with the same peculiarly swaggering gait, while Shevchenko stretched himself out on the bunk as before, but sleep would not come to him. Snatches of thoughts revolved in his mind in a restless swarm. The future rose before him in a black impenetrable curtain, while everything surrounding him seemed like a cesspool in which his life would have to ebb away. He got up, went to a water keg, drank of the water, and asked the orderly, making besoms of saltwort, to give him something to read.

"We're permitted to read only divine books," the orderly

answered after a thought. "Only those who belong to the Old Believers really care for such reading, but the nobility aren't interested much!"

"Give me something divine then," Shevchenko said with a smile. "An intelligent person can find a lot of interesting things in the divine writings as well."

The orderly took a thick Bible in a half-torn binding down from a shelf, blew a cloud of dust off it by the door, and gave it to Shevchenko.

"But mind you don't tear any pages out of it for rolling cigarettes," he added, and went back to his work.

On approaching the man lying on the bunk, Lazarevsky stopped in indecision. His excitement made him suddenly forget the name of the poet and all the words expressing rapture, love and idolization he wanted to tell him.

"Excuse me, are you Shevchenko, our Bard?" he asked in a stutter.

Shevchenko leisurely put the Bible aside, looked Lazarevsky over with distrustful and rather unfriendly eyes, and sat up unhurriedly. What did this young civil servant want of him? After everything he had gone through since his arrest, he suspected every official to be either a spy or provocateur the gendarmes used to plant in the prison cells of the Third Department. At best it might be simply a provincial philistine, for whom the appearance of an exiled "versifier" would be, if not a sensation, in any case interesting news which could be broadcast to the Orenburg ladies and matrons whom it was easy to "take in" on what was presented as a big secret.

"What can I do for you?" Shevchenko asked so coldly that any other visitor would have instantly lost every desire to continue the conversation.

But Lazarevsky did not notice anything. He only knew that this was Shevchenko, the marvelous magician of the word who for the first time had made the Ukrainian language sound with the same force and beauty as the Russian under the magic pen of Pushkin and Lermontov or the German in the fiery verse of Friedrich Schiller.

"My God! Where can I find the words to express what joy, what wonderful moments I experienced reading your Kobzar," he said. "Serhiy Levitsky and I have been reading and rereading it the whole winter through! We've learned almost all of it by heart. After we subscribed to *The Haidamaks* we counted the days when the book would arrive at last. We could have hardly dreamed to meet you! Why, it is such a ... such a –"

He stopped abruptly, realizing that he could not call this soul-trying meeting either joyous or happy and, carried away by his reverence and sympathy, he enclosed Shevchenko in an embrace.

Shevchenko freed himself with a light shrug of the shoulder, and without looking at Lazarevsky, answered dryly as before:

"Thank you for your appreciation of my work. I am glad you have enjoyed it."

"*Enjoy* just isn't the word. I was happy. We're missing our homeland terribly, for we are countrymen after all — from Chernihiv Province, and were assigned to this place after graduating from the university. We're in our third year of service here, and it's boring." The young man sighed so sincerely that for the first time Shevchenko looked at him attentively with an inquiring, although still distrustful look in his eyes.

Lazarevsky sat on the outermost edge of the bunk and looked at his favorite poet like a schoolgirl would have regarded a famous actor after a breathtaking stage performance. At the same time there was such a painful sadness in his look, and Shevchenko felt awkward for his distrust and reserve. But the bitter experience of the past two months had opened to him a facet of life which made him unwontedly cautious.

Lazarevsky wanted to tell him everything that was on his mind and to hear at once everything from the poet he adored. But he felt uneasy about asking him, lest he touch the fresh wound in the poet's soul. He faltered in embarrassment, not venturing to raise the most horrible, albeit most important question: Who had dared do such a thing to the poet, and why? Shevchenko had not been simply banished to this place like some of the other political prisoners, but conscripted by arbitrary force into twenty-five-year service as a private in a line battalion of the Orenburg Military Border District adjoining a wild steppe, where the ungovernable tribes of Kokand and Khiva frequently attacked the improvised forts and border posts.

In the meantime, the two suspicious characters squatting at the oven had stealthily moved up closer and, pretending to be looking for something in their tattered greatcoats, overtly eavesdropped on their new neighbor and the lanky bright-haired official. Shevchenko noticed them and chose his words with extraordinary caution, trying to speak quietly and vaguely.

Lazarevsky, however, did not see anything and was suddenly carried away.

"But how did they dare? Who, and why?" he almost cried out, throwing up his arms.

Shevchenko winced at such a display of emotion, and replied with deliberate clarity, sternly and dryly:

"By the supreme command of His Imperial Highness I, being of strong physical constitution, have been sentenced to military service as a soldier."

"Where are you being sent to serve?"

"I don't know. I've been assigned to the Fifth Line Battalion and will be shortly sent to my place of service," Shevchenko repeated, in an even voice, what he had been told by the commandant that morning.

"I wish they'd let you stay here," Lazarevsky said with a sigh. "Life is easier in a town anyway. I'll intercede for you and achieve my purpose. We have good, honest people here," he said, turning with a desire to act immediately. "You tell me what you wish and what I can do for you, and I, for my part…"

"Thank you, but I do not need any help," Shevchenko said, shaking his head. "I will help myself, and earn something for my livelihood. Even today the warden of the deportation prison asked me to teach his children. I'll manage somehow..."

Lazarevsky hung his head in confusion and embarrassment.

"And still... I am so inextricably indebted to you for all the beautiful things I have thought, reading your *Kobzar*! I see the common people and even the Kirghiz absolutely differently now. You yourself do not know what light and truth emanates from every one of your words!"

Emotion took his breath away, and his lips quivered.

"All right," Shevchenko said softly. "If I need anything, I will let you know, and you will help me."

"Yes, yes! Certainly!"

Lazarevsky clasped Shevchenko's hand and pressed it with both of his.

"Do not lose courage. It's just a temporary affair! Everything will pass! It cannot but pass. So hold out!"

Shevchenko looked round. The two suspicious characters in tattered greatcoats had come still closer and eavesdropped openly. Somehow he had to warn this trusting and exalted young man. Recalling nothing better than a phrase he had frequently heard in the aristocratic homes when the nobles warned one another not to speak without reserve in the presence of the servants, he said:

"Prenez garde: les gens!"

Shevchenko got up, letting Lazarevsky understand that it was time to terminate the conversation. Lazarevsky turned red in the face and jumped to his feet.

"Yes, yes. You are quite right, Taras..."

"...Grigorievich," the poet prompted, seeing off his new friend; and this time he shook his hand in a warm and strong manner.

Lazarevsky rushed out of the fortress as though he took wing, passionately determined to plead for Shevchenko, regardless of whether the poet wanted it or not. Without knocking on the door, he flew into the office of the manager of the border commission, General Ladizhensky, which he usually entered only on official business and timidly at that.

"Your Excellency!" he cried out from the threshold. "Shevchenko has been brought here. Our famous Kobzar! I saw him and spoke to him. What misfortune! We must help him somehow!"

The general looked up in surprise, regarded the young man attentively, tiny wrinkles fanned out from the corners of his usually stern, steel-cold eyes; a kindly smile fluttered and disappeared under his gray mustache. He understood that passionate and sincere impulse of the soul, but it had to be dampened somehow lest the cruel blow rebound on that bright-haired head. So lending his voice a ring of stern officialdom, the general said:

"First of all, young man, you forgot to greet me on entering, and secondly, Shevchenko most probably deserved such a bitter fate. Besides, such things have to be approached with particular care and thought before voicing one's sympathy for the convict, the more so before resenting the verdict of a court of law. And generally," he raised his voice, "I am utterly surprised that you approach me with such a request. The office I head is unrelated whatsoever to the Third Department of the Office of His Imperial Highness, which considers such matters, nor to the war ministry, under whose authority Shevchenko finds himself right now. So from all points of view I have no possibility or right to interfere in the fate of your protégé."

Lazarevsky was taken aback, his face turned red, he muttered something incoherently, his cap slipped from his fingers, and he darted out of the office. The general gave a sigh and shook his head. "That's how such effusive young men destroy themselves. He could get into an ugly mess now. But what a fresh and unspoiled nature he still has! He is on active duty for the third year now, but he is still as fervent as a student."

The general got up from behind his desk, picked up the cap, shook his head again, and rang a bell.

"Catch up with Mr. Lazarevsky and give him his cap," he ordered the courier.

Sad and oppressed, Lazarevsky returned to his office where he, together with Levitsky and Galevinsky, started to think how they might help Shevchenko. After some lengthy arguments they came to a unanimous decision to appeal to Colonel Matveiev, the official who was responsible for special missions in the office of the Orenburg military governor and who was considered omnipotent in Orenburg.

Matveiev came from the Ural Cossacks and in his heart condemned Czar Nicholas' regime which had considerably curtailed the old traditional privileges of the Yayïk Cossacks. A sincere and straightforward person, Matveiev hated to give ungrounded promises and dispense perfunctory consolation. After hearing out Lazarevsky, he was obviously moved and even excited. Lazarevsky pleaded that Shevchenko be left in Orenburg, where there were humane and educated people, good doctors, a library, and a kind of cultural life. The colonel did not promise anything, but the young man left his office inspired with hope and confident that their request would at least not be forgotten.

But when Matveiev had looked through Shevchenko's papers the next day, it turned out that the order on his assignment to the Fifth Battalion, billeted partly in Orsk, partly in the neighboring forts, had already been signed, while a copy of the order had been sent to the war ministry in St. Petersburg by special messenger.

Such hurry surprised Matveiev very much. He even had a horseman sent after the messenger, but the courier Widler had left Orenburg that very same morning and taken the messenger along in his *tarantass*. Matveiev's man, nearly riding his horse to death, turned back from the first post station, without having carried out the order.

3. TO THE JAILIAOU!

Ten days after the death of Shakir, the scouts Djantemir had sent to choose, secretly from the other *auls*, and lay claim to the best summer pastures in the Alatau mountains, returned from their mission. Everyone had guessed by now that this year the *aul* would wander much farther than they usually did, but no one dared ask the terrible *bai* about it.

On dismounting, the scouts went directly to Djantemir.

"Well?" the *bai* asked, without responding to their salaams.

"Glory be to Allah and his Prophet," Murzabai replied; Djantemir trusted this forty-year-old man, more than the others, for his thriftiness. "Beyond the river Hi it's already warm, but in the mountains the snow is still knee-deep. We have chosen a good place by a river fed from the huge glacier on the Kungei mountain ridge. Down below there are forests all around, full of berries, nuts and all sorts of fruit."

"I know!" Djantemir interrupted him. "Did you lay the *aul*'s claim to it?"

"Of course! We've tied the grass in bunches in nine places by the waterfall, shoveled away the snow, and laid out your *tamga* with black stones on the ground."

"And then the snow will fall and cover up 'my *tamga*' so that it will be impossible to find!" Djantemir remarked derisively. "You've made me happy indeed!"

"There is no reason for you to be angry, Djantemir *Aga*," Murzabai rejoined calmly. "We've painted your *tamga* in yellow on the steep cliffs, then we made notches with axes on the fir trees in a lot of places, and here and there we stripped the bark and branded your *tamga* on the fresh wood with red-hot knives."

"Oh, that's much better," Djantemir gave a nod of satisfaction. "A good thing you thought up. All right, go and have a rest. If it doesn't rain, we'll set out tomorrow."

In the sheds near the *bai*'s white yurts stood the light yurts intended for the summer pastures in the mountains All of

Djantemir's three wives — Zeineb, the thick-set Nurina, and Shauken — were taking down the yurts with the assistance of two servants, and the agile Kuljan was carefully looking them over and telling the servants which of the yurts needed cleaning or patching. Not far away the *jigits* were sharpening their *soyils*, knives and Bukhara yatagans on whetting stones, as if they were preparing not to travel but to engage in a *barimta* or some other kind of raid. In the yurts the women were emptying their trunks and packing separately everything they would be needing for summer, and chose for themselves and their children the best adornments and holiday dresses for the ceremonial departure, while the old people got ready their fishing gear, nets, hooks, and what they called "muzzles" to catch fish in the numerous steppe rivers they would be crossing on their way.

The trek was to be a long one. It would be a happy event only for the children and teenagers riding on camels beside their mothers or on horseback. Everything they would be seeing on the way would be entertaining and joyous. But the shepherds and herders scowled sullenly, since nomadic wandering spelled the hardest and most responsible work for them.

Kumish was worried: she understood that Djantemir would not postpone the departure even for the sake of his own son, but Jaisak could neither ride on horseback nor even get up on his feet without somebody's aid. Kuljan, who brought them milk and mutton every day as she had done when Shakir was still alive, met a weeping Kumish.

"What has happened, dear auntie Kumish?" she said, rushing to the widow.

"It looks like we will have to stay here guarding the winter camp," Kumish replied, swallowing her tears. "Jaisak cannot ride on horseback yet. And without any cattle we'll die here."

"But isn't he strong enough to ride a camel? Didn't my father fulfill his promise and give him a horse and a camel?"

"He did, hut where can I get a saddle for a man who still cannot sit or stand?"

"Zeineb has such a saddle," Kuljan exclaimed joyously. "I just saw it by her cattle shed."

"But will she give it to me?"

"I won't even ask her," Kuljan said with a jerk of her braids, her eyes flashing with an impish light. "Just don't ride with all the women up front. If anyone asks where you are, I will say that you went to the grave of Shakir *Aga* to bid him farewell and will catch up with the *aul* at the summer camp. So get on a horse, we'll put Jaisak on the camel, and you'll follow us way behind the *aul*. The horses and sheep will raise such a cloud of dust nobody will see you behind it, and if anybody sees the saddle when we make a halt for the night, they're not going to take it away from you, because I'll be doing the explaining then."

"May Allah bless you, girl," Kumish thanked her from the bottom of her heart, as a pale smile of joy touched her prematurely withered lips.

The morning of the next day was sunny and cloudless. One hour after dawn the *aul* was ready to depart.

The caravan set off in a strict, traditionally established order: the first to gallop ahead were three scouts who were to explore the lay of the land, warn the *aul* of danger if there be any, and choose a place for a halt or for the night. When they disappeared behind the horizon, they were followed by thirty *tyulenguts* who were well armed with *soyils, shakpars*, knives, slings, and Bukhara yatagans, and after them came the slowly and solemnly strutting camels.

Up front on the two-humped camels rode the women with their infants and children — all of them dressed in varicolored holiday garb which stood out vividly against the tender green of the vernal grass.

Behind the women the one-humped camels strode along with great dignity, burdened with light travel yurts called *jolim uyami*, and little summer yurts known as *turlin ujami*. Then came the cattle surrounded by mounted shepherds and herders, wolfhounds and sheep dogs. After them walked the camel bearing the sick Jaisak, alongside Kumish riding an old peaceful mare. A second detachment of armed *jigits* brought up the rear of the caravan.

They moved right across the steppe, without keeping either to streams, caravan tracks or even wells, because with the arrival of spring there was plenty of water everywhere.

After midday the caravan made a halt. The sheep and mares were milked, the flocks and herds were allowed to graze, but the men did not unsaddle the horses: they only slackened the girths and took off the bridles, while the guard intently watched the steppe lest any marauding band of Khivans or other Kazakh tribes at odds with Djantemir might fall on the traveling *aul* and snatch an easy booty. But the halt was uneventful, and three hours later the *aul* set off again after a good rest.

The camel bearing Jaisak strutted forward with a swinging gait, rocking the sick rider to sleep. His youth was gaining the upper hand, and his wounds were slowly healing. Jaisak was happy to stir the fingers of his maimed hand and feel the pain receding with every day. He was disgusted with having been laid up in the yurt, choking on the smoke and steam, and seeing day in and day out how his mother's slave labor for the *bai* was draining her last strength. He dreamed of catching an eagle in the mountains, training him for hunting fox, and selling a lot of furs for which the Russian "mayirs" paid lavishly — and then... The first thing he would do then was put up a good yurt, warm and clean, and maybe leave Djantemir's *aul* completely and wander about with his own flock. Occasionally a number of poor nomads got together into a wandering *aul* and gradually became not exactly rich, but in any case not as poor as they had been before. And then... then his sweet dream about a young wife — a gentle, bashful girl — made his chest rise and fall with deep, stealthy sighs.

4. THE FIRST FRIENDS

Levitsky and Lazarevsky sat by the window, drinking tea, as they leafed through the latest issues of *Sovremennik* (The

Contemporary), *Otechestvennye zapiski* (Annals of the Country) and *Severnaya pchela* (The Northern Bee) and exchanged occasional phrases. Suddenly Lazarevsky put the magazines aside, pushed back his chair, and looked out of the window. On the street in the distance he saw a man of medium height, wearing a round felt hat and a gray tailcoat. The man walked slowly down the street, at times stopping and regarding the buildings attentively.

"That's him! Shevchenko!" Lazarevsky exclaimed and dashed out.

Levitsky had not yet finished buttoning up his embroidered Ukrainian shirt when Lazarevsky led the poet into the room.

"Dear Taras Grigorievich, may I introduce you to my countryman and best friend, Serhiy Levitsky. Both of us studied at the Chernihiv Gymnasium and graduated from university at one and the same time — he in Kiev, I in Kharkiv. Now we're here serving on the border commission."

Levitsky was a broad-shouldered, sturdy man, tall of stature and seemingly much older than the somewhat lean and lanky Lazarevsky. His lively black eyes had a joyous expression, while his swarthy face bubbled with health.

Lazarevsky talked animatedly, not knowing where to seat his famous guest. "I have an elder brother, Mikhailo, here, too. He also works with the border commission, not in Orenburg, but in one of the forts."

"Could it be Orsk by any chance?" Shevchenko asked, sitting down.

"No, Troitsk. Why did you ask about Orsk?"

"It's where I am to serve. At least that's what the colonel told me this morning."

The friends exchanged glances in despair. Had Matveiev deceived them? Shevchenko continued speaking, after he had put his hat on the windowsill and wiped his sweating face.

"He called me over this morning and received me like a good friend: shook my hand, offered me a seat, and said that he had wanted to leave me in Orenburg, but the order on my assignment had already been signed and he had no right to rescind it. He asked me about St. Petersburg, Brüllow and Zhukovsky, and recalled Pushkin who visited these parts fifteen years ago to gather material about Pugachov. We had a lengthy conversation, and he issued me a leave warrant for two days."

The young men from Chernihiv exchanged glances again.

"Well, we can confess to you now, dear Taras Grigorievich that we went to see him about you yesterday evening. That's Matveiev. He's a decent and humane person, and if he could... It is very difficult to help you now, but I am sure everything will be managed with time. Oh, but why are we just sitting like this? Axinia, bring a samovar, quick!" Lazarevsky called to the housemaid. "Also bring from the cellar everything we've got from home. And fry some eggs for three."

Shortly after the samovar was humming and a sausage was sizzling on a frying pan Levitsky poured *horilka*, steeped in caraway seeds and anise, into glasses. The conversation flowed easily and without restraint. It turned out they had common friends in Kiev and throughout Chernihiv Province, the length and breadth of which Shevchenko had traveled. Soon it became clear to him what sort of people he was talking to and he told them about the Society of Cyril and Methodius and what he had been accused of by the czar's secret police. Both of the young men were overwhelmed by the tragic fate of Professor Kostomarov who in their student years had not been a professor, but was already known as a talented historian and connoisseur of antiquity. They were appalled by the actions of the traitor Yuzefovich and the careless Andruzsky whose unbridled tongue had caused the greatest harm to the poet. There was a ring of profound sadness in Shevchenko's voice when he told them what a cruel blow was dealt to Alina Kragelska, Professor Kostomarov's bride, when she learned about his arrest on the day of their wedding.

"That is why I am still wearing my tailcoat," Shevchenko

concluded with a bitter smile. "I was in a hurry to get to Kiev for the wedding. Kostomarov had invited me as his best man, but instead of a wedding the gendarmes rushed me off to St. Petersburg. I was apprehended in my summer clothes, because it was already warm in Kiev, the cherry and apple trees were in bloom and so were the chestnut trees, while in St. Petersburg there was deep snow."

He did not say anything about the interrogation. Levitsky and Lazarevsky tried to divert him somehow from his dark recollections, since they did not know yet that keeping silent and nursing his grief made if even more difficult for Shevchenko.

Every conversation has some unexpected break, and when such a moment of silence interrupted the conversation's flow, Shevchenko got up, went to the window and looking at the first stars on the sunset sky, suddenly started to speak about what had grieved him most.

"Worst of all were the sleepless nights in prison when there was no oblivion or rest. I felt as if I were in a stone grave; I looked enviously at the sparrows chirping outside, although I knew pretty well that every single moment they could fall a prey to a hawk or a cat which are as implacable as the gendarmes in their blue uniforms. And still I envied the sparrows.

"You know" — he dropped his voice to a whisper — "at such moments I wanted to turn into hundreds, into thousands of sparrows and fly in a flock through the bars of that cursed prison; or turn into hundreds of mice to burrow under the walls and come out into the light of the other side or, maybe, much farther — abroad, where I'd turn into a human again. I would lie on my bunk, sleeping, or sometimes I'd sink into a nightmare and it **seemed** to me that the executioners eavesdropped on my thoughts and were waiting to rush forward to look for me on the other side of the prison wall and trample the helpless mice in which my human essence rested, and when I became a human again I'd see that they had crushed my hands or eyes or ripped my liver, like Prometheus'."

Shevchenko's lips quivered. He poured himself a glass of wine and emptied it in one draft.

Tears had welled up in Lazarevsky's eyes; Levitsky stared at the floor.

"Did you write anything there?" Levitsky asked, pulling himself together with effort.

"I did — I'll title those poems *In Prison.*"

"Read something to us, if it won't distress you," Lazarevsky asked.

Shevchenko fell to thinking.

"Some of the verse I dedicated to Kostomarov," he said at length. "He is a good honest man, but he lives as if in a cloud, believing that schools and education alone will make people more humane and noble. A dreamer, a starry-eyed dreamer. No, that's not the way out! Around us there are tears, misery and slavery, cruel slavery, into which I was born as well. Tears won't move a crocodile! You have to have power, armies, guns and guillotines. Kostomarov, though, is not a fighter. But I like him. I like and respect him. He has been sentenced to imprisonment, after which he will be exiled."

Shevchenko lapsed into silence, probably recalling the opening lines of a poem, and then he recited. At first his voice sounded even and soft, but gradually it gained in force and rang out with tragic power.

"How wonderful!" the young men said of one accord. "Recite us some more, please."

Shevchenko recited again.

Lazarevsky could not restrain himself, turned away and ashamed of his tears, wiped them off with his fist.

"More," Levitsky asked in a dull voice.

Shevchenko's eyes glistened with struggling tears as well, but he checked himself and said: "All right, enough of fraying your nerves. I'll read you another, jollier verse, though written in prison as well." With a voice grown unexpectedly steadier, he recited:

> *A cherry garden at the cottage,*
> *Above the trees cockchafers buzz...*

Levitsky and Lazarevsky raised their heads. In their mind's eye they saw a peaceful evening in spring, with dancing chafers and trilling nightingales. The lyrics sounded so simple it seemed that this was not a poem at all, but a real landscape with recreated sounds, smells, a light warm breeze kindly fondling their faces. The walls of their bachelor's home seemed to have disappeared and opened onto their homeland, revived by the charming force of Shevchenko's talent.

Shevchenko fell silent, his hands pressed tightly against his temples.

"I am sure your friends in St. Petersburg will do everything possible to have you freed. They are influential people after all," Levitsky said.

"The dying man is always told that he will get well, and the prisoner sentenced to death that he will be pardoned," Shevchenko said with a bitter smile. "I haven't seen much of freedom anyway: I was born a slave, grew up a slave, and then became free, but not for long. And then, do we really have such a thing as freedom here in Russia?

Every one of us is like a dog on a chain, with the only difference that one's chain is a bit longer, while another's shorter. Well, enough about that," he said, bringing his fist down on the table. "All that is nerves, and I'll have enough strength to cope with the rest. We'll see yet who'll win!"

Axinia brought in the samovar. She brewed some fresh strong and aromatic tea. Shevchenko drank it with rum, delighted to feel its pleasant, invigorating warmth flowing through his body.

"How good it feels," he said, placing the empty cup on the table. "Last night and the night before I came down with a cruel fever. I caught a chill on the way: in St. Petersburg and right up to the Volga the nights were dreadfully cold, and the greatcoat they gave me is thin and threadbare."

"So go to the military hospital tomorrow," Lazarevsky said, happy to have hit upon the idea. "Maybe they'll let you stay here while you're ill."

"No," Shevchenko refused flatly. "Shirking isn't my cup of tea. The fever will rattle me some and then everything will be all right. Better tell me about the Orsk Fortress. It must be a pretty hole, since I am being put away there by the 'most pious autocrat'?"

"Well, how can I put it... We have never been there, but all our forts are very much like the Belogorsk Fort in Pushkin's story *The Captain's Daughter*. Orsk Fortress is to the south-east of Orenburg."

"How do you like our town?" Levitsky asked to divert Shevchenko from his thoughts of the bitter future.

"A wretched place I must say," the poet told him frankly. "When you walk down the street, you see only high-jutting fences on either side without a single tree or shrub, and all the buildings look so naked; they might have been covered with ivy, hops or vines at least. I haven't seen a single flowerbed under the windows. Its name, too, sounds so asinine: Orenburg. Does it stand for *long-eared town?*"

The young men burst into hearty, spontaneous laughter.

"That's where you are wrong, dear Taras Grigorievich. *Burg* really is from the German, but *oren* does not mean *ears* in German. It takes its name from the river Or on which now stands the Orsk Fortress, which itself was the original Orenburg. Later on it was thought that the upper reaches, of the Ural were poor in water for a big town, so the town was moved to this place where the river is much fuller."

"Oh, I see," Shevchenko said. Suddenly he began to sing in a pleasant, powerful baritone:

On the meadow, by the birch tree...

Levitsky, who had a wondrously beautiful tenor, immediately picked up the song, and their voices flowed forth, intertwining melodiously and harmoniously. Lazarevsky also tried to join them, although his voice was much weaker.

After that they sang a second, then a third song. The singing was interspersed by recollections about Kiev, their student pranks and sport, the boat rides down the Dnieper, the merry and noisy Kiev fairs, and the wonderful church choruses ringing under the ancient vaults of Saint Sophia Cathedral which was built eight hundred years ago and held the remains of the great lawgiver of Kievan Rus, Yaroslav the Wise, in a marble sarcophagus.

Levitsky produced another bottle of strong blackthorn homemade liqueur and poured everyone a full glass. It inflamed their minds and they burst into another song when suddenly a wooden cuckoo popped out of its neatly carved "house" on the wall clock and announced the hour. Shevchenko clutched his head.

"Oh, my goodness! It's half past one! The gates of the fortress are closed at midnight!"

"Stay the night at our place," the young men said, unabashed. "Tomorrow, that is, today is a Sunday and we'll deal with the unpleasant consequences through the very same Matveiev."

"I don't think you'll have to, because I've got a leave pass for two days," Shevchenko put their minds at ease. "But I'm afraid I'll be too much of a bother to you."

"Oh no!" Lazarevsky exclaimed. "We're very glad to have your company."

Nobody was in a mood to sleep, however. Only after the lights were out did the young men pluck up enough courage to ask Shevchenko to read the verse for which he had been so cruelly punished by Czar Nicholas.

Shevchenko recited them his epistle *To the Dead, the Living and the Unborn...* as well as his long poems *A Dream* and *The Caucasus*.

Levitsky and Lazarevsky listened spellbound. Some of the allusions, though, they did not understand, but they dared not interrupt the great Bard with questions. New and hitherto unseen and unknown horizons opened to their minds as they listened to his poetry. They seemed to hear the moans of the tortured and see the tears of slaves, as all these sounds merged into a single outcry of suffering, a mighty torrent of indignation and anger as mighty as the Dnieper's cataracts and as dazzling as a thunderstorm in the steppe. Here was an absolutely different Shevchenko, not the sad bard deploring the lot of a betrayed and abandoned country girl, neither a chronicler of the hoary past, nor a landscapist fascinated by the beauty of Ukraine's scenery. Before them was a formidable exposer whose words lashed out at the provincial lordlings, ludicrous in their aping of all things foreign, and at petty tyrants whose liberal word mongering did not stop them from committing any crime or exercising wanton and barbarous despotism.

Here was a champion advocating the overthrow of the obsolete czarist machinery of state. He censured the arrogant and adulating officials, bribers, vanity-minded persons and toadies, and he called on the people to shed their shackles and build a free, honest and new life, in which every man would find his place and his work — not that of a slave, but work chosen as a vocation to bring joy and lend a purpose lo human existence. And the young men understood that the verdict which had doomed the poet was prompted to the czar not so much by personal offense as by fear of the tribune of the people.

"I wonder whether he himself read that poetry?" Levitsky asked, after the poet fell silent.

Shevchenko shrugged his shoulders.

"Probably it was read to him or simply retold."

Nobody wanted to sleep. Their conversation was alternated by songs, in which they gave vent not only to their feelings and love for their homeland but also to what they had experienced, which a great Greek philosopher called catharsis — the purification of the emotions through art.

In the east, dawn was breaking, heralding the birth of a new day.

During breakfast Shevchenko's new friends asked him about his personal belongings.

"The manuscripts and drawings were taken away by the gendarmes, and the rest remained in prison," be answered indifferently. "With the little money I have about me I'll have to buy myself something for the summer, because it will be too hot and I'd look funny going around in a tailcoat."

That was enough for Lazarevsky to plunge into a flurry of activity. He called the housemaid Axinia and told her to clean and press Shevchenko's tailcoat, and to wash and starch his shirt. Levitsky offered to lend some money and a canvas suit. Shevchenko refused to accept the money but tried the suit on, and Axinia volunteered to shorten its legs and sleeves a little bit. Then she recalled that the husband of the landlady had recently died and left quite a few of his things. The young men took him immediately to the landlady who, on learning that Shevchenko was an artist and in exile besides, brought a summer coat from her wardrobe and flatly refused to take any money for it, adding to the coat several pairs of underwear, a straw hat, and a pair of warm winter trousers.

"This is not a present, but rather a down payment," she said to ease his embarrassment. "Once you are freed, you will paint a portrait of my late husband from this little daguerreotype. Consider me your first customer."

After parting with his new friends, Shevchenko took a walk around the town.

Dust and sweltering heat hovered over Orenburg. Its central part was a cluster of public buildings: the two-storied palace of the governor, beside it a large building occupied by the military district commander, a little farther away the Gymnasium, the building of the provincial revenue department, a military school, and a school for the girls of the nobility — all of them dull-looking in the heavy architectural style of Czar Nicholas' reign, and all of them painted with bright yellow ochre. On the square was a clumsily designed cathedral with a huddle of beggars on the porch, an arcade with short smooth columns painted white, and a little to one side was a prison castle — simply a prison with guards on the watch towers behind the tall brick walls. All around there were innumerable monotonous single-storey buildings of wood, with blackened, unpainted tiny windows, tightly shut gates, and tall enclosures without a single chink.

There were practically no civilians in sight, except for some occasional old woman carrying a couple of wicker baskets or pails of water.

Helmets and epaulettes. Epaulettes and helmets. Soldiers and Cossacks, Shevchenko thought as he walked across the hot velvety dust. It's not a town but a military camp.

The streets all looked alike: on the dirt road lay heaps of ashes, at the crossing was a pile of rubbish, and on the market place the wind was whirling around wisps of hay, dirty paper, husks and. dust. Salesmen or a proprietor-merchant yawned from boredom in the shops scattered here and there, and gawked at the strange pedestrian; and in the lower part of the town stood a green nondrying puddle in which two ducks splashed about and a mud-covered sow lounged. It seemed that the silence was suspended in the air along with the dust and sweltering heat, occasionally interrupted by the barking of a dog or the soul-rending sounds of a waltz coming from a barrel organ.

Without realizing how he came there, Shevchenko found himself in the steppe and suddenly saw on the horizon the outlines of the caravanserai and beside it the dome of the mosque and the tall stone needle of the minaret.

The minaret was much farther away than he had thought at first. Its narrow door was open. Behind it, in the semi-darkness, he saw the barely distinguishable stairway rising in a spiral. Shevchenko stopped in indecision: he wanted to climb the stairs and look at the steppe, the town, and the deep churning Ural River from thirty meters up, but the heat and walk had exhausted him, and it occurred to him that the faithful might take his unwonted intrusion as an offense against their holy shrine.

So Shevchenko only walked round the minaret, admiring its revetment of rose granite and the facing of intricate cornices of colored tiles covered with clear-cut geometrical ornaments girding the wall in several bands. Then he came up to the mosque and was about to cross its threshold when an old Kazakh wearing a white turban shook him by the shoulder and angrily gestured at his feet. Shevchenko stopped in surprise, but seeing that everyone entering the mosque took off their footwear first, he pulled off his shoes as well. The old man in the turban gave him a nod and motioned for him to enter.

It was cool and quiet inside the mosque. The air in it smelled pleasantly of the steppe grasses. Shevchenko wearily sat down on the deep-pile carpets covering the marble floor and crossed his legs in Oriental fashion. He did not notice how long he was sitting like that, engrossed in dreamy contemplation, while his tortured soul found respite and all his anxieties faded away in his torpor.

Loud voices from the threshold of the mosque jolted him back to reality. He got up and went outdoors.

Opposite the mosque rose the tall blank wall of brick of the caravanserai. A motley crowd milled about on the huge square of the caravanserai. There were quite a few Kazakhs, or Kirghiz as they were called at that time, and Russian merchants. Shevchenko was dazed by the varicolored and unexpectedly thrilling scene that unfolded before his eyes. He could not make up his mind what was better to look at: the arrogantly disdainful camels looking down on this feverish bustle, or the proudly dignified Bukharans in shiny silken robes and with faces the color of dark bronze, murky black eyes and aquiline noses, or the Kazakhs with their mysteriously calm slitlike eyes looking down from light-footed steppe horses, or the Uzbeks wearing lavish turbans bobbing above their gray little donkeys.

"Taras Grigorievich, can it really be you?" a familiar voice asked from behind him.

Shevchenko turned round: before him stood Levitsky in the company of a tall slender officer with the epaulettes of a staff captain.

"Let me introduce you to Karl Ivanovich Gern," Levitsky said. "He's a good friend of ours and a great connoisseur of literature and art."

"Connoisseur is a bit far-fetched," Gern said reproachfully, as he shook hands with Shevchenko. "It's just that I love honest, good and beautifully written fiction, but I regret being introduced to our best poet under the circumstances which have brought you to Orenburg."

Shevchenko took an instant liking to Gern.

"How did you get here and what are you doing in this place?" Levitsky asked.

"Just admiring and suffering. What torment it is to see such a lot of new, original and exotic things, without having the right to paint them!"

"I know! I understand and sympathize with you," Gern said after a moment's pause. "Look, admire and store in your memory everything. One of these days it may be useful and, the main thing, you must take care of yourself... for the sake of the people," he added quietly.

Shevchenko glanced at him silently.

"Still, what wonderful figures of people," he said after a while. "What faces!"

"As for us, we're here because life is so dull back in town. The appearance of a caravan is a great event that does not occur too often. Besides, you can buy wonderful things here at times."

"I, for one, am looking for a good English sporting gun," Gern joined in. "Unfortunately, I have not seen any today."

"An English gun?" Shevchenko asked, bewildered.

"Of course. The British are not at war with us, as you know, but secretly they supply arms and funds to those who do fight us. They are thus arming the Circassians. The Khivans, Bukharans and Kokandians have such wonderful carbines, shotguns, and rifles which our Christ-loving soldiers with their pathetic bullet belchers can only dream of. Generally, we – "

Gern fell silent abruptly on seeing the blue uniform of a gendarme.

"I am trying to find something for my parents who are lavishing Fedir and me with their parcels," Levitsky said. "Here's a shawl I bought for my mother. I wanted to buy a Bukharan robe for Father, but the price was formidable."

"The day after tomorrow the caravan will be moving on. Just before it leaves the prices will drop," Gern put Levitsky's mind at ease. "Let us go to a Turkish coffee house for a cup of the finest Turkish brew."

After coffee the friends strolled through the caravanserai, showing Shevchenko the performance of a Chinese acrobat, or stopping to listen to the singing of an *akyn*. Gern understood the Kazakh language and explained to Shevchenko that the *akyn* was singing of Koblanda *Batyr*, a hero of a Kazakh epos, and about Isatai Taimanov, the Kazakh leader of the uprising which had spread throughout this land some twenty or thirty years earlier.

"They have many wonderful ancient legends," Gern said. "The *akyns*, just like the rhapsodists of ancient Greece, bring them together into endless poems."

Gern must have taken an interest in Shevchenko For a long time he asked him about Ukraine, the Academy of Arts and Brüllow, Venetsianov, Tropinin and Shchedrin, and recalled how he had made the acquaintance of Alexandr Brüllow the previous year when he came to build the minaret. Soon they learned that they had common friends in St. Petersburg where Gern graduated from the Military Academy several years past. At long last they made to leave the square when Shevchenko stopped to look how water was being drawn from a well in the center of the square.

On either side of the well pit two inclined poles rose out of the ground. Their top ends were held together by a thick iron bolt with a pulley over which passed a strong rope. One end of the rope was tied to a large leather bucket holding about eight pails of water, and the other end was attached to the neck of a horse. To lower the bucket into the pit, the horse was slowly backed toward the well, and when the bucket filled with water, the animal was made to move toward the gate and stopped only when the bucket appeared over the well curb. After that an old overseer ladled out the water to the people with a huge scoop or emptied it into a stone-lined pool for the cattle, for which he was given several coppers.

"An interesting invention," Shevchenko said. "It must have survived from the hoary past."

"In this way, over three thousand heads of cattle can be watered within a day," Gern remarked. "Such a well is called a *shingrau*. It is dug wherever the ground water table is very deep and there are no rivers or lakes nearby. Where the ground water is high, the Kazakhs dig themselves a well in a day at every new camping site, and then, when they move to another place, they leave it behind to be used free by anyone. A *shingrau*, however, is not that easy to dig. It can be afforded only by a rich *bai* or khan. To dig and line the pit with stone costs no less than one hundred sheep. You must know perhaps that the Kirghiz do not pay with money but with sheep like our ancestors once did with marten furs. The owner of such a *shingrau* makes a good profit. The *shingrau*, though, was built by the Russians to revive caravan trade with Persia and Bukhara, and in the next few years with India perhaps."

"What a lot of things yon know about this place," Shevchenko said with a sigh. "I'd like to have a better knowledge of all this. But they'll be sending me off to Orsk in a few days. Back at the barracks I was told that an escort of guards is getting ready."

Gern fell to thinking.

"You know what, Taras Grigorievich, come to me tomorrow in the evening, and in the morning I will try to find out what will happen to you. Come by all means. My wife will be very glad to see you. She's a Pole; we have many Polish acquaintances in exile here, among them students, musicians, and even an artist. They have been forced into military service just like you, but most of them lodge out of barracks."

5. KULJAN

Kuljan was an orphan. Her mother, Djevger, a Turkmenian by origin, bore no resemblance to the Kazakh women inhabiting the foothills of the Urals. Slim, with large black eyes and unusually long eyebrows, and braids reaching below her knees, Djevger looked like a graceful statuette of ebony brought from India by some accident. At the age of seven she was engaged to an oldish Bukharan merchant who traveled with his caravans to the banks of the Volga and to the Urals. He often took her on these distant and difficult treks; when she was barely seventeen, he died of cholera not far away from the camp of Djantemir. Nobody knew where and how the libertine *bai* had cast his eye on her but, with the merchant buried, his brothers and commercial partners bartered the young widow for sheep the very next day — and the tender beauty Djevger shed her paranja and became the wife of Djantemir *Bai*.

The next spring she bore him a daughter, Kuljan, and two years later, a son, Rahim.

Kuljan was not fated to enjoy her mother's tenderness for long. Djevger was gradually fading away in the boundless steppes of the cold northern Kazakhstan, as she recounted to the girl the stories about the luxuriant orchards and vineyards of her homeland. At the age of six Kuljan became an orphan.

Without her mother near her, life became sad and dreary for Kuljan. Zeineb, Djantemir's eldest wife, did her no wrong; but beset with the cares for her own children as she always was, she paid the orphan as much attention as she did the watchdogs, while Djantemir did not like little children at all. Kuljan grew up a sensitive and dreamy girl who remembered her mother's fairy tales for years to come. Djevger was a remarkable storyteller: she changed her fairy tales every time, which made them always interesting to listen to. As she grew up, Kuljan started retelling the fairy tales to her little brother. She would find a secluded nook, sit down, gently put her arm round little Rahim's shoulder as if giving him a part of the motherly affection he had lost, and relate the fairy tales.

After Djevger's death Djantemir remarried and took a corpulent and lazy woman, Nuripa, for a wife. All day long she lounged around in her yurt, chattering with the servants, while the orphans, Kuljan and Rahim, grew up like the steppe feather grass, knowing no care, tenderness or kindness, .except for the moments when they visited the black yurt of old Shakir, who would make them a reed pipe or else give them something for a present, while his wife, auntie Kumish, treated them to a bowl of *airan*, stroked their heads, gave them a piece of still hot flat cake of corn, and then hurried back to milking the *bai*'s sheep or mares to make kumiss, and sometimes Jaisak would give them a ride on his back, kicking his legs and shaking his head in imitation of a mettlesome horse.

During the first few years of their orphanhood they never parted. But gradually Kuljan was being schooled to do a woman's work, while little Rahim, like all the boys, took a fancy for weapons, hunting and horses, and little by little brother and sister became estranged.

When her mother was still alive, Kuljan, just past the age of five then, was engaged to the son of a rich *bai* who camped far away from her *aul*. Djantemir received from the *bai* a substantial down payment in lieu of bride money, and, for his part, he paid the parents of the intended husband what was called a *kyit* which was always a little bit less than the bride money, because the kin of the bride-to-be was losing, while the kin of the future husband was gaining a worker instead. It was also agreed that the wedding would take place once the engaged children reached the age of fifteen.

Kuljan was past sixteen already, but her betrothed did not show up. Djantemir decided to wander that spring not to the Syr Darya River as he usually did, but much farther to see the *bai* and finally clear the arrangements for Kuljan's wedding.

The thought of leaving her *aul* forever frightened the girl. What was her intended husband, the strange *bai*'s son Ibrai, like? What if she would never be able to love him? She felt sad to leave even this desolate and monotonous steppe, so dreadful to every new arrival, yet so beautiful to her. Neither did she want to leave *baibishe* Zeineb, Djantemir's eldest wife. Zeineb never did anything wrong to Kuljan, and now after her daughters had been married off to other *auls*, she even invited Kuljan kindly to her yurt to tell her something interesting or to teach the girl the native customs. Kuljan was also loath to leave old Kumish and her son Jaisak who was maimed so horribly by the wolves.

Whenever she recalled the young herder, she blushed against her will and a peculiar tremor rippled through her body. But for nothing in the world would she tell anything about it either to Rahim, Zeineb, her girl friends, or even to her favorite dog Jolgusta, which followed on her heels everywhere and crept into her yurt during the nights to guard her against snakes and scorpions.

Yes, it would make her awfully sad to leave her *aul* forever. But on the other hand, she would get rid of her stepmother Shauken, Djantemir's fourth wife, who appeared in the *aul* in the spring of the previous year.

Djantemir did not tell anyone about his intention to have a fourth wife. Shauken was a rich widow from a clan living on the banks of the Irghiz River. Her husband had died some years earlier, leaving her with no children or relatives. Shauken managed her household alone and even set up her own *aul* which kept away from the others. Djantemir paid occasional visits to her, and only the old bonesetter Abdullah and Monbasar vaguely suspected the true purpose of his visits. Then suddenly the news flashed through the *aul*: the *bai* was preparing a *kade*, that is, a wedding present for his intended wife, and was about to visit her again with a large retinue of *nukers, tyulenguts* and relatives.

Several days later the *bai* returned, exhausted but pleased and merry, and for a long time thereafter the *jigits* were telling stories how they had been lavishly treated to food and drink, what a pompous and gorgeous *baiga* there had been, and how Djantemir's son Iskhak had beaten everyone on his stallion, the offspring of the famous Karligach.

Three weeks later Djantemir was again preparing to leave with his retinue — this time to celebrate his wedding. He said that he would return with his new wife in a week.

The whole *aul* was getting ready to meet the *bai*'s wife. Most of the men had left with Djantemir, while the *jigits* who stayed behind started to choose the best racers for the *baiga* and chased them wildly around the steppe, getting them accustomed to runs over long distances.

In the meantime, the white-bearded *axakals* made new and repaired old ceremonial saddles of polished wood with ivory inlay, the old women made new caparisons reaching down to the horses' hooves.

The women dressed in their holiday best. Kuljan was agitated and abustle more than anybody else. Her father's wedding had introduced a merry diversity into the dull life of the *aul*. Without a moment's rest she worked hard to get the *aul* ready for the feast: she lugged heavy pails of water from the well, dusted the thick carpets, cleaned the white yurts inside and outside, and only after all the work was done did she manage, with Zeineb's help, to make herself a new skirt and fit to her figure her mother's sleeveless jacket of velvet, and don a new gold embroidered skull cap with feathers. She was on her feet from the earliest hours of the morning when the bride and groom arrived.

Presently the ceremonial train of the bride entered the *aul*. The buxom Shauken seemed to be stouter and ruddier than usual. Her flat face, round as a full moon and marked with smallpox here and there, was glowing with triumph and self-importance.

The tall velvet *saukele* wedding headdress glittered with golden embroidery and the golden coins sewn onto it jangled. Similar gold coins sparkled on her sleeveless jacket of silk, and a light white veil — an invariable attribute of a married woman's dress — fell like snow-white froth down her back. Twenty strong one-humped camels carried parts of her new white yurt, and another five camels were loaded with numerous trunks holding her belongings. In half an hour the white yurts of Djantemir's family were increased by another one, the largest and most luxurious of them all, displaying the trousseau of the rich new wife.

The numerous guests and the entire *aul* admired enviously the sumptuous carpets, sheepskin coats lined with silk and velvet, the holiday dresses, china, saddles, *chaparis*, and colorful robes. The young *jigits*, as ancient custom demanded, surrounded the bride and sang a jocular wedding song with which an *aul* of the bridegroom met the bride.

The bride bowed low by custom as if taking seriously the song's advice to live by the commandments of Allah, but her appearance showed, in fact, that she did not intend to be a submissive worker in the *aul* and would bring it under her heel.

The guests broke up into groups, conversing, drinking tea and kumiss; then they were treated to a generous and tasty meal. While the *jigits* were lining up for a *baiga* far out in the steppe, the guests in the *aul* were entertained with wrestling, competitions in strength and dexterity, the archers shot their arrows at a gold *jamba* fixed on top of a tall pole. When the first horseman showed up on the distant horizon at long last, everyone rushed to the finishing line where the winner was to rein in his horse opposite the place of honor where Djantemir and his new wife sat in a circle of *axakals* and the most respected guests.

This time, too, it was Djantemir's horse which came first, although there had been a lot of wonderful racers from other *auls* taking part in the competition. Djantemir rejoiced openly, because when a horse of a bridegroom or bride won in a race it was considered a good sign for the newlyweds.

After the races other entertainments were staged.

By custom, the bride and her husband had to perform the first dance, but Djantemir was too corpulent and old for such frivolous activity. Following the generous meal and fat mutton with strong kumiss, he could not even get on his feet, so he accorded the honor of dancing to his younger brother Adilov.

The guests formed a big circle and clapped their hands in time with the music. Shauken made three rounds of the circle, and, fanning her sweating face, returned to the place at her husband's side, after which Kuljan entered the circle. She was all atremble with joyful impatience to dance. The *jigits* became animated and met her with joyous outcries. Her holiday dress emphasized her rare beauty. She looked like a gorgeous tropical butterfly which had unexpectedly flown out of the gray cocoon of an everyday dress.

Among the guests there were three *akyns,* Abdrahman being the oldest and most famed of them. This was not the first time he was seeing Kuljan, but it was only now that he discerned how beautiful she really was. Here was a delicate and graceful southern beauty, especially when compared with the heavy and obese Shauken. He even leaned forward, sensing how instead of a song in honor of the newlyweds, there originated in his heart the lyrics of another song devoted to the youthfulness of this girl who had suddenly ceased to be a child.

Kuljan continued to dance. The strings of the *dombras* and *kobyzes* sang for her. It was for her that the spring larks trilled in the heavenly blue up high. It was for her that the eyes of the *jigits* flashed with rapture.

Nothing escaped Shauken's attentive eye. The thick covetous lips on her flat copper-red face were tightly pressed together. Her small eyes seemed to have become smaller, and they flashed a bear-like rage lurking rapaciously under her eyelids. She leaned toward her husband and whispered something in his ear. Djantemir looked at his wife stupidly, without understanding what was up, then he gave a drunken smile, got to his feet heavily, and reeling, went toward Kuljan. Her arms were raised just then and she waved them over her head as if prepared to take wing, when suddenly she felt the heavy hand of her father on her shoulder.

"Go and tend to your household work! It is time you got used to helping your elders! I see all of you have got out of hand while I have been away for several days," he said hoarsely.

Kuljan stopped, surprised and lost, dropped her arms helplessly, and deep in her eyes, shaded by dense eyebrows, glistening tears welled up. She hung her head low like a cut flower, went out of the circle, and disappeared behind the farthest yurts.

What for? her pain-stricken heart screamed. What have I done to be put to such shame and abuse? Even the servants dance together with the guests today. Didn't I work before they arrived, or didn't I do well enough?

Bitter, undeserved tears dropped on her mother's sleeveless jacket, and there was no one she could share her first maidenly grief with.

The wedding party was getting ever noisier. Now the *jigits* were dancing an ancient militant dance with knives to the rumble of one big and three smaller drums, the jangling of tambourines and the whistling of the pipes of the hired musicians. After that it was the girls' turn to dance.

When the musicians grew tired of playing, the young people gathered by the bride's yurt, the *akyns* picked up their *dombras* and cast lots to determine who would be the first to sing. The first lot fell to the young *akyn* Azat. He went out of the guests' yurt, salaamed Djantemir and his wife, and struck the strings.

Azat's song did not last long, but it had captured everyone.

"*Oi boi*, what a wonderful song!" the *jigits* broke out of one accord when he fell silent. "He understands the horse like his own soul."

"Yes, it is a wonderful song!" the *axakals* joined in, nodding meaningfully.

"Thank you for the song, Azat," Djantemir said, and pressed the young *akyns* hand with both of his. "Sit by my side, drink some kumiss, and listen to the glorious Nurbai not as to your rival but as to a master of masters who rejoices in the successful performance of his friend and does not envy him."

Nurbai was a man of middle age. He was a frequent guest of Djantemir and always stayed long at his yurt. More than once did Djantemir bestow expensive gifts upon him. That was why Nurbai considered it his duty to be present at the wedding and compose a song in honor of the newlyweds. But on meeting Azat and the famous Abdrahinan at the *aul,* he was unpleasantly surprised. Instead of the role of an honored famous guest and adornment of a *toi,* he was offered the role of a common participant in a competition of *akyns* that was usually staged during the holidays of a *bai*'s kin. So when the exclamations of approval and praise in honor of Azat died away at long last, he picked up his *dombra* unwillingly and started to sing his song.

Shauken's face was wreathed in smiles on hearing Nurbai referring to her as a masterful woman leading her *aul* through the steppe by the call of her heart, the heart of a rich woman priding in her power. Her smile of self-satisfaction spread more and more across her face until she could not check herself and started nudging Djantemir to make him realize what a wife fate had sent him. Struggling with the overpowering drowsiness caused by the abundant food and drink, he responded with a sweet and complacent smile.

When Nurbai finished his song, a merry chatter broke out. The guests rushed to congratulate the bride who had earned such compliments from a famous *akyn.* The relatives nudged Djantemir in fun and whispered in his ear that now he'd have to be on guard lest his rich wife take his *aul* and Djantemir himself in her hands. For all the noise and jokes, everybody forgot about Nurbai or else remarked to him by the way:

"That's something yon noticed quite cleverly: it's the end of our *bai*'s rule."

"Now he'll be under a high hand and will be paying her a *zakat* and *yassak* like to a sultan or czar."

What could have been more abusive for an artist or poet? Everybody had forgotten about him! He bit his lips, clenched his fists, and was almost glad when Faizullah clapped his hands and exclaimed:

"*Axakals! Jigits*! Girls and young women! Enough of that noise! Let us better ask the famous Abdrahman to sing us his songs which bring joy to people and make the sun shine even on a cloudy day."

"Yes! Yes! Sing for us, our wise Abdrahman," the guests supported the suggestion. "We would be happy listening to you till dawn and even till the next midday!"

"Where is your daughter, Djantemir?" Abdrahman asked, tuning up his *dombra*.

"Indeed, where has Kuljan disappeared to?" Djantemir wondered, having forgotten by now that he himself had sent her away. "Hey, women, call Kuljan!"

Abdrahman had a good enough reason to ask Djantemir of his daughter's whereabouts. He had seen how the *bai* came up to the girl when she was performing her wonderful dance, and how his heavy hand placed on her shoulder suddenly clouded her eyes. He had also noticed with what rage and envy Shauken was looking at Kuljan, and decided, through his song, to open Djantemir's eyes in regard to his daughter.

The guests fell silent, and involuntarily their eyes glowed softly and joyously, while the girls sighed deeply and excitedly as if taking in the fragrance of invisible flowers. Even Djantemir grew sober. Heavy and huge like a bear, in an expensive oriental robe of silk, he got to his feet, went up to the *akyn*, and clasped him in an embrace.

"I thank you, Abdrahman *Aga*," he said, his voice quivering. "Thank you... Yes, Kuljan is a fine girl, pretty and gentle like a baby camel. But I did not want her to be in the way of the guests, because guests, after all, have to be given the first place of honor and the best piece of food," he explained lamely, and returned to his place at Shauken's side.

The guests suddenly started to talk and rushed over to the old *akyn*.

"Thank you, Abdrahman *Aga*," they said, interrupting one another. "None of the *akyns* will deny that your song is the best."

"Yes, yes, the best!" echoed the *jigits, axakals,* girls and young women, surrounding him in a tight circle.

"And Kuljan is worthy of such a song: she is spring incarnate."

"She is like a fairy bird that brings us happiness."

"Like the flower from the gardens of paradise," added the white-bearded close-mouthed mullah of Bukhara who had not spoken a single word since the beginning of the *toi*.

For Djantemir he was the highest authority.

The competition was over. On Djantemir's sign, Zeineb and Nurina brought a crimson robe of heavy Bukharan silk out of the yurt and presented it to Abdrahman with a low bow as the prize he had won in the competition.

Hardly anyone noticed what a furious glance Shauken shot at the mullah, and with what savage anger her little eyes flashed at the *akyn*, the guests and Djantemir.

From that day on she conceived hatred toward Kuljan, and at every opportunity kept ramming into her husband's head that the girl was dissolute, lazy, given only to dressing flashily and singing, without any desire and ability to work. At times Djantemir tried to argue, recalling Abdrahman's succinctly worded song and the mullah's opinion, but he fell silent the moment Shauken raised her voice, because an old man regards everything through the eyes of his youngest wife, happy that he is still loved or rather made to believe that he is loved.

So Djantemir silenced his tongue and ordered Kuljan to do all sorts of work around the *aul*. In winter when the old herder Shakir was taken ill, and then Jaisak took to his bed after he fought the wolves, Shauken went after the girl again, and to humiliate her stepdaughter before the whole *aul*, she made her take meals to the black yurt. The stepmother did not suspect, though, that only in Shakir's yurt could the orphan recall her late mother out loud, find peace for her soul, and talk freely about her dear brother Rahim whom Djantemir had sent to study at a *madrasah* in Omsk not so much out of respect for education as exclusively for the sake of prestige.

Although the *aul* had set out in the middle of April, it was dry and unusually hot in the steppe; the next day would be the beginning of the most difficult trek across the Karakum Desert. Broiling heat and calm portended a storm which in the Karakum was much more terrible than the wildest blizzard in February; not without reason did Djantemir call all the *axakals*, shepherds and herders for a council during a halt.

"The main thing is to preserve the cattle," he said. "We'll have to walk across the desert for three or four days, and there will be only two wells along our way."

"There's a third one beyond the valley swarming with snakes," old Mirzabai added, hacking into his fist.

"I know. But it has too little water, whereas we have over five thousand cattle and ourselves to think about. Then there are also the camels. So water them today as much as they can drink, and apart from the usual load, put two water skins on each. Water the horses as much as you can, too. A clever horse will drink more when its master asks it to. We'll move on at midnight so as to cover as long a distance as possible by dawn. Throughout the day we'll be resting. Mind you, the nights in the desert are very cold now. Let your women dress the children warmer, and don't forget about quilted robes and mittens yourselves."

Up till then the *aul* had been crossing a damp green plain where puddles of snow water stood out in silent blue. Then they entered the realm of drifting sand with steep dunes up which the heavily loaded horses could barely clamber as they sunk knee-deep into the sand. The worst off were the sheep. One mile across such sandy terrain exacted much more effort than five miles of green steppe, and the people gladly swerved to the rocky places they came across here and there in the sea of sand.

The caravan made a halt when the sun was already high. By midday the heat was so intense it blistered bare feet. A slackless thirst plagued the people. All the pails, water skins and bottles had been emptied by now, and there was still a day's trek to the first wells. During the night the *axakals* remembered a trick of the Khivans, and when the caravan passed salt marshes, they picked up handfuls of salt that sparkled like snow in the moonlight. In the daytime they dissolved it in water and rubbed their bodies with the solution which made their pores contract and secrete less sweat. Those who had failed to pick up the salt looked at the sagacious old men with envy.

At six in the evening the caravan set forth again. The sinking sun was bright, but the sky in the west seemed to have been reddened with blood or the flames of countless fires raging behind the skyline. Looking at the fiery sunset, the *axakals* exchanged alarmed glances and shook their heads.

Walking became ever more difficult, because the respites under the blistering heat of midday did not augment anyone's strength. Djantemir sent out thirty horses and twenty *jigits* to help the shepherds pick up the exhausted sheep and carry them on the unloaded horses.

Just before dawn they reached the first wells full of spring water. The people drank greedily and could not have their fill, after which they watered and fed the animals.

By the time the sun started to beat down on the desert the people were fast asleep after the trying night march. Nobody knew how long they had been sleeping when a piercing whistle made them jump to their feet. Bleary-eyed, nobody could understand what had happened. A dry yellow mist hung in the air, shielding off the sun. Clouds of dust rose from the crests of the dunes like throngs of apparitions, the wind chasing them somewhere into the distance. The storm toppled the light summer yurts and tents, scattering dishes, carpets, clothing, and pails on all sides. People shouted and caught all these things flying about them, or else tried to find refuge from the storm as they pressed to the camels' sides. Swept off their feet under the onslaught of the wind, they covered their heads with whatever tatters they could catch. The camels, however, remained lying quietly on the ground, feeling instinctively that this was the best way to survive.

The storm raged on. A sharp stone cut Kuljan's cheek and a heavy piece of felt hit her side. Horror-stricken, the girl clasped a *kerege* and shielded herself with the felt from the driving stones. Her dust-filled eyes watered with tears and squinted in pain. Kuljan tried to go round a yurt to hide behind it from the wind, but a new gust, more violent than anything before, picked her up and swept her away. She tried to catch hold of something but the wind carried her farther and farther away. Then she suddenly slipped down a steep slope and rolled into a deep ditch between the dunes, gasping for breath and stunned, unable to get up or even stir. A hot dry dust kept piling on her from above, pinning her down under its heavy burning burden.

I have to get up; I must get up, the thought flashed through her mind. But she only stirred weakly and then lost consciousness.

The storm raged for another hour, turning the desert into a choppy sea of huge dunes which lifted their heads and dashed away with incredible speed like tumbling billows.

When the storm had spent itself, the people rushed about, looking for their wives, children and relatives, while Djantemir yelled in his yurt which had been half buried by the sand. The *aul* poor started to dig into the sand with their hands, because no one had any spades, *ketmens* or even a piece of board to work with. At long last Djantemir crawled out of his yurt and clasped his head in despair.

"Where is the flock? Where is the herd?!" he screamed at his kin and servants.

The people looked at each other in confusion. The camels were already on their feet and their usually contemptuous eyes looked calmly and proudly at the people. The saddled horses with slackened girths snorted and shook the sand off their pelts, but there was no more than half the horses left and the sheep had disappeared altogether.

"Where is the flock?! Where is the herd?!" Djantemir kept yelling ever more loudly.

Presently Shauken came out of her yurt.

"Do not ask, but order!" she interrupted her husband sharply. "Make the women and old men dig up the belongings of the *aul* and the men look for the animals."

Shauken's words seemed to have made Djantemir sober, and the *jigits* themselves had realized by now that finding the flock would save them from death by hunger. They quickly tightened the saddle girths, jumped on the horses and galloped off into the probable direction the storm had driven the flock.

First of all the people of the *aul* raised Zeineb's white yurt which collapsed at the outset of the storm. The elderly, corpulent Zeineb had almost suffocated under the weight of the *kerege*. When she had come to, she joyously pressed her little grandchildren to her side, and asked:

"Where is Kuljan?"

"What? Wasn't she together with you?" Djantemir asked. "She was but when the yurt collapsed she disappeared somewhere."

"Call Kuljan!" Djantemir ordered. "Who saw her during the storm?"

"She dropped in at my yurt," Shauken said reluctantly. "She opened the flap and let a lot of sand in, so I ordered that she lower the flap, but she got angry and left. I haven't seen her since," Shauken lied, concealing how she had actually chased Kuljan out into the storm.

Everyone started looking for the girl, but she was nowhere to be found, neither in the yurts nor in the collapsed *jolim uyami* by the rocky hills. So people started probing the sand with poles, and whenever a pole struck against something soft, the sand was carefully dug aside and either a rug, a rolled up carpet, or at times an unconscious person was unearthed. While the unconscious were coming to, the search continued, but there was no trace of Kuljan.

Jaisak was lying off to one side and moaning quietly: when the sandstorm had broken, he dropped to the ground between the camels and shouted to his mother that she quickly take cover at the foot of the rocky hill

On learning that Kuljan had disappeared, he got up and made a second round of the camping site, probing the sand with a *soyil*. But his search was in vain, he only found the dead Faizullah who had suffocated under a dune, and his teenage grandson. They managed to bring the boy back to life. But still there was no trace of Kuljan. Crushed with despair, Jaisak stuck a hand into his pocket and found something soft and silky in it. It was a ribbon from Kuljan's braid he had found in the morning and forgotten to give her back. He clutched it with a feeling of sadness and suddenly recalled his wolfhounds and Jolgusta, Kuljan's favorite dog. There were only four of his bold four-legged friends left after another two had died fighting the wolves. Jaisak called the dogs, let them sniff the ribbon, and ordered them to seek the scent.

The wolfhounds started to run in circles, their snouts close to the ground. Jaisak went up to his workhorse, tightened the saddle girth with one hand, and taking hold of the horse's withers, swung into the saddle with an effort.

"Where are you off to?" Kumish asked, frightened.

"To look for Kuljan," he answered matter-of-factly.

"But you're not well yet! Stop!" she cried.

Jaisak did not so much as turn round. He rode slowly, looking intently at every bump and wrinkle on the ribbed sand. The wolfhounds and Jolgusta circled around him. Now they seemed to have picked out the scent, then they stopped again, raising their snouts and barking in confusion. Some time later all of them suddenly dashed ahead, ran up a high drifting dune, and rolled down its opposite steep side. Here they sniffed the ground again. Then Jolgusta went down on her haunches, lifted her head and broke out in a drawn-out howl, while Koskar and Barbass started to dig the sand for all they were worth.

Jaisak's heart missed a beat on hearing that dismal howl. He jumped from his horse, slid down the slope of the dune, and helped the dogs with a spade.

If it had not been for the piece of felt which Kuljan covered herself with against the hail of stones, she would have suffocated long ago. The felt had bent over her head in a small vault and had thus trapped some air. She had lost consciousness during the last burst of the storm, and so was buried not too deeply under the sand. Jaisak dug the sand with quick strong movements, which made the pain in his shoulder so unbearable he bit his lips until they bled. A corner of the felt came in sight, then a limp suntanned hand. After throwing aside another five or six spadefuls of sand, he raised the felt, picked up the unconscious Kuljan by the waist and pulled her out. Jaisak started to force air into and out of her lungs as he had once seen the Yayïk Cossacks doing to a drowned man. He did it awkwardly and unrhythmically, but still after some minutes the deathly yellow face of Kuljan turned a dim pink, and a light breath escaped her parched lips. She stirred them, trying to open her eyes, which made her moan faintly.

"Oh, my eyes," another moan escaped her lips. "Sand…"

He did not have a drop of water about him nor a clean handkerchief to wash and clean her eyes under the heavily ringed swollen eyelids. He had nothing, except for the ribbon by which the dogs had picked out her scent. He lifted one of her eyelids with a gentle touch of his finger and cautiously started to pick out the sand with the ribbon folded in two. She gave a moan, tore herself from his hands, but he checked her gently and said:

"Have patience, Kuljan *Djan*. Your eye is full of sand, have to clean it. So be patient, my dear."

"It hurts," she said with a moan again, but did not struggle in his hands anymore.

When one eye was clean, Jaisak, not knowing how to ease her pain, licked first one and then the second tear-filled, bloodshot eye. His spittle soothed her eyelids and allayed the burning pain.

"Do it again!" she asked quietly, when her eyelids had dried. "I feel better when you lick them."

He bent forward, pressed his temple against hers for a moment, and her eyelids brushed against his cheek several times with a barely felt touch like the petal of a flower or the wing of a butterfly.

Kuljan started. Overcoming her pain, she opened her eyes for a moment, and their eyes met. It was no more than a fleeting glance. No more than a brush of his eyelids against her temple — the lightest breath of tenderness — had made both of their hearts miss a beat.

A delicate blush beautified her cheeks. Shyly and carefully he helped her to her feet and onto his horse with his sound hand, and walked alongside the horse, going round the steep slope of the dune.

They did not exchange a single word nor did their eyes meet anymore, but both realized perfectly well that a cherished secret had penetrated their hearts, a secret which they could never tell anyone in the whole world, because human language still lacked such limpid, fragrant and ethereal words.

6. THE VISIT TO THE GERNS

The next morning the battalion's quartermaster-sergeant brought Shevchenko the full set of a soldier's outfit.

Putting on the uniform, Shevchenko seemed to awaken for the first time since his short rest among kind people. The thought that he would be wearing this uniform through his twenty-five-year stint in the army beaded his forehead with cold sweat.

Of the three uniforms he was offered none fit him. Marking with a piece of chalk the places that had to be expanded on the largest of the uniforms, the quartermaster-sergeant grumbled angrily:

"My, what a paunch to grow, God forgive me for saying so! What's good for you in height doesn't come together at the belly. Never mind, our drill will get the fat out of you in no time."

For some reason Shevchenko believed that he had to pay for the uniform, and as he sadly calculated in his mind the expenditures he would have to incur, he asked:

"How much do I owe you for all that?"

"Forty rubles," the noncom answered, without batting an eyelid.

Shevchenko counted out the money without arguing. Two skinhead recruits, who had come to receive their uniforms as well and had witnessed the scene, could barely swallow their laughter and ran out of the barracks where they gave vent to their bridled passions.

"What a fool!" they roared with laughter, almost going down on their knees and clutching their bellies from the fun. "Did you ever see such a freak?! And he's supposed to be a nobleman! An artist, they say. Studied at some sort of 'cademy!"

"What is going on here?! Why this wild laughter?" the stern voice of an officer suddenly rang out.

At the sight of the officer the soldiers snapped to attention. "Your Exlency, we've got a fool of a transit convict here. The quartermaster-sergeant brought him a uniform for which he paid money."

"Who is the fool you are talking about?"

"We don't know. Shevchenko's his name."

The officer went into the barracks. The orderly on duty jumped to his feet and rattled off the report.

"At ease!" the officer waved his hand, and asked, "Who's Shevchenko here?"

"I am," said Shevchenko, who had changed into his canvas suit again.

"That's no regulation response!" the officer remarked, not

knowing yet how to react to the man's liberty for which an old soldier would have been dispatched to the guard-house at once. "What is the proper regulation response?"

"Excuse me, sir, but ... I haven't learned it yet," Shevchenko mumbled, snapping to attention.

"All right, you'll have enough time for that." The officer smiled involuntarily. "So tell me the truth only: how much did you give the quartermaster-sergeant and what for?"

"I paid forty rubles to the soldier who brought me the uniform. He said that it costs that much."

"Did he demand the money?"

"Oh no. I just asked the price and he told me."

"Did he take the money?"

"Of course he did."

"What a scoundrel!" the officer said bursting into laughter. "Never mind, he will return you the money right away, Do not worry. But I advise you to learn the regulation responses as fast as possible in order to avoid trouble."

What the officer said to the quartermaster-sergeant remained unknown, but fifteen minutes later the sergeant, raving mad and his face brick-red, flew into the barracks and threw the crumpled bills on Shevchenko's bunk.

"Here you are! Choke on your money for all I care, you mutt! You damned squealer! I don't need your forty rubles. I didn't ask for them, did I? Or demand them? I just took them, because you're such a fool who doesn't know what's what in life!" he spat out angrily, and without waiting for a reply, rushed out of the barracks as madly as he had entered it.

In the end, toward the evening, Shevchenko received the niform not from the quartermaster-sergeant, but from the battalion tailor.

Then he was called to the battalion office and given a leave pass for a total of eight days during which time, as it was explained to him, he did not have to show up in he barracks at all or, if he wanted, he could come for breakfast, dinner and supper.

It warmed Shevchenko's heart to realize that kind people could exist everywhere.

Neither did Gern forget about the poet. He read attentively through Shevchenko's entire dossier and was struck with surprise: there was everything in it — the indictment, examination records and the verdict, but not the verse which had sealed his cruel fate. That was why Karl Ivanovich could not fully grasp the utter hopelessness of the poet's situation.

Shevchenko arrived at Gern's home at the appointed hour. Gern immediately saw him into the dining room and introduced him to his wife.

Gern was on the wrong side of thirty, a tall, slender man, which made him look like a twenty-five-year-old. Everything in him — his face with its high forehead lined by wavy chestnut-colored hair, lively clever eyes, well-cut nose, and groomed silken mustache — was consonant and refined.

His wife, Sophia Ivanovna, had a typically Polish appearance: blond hair, dazzling white face with a faint blush, roguish dimples, and full rosy lips. She invited him to the table, poured him a cup of tea, and offered him rum and tasty patties with cherry filling.

A lively conversation began. Some minutes later Shevchenko had a feeling he was among old kind acquaintances. Sophia Ivanovna told him that there were a lot of her compatriots living in Orenburg as exiles. Among its residents was also the artist Chernishov whom Shevchenko would have probably met in St. Petersburg. She asked him to visit her home more frequently and was sincerely saddened when Shevchenko informed her about his approaching departure to the Orsk Fortress.

"Oh those fortresses!" she said with a sigh. "Many as they build them, there is still no peace."

"My dear, there is nothing you can do about it but getting used to being the wife of an officer. We have built twenty-nine forts now, if we add to them the Raïm Fort and another two on the rivers Irghiz and Turgai, for which I myself chose the sites the year before last."

"What do you mean? I thought you simply took back Kenessary's wife who had been held as a hostage," Sophia Ivanovna said, surprised and even excited.

Gern gave a smile.

"A Russian officer's wife is not permitted to know everything" he said. "At times there are such things as official secrets." Turning to Shevchenko, Gern explained: "Here we have to be actors performing a variety of roles: now we're simply military men, then diplomats, and sometimes itelligence officers or topographers. Indeed, two years ago I went with a mission to a chieftain of the rebellious Kirghiz. You've probably never heard about him, or have you?" He interrupted himself, and when Shevchenko shook his head, Gern continued: "The Kirghiz have rebelled against us frequently, right from the times of Pugachov, but throughout the past ten years the rebellions of Kenessary Kasimov ave been the most significant and, I should say, the most organized. He is a man of no average standing. Probably he dreamed of uniting all the scattered tribes — the ones in Siberia, around Tashkent, Khiva, Kokand, and our local Kirghiz — into a single nation. That is why he not only fought battles, but also wrote laws for them. For instance, he abolished the kin courts and introduced a single court of law instead, codified the ancient Muslim tax, the *zakat*, which every sultan or khan levied for his own interests, and made it into a single state tax that goes to the state treasury — not to the Russian, of course. In short, he tried to become a unifier of the Kazakh lands. Under the aegis of Great Britain, as you might well understand. In general, he is a rather narrow-minded nationalist and by no means a champion of freedom. A typical despot and slave owner.

"We, that is, our command, suspected for a long time that Kenessary was playing a double game. That was why General Obruchev decided to show him up and had him summoned. Our adversary was rather dangerous, because the Emir of Bukhara had supplied him with six hundred rifles and fifteen pieces of artillery along with hundreds of shells.

"We realized pretty well that behind the Emir of Bukhara stood the Britons who had been dreaming of seizing our Central Asian markets long ago. At the same time the Khan of Khiva sent Kenessary fifteen *argamak* horses, two saddles covered with gold leaf, and a whole caravan loaded with gun powder. Understandably, all these presents had one and the same label: Made in Great Britain.

"So we, too, marshalled a substantial force against him when suddenly we received a strange order from St. Petersburg: Kenessary was to be pardoned for all his previous rebellions, as were his family and all of his relatives; even his favorite wife Kulimjan was to be returned to him. To compromise on all controversial points, a mission or delegation with Dolgov at its head was to be sent, and I, as a general staff officer, was to accompany Kenessary's wife, with secret orders to choose two strategically useful sites — one on the river Irghiz, and the other on the river Turgai — for the forts.

"I carried out the orders, and did it so shrewdly that Kenessary did not suspect anything — otherwise we would not be sitting here at this table drinking tea.

"When we arrived at his camp, he isolated us completely from his people and started to delay the negotiations, not letting us leave either. We wandered around with him for a month and a half, but did not achieve anything. In the meantime, Kenessary had written to St. Petersburg that he would cooperate with Russia, provided we destroyed all our forts built on Kirghiz land. Obruchev got mad at that, and we immediately laid the foundations of the forts on the Irghiz and Turgai, while Kenessary wandered off to the Syr Darya on the banks of which we laid the foundations of the Raïm Fort as well.

"Officially, we are not at war with anybody, but a lot of blood keeps flowing. The old soldiers will tell you quite a few things about the local campaigns, attacks and sieges," Gern concluded, sipping his tea that had become cold by then.

The story impressed Shevchenko immensely. Neither in St. Petersburg nor in Ukraine had he ever heard about this undeclared war.

"I simply cannot understand — who needs this steppe? It's just a desert and nothing else!"

"That's true, but this steppe is crossed by trade routes running to our Central Asian markets — to Bukhara and Persia, to Afghanistan and, in the future, to the fabulous India. We must render them safe. Central Asia is a gold mine for commerce. Small wonder the Britons covet it so much and send rifles and guns to its semi-savage chieftains."

"So that's the reason. I see," Shevchenko said. "A little less than a hundred years ago the poets called the czarina 'the Godlike Czarina of the Kirghiz-Kaissak Horde' in their odes. The tribes pledged loyalty to her back in those years, but I see they are still fighting us."

"Oh, old chap, there is more to it than you realize," Gern said. "Just count what a lot of taxes we have levied on them: on the yurts, fishing, salt from the salinas. Could you really survive even one day in such broiling summer heat without salt, eating not bread but meat and milk? Even the wood for the *kereges* is taxed. These people have never held money in their hands, because they trade in sheep. Their poverty is appalling. It's a wonder they still exist in this world. To tell you the truth, it is their *bais* who have reduced them to such misery. But we, for our part, are not too eager to offer these people any salvation either. All right, Taras Grigorievich, let us repair to my study for a smoke and chat about your affairs."

When they were in the privacy of the study, Gern asked the poet to recite the verse which had made him a convict. Shevchenko complied.

After hearing him out, Gern remained silent, reflectively drawing on his cigarette and flicking the ashes into an ashtray now and then.

"Yes," he said at length, "now everything is clear to me: your poetry does not simply call for a peasant rebellion, but for an assault on the Bastille. The gendarmes have a good nose for such things. They smelled right away where the smoke was coming from, and to make your punishment the more direful, they drew the czar's attention to the very lines in which he and the czarina were mentioned. Ours is a rancorous and vindictive monarch. There is one thing I want to tell you frankly, like a friend, and I beg your pardon for my frankness. Your poem *A Dream* has one verse which, as I see it, does not sound ... too good: you make fun of the empress for her illness. She is a fairly old woman, by the way, who does not interfere in state affairs."

Shevchenko gave him a look of disguised irony.

"I am a peasant and a serf," he said. "No one has taught me how to treat a sick empress. But, unfortunately, I know only too well how fairly old, sick serf women, who don't meddle in politics either, are treated by the blessing of the czars, czarinas and their courtiers. I wrote the way people see it. Although ... from a narrower, human point of view, as it were, you are probably in the right."

"I told you that, because I took a liking to you," Gern said, confused, and strongly pressed the poet's hand. "I pray to God that back in St. Petersburg these lines will be forgotten as soon as possible."

After seeing Shevchenko off to the wicket gate, Gern went back into the house and, deep in thought, made for the bedroom. Sophia Ivanovna was already in bed, reading the *Kobzar*.

"Has he gone?" she asked, raising her eyes from the book. "You know, I am not too good at Little Russian, but I really like his poetry. It is written in such a novel way, simply and touching. Did you find out what he was convicted for?"

"I did. His affairs are bad. I am afraid that neither the czar nor the czarina or even their descendants will ever forgive him several lines from his poem. He was not simply forced into the army, but prohibited from writing and painting. Besides, in his dossier there is an order to have the poor chap transferred to the farthest fort, from which it would be difficult to bring him back that fast. He has been assigned to Orsk where the battalion is commanded by Major Meshkov, an unusually hidebound person and a blockhead: a martinet of an officer who rose in rank from the noncoms. I am afraid his Prussian drill will plague the life out of the poor chap. General Fedyaev and I had a talk about him and wrote a letter to Meshkov, asking him to pay particular attention to Shevchenko and help him in whatever way possible."

7. ON THE WAY TO ORSK

The sound of a bugle roused Shevchenko from sleep in the transit barracks. He got up quickly, dressed, had his breakfast, received his travel rations, and packed his personal belongings. At seven sharp he was summoned to the office where a young officer he did not know was waiting for him.

"Shevchenko?" the officer raised his eyes inquiringly.

"Yes, sir!" the poet said, snapping to attention.

"Good morning" the officer said and extended his hand. "I am Ensign Dolgov. I am off to Orsk and am taking you with me. Are you ready?"

"Yes, sir!"

Beyond the town the road followed the winding course of the river Ural. The riverside meadows were gray with the dew, and the dust did not whirl about yet on the road. Dolgov shot sidelong glances at his companion, probably studying and observing him. The poet kept silent as well, not knowing how to behave in regard to someone who might probably be his future commander.

"Tell me, please, what is dearer to you — painting or poetry?" Dolgov asked suddenly.

Shevchenko did not reply at once.

"I don't know. When I was a boy, I was fond only of drawing. Then I was captured by poetry, but now... now I am like a mother of two children who have been committed to prison. They will die if nobody helps them, because their mother's hands are too weak to pull down the walls of that prison," he said and fell silent, angry at his unexpected impulsiveness.

"Hm-m... I see," Dolgov mumbled and suddenly turned to Shevchenko. "You know, you are the talk of the whole town. There is an old captain in Orenburg. He should have been discharged a long time ago, but he's still serving. Some days ago I was talking with Karl Ivanovich when that captain ran up to us and said, 'Did you hear? There's some versifier arrived here who's got a horrible verdict: he's prohibited from singing and talking. But that makes life impossible!'"

Shevchenko smiled wryly.

The conversation came abruptly to an end. Dolgov had never met a real poet or artist before. From his childhood he believed such people to be next to supernatural, something like prophets or clairvoyants, so usual simple words did not come to his mind to keep the conversation flowing. Shevchenko, on the other hand, knew that most of the army officers were either drunkards, gamblers, or duellists, and though Dolgov did not exactly resemble such a type, Shevchenko tried to keep a low profile and answer the questions as tersely as possible.

Every twenty or twenty-five *versts* they changed horses at a station. The road twisted along the Ural as before. The meadows around were grassy and luxuriant. Occasionally they came across shady groves and little gullies, at the bottoms of which gurgled cold streams, where they stopped several times for a drink of water. The sand gritted under their teeth, and soon Dolgov's snow-white service jacket and Shevchenko's white shirt turned gray. But the heat was gradually subsiding.

"When's the next station?" Dolgov asked impatiently.

"Over the hillock there, sir, will be the *stanitsa* of Ostrovnaya, and then it's another ten *versts* to the station," the coachman said, taking the whip. "Giddup, you sluggards!" he laid the whip across the horses' rumps.

The *tarantass* went up the hillock like a whirlwind.

Shevchenko almost let out a cry of pleasant surprise at what appeared before his eyes: down in the valley spread a large *stanitsa* immersed in the dense verdure of orchards and tree-enclosed meadows. Snow-white cottages shone in the sun with a dazzling cleanliness. The green unbound tresses of weeping willow trees dropped languidly over a pond, and a girl with a garland of live flowers and a varicolored, neat *plakhta* skirt drove a long-horned cow down the road.

For a moment Shevchenko thought he was back in his Ukraine in the environs of Sedniv on his way to pay a call on his friend Andriy Lizohub — and his heart gave a jump.

"Where do we spend the night?" Dolgov asked the coachman.

"Wherever you wish: some stay at the *stanitsa*, others go to the station of Ozernaya. The officers mostly drop in on the *stanitsa* ataman or the Cossack Captain Stesenko."

"Let us spend the night here," Shevchenko suggested suddenly.

"It reminds you of your homeland, doesn't it?" Dolgov said with a smile. "Agreed. Let us go to the *stanitsa* ataman."

"Permit me to seek a humbler lodging," Shevchenko asked.

"As you wish. But mind you don't oversleep. We'll be setting off early, while it's still cool."

Dolgov ordered the coachman to stop. Shevchenko got off. He slowly walked down the road, inhaling the hot air which suddenly became near and dear to him. In the distance he saw a cottage under a thick straw thatch. Sitting outside was a Cossack with a long mustache, reflectively sucking on a pipe, and only by the faded blue strips on the sides of his wide trousers Shevchenko could tell that this was not a Zaporozhian but a Ural Cossack.

"Hello, Cossack," Shevchenko said, and bowed as he came closer.

"Hello," the Cossack responded cordially. "Where have you come from?"

"Now it's from Orenburg, and earlier from Kiev. Could I stay at your home for the night?"

"Sure! We're always glad to take in good people. Have you come alone or with somebody else?"

"With an ensign, but he went to the *stanitsa* ataman," Shevchenko replied, sitting down beside the Cossack.

As was the custom with every real Ukrainian, the host answered the guest's questions briefly and unhurriedly, while the hostess, on looking outdoors and seeing them, immediately went into a bustle of preparing an evening meal. To make the conversation livelier and pay indirectly for the lodging, Shevchenko asked casually:

"Do you have a tavern at your *stanitsa*?"

"We don't, but people distil their own vodka and brew their own beer. If anyone needs it, he can buy it."

Shevchenko took some bills out of his pocket, and on noticing a girl of about ten bashfully hiding behind the door, extended the money to her, saying:

"Run, child, and bring us some *horilka* for supper."

On hearing this, the hostess rushed behind the house to kill some chicken for the meal, and then went to her neighbors for eggs, because her own stock had dwindled.

During supper Shevchenko treated the hosts to one, then to another drink; for the girl and her five-year-old brother he found a lump of sugar for each in his pocket. On the table stood a bowl with pickled cucumbers, fried potatoes, and the smell of garlic-spiced sausages tickled the palate of the famished traveler.

The drinks made the host talkative, and he told the guest that his grandfather had come here from Ukraine with a company of Cossacks during the reign of Czarina Catherine. The Ural Cossacks received them eagerly.

"Of course, this was no *Sich* but a *stanitsa*, so our young men married either our or the local girls. We were given land to till — that's how our forebears built this *stanitsa*," the host added, accepting the third drink.

When their initial hunger was appeased, they started singing Ukrainian songs, according to ancient custom.

The lights in the *stanitsa* were going out one after another, but Shevchenko remained sitting at the table with his compatriots, recalling the past and singing songs.

Shevchenko's fate touched the hosts to the bottom of their hearts. The hostess did not know how best to please and treat him. After hearing out his story, the host lapsed into a long silence, and then said with a deep sigh:

"All our troubles come from the czars, but people don't know yet how to do without them."

The next morning they left the *stanitsa* only at nine o'clock when if was already hot in the sun, and they reached the station in an hour and a half. At Ozernaya they had to wait for a long time again until they could get a pair of fresh horses.

The ensign and private of the Fifth Line Battalion felt less inhibited by now and the conversation flowed easily and unrestrained. The son of an Orenburg general, Dolgov asked Shevchenko about St. Petersburg, a city he had never visited. He had never traveled any farther than the town of Ufa after graduating from a military school in Orenburg. On learning that Shevchenko had been a student of Brüllow — who had painted a portrait of the poet Zhukovsky which was raffled off to buy Shevchenko's freedom from serfdom — and that he was acquainted with Prince Repnin, the former viceregent of Saxony, Dolgov fell into complete confusion and apologized for having let Shevchenko stay at the home of a minor *stanitsa* dweller instead of inviting him to dinner at the station and taking him to the *stanitsa* ataman.

Shevchenko put his mind at ease. "On the contrary, I am very grateful to you for having permitted me to stay with my compatriots."

Dolgov fell silent: the future confronted him with a big question mark. He did not know yet whether he was fated to get out of this steppe; he could be killed by a bullet, lariat or soyil of a rebel Kireghiz, and so he kept silent, just as depressed as Shevchenko.

"And there is Orsk," the coachman said as if to himself.

Shevchenko started and looked intently into the steppe, across which gray shadows of clouds drifted like huge hats. It took him some time to make out the barely discernible hill topped by the white speck of a fort that seemed to be outlined in red against the skyline. There was not a single green tree around it, just like throughout the entire desolate desert.

The horses went at an easy but eager trot. The white speck on the hill soon turned into a diminutive church surrounded by public buildings. From a distance their roofs looked like red stripes. On the road a group of people were reparing the road under the watchful eye of armed guards.

When the *tarantass* came level with them, Shevchenko recoiled at the sight: every broad-cheeked Mongol face was scarred by a brand on the forehead, and many had their nostrils and ear lobes torn.

"What are these people?" Shevchenko asked the coachman.

"Oh, these are rebels — convicts, that is," the coachman replied. "They must be from Kenessary's band. Well, our soldiers gave them a good drubbing. Some were sentenced to death, others were branded."

The convicts followed the passing *tarantass* with a mysterious indifference, but Shevchenko realized that under this outward indifference there blazed an inextinguishable hatred.

There it is, my grave, Shevchenko thought. Suddenly he asked himself: Can a song really ring out here? And he answered himself: No, a song cannot resound here, nor can joy come to flower.

8. BARIMTA

The *aul* stayed at its ruined camp throughout the entire day. An additional number of people were dug out of the sand and brought back to their senses, but three of Djantemir's people were beyond rescue. The broken *kereges* and the pieces of felt were dug out as well and brought together. A part of the *aul's* property and most of the sheep were saved, but still over two hundred cattle from the huge herd of Djantemir and his kin had perished.

After the sandstorm a spell of cold set in, but it was thirst which tormented man and beast most of all.

The dead were buried, the bitter tears of their relatives being substituted for the last ablutions. Several days later the desperate crying of orphaned children died away as did the laments of berieved mothers and wives.

Now Djantemir's *aul* was not alone: it had joined a huge noisy stream of *auls* moving to the summer pastures — the *jailiaou*. The shepherds and herders had to watch carefully lest the herds got mixed up. Nights were the most trying stages of the trek. Each *aul* branded its camels and horses with a kin *tamga*, but the goats, sheep and rams were unmarked and belonged to almost one and the same breed. Every hour of the day several score of sheep were found missing in one or another flock which provoked arguments and squabbles, shouts, cursing, and at times spontaneous fights. As is usual in such cases of confusion, it was not the thieves who suffered, but those who had weaker fists, a lesser number of herders or well-armed *tyulenguts*.

The Aral Sea had long been passed, and to their right, beyond the low horizon of the steppe, flowed the mighty Syr Darya. Some *auls* left the caravan and turned to the banks of the river to spend the summer amid the luxuriant wet meadows, but Djantemir persistently pushed on to where the most powerful and the richest *bais* were heading.

Djantemir was close-mouthed and gloomy like a black cloud. He could not reconcile himself with the disappearance of such a large number of cattle, and brooded day and night over how to regain his losses.

Jaisak did not see anything of the strange things going on about him. As a senior herder and shepherd, he was up to his ears in daily work and troubles. But Kumish had a rich experience of life and made out a lot of what was up.

"Today he sent Iskhak and his lazybones somewhere," she told her son in the evening. "No sooner had we set forth in the morning than they galloped off to one side and caught up with our *aul* toward the evening, after which Djantemir ordered Taijan to sharpen the yatagans, knives and *soyils*, and drive more nails into their *shakpars* as if in preparation for a fight."

"To hell with it, *apa*!" Jaisak said drowsily. "I've got other things to worry about. We'll have to get on our feet firmly and throw off this yoke, because I cannot keep on looking quietly how the *bai* is sucking the last dregs of life out of you."

"Oh, my dear son," Kumish sighed. "Shakir and I thought the same once, but our fate must have been ordained to be bitter. I beg only one thing of you — if the *bai* sends you on a dishonest job, don't go! It's enough that the wolves maimed you, and for him it's enough that you saved the flock and daughter who will bring him such big bride money."

His mother's words caused him pain. Yes, Kuljan was engaged, and no force could undo that.

"Don't you worry, *apa*," he said with a sigh. "He won't make me do his dirty work for him. As for Kuljan, I saved her not because of the *bai*, but because she's got a heart of gold. It is only thanks to her that we meet with any good here."

Kumish was right. In the morning, Iskhak stayed in his father's yurt for a long time along with his stepmother Shauken who had stationed the deaf Abdullah before the entrance to keep anyone from eavesdropping on their conversation. Come night, Djantemir roused his *tyulenguts*, had them gathered in his yurt, gave each a *soyil* and *shakpar*, and his eldest sons — Baisali, Undasin and Iskhak — a rifle and yatagan, and all, under the command of Iskhak, quietly left the sleeping *aul*, each leading a saddled horse by the bridle. At dawn they drove into the *aul* a flock of no less than six hundred sheep they had rustled.

The happy Djantemir ordered the slaughtering of six fat sheep and had the whole *aul* have its fill of *bishbarmak* and *manty*, then he treated each *tyulengut* and shepherd to a full bowl of kumiss, and gave orders to set off.

During the heat of the departure, when the last *jolini ayami* were already loaded on the camels, a number of women and *axakals* came riding into the *aul*. They immediately made out who the *bai* was and all as one went after Djantemir with shouts and laments, imploring that he give them their sheep back.

"We are Kazakhs just like you, *bai*," a gray-haired woman with a proud face said, a tremor in her tearful voice. "Wasn't it enough that the Khivans fell on us in winter, ransacked our *aul* and took away our men and sons into slavery — and then for you, one of our own people, to come along and finish us off? You're dooming us to a death of hunger."

"Give us our sheep back! We are not to blame for Allah having punished you in the Karakum," an old *axakal* with a sparse beard and a copper-bronze face said. "Give it to us as the law of Allah and his Prophet wills! We are not some giaours but true believers like you."

"There is no such law that permits people of our blood to rob each other!"

"You murdered people!" the others shouted, interrupting one another.

"So go to Allah with your complaints," Djantemir snapped back, baring his teeth savagely. "There are no brands on the sheep to tell who they belong to. It could be my flock which had run away during the sandstorm. I don't know anything and don't want to know!" he shrugged his shoulders. Picking up the ends of his *chapan*, he walked up to his horse, jumped into the saddle with unexpected agility, and ordered:

"Move on!"

"So that's the way you're putting things." The strangers rushed at him. "The sheep might not be branded, but your horses have your brand on them. When one of your *jigits* was killed and fell from his horse, our people captured the horse, and we'll prove to every khan and sultan that you plundered us like a Khivan robber."

"Like a highwayman, and not a *bai* who enjoys respect!"

"Give us our flock back, and we won't complain to anyone!" the woman with the proud face implored Djantemir again.

"And Allah will reward you tenfold!" the other women joined her, weeping.

"Move on!" Djantemir shouted at the top of his voice. "And you," he turned to his *tyulenguts*, "turn them out neck and crop."

The *jigits* exchanged glances, wavering: young that they were, it was unfit for them to chase away gray-bearded men, let alone gray-haired women.

To put an end to it all, Djantemir spurred his horse and intentionally rode up to the front, bypassing the camels. The people he had had plundered shook their fists and hurled shrieking curses at his back.

Jaisak heard everything that had been going on. He was ashamed and it pained him to look at the plundered and unhappy people who were really doomed to death. A fierce hatred blazed in his heart, but he did not dare give the people back their sheep. Suddenly Taijan rode up to him.

"Ride ahead, my friend, and I'll give if not everything, then at least three hundred of the sheep to their true owners. Our skinflint won't notice anything for the dust, and then we'll find an explanation later on."

"All right!" Jaisak agreed with righteous rage and rode toward the dense cloud of dust hovering in the wake of the *aul*, behind which the heavy figure of Djantemir had disappeared a long time ago.

When Jaisak left, Taijan whistled for the dogs, directed his horse into the flock, cutting from it some 250 to 300 sheep, and drove them back where the plundered people were still standing.

"Here you are, *axakals* and mothers. It's part of your flock for breeding. We can't give you more, because, as it is, our shaitan will make the place too hot for us when he finds out," Taijan said.

"Don't despair; better tell me your names and where you come from. If our Djantemir makes life unbearable for us, we'll take our sheep and join your *aul*. Would you take us then?"

"May Allah bless you, *jigit*," the old woman with the proud face said. "We are wandering to the north of Balkhash. We'll accept you like one of our kin, give you the best girl in marriage, and put up a yurt for you," the woman added with a tearful voice. "You tell us your name, too, *jigit*, so that we know whom to pray to Allah for."

"There are two of us: Jaisak and Taijan!" Taijan replied, and turning his horse round, galloped off to catch up with the *aul* which was disappearing in the gray cloud of dust.

9. PRIVATE 3RD COMPANY

After rattling across the trembling bridge spanning the river Ural, the *tarantass* rolled up a hill and drove into the Orsk Fortress.

By the bridge another crew of convicts with ugly brands on their foreheads was repairing the road (probably in preparation for the reception of some bigshots), and on a large parade ground soldiers were going through drill.

The parade ground was surrounded by barracks headquarters, offices, a prison, stacks of logs, stables, storehouses with huge padlocks on their doors, and only the brick church painted dazzlingly white at the opposite end slightly enlivened the gloomily dully sight of the parade ground and the whole of Orsk which was devoid of any vegetation.

All the public buildings were covered with tin roofs of a dark-reddish color, and behind them were scattered fifty or so log cabins of the Ural Cossacks. The scene resembled a tiny sad island in a boundless sea of a bleak steppe.

Gloomy and depressed, Dolgov stepped off the *tarantass*. This was not the place he had dreamed of when receiving his first commission! Shevchenko was sadly silent as well. Here, perhaps, he would be fated to die a martyr of his cause.

Dolgov gave the coachman a ruble to buy himself some vodka, ordered the soldier, who came running to meet them, to pick up his things, and went into the headquarters. The *tarantass* slowly rolled away from the porch, but Shevchenko kept standing in one place, gripped by a depressing melancholy.

Suddenly the very same soldier ran out onto the porch and called to him:

"Hey you, Shevchenko! Come to the commander! He's calling you!"

Shevchenko silently picked up his things and went up the porch steps.

"Halt! Where do you think you're going! Put down your riggings! That's no way of entering the chief's office!" the soldier cried out with what sounded like anger or mockery. "Where do the likes of you come from?!"

Shevchenko put his things in a corner and entered the office. The company commander, Captain Globa, was sitting at his desk, looking through the papers Dolgov had brought with the parcel, and Shevchenko recognized the bluish stationary with the seal of the Third Department.

"Shevchenko?" the captain raised his eyes to him.

"Yes, sir!" the poet snapped to attention.

"Did you get your uniform?"

"Yes, sir!"

"Why are you in civvies then? Change at once and hand all non-regulation items to the storehouse. And mind you, no civvies whatsoever will be tolerated around here. Do you understand?"

"Yes, sir."

"Sidorchuk! Take him to the company clerk Lavrentiev. Let him issue orders to have this man put on the allowance list and write out the proper record card."

He gave Sidorchuk all the papers from the packet and again turned to Dolgov, immediately dismissing the exile from his attention.

"So you've come to serve in our battalion? Wonderful. But

you'll yawn yourself to death from boredom in this place. Every new man is like a heavenly grace for us. Believe me, there is no one you can exchange a sincere word with. Tomorrow morning you'll be received by the general and assigned to one of the companies, and in the meantime — please be my guest for supper and stay the night at my home. We haven't got any taverns or hotels around this place. But we can take a nip or two anyway."

"Thank you," Dolgov said with a bow. "The sight of the fortress is really depressing, but with good people around it can be fine anywhere."

"It depends. But good people are something you cannot order from a pharmacy by prescription."

"I am not such a pessimist as you," Dolgov said with a forced smile, trying to be amiable. "I believe there are some interesting people among the soldiers as well."

"God forbid! There is nothing you can talk about with these swine. They have to be hold in check like this!" Globa clenched his hairy fist. "We don't get the usual recruits, you know. The regiments send us offenders, and of the recruits we got mostly those who have been brought to book for rebellion or outrage: drunkards, thieves and villains of the highest order!"

"It's a pity! Now this Shevchenko — he's an extraordinarily interesting man. An artist who graduated from the St. Petersburg Imperial Academy of Fine Arts and was a professor at the St. Vladimir University of Kiev. Besides, he is a famous Little-Russian writer. An educated and tactful man, he was accepted in the highest circles," Dolgov emphasized intentionally.

"And still he landed in a penal line battalion to serve with inveterate rogues," Globa guffawed. "Believe me, my dear ensign, they all are tarred with the same brush: both the criminals and the rebels, and all those various Voltairians and authors of libellous rhymes. But we'll knock the nonsense out of their heads in no time. Theirs is a very simple job to do — marching left! right! — that's all. A soldier is not supposed to think."

Suvorov looked at the soldier quite differently, Dolgov thought, but kept his peace.

"Sidorchuk! Take the things of his Excellency to my homo!" Globa called again. "And mind that nothing disappears, you son of a bitch!"

Taking Dolgov by the arm, Globa saw him to the door.

In the meantime, the clerk Lavrentiev, with the assistance of the battalion medical attendant, was putting the novice on the staff. Shevchenko had to undress completely to have his weight, height and chest volume measured and his lungs and teeth examined. Then Lavrentiev wrote out the form, glancing now and again into the papers he had received from Captain Globa.

This was a usual but at the same time a difficult job for him to do, because his knowledge of reading and writing were imperfect.

After Private Shevchenko was put on the allowance list, Lavrentiev took him to the cook and asked him to feed the man properly. On parting, he slapped Shevchenko amicably on his back.

"Life is possible everywhere, old chap. You, too, will live your days in Orsk. Now if you'll teach my boys to read and write and all the other subjects, I'll be your friend and protector against our officers."

The barracks had been built for fifty men; inside, it was uncomfortable looking, dirty, big, and badly lit. Shevchenko stopped in indecision at the threshold and involuntarily recoiled at the stench that hit him; it was difficult to determine what was more nauseating — the smell of sour borshch, rotten cabbage, sweat, foul foot rags, shag smoke, or the stench of the latrine bucket. Shevchenko forced himself to cross the threshold, his eyes roving to find an orderly in the semi-darkness. The orderly motioned at a free bunk in a corner, told him to put his things in a separate wardrobe that had no lock or latch, and considering his duties thus discharged, disappeared.

Shevchenko looked round. Forty-five pairs of eyes followed his every movement with interest: some derisively, others malevolently, especially when he produced a handkerchief and put it to his nose to banish the intolerable stench somewhat at least.

A minute later a bugle blared on the parade ground. The soldiers jumped to their feet, started to dress, did up all their buttons, and tightened their belts.

"What's that?" Shevchenko asked an elderly soldier who occupied the bunk next to his.

"Roll call, brother. Then come evening prayers — and that ends the day," he explained readily. "Is it any different in other garrisons?"

"I don't know. This is my first day in the ranks," Shevchenko answered quietly and gave a sigh.

"Never mind, old chap. You'll get used to it. This is my twentieth year," the soldier said, just as quietly, tightening his belt. "Just don't clash with the commanders, and you'll be all right anywhere."

Shevchenko was restless that evening. He kept running out of the barracks for a breath of fresh air, but on returning to his bunk, he could not fall asleep for the pandemonium of talking, laughter, swearing, and the screechy sounds of an accordion, and when the men quieted down, he was attacked by swarms of bed bugs that made his body burn like he had been stung by nettles.

"Oh, my God! However can you sleep here?" Shevchenko whispered to his neighbor in horror. "The bed bugs are eating me alive."

"After you stomp around with us for a whole day, brother, no archangel's trumpet, let alone our battalion bugle, will be loud enough to rouse you," the old man said with a sigh. "On holidays the bed bugs are really a nasty plague, but on ordinary days they're the last thing on your mind." His steady voice betrayed the hopeless, submissive sadness of a man who was reconciled to everything in the world.

"Listen, neighbor," Shevchenko said in a whisper again, moving closer. "I was told back in Orenburg that you've got

Polish exiles here. They were supposed to have been forced into the army just like me. So where are they?"

"Are you a Pole?"

"No. I'm from Kiev Province. A *khokhol* as you call us."

"I see. We have got some Poles around; not in our battalion, though. Most of them lodge in homes. Previously there were a lot of them, but now there's no more than five in all."

After morning prayers and breakfast, the company was marched off to the parade ground for the soldiers' basic science — drill.

They marched in twos, fours or eights in a line. The company commander and a young officer stood at one end of the line and a corporal and a noncom at the other, watching that all the men, lined up in order of height, raised their feet simultaneously to one and the same level, with toes stretched out, and brought them to the ground simultaneously and with equal speed and force.

From the first minute Shevchenko felt himself helpless in the line. The new Russian-leather boots did not fit his feet properly yet. They were tight at the instep, while the legs bent in the knees against his will, the toes sticking upward and upsetting the orderly alignment of the raised feet.

"Hey you swag-bellied character! Come out of the line here!" the company commander shouted angrily. "How are you marching, you rogue?! Zlishchev! Let an old soldier take charge of this dolt and teach him to march properly. And you" — he turned to Shevchenko, — "mark my words: I'll flog the daylights out of you, if you play the fool. Understand?!"

"Yes, sir!" Shevchenko said and dropped his eyes lest their expression betray him.

A ruddy-cheeked noncom ran up, called Shevchenko's bunk neighbor Kuzmich out of the ranks, and said:

"He's going to drill you now. Listen to him and learn. If you won't of your own free will, we'll make you by force. This is no place where honey and cakes are handed out."

Kuzmich took Shevchenko aside, stood beside him and, leaning upon his left heel, raised his right leg with an ease that was remarkable for his age; he stretched out his toe like a ballerina and solidly brought the sole of his foot down to the ground, after which he raised his left leg with the same agility and made a second step.

"When an ordinary man walks along," Kuzmich explained, "he always puts his weight on his heel first. But as a soldier you have to hit the ground with your sole like you're putting a brand or seal on the ground."

Shevchenko tired quickly from the drill. His entire being protested against the compulsion and senseless physical exertion, and his inward opposition unconsciously lent all his movements an awkward unwieldiness.

"Left! Right! Left! Right!" Kuzmich called out boisterously as the poet bathed in sweat. His shirt was dripping wet, his heart pounded wildly in his chest.

The drill went on for another two hours. During a five-minute break for a smoke, Dolgov was crossing the parade ground together with the battalion commander, Major Meshkov. On seeing that all the soldiers were having a smoke sitting on the grass and only Shevchenko was carrying on, Dolgov turned aside and made Meshkov follow him.

"I want to draw your attention to this man. He is a gifted poet and artist from St. Petersburg," he said to Meshkov. "Today he is in disgrace, but tomorrow circumstances might suddenly change and he will reappear in high society in the capital and ride the crest of popularity after creating a new book or a new painting. Who knows, but you and I might one day be asking favors of him. I was told in Orenburg that very influential and highly placed people had already interceded for him."

At the sight of the officers Kuzmich and Shevchenko stiffened to attention.

"At ease!" Meshkov said with a wave of his hand and Dolgov walked up to Shevchenko.

"Good morning, Taras Grigorievich!"

"How do you do, your Excllency!"

"So that's what this artist and famous rhymer looks like," Meshkov drawled as if thinking out loud. Then he addressed the poet: "General Fedyaev, a man with the kindest of hearts, has written to me, asking me to help you. Since you're here with the right to clemency you can receive an officer's commission with time. I, for my part, will try to justify his Excellency's trust in me and make a good combatant and exemplary soldier out of you," he added.

Struck to the quick by such a turn of Meshkov's mind, Shevchenko could not find his tongue to respond with the conventional, "Glad to do my best, your Excllency!"

What a blockhead! Shevchenko thought in despair. Fedyaev could not have written to have me relieved of my daily exercise just like that, and here this churl got him all wrong. He'll drill mo to my grave.

The break for a smoke had come to an end. The drums rolled again, and again the heavy footfalls of marching men filled the air. And again, dripping with sweat under the stuffy uniform, Shevchenko went through the motions of the drill, utterly confused and crushed by Meshkov's words. The feeble hope of having his sentence commuted had snapped like a thin thread.

Day passed after day, each an exact repetition of the previous one. Shevchenko had a feeling he had been there several weeks, while in fact it was only the first week of his soldier's life. Then it was Sunday.

As always, the drum roused him in the morning. As always, they were marched outside for the roll call. After breakfast they were taken to church, after which some went to sleep, while most of the men went whichever way they chose.

Feeling like be had slept through a racking nightmare, Shevchenko went outdoors and came across Kuzmich who was sorting out a bunch of fishing rods with self-made hooks of wire.

"Off fishing, Kuzmich?" Shevchenko asked.

"You guessed right. I'll go to the Ural or else to the Or. There are some fine sterlets in these waters, and such carp you won't find anything like them anywhere. In a single day you can catch two pailfuls for a mouth-watering fish soup. I've even bought bay leaf for this purpose. Some of the fish I take to the general. His daughter always buys them from me and treats me to a drink into the bargain. Let's go together!"

"All right!"

After going round the church, they walked down a dusty road littered with dung and piles of ashes, passed the new cottage of the priest and the homes which belonged to the officers, as Shevchenko learned from Kuzmich.

"And where does Ensign Dolgov live?" Shevchenko asked.

"What Dolgov?"

"The one I came with."

"We haven't any Dolgov here. Our staff of officers is filled. He must have been transferred to the fourth company at the neighboring fort. An officer is said to have died there."

Shevchenko gave a sigh. So this hope had betrayed him, too. The mail, as he had learned, arrived only once a month, when an opportunity occurred. So he would not be able to write to his friends so soon. And the poet's eyes, rekindled to life a moment ago, became listless.

At long last they came to the Ural and ran down its steep bank. The old soldier started immediately sorting out his fishing rods, while Shevchenko pushed his peakless cap to the back of his head, and said:

"Well, I'll be moving on so as not to be a bother to you. Fish prefer quiet. I'll wander around this place and have a swim perhaps."

Kuzmich gave a nod silently, preoccupied as he was hooking the worms, and Shevchenko started out along the Ural.

Orsk was gradually disappearing behind his back, merging into one line with the bare desert. The river bank turned sharply, and Shevchenko kept walking on and on. At last he stopped and looked around.

The illimitable steppe ringed him like a round flat bowl topped by the blue cupola of the sky. It was quiet and empty here, without a single bird, jerboa, or curious gopher in sight.

He felt lonely, all on his own, unable to do anything for other people and his oppressed brothers. In banishing Ovidius from Rome to the estuary of the Danube, the heathen Octavius could not have thought up a more subtle punishment. For an artist there is no greater torment than to be deprived of creating the beautiful for the happiness of people.

He dropped to the ground, buried his face in the wilted grass from despair, and burst into tears.

His despair seemed to melt in the tears and retreat from his heart like a spent thunder. The despair that was racking his heart gradually gave way to rising hatred, one drop of which could have reduced to ashes Czar Nicholas along with all his satraps from Dubelt and Orlov, Funduklei and Yuzefovich up to Globa and Meshkov.

His hatred bred a protest, a power and will to fight.

"I will write! I will! I shall not be broken! You won't stop my mouth!" he shouted into the empty steppe. "I cannot but write, just like the sun cannot but shine, just like the air cannot become solid and motionless! I will write! And all your prohibitions are impotent against the spoken word! Your sentence has only proved that my word is a weapon as well! And you are afraid of it!"

Shevchenko got to his feet. There was determination and firmness in his eyes.

The barracks was almost empty. A number of utterly drunken men were snoring on their bunks, the orderly was nowhere in sight. Shevchenko opened his locker, pulled out his suitcase, took a number of sheets of paper, bosomed them, and went into the steppe beyond the ramparts. There, on the bank of the quiet river Or overgrown with dense reeds, he made himself a little notebook out of the sheets of paper, and wrote in it his first poem in exile.

10. WHERE THE ALATAU SLEEPS UNDER THE ICE

Djantemir's *aul* passed the cheerful and clear waters of the river Ili and stopped for its last night on a plain. The sun slipped slowly behind the black mass of the Suuk Tiube Mountains and twilight descended on the plain, while a foamy strip of sun-tinted clouds glowed high over the horizon for a long time thereafter.

Kuljan was seeing mountains for the first time and admired them with fascination. Three weeks had passed since the sandstorm, but she felt so weak that even Shauken did not pick on her and force her to work. While recuperating, the girl looked on everything she met with the joy of a person who had been brought back to life, and together with her brother Rahim she rejoiced at everything that was new and strange to her.

Rahim loved his sister with a particular, gentle and deep love as orphans do their elder sisters who give them the motherly tenderness that has been lost. Now he rode the same camel with her and whenever they halted, brought her a lump of sugar he had stolen from his father, or else a strange colorful butterfly, or a splinter of rock with a silvery glitter.

"You know, Kuljan," he told her quietly once. "I'll love Jaisak like a brother for him having saved you. That's a real *jigit*! He's a *batyr*, just like Koblanda. I'll ask him to teach me fight with a *soyil*, *shakpar* and yatagan. I, too, will become a *batyr* and always protect you against any danger."

Kuljan gave him a tender smile.

"You might save me from a tiger or a poisonous snake, but hardly from Shauken. She poisons my life much more than the witches from the fairy tale the old Bukharan told us when he brought Father the carpets and dried apricots."

"I hate her!" Rahim said with flashing eyes. "She chased you out of her yurt to certain death. I'll never forgive her that. Once you're married to Ibrai, I'll run away from our *aul* and join you so as not to see her anymore. But I'll be sorry to part with Jaisak," he added with a sigh.

The next morning the *aul* set off at dawn. It was hot already and spring reigned supreme. The terrain was getting hilly. It seemed that a sea had once raged here and its huge waves had suddenly frozen. Through the mist in the distance showed the faint outlines of the mighty mountain ridge of the Zailiysky Alatau.

The *aul* reached the valley it had been seeking. The scouts Djantemir had sent ahead met him at the intermontane plain and took him to the sheer granite cliff where they had left the *tamga* of his kin three months ago.

It was an exceptionally well chosen place. Two mountain streams, swollen enough to water twice as many sheep as Djantemir's, crossed the placid valley where the *aul* pitched their summer yurts on the leeward side. All around were luxuriant alpine meadows of fragrant grasses, many of them medicinal herbs.

At the mountain camp Shauken seemed to become aware of Jaisak's existence for the first time. Either she had been impressed by the young *jigit's* courage or else was sick of breaking her head over her household affairs all the time and having to while away her days with the old and grouchy Djantemir, because she invited Jaisak to her white yurt again and again, treating him to kumiss or fresh mutton. Jaisak thanked her for the treat, did not refuse to accept an extra piece of food, but he never abused this favor from his cunning and talkative hostess and was always restrained, polite and chilly.

"You must value such a man," Shauken told Djantemir. "Jaisak has done you more than all the other shepherds and herders taken together. He saved the herd from the wolves, tried to keep up order during the trek, and saved your Kuljan from death. The girl's mischievous and foolish: the shaitan knows why she had to traipse around the camp during the storm, and if it had not been for him, you would have lost the big bride money you will get for her. Jaisak can be useful to us yet. You must arouse his interest in something, do something for him."

"I know," Djantemir retorted gruffly. "What's made you so generous all of a sudden? Isn't it enough that I gave him a camel, sheep and a new sheepskin coat? I won't give away the last thing I have! Such a lot of cattle died, and that *barimta* proved to be a miserly gain. We got no more than four hundred head. I suspect that your Jaisak blinded my eyes, because Iskhak swore there had been twice as many sheep."

Djantemir realized dimly that he had been deceived, but he could not prove anything. He did not dare make a repeated raid: what he had permitted himself during the trek would now only dishonor him as a gross violation of an ancient custom, so Djantemir decided to occupy himself with other matters

He had Iskhak and two elder sons ride round the mountains and valleys to discover the whereabouts of Zulkarnai whose son Ibrai was engaged to Kuljan. A week later his elder sons returned without finding out anything, but the acute Iskhak heard people say that Ibrai was terribly ill now and would hardly be ready for this summer's wedding.

The news made Djantemir gloomier than ever, and when Shauken mentioned Jaisak once, he bared his yellow teeth at her and madly waved the whip in front of her face.

"You've gone mad, woman! Here I'm grappling with failure after failure, while you can't get that swindler out of your head! Have you fallen in love with him, or what?!"

The next day he unexpectedly called for Iskhak and two *axakals* and rode off to Zulkarnai's camp.

Left on her own, Shauken felt herself the sole mistress of the situation and started fulfilling her schemes step by step. Djantemir's angrily dropped remark was not fruitless conjecture. The handsome herder Jaisak had really stirred her blood, and his dry restraint teased and fired her more than if he had met her flirtations halfway and responded to them with off-color and frank jokes. But no opportunity offered itself to simply invite him to her yurt. So Shauken ordered one of her servant girls to call Jaisak's mother Kumish.

"Did you call me?"

"Yes, Kumish. I want you to ask one of the women to take charge of milking the mares while you assist me in sorting out the pieces of felt. Since your son saved Kuljan and a lot of sheep, I want to present him with a new warm winter yurt; your old one is being blown through by the winds on all sides."

Keeping up her role of benefactress and proficient keeper of her kin, she added:

"Tell Jaisak to see me tomorrow. We'll think of what should go on the *kerege* and what else would be needed. If it's a question of putting up a new yurt, everything must be done properly."

Kumish hurried to bring the good news to her son.

"A new yurt is a good thing, of course," Jaisak said. "But don't let Shauken get the idea that she and Djantemir are going to tether me to their will like a dog to a chain. We have to throw off their yoke. Taijan and I are seriously thinking about it. I won't go to Shauken. Djantemir is away now, and I don't want any gossip and trouble. By the way, Taijan and I agreed to try and catch a royal eagle tomorrow."

"How can you without the *bai*'s permission?"

"I had a talk with him about it. He asked me to get an eaglet for him, too. As to Shauken, I don't want to have anything to do with her. If you like, you can tell her that I am very happy to receive the present, and in gratitude I'll bring an eagle for the *bai* by all means. But don't you say more than that. Do you hear me, *apa*?" Jaisak said with determination, lay down on his bedding, pulled the blanket over his head and turned toward the *kerege* to indicate that he wanted to sleep.

The horses went slowly and warily down the rocky slope of the narrow valley which cut the huge mountain ridge in a twisting crack. This was not the first time Taijan visited these gorges and so he rode confidently up front, followed by a horse loaded up with food, lariats, sacks, fur-lined mittens, and thick padded robes. All this was absolutely necessary for catching royal eagles and camping in the mountains for the night.

Rahim and Jaisak rode behind, taking in and listening to everything going on along the way. At their side trotted two wolfhounds. Jaisak regretted having taken along the boy who could fall prey to his inquisitiveness and inexperience but it was too late to correct the mistake, and now the only thing that remained was to be on guard.

Suddenly Taijan saw two bird feathers slowly drifting in the air. This meant that somewhere high up a bird of prey was clawing its catch. In this place, the opposite side of the valley was sloping, and after he had climbed the slope, he saw the crest of a sheer cliff from which the feathers had fallen. To the right, almost on the very top of the cliff, was an eagle's nest clinging to a ledge. From there several feathers were slowly drifting down.

There it was — the nest of a golden eagle. But even an ibex would have been unable to clatter up such a steep cliff.

"We'll have to go round the mountain, and there we'll think up something," Jaisak said, as if reading Djantemir's thoughts.

Rahim intercepted the look of the men and said with a tone that brooked no objection: "I will stay with the horses."

When they had crawled almost up to the nest, Taijan suddenly muttered a curse: a she-eagle was sitting on the eggs, while her mate was wheeling over her with some small prey in his talons.

Angry and disappointed, the *jigits* descended into the valley.

"How did it go?" Rahim cried merrily. "Did you catch it?"

"There was nothing to catch. She's still sitting on the eggs," Taijan grumbled, annoyed.

"Really? I spied another two nests here, both of them a little bit lower," Rahim's eyes flashed cheerfully. "Let's go, I'll show them to you."

Chasing away the wolfhounds which wagged their tails eagerly, Rahim jumped on his horse.

"There is an eaglet," the boy insisted heatedly. "I saw the eagle bring it some food."

In the nest, as was usually the case with golden eagles, sat only one eaglet, already big, with a long bare neck and bald head. When Taijan had lowered himself on a rope to the nest, the eaglet hissed viciously, gave a piercing cry, and was ready to peck and tear him with its talons. Taijan unfolded a heavy, sturdy piece of cloth and threw it on the nest and eaglet with one precise movement. The eaglet thrashed under the cloth, but Taijan did not give it time to come to its senses and tear the cloth: he quickly rolled it up in a thinner cloth, tied it strongly with twisted string, and put it into a sack tied to the rope hanging at his side. The noose of the rope he slipped down to his hips, settled in it like in a swing, and called to his companions:

"Pull me up! I'm ready!"

Jaisak and Rahim were anxiously waiting for the call. Now they started pulling up Taijan slowly, while Taijan, lest he hit against the cliff, carefully moved his feet up the rock face. At last his head appeared over the ledge. Jaisak gave another pull, Rahim stretched out his hand and helped Taijan scramble to the top and bring up the sack with the catch.

The hunters knew that a male eagle did not always fight for his nestling: they were more afraid of the mother which, on returning to the nest and finding it empty, could attack the thieves, and so they hurried to get away from the danger as fast as they could.

About three *versts* from the empty nest they stopped under an overhanging cliff to decide what to do next. To leave Rahim with such a restless catch and look for another eaglet was hardly expedient. Besides, no other nest was in sight.

"Let's go home," Rahim suggested. "I'll tell Father how you caught the eaglet and he'll let me go with you again. We might take another *jigit* along. Then we'll shoot some game on the way back. Father just loves roasted game. He'll be very pleased."

The hunters agreed that the boy's advice was sound enough, and after a good rest set off back for the *aul*.

II. THE CONSOLATION

For the third week now Shevchenko was going through his exhaustive life as a soldier. Now he knew all the commands well, and brought his whole sole down onto the ground when he marched in the ranks. During firing practice and soldiers' "colloquy" he even earned a commendation. But he himself was far from having developed that stalwart bearing which Meshkov demanded of him so insistently.

He lived a double life. One was for everyone to see: on the parade ground, in the stenchy, noisy barracks, and during the soldiers' "colloquy." Yet he also had another, deep-bosomed, sustaining love which only his friends could have surmised. An outsider did not suspect that in his heart inaudible songs rang out, verses rhymed into poems, images were conjured up, and observations crowded his mind. Even on the parade ground the dry and rattling roll of the drums generated ironic verse inside him in time to the blasted beating.

At such moments the toe of Shevchenko's boot stuck out mockingly above the rest in the line, and Globa would run up to him and yell madly:

"Where are you looking, you dolt! Don't you see your toe is higher than the others' again?"

"Your Excellency," Shevchenko said in justification, "believe me it protrudes like that from birth! I try as hard as I can but…"

"Shut up, you fool! No gabbing in the ranks!" Globa shouted and flourished his hairy fist in front of Shevchenko's eyes, not daring, though, to cuff him. It was not for nothing that Dolgov had told Meshkov that some high-placed persons were interceding for the poet in St. Petersburg. Globa thought it better not to put his career in jeopardy for the sake of a number of knocked-out soldier's teeth.

"I'll have you caned! I'll have you run the gauntlet if you have your head in the clouds!" he raved a key lower and rushed over to another platoon on seeing something wrong there.

On holidays and during red-letter days, of which, apart

from Sundays, there were no less than two or three a month, Shevchenko went to the Or River which flowed into the Ural some two to three *versts* from the fortress. There, convinced that none of the barrack drunkards, let alone the officers, had followed him, he settled in some dense shrubs, took the little notebook out of his bootleg, and wrote poetry in his native Ukrainian language which nobody spoke or even understood here.

Shevchenko's thoughts always took him back to his homeland. It was enough for him to close his eyes or simply fall to thinking and his mind revived the village of his childhood Kirilivka, or his boundlessly loved Kiev sprawling along the green banks of the Dnieper, or else the hospitable home of a friend where he had lived for a long time, painting portraits of the hosts and writing his poems. At all times his heart was with his dear nation, his brothers and sisters were suffering, and like Antaeus touching his native land in his thoughts at least, his spirit buoyed and he wrote. He invited these thoughts, sweet and bitter as they were at one and the same time, pleading with them not to leave him in a foreign land; in his poetry, he drew pictures of the Ukrainian village immersed in the lush verdure of orchards, with snow-white cottages between slender poplars, with the clean mirrors of ponds, with meadows and the cheerful frothing of water on the water-mill wheel.

Yes, it was an Eden on earth, but nearby, on a hill, loomed the landowner's palace where money was always needed to hold the unending banquets — and so the peasant was robbed of his last cattle, of his last jaded nag, without which he could not plow his miserly strip of land, and his harvest was sold to the merchant, which doomed the village to hunger.

In this way he wrote the poem *The Princess*. His heart boiled with wrath and hatred, the poem's words becoming as cutting as the lashes of a whip. These verses were fated to reach the reader only many years later when serfdom was abolished. After having had his fill of the sweet torments of creativity, Shevchenko returned to the barracks, conscious of the fact that even here, in exile, he served his native land, preparing a weapon to struggle on for the freedom of his people.

Once on a Sunday in late July he decided against walking far into the steppe to the Or, because storm clouds had overcast the sky, here and there a gray net of rain screened the horizon, and a barely audible rumble of thunder reached his ears. Sitting in between the shrubs on the high bank of the Ural, he looked through the pages of his notebook and his "children," as he called his verse with a sense of pain; then, wearied by the stifling heat of the approaching rainstorm, he undressed and jumped into the cold waves of the Ural. The bathing refreshened him. He dived a number of times, swam some more, and was already dressing when a pleasant baritone with a discernible Polish accent asked suddenly:

"If I am not mistaken, the gentleman is the poet Taras Shevchenko?"

Shevchenko started and impulsively reached for his boots: the cherished notebook was in place.

"Excuse me, but who do I have the honor of speaking to?" he asked, calmer now.

"Let me introduce myself. Your comrade in misfortune: Otto Fischer, an exiled Pole."

The introduction relieved Shevchenko's tension.

"I am very pleased to meet you! I, too, wanted to get acquainted with you, that is, with all the exiles," Shevchenko said, shaking Fischer's hand genially. "But how did you learn about me?"

"My colleague Ludwik Turno wrote to me about you from Orenburg."

"Turno? Oh yes, I remember meeting him at the Gerns'. He is an extremely likeable person. But as far as I know, you're not the only exile here?"

"There are three of us at the Orsk Fortress now. One died of consumption this spring. The rest were transferred to other battalions. How was your swim? Is the water good?"

"Just wonderful. Cool and healthfully refreshing."

"With your permission, I will take a dip then."

It was only now that Shevchenko noticed how smartly Fischer's uniform fitted his figure, and he suddenly felt uneasy about his own untidy appearance. While Fischer was swimming, Shevchenko combed his hair and mustache, shook out his uniform, and wiped the dust off his boots with grass, and when Fischer settled at his side, he extended both hands to him for joy: "Oh, how I've missed a friendly conversation here!"

They were oblivious to the flow of time as if this was not their first meeting and they had been good friends and seeing each other after a long separation. A furious whirlwind jolted them back to reality.

"A rainstorm!" Shevchenko jumped to his feet.

When they had reached the first houses, a warm, blessed downpour spattered around them, the wind chased the pallid waves of rain which made them look like some formless apparitions with loose gray hair.

After they shook the water out of their clothes on a porch, Fischer took Shevchenko into a log cabin built in Oriental fashion, with the windows facing the yard and a blank wall giving onto the street.

A tall dark-mustachioed man of about thirty rose to his feet to meet Shevchenko.

"Let me introduce you to my friend Stanislaw Królikiewicz," Fischer said.

"We were looking for you last week," Królikiewicz said genially in a mellow bass. "We dropped in to the barracks and looked for you in the steppe. I am sincerely glad to see a dear poet and a likeminded adherent."

"Thanks for your kindness!" Shevchenko said with a bow. "But I have no right to claim any personal merits in fighting for your martyr — Poland."

"You are wrong to think so! We have a common enemy —

czarism. Hence a common purpose as well: to gain freedom for all nations who groan under the heel of czarism," Królikiewicz said.

"You know, Taras Grigorievich," Fischer intervened, "Monsieur Królikiewicz and Monsieur Zawadzki, our third comrade, were laid up in hospital for three months after running through the 'green street.'"

"What? After running the gauntlet?" Shevchenko clenched his teeth.

"Yes. We were chased between a double file of five hundred men twice," Królikiewicz confirmed. "For instigating rebellion. That's how the verdict ran."

At that moment a drenched Zawadzki, a thick-set man with gray hair, entered the room. He carried a big roll of tobacco leaves in gray wrapping paper.

Fischer hastened to introduce him to Shevchenko. After shaking hands, Zawadzki threw off his wet uniform, and sitting down at the table, asked the guest:

"Do you smoke?"

"Yes. Not cigarettes, though, but a pipe."

"I've just got some fine *kafan* from a Bukharan. It's one of the best Turkish tobaccos around. What about trying it? It's really wonderful."

"I have an extra pipe," Fischer went into a bustle. "Here you are: as a token of our future friendship, let us smoke a 'pipe of peace.'"

"Well, if you put it that way..." Shevchenko gave a smile as well, as he accepted the pipe.

After the shag and the cheap cigarettes, the poet inhaled the fragrant *kafan* smoke with pleasure when he suddenly saw a big shelf lined with books on the wall. His eyes flared up like those of a hungry man seeing bread. Królikiewicz intercepted his look and his stern eyes softened.

"Are you fond of books? They are really difficult to get here. Our compatriots got us these to save us the trouble occasionally;

our parents send us some with the travelers who come here. Our library is at your service."

Shevchenko went up to the bookshelves: there was Mickiewicz, Słowacki, Schiller in Polish, Jan Kochanowski, Ignacy Krasicki, Walter Scott, and German, Polish and French novels. Only three books were in Russian: Pushkin, Rileyev and Odoievsky's *Heterogeneous Tales*.

"Do you have Herzen by any chance?" he asked.

"We do, but it's in Rover's kennel," Zawadzki responded as he cut the tobacco leaves on the table.

"Everything that is prohibited we keep outdoors in the dog's kennel," Fischer explained with a laugh. "Rileyev is normally there too, but today we failed to hide it, because the masters of the house were at home. We visit Rover when they are away, or at night when they're asleep. Rover is guarding the books honestly. He loves us ... that is, the bread and the bones from our borshch he gets."

"You should see his fangs — they're like a wolf's," Zawadzki added. "No stranger dares go near his kennel."

"And what about the masters of the house?"

"They don't know anything about our cache. We built it when we were repairing the kennel. No search in this house will reveal anything."

Shevchenko picked out the *Heterogeneous Tales* and a pocket-size volume of Mickiewicz. In the meantime, a samovar and cold collation had appeared on the table, and a lively conversation began during tea.

"What happened in Cracow, after all?" Shevchenko asked. "The Russian papers wrote next to nothing about it."

Królikiewicz lit up his pipe and drew on it deeply.

"We wanted to rise as one nation, so that the enemy would not have known a moment's peace in every village, city and town; so that he would be fired at or watched furtively from every wood and orchard, from behind every cliff in the mountains and from every home and thus be drawn into an ambush or trap. It was to be a fight just like the Spaniards' with Napoleon who overcame powerful states but could not subdue the Spanish patriots. We set the date of the uprising for the twenty second of February, but our cause was betrayed by traitors from among the gentry who warned the enemy. The Austrians dispatched a unit to help the government that was well-disposed to them, and several days before the uprising most of our leaders were arrested. That is why only Cracow rose up in arms. Its main force was the town's poor citizens. They captured the town, and the Austrian troops had to flee. We established a provisional government which immediately issued a manifesto calling on everyone to struggle for the independence of Poland, at the same time eliminating all taxes and proclaiming democratic freedoms. Unfortunately, arguments flared up within the government: some wanted to limit themselves only to the national question, while others pointed to the peasantry's demands for the abolition of serfdom, the workers' demands for more pay and cheap bread, and the townspeople's demands for civil rights. All these demands frightened the gentry and bourgeoisie, and the Austrians started to advance with substantial forces. Battles ensued. A unit of workers from the Wieliczka salt mines under the leadership of Dembowski came to the town's assistance. He reorganized the town's defense, under his influence democratic reforms were effected more broadly, which drew masses of the peasantry to the uprising. We were expecting insurrections in Silesia, Poznan, on the Vistula and in Galicia. Peasant riots had actually broken out there, but the forces were unequal. Dembowski was shot by the Austrians who then captured Cracow in early March. And we landed up in Orsk..."

Królikiewicz fell silent, but a nervous twitch lingered on his thin lips, and grief spread across his stern face. After regaining self-control, he told about his arrest, the inquest and the trial.

Then Shevchenko told them about the Brotherhood of Saints Cyril and Methodius and about his copy of the manuscript *Three Years* the gendarmes had taken away from him. He read his poems *To the Dead, the Living and the Unborn...* and *My Testament,* as well as one or two others.

The Poles looked reverently at him, feeling happy for the first time since they had landed in this horrible prison without walls.

Back at the barracks, Shevchenko lay down on his bunk and opened a book, pretending he was reading it, but instead of the *Heterogeneous Tales* and Mickiewicz he saw before his eyes the events of his distant youth.

In the days when he lived in Vilnius an uprising was about to break out. Even the tender and bashful Dziunia Gusikowska — his short-lived love — burned with the sacred fire of struggle for her people. At that time he was already reading Mickiewicz in the Polish language and was just as raring to take part in the uprising. He had studied the Polish language which stood him in good stead today. He sincerely envied the Poles who had learned to unite so strongly and were capable of real struggle.

If only the Russian, Ukrainian and Polish peasants, the Caucasian highlanders and these naked and hungry Kirghiz were capable of uniting and attacking czarism!

How had it happen, after all, that two fraternal Slavic nations had become enemies? They should have lived in lasting peace as good neighbors, stood shoulder to shoulder against the enemies as they had once done against the Turks at the walls of Khotin and confronted the Teutonic knights on the shores of the Baltic Sea and Lake Chud.

Twilight was falling. Evening prayers and roll call were over. The barracks gradually quieted down. But Shevchenko was deep in thought about the past, and sleep evaded him. In his heart he felt compassionately for a Poland that had been torn into three parts, a nation that had produced such courageous and staunch people.

The men in the barracks were asleep. Discordant snoring, sighs, and mumbling came from all sides. Shevchenko hid the book in his locker, settled by a wick lamp, unfolded a piece of paper he had found between the pages of the book, and became thoughtful.

Yes, they were set at variance with one another by the rapacious magnates, and the predatory, cunning Jesuits.

Shevchenko reread what was written there, carefully folded up the paper, and hid it in his pocket.

He impatiently waited for the end of that week during which he read the *Heterogeneous Tales* twice and learned many of Mickiewicz's poems by heart. But when he was getting ready to leave for his new friends and opened the locker, he saw that the *Heterogeneous Tales* had disappeared.

Shevchenko's face paled.

"The book! Where is the book I've been reading?" he said, turning to Kuzmich who was sewing a button on to his uniform. "The book isn't mine. I have borrowed it."

"I'm no crook," the old soldier said, giving him a stern, but open look. "Ask them." He gestured contemptuously toward the far corner where Kozlovsky was boisterously playing cards with the demoted Ensign Belobrovov and the drunkard Schulz.

Shevchenko went up to them, and looking straight into Kozlovsky's eyes, asked:

"Where is my book?"

Kozlovsky did not bat an eyelid.

"Whoever wants a book that's already been read?" he answered the question with a question.

"Must have been used for rolling cigarettes," Belobrovov retorted carelessly.

"I demand the book be returned at once!" Shevchenko said sharply.

"Oh, *pardon*." Kozlovsky clicked his heel pieces together. "I forgot to inform you that it's now in the possession of the merchant Ghalhushian in the settlement. He eagerly buys up books for twenty kopecks. Go and get it. He probably hasn't torn it up for grocery bags yet."

Shevchenko left for the settlement almost at a run. Chalhushian's store had a profuse display of goods: barrels of herring, kerosene and plant oil, sacks of flour, millet, sugar and groats, crates of soap, shag, nails, macaroni, candles, jars of fruitdrops and cheap candy, boxes of cinnamon, raisin and laurel leaf, and under the counter stood huge carboys with vodka and cheap Caucasian wine.

"Has anyone offered to sell you a book recently?" Shevchenko asked.

"One soldier brought a book yesterday," the fat, short-legged shopkeeper answered impassively. "Look! Yours — not yours?" he threw the *Heterogeneous Tales* on the counter.

"It is! It is! The book was stolen from me," the poet said and noted with horror that the book's list of contents and last page had been torn out. "There was a page here. Do you still have it?"

"Soldier brought book," the Armenian repeated indifferently. "Me doing you service: we need paper for herring, need for sugar, need for raisins. Soldier bring — we take, we give vodka, shag. Pay thirty kopecks and take it."

Shevchenko paid the money and hurried to his friends. Zawadzki and Królikiewicz were not at home: they were on guard duty that day; only Fischer was awaiting the poet. Shevchenko told him what had happened and apologized for the missing page in the book.

"Don't take it so much to heart," Fischer said with a smile, seeing how overwrought Shevchenko was. "It would have been much worse if the entire barracks were to use up the book for rolling cigarettes. Sit down and tell me what's new. Then we'll take a swim in the Ural and do some fishing. Today is a cool day, and fish bite well in such weather. As for dinner, we'll go to General Isaiev.

"What?" Shevchenko asked, bewildered.

"Very simply. The general is a widower living with his daughter Natalia who recently graduated from the Smolny Finishing School in St. Petersburg. His elder daughter, the widow of an officer killed in the Caucasus last year, has come to visit him. She has a boy I am tutoring for the entrance examinations to a Gymnasium. Frequently I stay the evenings with them. The general wants to meet you, and his elder daughter is fascinated by your poetry. They asked me to bring you along at all costs."

Refreshened by the swim and walk in the steppe, they went to the general's home.

The principal adornment in the modestly furnished but large parlor of the general's home was an Eberhardt grand piano and a number of magnificent date palms and rubber plants. A red-breasted gray parrot was squawking merrily in a tall round cage.

Lidia Andreievna, the general's elder daughter, came out to meet them.

"How do you do," she said simply, extending her hand to Shevchenko after he had been ceremoniously introduced to her by Fischer. "I am glad to meet you. But why are we standing? Do sit down, please. Papa is in a bad mood as always. He will join us in no time. I have read your *Kobzar*. It was back in the Caucasus when my husband was still alive. You certainly have a distinctive talent. At times your poetry is so delicate, so lyrical, and at others tempestuous, sharp and courageous. Like a storm on a sea. You must take care of yourself and go through whatever suffering you have to so as to write another book as good as this one."

Shevchenko bowed formally, without saying anything in reply.

That moment Natalia entered with Petya, Lidia Andreievna's ten-year-old son. Petya carried a little basket with cherries he had picked in the orchard; Natalia threw a stack of sheet music on the lid of the grand piano and, after greeting the guests, turned to Fischer:

"Monsieur Otto, help me find a remedy against boredom. Organize a concert, please. We've just received wonderful romances by Varlamov, a part of Glinka's opera *Life for the Czar* and one or two other things of the sort. You'll be playing the violin, Lidia and I the piano. Globa has not too bad a bass, and Stepanov a tiny tenor. Besides, we could *get* a choir together. Mother Stepanida has a fine voice, and I could just as well squeak away two romances or so."

"And let Meshkov organize a Prussian-style *corps de ballet*," Fischer added ironically. "He's good at drilling us soldiers to stretch out our toes like on the opera stage, but without tutus and tights, which would make the picture complete. Perhaps Miss Natalia would make them for the whole company out of the hospital gauze and tarlatan."

Everyone laughed merrily. Lidia Andreievna sat down at the piano and looked through the sheet music.

"This is an exquisitely melodious duet," Fischer remarked, putting a sheet of music in a colorful cover on the music stand. "I used to sing it back home in Warsaw."

"You don't say! So let's try and sing it now," Natalia said, "Come on, play, Lidia. Pardon, monsieur Shevchenko, for not having asked. Do you sing too?"

"I do; not romances but folk songs. Please, sing. I have missed music so much."

Following the introduction, Natalia sang with a ringing and clear soprano, then Fischer joined in, darting amorous glances at her. Their young voices blended beautifully; Shevchenko shut his eyes and forgot for a moment that he was in Orsk. He seemed to be back in his Ukraine at Zakrevsky's estate in Berezovi Rudki.

Lidia Andreievna underscored the voices of the singers the more by alternating ringing chords with velvety, rolling tremolos.

"And now we'll ask Taras Grigorievich to sing!" Natalia cried out and clapped her hands. "No, no! Do not refuse. This is a concert after all. We are but amateurs!" she said passionately seeing how Shevchenko became timid and waved off the idea. "Sing for us, please! We love Little-Russian songs!"

"My mood is not fit for singing now," he said sternly. "I will sing a little later on."

"How I understand you!" Lidia Andreievna suddenly said as if she were talking to herself. "It's a year now since my Alexei died, but I still cannot reconcile myself to his death. Are those unfortunate Caucasians to blame for his death? Oh no! It's the czar!"

"Dear Madame Lidia," Fischer stopped her. "It's inadvisable to say such things out loud. Before you is a living example: Monsieur Shevchenko wrote about all that and here he is a soldier in the Orsk Fortress. We know and understand this, but you cannot talk about it frankly in the Russian Empire, because if Monsieur Globa or Monsieur Meshkov or any other officer were to hear you, it would spell a lot of trouble both for you and your father."

Lidia Andreievna gave a bitter laugh.

"I know! But at times even a dumb man starts to shout. I lived in Piatigorsk in eighteen forty and remember Lermontov. He, too, was in disgrace and could not keep silent…"

"…and died from the bullet of a mercenary assassin," Fischer concluded her thought.

Shevchenko listened to the conversation with deep excitement. What a happiness it was to have crossed the threshold of this home!

Fischer diverted the conversation to music, opera and the concerts he had attended in Warsaw, and Natalia started passionately recalling her days in St. Petersburg. Then they talked about drama and the stage appearances of Shchepkin and Karatigin. Soon they learned that they had common friends. At the height of the conversation the general entered the parlor. In the morning he usually retired to his study where he read the *Russkiy invalid* or *World History* and always appeared for dinner in full dress uniform. But today, intrigued by Fischer's stories about the exiled artist and poet, he came into the parlor an hour earlier to meet Shevchenko before the arrival of the officers, who had dinner at their commander's every Sunday.

Seeing the general, Shevchenko got up and snapped to attention. The general smiled and extended his hand.

"Drop these formalities, old chap. I have enough of them during duty hours as it is. Sit down and tell me how you live here."

"I try to get used to it all, your Excellency, and be no worse than the others," Shevchenko replied.

"It must be difficult, mustn't it? Don't say no, old chap! I know it myself and regret not having done anything for you yet. It's all because of my ill health, the devil take it. A military man has it hard, but for a civilian our *corps de ballet* might be out of his depth altogether. I am a soldier of the Suvorov school and abhor that damned foot drill. The army exists so as to fight and defend the country, not for parades and humiliating people," the general thundered, getting ever more excited. "They teach you to march all right, but the officers themselves are not always good shots! In a war this *corps de ballet* is absolutely unnecessary. It wasn't by parading that we defeated Napoleon, and it wasn't by parading that we attacked Izmail, and we didn't cross the Alps to the tune of marches either. This damned order of things made me leave the Guards, because I am used to speaking the straight-out truth. So they decided that this hero climate would be the healthiest for me. Oh well, let the devil take them!" He suddenly waved his hand dismissingly, fell silent and hung down his head.

After the general had regained his breath from his passionate outburst and asked Shevchenko how he could help him, the poet said simply:

"Drill is a cursed thing to go through, but life in the barracks is much worse, what with that horrible dirt, unbearable stench, lice, millions of bed bugs, flies and cockroaches which don't give me a moment's rest. I doze off from fatigue only toward morning and wake up with a headache, an exasperated, crushed man. I grew up in misery, in a wretched peasant's home, but I have never seen anything like this even in a nightmare."

"That's my fault," the general muttered. "Whatever else, but bed bugs and dirt can be dealt with and... and everything else, too. Never mind, we'll get that done. Don't you be sad: I'll have something arranged for you."

He asked Shevchenko in great detail what the soldiers received for rations, and suddenly noticed that Shevchenko seemed to be holding something back.

"What's the matter? Once you've started to speak up, make a clean breast of it."

"I wanted to mention about the sick men. There are some soldiers who are marched off to drill while they should be ... well, they ought to be in hospital."

"So why haven't they reported through the proper channels themselves?"

"They reported to the noncoms and the corporal. There is one such novice, an utterly quiet character who is afraid of everything. He's got a hernia hanging like a bag."

"What is his name?"

"Ivan Karpov."

"I see... On the other hand... All right... Although... Inteesting... Who else?"

"There is Foma Berezin. He has a festering abscess on his foot. And Petrov obviously has scabs."

"And what do the noncoms do about it?"

"I don't know... The men say that only vodka makes the reports get through to the superiors. But otherwise..."

"What scoundrels!" the general burst out laughing. "Well, it's nothing unusual. In a soldier's life a lot of things depend on the noncoms. You were right in calling them bribe takers and leeches," he added with a twinkle in his eye.

Shevchenko squinted slightly.

So I've been squealed on, he thought. The general must have read his thoughts, and said in his deep voice:

"That's it, old chap. Let this be a lesson to you: you say one word, and your superiors get three words reported. In your situation you should keep your mouth shut."

Then the general settled in his favorite rocking chair and asked Lidia Andreievna to play something for him. His daughter played with feeling and under her fingers Chopin's nocturnes sounded deeply lyrical.

Presently, loud voices, the jingle of spurs and coughing came from the vestibule, and in the parlor there appeared Meshkov,

Globa, Stepanov, Ensign Bogomolov, and some tall, red-haired officer from the Second Company Shevchenko had seen on the parade ground only from afar. While the officers greeted the general and ceremoniously kissed the hand of Lidia Andreievna, Shevchenko and Fischer retired to a corner, but the general immediately remembered them.

"Gentlemen, let me introduce you — not in the line of duty but privately — to the only real artist and poet in Orsk. I ask you to like and respect him."

After such an introduction the officers had no choice but shake hands with Shevchenko, feeling deeply embarrassed on recalling how they had addressed him rudely on the parade ground and called him names for every awkward step, turn or movement.

"Monsieur Stepanov, and you, Captain, look what wonderful music I have been sent from Orenburg," Natalia warbled away to offset the moment of embarrassment. "Here is one of Susanin's arias from Glinka's opera. That's especially for you, Captain. And here is a romance for you, Ensign," she turned to Stepanov. "Otto and I have just had a try at a very melodious duet. I want every one of you prepare some musical item for my birthday. Monsieur Fischer will play his violin, and i will sing a duet with him. I'd like it to turn into a real concert like they have in the big cities."

"But only without the ballet troupe under Major Meshkov's direction," Fischer whispered to her.

Natalia could not check herself and burst into a giggle, covering her nose with a handkerchief to make it look as if she had a cough.

Meshkov sat by the general, and Petya claimed the fullest attention of Stepanov, as he showed him a model of a Roman catapult he had built out of pieces of wood, rubber bands and cork. Lidia Andreievna asked Shevchenko to sit at her side and tell her about Varvara Nikolaevna Repnina whom she had once met in St. Petersburg, while the officers looked through the sheets of music and commented on strictly military matters and news.

The dinner that followed was a noisy and lively affair. The officers had a few drinks and conversed with the ladies in an easy manner. After coffee the general invited Meshkov to his study and asked him about Shevchenko.

"He is a quiet man, sober and polite compared with others, but for the death of me he remains the same clodhopper he was when he arrived. He just hasn't got any military bearing — you might as well write finis to it," Meshkov said, spreading his arms in despair.

"All right, let him remain how he has been made by the Creator," General Isaiev said with a smile, puffing on his long pipe. "I think that as a political prisoner he should be transferred to civilian quarters."

"But, your Excellency, that is against regulations."

"What makes you think so? Fischer, Zawadzki, Królikiewicz are also soldiers and live out of barracks, don't they?'

"As to the Poles, we have a special instruction. The czar deems it necessary to keep them isolated from the soldiers, for they might be a bad influence. But this Shevchenko…"

"…this Shevchenko is no ordinary character. Today he rails at the noncoms, and tomorrow he might go after royal dignitaries."

"But he'll be under surveillance."

"Yes, that is so. But still … A word spoken is past recalling; his word might awaken a harmful thought in a soldier's head. I know such types, he must be isolated immediately. I know what I am talking about. It was not for theft or murder that he was forced into the army. His is a more serious case. What if he manages to induce adverse sentiments in the barracks and it becomes known to the higher-ups? What will happen then? Why, you'd be made responsible for it in the first place as battalion commander, and Captain Globa as company commander."

Such an unexpected argument overwhelmed Meshkov.

"Let me call Globa, and we'll think it over together," he proposed.

"All right, call him."

Globa heard out the general, and retorted:

"But that's against regulations."

"Come on, old chap," the general cut him short brusquely. "Regulations are written to maintain order, but every one of us breaks them once in a while. You, for instance, Captain, are entitled to a leave of twenty-eight days in a year. But who else but you, and twice for that matter, went to Orenburg for a length of ten days each time, and I didn't say a word to you, because not every feast is supposed to end in a reckoning, so to speak. And you, Major, asked me to give you help in building your house. Thirty soldiers worked on it without any pay for forty days, raising walls, setting rafters, building the roof and stove — everything. They even worked on holidays" — the general raised his index finger, — "and this at the expense of drill exercises, which by the very same regulations are prohibited from being replaced by anything whatsoever. I looked at all this through my fingers as well. But here we have an absolutely special case. I am serious about it, because such a quiet character might make a political rebellion flare up. Just imagine the Kirghiz rebelling against us as they did ten years ago. They come up to Orsk, and this here man juts it into the soldiers' heads that the Kirghiz have no serfdom, and our men side with the rebels out of stupidity. What tune will you be singing then? That is why I advise you not to argue the point. The first thing I'll do tomorrow morning is sign an order, because I've made up my mind to guard my own and your security by isolating him promptly from our 'drab riffraff,' " the general concluded and got to his feet, making everybody understand that his decision was final.

On leaving, he stopped at the threshold for a moment, and added:

"I advise you, gentlemen, to treat him circumspectly when he's in formation. Don't make a martyr out of him in front of the men."

While visiting the general, the officers felt themselves a little restrained: they liked to drink without measure, and after getting drunk, burst into song or dance, but the presence of Lidia Andreievna, a lady from the capital's high society, hindered them. For propriety's sake they asked her to play something on the piano, and while she played, they had a tedious time, pretending to be listening to her performance attentively. When she finished her number, they applauded all as one, and then did not know what else to do.

"Oh my," the red-headed ensign from the Second Company sighed all of a sudden. "Last year I was stationed at Nizhniy Novgorod. While the local fair was on, there was no end to the fun: gypsies, comedies at the theater, carousals at the restaurants every evening. We had an ensign there. He did not know music and his voice was not of the best, but he could sing those *khokhol* songs so well it wrung your heart to tears. We could listen to him for hours."

"Our Taras Grigorievich here also sings Little-Russian songs," Fischer dropped an offhand remark, realizing quickly that it was in Shevchenko's interests to produce the best impression on the officers. "Ask him. He is a wonderful singer."

Shevchenko, however, remained implacable.

No sooner had Shevchenko entered the barracks the next day after dinner than the orderly called out to him:

"Hey, Shevchenko! Off to the office! Clerk Lavrentiev wants to see you. On the double!"

Such a summons never portended anything good: it would mean either confinement in the guardhouse, extra duty for some minor infringement of regulations, or something else of the sort. But Lavrentiev met him amicably.

"This deserves a treat off you, greenie, because I've got orders to have you transferred to civilian quarters but with daily report for drill and other company exercises. So pack up your wearables, draw your rations in kind, and foot it to the settlement. You'll be issued your ration of bread every day before drill."

Shevchenko made the sign of the cross on himself for joy and was ready to embrace Lavrentiev. The latter smiled and asked:

"So where will you go now? Come to my place! My house is one of the best. The old lady, I mean my mother-in-law, died last winter. I'll have you settled in the living room. It's warm, clean and without any bed bugs. Now mind you don't bring any along from the barracks. My wife will plague the life out of you and me if you bring in that vermin. She's a compatriot of yours, a dumpling eater from Poltava, so her home is as clean as the general's."

"How much will you charge?" Shevchenko asked foresightedly, because his resources were depleted.

"People charge a ruble a month, but I'll take you in for nothing, if you're willing to teach my boys, Vasiliy and Stepan, reading, writing, 'rithmetic and all those other fancy school sciences."

"Agreed," Shevchenko said happily and hurried to the barracks to pack.

That day he could not get over his excitement. Meshkov unexpectedly relieved him of attending "colloquy" classes to let him get settled at his new place of residence. Shevchenko asked the hostess to lend him a scythe, cut himself some grass for a mattress, stacked the books by Schiller — miraculously saved from Kozlovsky and Belobrovov's greedy eyes — on a simple, rough-hewn table, but did not take the notebook out of his bootleg, because in his private quarters he would nonetheless remain under surveillance, an unexpected search was possible at any hour of the day; his bootleg notebooks were dearer to him than life itself.

By evening the hay had dried under the sun. He stuffed a mattress and pillow case with the hay, covered his bed with a gray soldier's blanket, hung his greatcoat on a nail, and sat down on a stool, taking pleasure in the quiet and inhaling the clean air of a tidy human dwelling. In the room stood a faint fragrance of dried herbs which hung along the wall in little bunches. Shevchenko recalled that Lavrentiev's late mother-in-law had been an herb doctor, and in his heart he wished that God rest her soul in His Kingdom.

That night he slept profoundly and serenely for the first time in days, and there followed a period in which he gradually regained peace of mind. Even drill seemed to him much easier after a healthy sleep at night. When his soldier's duties were over, he immediately hurried to his poorly furnished but nonetheless quiet and tidy room. He never said that he was hurrying home, because *home*, as he saw it, merged with *Ukraine*.

At first the boys, Vasiliy and Stepan, were afraid of their tutor, but eventually when "uncle Taras" made them an ABC out of cardboard Lavrentiev had got from somewhere, and painted an animal or bird on the reverse side of every card, they were suddenly overcome with a trusting love of him, not letting him leave them for hours on end and begging him to tell them a fairy tale or some interesting adventure.

At first Shevchenko taught as he himself had once been instructed to relate every letter with a whole word: *P* stood for *pan*, *M* for *man*, and *G* for *good*. When he visited the Isaievs again the next Sunday and told Lidia Andreievna about his lessons, she advised that he explain to the children that a letter is no more than a symbol representing one speech sound: *M* in the word *moon*, for instance, conveys the sound of a mooing cow, *S* the hissing of a snake, and *Z* the buzzing of a fly or bumblebee. Shevchenko had not heard about this new phonetic method of teaching the ABC before and was fascinated by such a simple and intelligible technique. He explained it to the children the very next day and their joy knew no bounds when they composed out of the scattered letters the simplest and dearest word for every child — *Mama*.

The new method of teaching made their pace of learning so rapid that within one month the boys could already read a printed text. Another thing that proved of help was Natalia Andreievna giving the boys her ABC by which she herself had once been taught to read and write.

Shevchenko had grown physically stronger while living in his private quarters, and his good mood made his verse sound mellower and tenderer. He even added a lyrical introduction to his mournful poem *The Princess*.

12. THE TAMING

Taijan's father had once been an outstanding hunter. He hunted with hound and falcon, but most of all he loved to hunt with a golden eagle. The old man was utterly deaf and barely moved around for his progressive rheumatism, but on seeing the eaglet he suddenly livened up and his eyes flashed in a youthful way from under his puffed up eyelids.

"He's not ours. We got him for the *bai*," Taijan shouted in the old man's ear, but his father understood him only when Taijan pointed first at the eaglet and than at Djantemir's white yurt which seemed to be tinted red in the setting sun.

In the morning Taijan went to the *bai*, but Djantemir had not yet returned from his visit to Zulkarnai, and Shauken was in charge. After a look at the eaglet, she flared up.

"What kind of a sorry scarecrow is that?! Take the creature away, away! We won't need such a freak. Call Jaisak! I'll tell him what sort of eagle we need."

After cursing her in his mind, Taijan threw a cloth over the eaglet and took him to Jaisak's yurt.

"Take him, auntie Kumish. Our mistress doesn't want him."

Kumish waved her hands with horror. "Oh no, Taijan, no! I'm afraid of him. Look how fierce and angry he is. Why, he might peck my eyes out. Take him to Jaisak. I don't have a place to put him anyway."

Taijan realized that old Kumish would really be unable to handle the restless bird, and took the eaglet to the pasture.

"All right, let's wait for Djantemir then," Jaisak said. "In the meantime, we'll have to tame this bully. Will you help me?"

While Taijan was holding the eaglet fast, Jaisak quickly tied jesses to the bracelets on the bird's feet. At each end of the jesses there was a copper ring through which he passed a strong *kulash-long* leash of raw camel leather with a metal ball at one end and a noose at the other. The ball was larger than the rings to prevent the leash from slipping out. Jaisak tied the other end of the leash to the *kerege*.

Then, after pulling on badger-skin mittens that reached to his elbows, he gathered the jesses along with the eaglet's feet in his fist and pressed them strongly. The bird let out a cry of pain and started to thrash, trying to peck the young herder, but Jaisak suddenly jerked the leash and the eaglet fell headlong to the ground; then he threw him up with a strong movement of the hand and settled him on his mitten again. The eaglet made to free himself, but Jaisak dropped him head down as before and threw him up on his mitten a moment later.

This contest of endurance between man and bird of prey lasted for another two or three hours. By midday the eaglet was completely exhausted. Rahim could not look on any longer. "Leave him in peace! Why are you torturing the poor bird?! You've been throwing him around like a rag half the day. He's hungry and tired. Sit him on a *tugir*."

"You can't!" Taijan replied. "He must be made to understand that man is stronger and must be submitted to. Grownup eagles are thrown like that for three days without any food and rest."

In the end, Jaisak took pity on him. He sat the eaglet on the mitten, stroked his sparsely downed head, and repeated tenderly:

"*Kal bopali! Kal bopali!*"

"Rahim, bring some raw meat and a lump of sugar," Jaisak called to the young lad, who at first took the contest between man and bird as an entertainment, but now was lying on the grass, his back turned to the scene of torture. These words brought Rahim to his feet and he dashed off to the herders' yurt where the meat was being cut for the evening meal.

At the sight of the food the eaglet started for joy and gulped several pieces of meat quickly and fearfully. Then Jaisak broke the lump of sugar into three little parts and put one of them into the bird's beak. He took the food out of his captor's hands warily just like he had out of his father or mother's beak the day before.

The weather was sultry and the sky cloudless. The short southern shadows clung to the ground, hiding under the belly of the horse and peeping shrinkingly out from under its side facing the north.

"Good day, Kuljan!" Jaisak called out when he rode past her. "Rahim is missing you terribly and asked that you come to our pasture. It's very fine there. You won't regret it!"

"I have no time," Kuljan sighed. "Here I'm shearing and shearing the sheep, with no end to the work in sight. My palms are covered in blisters."

"Take a rest then. The women will manage without you," Jaisak suggested. "When your father comes home, show him your hands and he will understand."

"He might, but Shauken won't," Kuljan said. "I also wanted to have a look at the herd and stay with Rahim for a while. How is Akbozad doing?"

"The colt's fine and healthy, may he be preserved from an evil eye," the superstitious Jaisak said by way of warning himself. "Don't be afraid of your *kshi apa*! Get on a horse and let's ride off!"

It was only now that Kuljan saw Jaisak leading a second saddled horse by the bridle. She gave another undecided look to the huge black sheep she had not finished shearing but the temptation to leave was much stronger.

"But what will I tell my father?" she asked.

"I'll do that, and all the herders will confirm that Rahim overate wild strawberries and is ill, and you came to treat him with strong tea and herbs," Jaisak quickly found an explanation.

"All right, I'll go!" Kuljan decided and called her friend: "Finish shearing for me, dear Karakoz!" She jumped into the saddle like a bird. "Let's go!" Jaisak cried out cheerfully. And they galloped off.

Kuljan spent an unforgettable day at the herders' camp. Rahim clung to her neck with a shriek of joy, and immediately started showing her his treasures. There were not many of them, though, because the songbirds did not let themselves be lured into his snares, and the cages he had prepared for them stood empty. Instead, he proudly treated her to two fried fish he had caught in the morning, and then led her to the forest to pick strawberries. Naturally enough, Jaisak joined them lest she be attacked by a panther lurking up a tree. His presence made her face red with blushes, and her eyes glowed with an inward light of a maiden whose love is pure and deep.

The herders liked Kuljan, and during the evening meal she was treated to the best morsels of mutton and the best kumiss. Since it was improper for a girl to spend the night away from her parents' yurt, Jaisak and Rahim saw her off right up to the *aul*.

"It's a good thing you returned, son," Kumish said happily. "The mistress gave us a new yurt as a present and keeps asking for you every day. Go to her and thank her for the present."

"Has the *bai* come back yet?"

"No. Baisali and Iskhak returned, but the *bai* is laid up at Zulkarnai's. He broke his leg in the mountains and won't be back until he's able to sit in the saddle. Now Shaukon is the leader around here."

Jaisak made a wry face.

"All right. If it's so, let us go together, *apa*."

Kumish threw a white veil on her head and minced along at her son's side.

Shauken was about to go to sleep when they came up to her yurt.

"You behave as if you were hiding. I hope you're not?" Shauken asked with an angry smile but nonetheless playfully, as she greeted them.

"I have a lot of work on my hands," Jaisak said with a bow. "Mother and I have come to thank you and Djantemir for the present. It's a good present, and it has to be deserved. That is why I stayed with the herd. My father died, so did Grandpa Faizullah, and the herders over there are young and inexperienced."

"That's what we appreciate in you," Shauken smiled. "You are a real *jigit* and deserve such a present. Live in your yurt to your heart's content. And now tell me how this year's lambs and calves are coming along."

Jaisak reported briefly and precisely, and although she tried to prolong the conversation, he precipitated the departure.

"Let us go, *apa*! At dawn the shepherds will come to me to drive the flock to another watering place. I promised to help them. Good night, mistress!"

Shauken could do nothing but let him go.

The day before his departure for the mountain pasture Jaisak stayed with the flock throughout the whole morning. When he was going back to the *aul* down a mountain footpath running along a stream and rounded a cliff, he stopped abruptly in his tracks, stunned. In a scanty creek he saw Shauken bathing.

"Oh, it's you, Jaisak!" she gave a cry, either from fright or for joy.

Jaisak turned away shamefacedly.

"Salaam, mistress," he mumbled, not knowing what to do.

"You greet me rather badly, Jaisak," Shauken said playfully, wringing out her wet hair. "You've turned away and don't want to look at your mistress."

He turned his face toward her and went rigid with shock. She was standing in the water only up to her knees, absolutely naked, the water dripping from her head and running down her legs. Blood shot into his head when he saw her plump body in its blooming prime. Summoning his will, he forced himself to turn his back on her.

"It is not fit for me to look at the wife of such a respected person as our *aga*," he said in a peculiarly dull voice. "Do not play such jokes on me, mistress."

Shauken shrugged her shoulders angrily, but nonetheless slipped into a long chemise and started to plait her braids.

"I am sick of the old man. Besides, the creek here is so warm and clear. And where do you water your herd?"

"Wherever I come across water. Sometimes here and sometimes lower down the stream," he replied, without understanding what she was leading up to.

"So I'll be coming here as well. And you'll be looking at me, because it is sweet for a young *jigit* to look at the body of a woman."

"You say bad things, mistress! Don't! Besides, it is dangerous walking these footpaths alone; not so long ago a panther tore a jackass to pieces here, and Ulagai killed another panther with a stone sling."

"But I won't be alone — you'll be with me. Wouldn't you protect me?"

"The herd is grazing far away from here. I wouldn't hear you, and people might see and censure us."

"Where do you see people here? Only the forest, meadows and cliffs all around. There will be but the two of us I am sick of Djantemir's grouching. I hope he doesn't return at all We'd have a wonderful time together."

"And do you know, mistress, what punishment we'd deserve by the *shariat*?" Jaisak said, trying to impart a polite tone to his voice. "They'll take a lariat, make a noose at both ends, throw such a noose round our necks each, bring up a camel, put it between us, make him lie down, and throw the middle of the lariat across his back, then the camel will get up, and you and me will dangle down his sides. I don't know about you, but I am not willing to die yet."

"They won't dare! What is not permitted to a common woman is permissible for a *bai*'s wife, and like all men Djantemir will be sleeping in his yurt, without suspecting anything. Who will dare tell him something against me?" Shauken went on, finishing plaiting her braid and drawing closer. "Don't you really want me? Why are you standing there like someone struck by lightning? Stop pretending to be an innocent lamb! I am telling you: nobody will dare to even hint."

"I will dare! I will tell" a strained boyish voice suddenly rang out.

Rahim, his face red with rage, darted from behind a cliff where he had been lying with a fishing rod on a flat stone, hoping to hook some evasive graylings. He had heard every single word of the conversation and appeared from behind the cliff, fearing that Jaisak would not be able to resist the woman's temptation.

"Oh, it's you, you pup!" Shauken hissed, her face going pale.

Her lips trembled, she felt sick in the pit of her stomach. Jumping from foot to foot as if the stones he was standing on were burning his bare soles, Rahim cried frantically:

"I'll tell everything! Everything! You alone will be punished by death. Jaisak isn't guilty of anything!"

"And what about him traipsing around the woods with girls? Do you think he was just picking strawberries with Kuljan there?" she hissed again, clenching her fists.

"What?! Don't you dare telling lies about him and my sister! They are young, and they enjoy being together. Ugh, you old hag!" Trembling with rage, he rushed up to his stepmother. "Just you try and lie about my sister. Just you try and chase her to work! She's no slave of yours! I'll tell everything about you! Both to my father and to the *jigits*! And to the women, too! To everybody!" Rahim cried out, jumping in front of her like an enraged rooster. "Just you try!"

"Hush, Rahim! Calm down! The mistress was only joking! Nobody will pick on Kuljan anymore! And she won't be chased to work! Go home now, mistress, and calm down as well: the boy will hold his tongue, but you had better forget the way to this place," Jaisak said sternly. "And thank Allah that the boy was alone here."

"Not alone!" Rahim cried out with furious anger. "Ismagul is here and Grandpa Ulagai! The three of us are fishing together. Hey, Ismagul, come out here, and you, too, Grandpa!"

An embarrassed Ismagul, Rahim's friend, came forward from behind the cliff, carrying a pail with about half a dozen graylings swimming in it, and then the gray-bearded shepherd Ulagai appeared. Shauken's jaw dropped; abruptly turning on her heel, she ran away, forgetting her mirror and towel on the stone.

"Aha, got scared, you snake! Running, aren't you? Run, run, you nasty creature!" Rahim cried after her. He fell silent only when Jaisak gave his arm a powerful jerk.

"Shut up, Rahim! Enough! If she was behaving indecently, so your behavior isn't any better. It's not your business to teach your elders. For this your father might give you a good whipping with a *kamcha*. She's been tamed as it is. She won't dare touch Kuljan now, but you, too, have to keep your tongue between your teeth. And you, Ulagai, and Ismagul, too! All right, let's go!"

Several days passed. Shauken locked her tongue; Kuljan had a brief rest after shearing the sheep and took to her favorite occupation — weaving carpets. Shauken did not pick on her anymore.

Kuljan visited the herders on several occasions to see Rahim who did not come to the *aul* for long, so as not to meet the "cursed harlot," as he called his *kshi apa* now. Under great secrecy he told Kuljan what had transpired at the mountain creek, and Kuljan understood why her life had suddenly taken an easier turn. Every time she met Jaisak, she blushed and was all aflame with the pure joy of first love. Even the thought of the distant Ibrai rarely crossed her mind now.

In the meantime, Djantemir had sent word that his leg had mended, and the *aul* was expecting him any day. That was why Taijan and Jaisak again made preparations to catch a golden eagle in the mountains.

Catching a large grownup eagle followed quite a different procedure from taking an eaglet from the nest. The first thing Taijan did was find three young slender pine trees over six feet tall each; he felled them and stripped them of branches and bark. On the tip of the first he wound a bundle of wool saturated with tar; to the top of the second he attached a ring, passing through it a thin but strong, twisted string with a noose at its end; and to the third he fixed a reflector made of a shining white tin plate. To find such a piece of tin in the mountains was next to impossible. Taijan's deaf father had one, but he would not lend it to his son for anything in the world. So Taijan had to pretend to have been taken sick and stayed in bed for two days, waiting until the old man would leave the yurt to warm himself in the sun so the plate could be taken out of the chest while he was outside.

"After we catch the eagle I'll put it back," Taijan explained. "He won't notice anything."

When they reached the mountains, Taijan did not inspect the crests of the cliffs, but galloped on, to where the intermontane trough became wide and a creek gurgled merrily in the middle. On either side of the creek grew centennial cork elms and gnarled oak trees. But none of them seemed to be fit for his purpose, because he passed them and galloped on and on. Then he suddenly reined in his horse and stretched out his arm, pointing to a huge dry cork elm standing in the middle of the plain. When the horses rode up to it, they saw it was dirty with bird dropping — a sure sign that an eagle was passing its nights up the tree. It was midday by then. Without being afraid of the eagle appearing, the hunters measured the poles against the highest branches. There was only one dry branch that was unreachable, so Taijan climbed up the tree without wavering and cut off the branch. Now he was sure that they'd catch the eagle. The hunters rode away from the elm and settled in the shade of a full-branched nut tree where they had a generous sunset meal and lay down to rest until the evening The hunters watched the eagle as long as twilight permitted and glanced in fright at its hooked beak and talons which could pierce a human skull with a single blow. Apart from Rahim, Taijan had taken along two *jigits* who had warned Rahim urgently not to approach the eagle closer than three full *kulash*.

At long last the eagle fell asleep. Jaisak carefully lifted the lid off a pot filled with glowing coals, lit the tar-saturated wool on the tip of one of the poles which he bound with leather thongs to the second pole topped by the reflector. The men quickly approached the tree, raised the poles to the level of the eagle's head, (the reflector at first turned away from the eagle) and instantly turned the poles round, throwing a dazzling light, multiplied threefold by the reflector, into the eagle's eyes. The glare roused the eagle from sleep; he closed his eyes the next moment, and hissed threateningly. Blinded, he stared then at the fire and saw neither the hunters nor the thin noose that was lowered over his head. Taijan did not miss his mark: the noose embraced the eagle's neck, clutched his throat, and sealed his doom when he was pulled down the tree with a jerk.

The struggle that followed was long and arduous. The ruler of the skies was not prepared to give up. His talons ripped the sturdy canvas, his ravening beak tore the sheepskin coats and mittens to pieces, but in the end metal rings fettered his feet, his wings were twisted behind his back, and a huge sack became the dreary night abode of the tough opponent.

For three days and nights, relieving one another in turns, Jaisak, Taijan and the other two *jigits* tamed the bird to their will. But every resistance has its limits. By the end of the third day Taijan threw the semi-conscious bird to the ground.

"Enough!" Taijan said, throwing the eagle up onto his mitten for the last time. "A dead eagle won't earn us even a bowl of kumiss, let alone a chunk of mutton from Djantemir. We have tamed both the nestling and this big one," he concluded, setting the eagle on the *tugir*.

"And what about the *bai*'s wife?" Jaisak asked with a derisive squint in his eye. "She's been tamed too. Ever since our boys gave her a good pecking she hasn't been pestering Kuljan and the other women."

The next day Djantemir returned to the *aul* at last. He was still limping slightly, but could already walk without crutches or cane. Shauken put on a show of happy reunion by throwing herself on his neck "for joy" before the entire *aul* and ordered a number of her sheep to be slaughtered and for everyone to be treated to noodles with mutton and badger meat. Djantemir could not help wagging his head in surprise on seeing his wife's unprecedented generosity, but as a husband, he was very much pleased by the attention accorded him.

When everyone had had his fill of the treat and settled round the *bai*, sipping the foamy kumiss out of their bowls, Djantemir told about his travel. Ibrai was already going on eighteen, but two years earlier he had been taken gravely ill. When still a teenager, he climbed a tree to pick some nuts and fell to the ground from a partly broken branch. At first nobody noticed any changes in him and he did not complain of anything, but one or two years later his back started to ache ever more terribly. He had difficulty in walking and could hardly bend down. He was rubbed with goat fat, the mullahs treated him with prayers and incantations, but his health deteriorated ever more until, last year, Zulkarnai took him to Orsk to a Russian physician who ordered the boy put in a plaster-cast bed, kept warm, fed well, and brought back for examination two years later.

"Zulkarnai gave the doctor two horses, and the doctor promised to restore the boy's health," Djantemir said. "Now he's laid up in his father's *aul*: the boy looks healthy, but he cannot get up, because if he does, he'll break his spine that has been smitten by a horrible disease, and then he won't be healthy to the end of his days."

"He asked about you, too," the *bai* turned to Kuljan who listened to her father with deep alarm. "I told Ibrai that you were waiting for him anxiously. Also, that you are capable of doing everything and are so pretty that even *akyn* Abdrahman composed a song about your beauty," Djantemir added, cunningly winking at his wife. Instead of shrugging her shoulder indifferently as was her habit and dropping a disparaging remark, Shauken suddenly gave a smile and said in a sugary voice:

"You should have also told him how industrious she is, how good she is at embroidering and weaving beautiful carpets."

"Oh yes, I forgot about the carpets," Djantemir said with a

sigh of regret/ "But Zulkarnai is so rich she'll live at his home without working, if only Ibrai gets well. And this is what he asked me to give you as a present." Djantemir stuck his hand into a pocket and produced a necklace bound in a tiny cloth. "Ibrai asked you to wear it and pray to Allah to make him well. Then we will celebrate your wedding in a year."

The girls darted over to Kuljan to have a look at the present, while Djantemir inquired about the flocks and commented on the bride money he was expecting from Zulkarnai, complaining bitterly that the prize would be his only in a year's time.

In the meantime, nobody had noticed that Kuljan had disappeared with her girl friends and a number of the *jigits*. This did not escape Shauken's eyes, but she had all too important reasons to keep silent, and Taijan, to divert the *bai*'s attention from the young people, brought him a huge eagle which he ceremoniously settled in the *bai*'s yurt on a *tugir* prepared the day before.

The *bai* was transported with joy. He feasted his eyes on the eagle like a child on a new toy or a warrior on a rare weapon, gave the eagle pieces of fresh mutton, lumps of sugar, and ordered Shauken to bring him from his trunk the most lavish *tomaga* he had, one that had belonged to an eagle he had hunted with when he was young and achieved fame throughout the entire steppe.

When Shauken informed him that she had presented Jaisak with a new yurt, Djantemir did not so much as utter an angry word, so timely was he overjoyed by the present from the young *jigit*.

"Oh, if only he were rich as the late Shakir had once been!" he said with a sigh, when he was alone with his wife. "I would have given him my Kuljan in marriage instead of that sickly Ibrai! I agreed to wait another year, but if he doesn't get well, I'll have to turn him down."

Djantemir did not know that Kuljan and Rahim were sitting behind the wall of the yurt at that moment. Blushing and trembling from excitement, she had heard her father's confession.

13. DAYS AND THOUGHTS

The mail arrived in Orsk with a supply transport in the latter half of the month. Everyone who was expecting a precious message from anywhere waited impatiently for it and, well in advance, prepared letters, parcels and money orders to be sent to all coiners of the vast Russian Empire.

Shevchenko was also anxiously waiting for the transport: he had to send Lazarevsky the address of Alexandriysky, a physician he had recently been introduced to at the Isaevs. Alexandriysky had immediately agreed to Shevchenko's mail being sent to his home. Besides, Shevchenko asked Lazarevsky to tell Gern not to send any more messages to the Orsk commandant — so frightened was he by the unexpected consequences of Gern's letter to Meshkov. And lest his letters from Orsk fall into the hands of the officers, Lidia Andreievna herself went to the post office and mailed Shevchenko's letters in her own name.

He could have written a lot and to many people, but at the thought that his letters would first pass through the hands of his superiors and the gendarmes, perhaps, the pen slipped from his fingers and he tore to pieces unfinished letters in which every line cried out in anguish.

In the middle of August he started counting the days and hours when he would get a reply from Orenburg and Ukraine. But his expectations were in vain: there was no mail for him that month. Neither Levitsky nor Lazarevsky, let alone Gern, had had the courage to send their letters openly by mail.

Shevchenko was assailed with grief, and on the pages of his bootleg notebook appeared verse deploring the sun not warming his soul in the faraway steppe beyond the Ural, where he wished the free wind would at least bring the dust from his homeland and scatter it on his grave if he were fated to die here.

The days became shorter, the nights colder. Every morning, on holidays and Sundays, he hurried to his new friends and returned with gratitude the books he borrowed from them, chose another one to read, and then settled down to hear the latest news which now and then reached them from Orenburg and sometimes even from the banks of the Vistula. They read to each other their letters in which every word was deliberately ambiguous — the state of the weather stood for public sentiments, convalescence for hope of imminent change, and surgical operations for arrest and trial.

These conversations invigorated Shevchenko and inspired hope for the reversal of the reactionary violence. It was not without reason that Europe was living through great changes.

"Mark my words, gentlemen: after dethroning Louis XVIII, the French will soon depose Louis-Philippe," Stanislaw Królikiewicz kept repeating with conviction. "There is a great sense in the proverb: 'Between two evils 'tis not worth choosing.' Previously the people suffered directly from the aristocrats, and now financial magnates and manufacturers have snatched the reins of power. At a factory the working day is between sixteen and eighteen hours long. The peasantry is disintegrating, swelling the ranks of the workers more and more. And when all the laborers come out into the streets of Paris at one and the same time, Louis-Philippe is going to be in difficulty. France is now setting the pace for Western Europe. And the reverberation of its revolutions is shaking both Prussian and Austrian absolutism. Soon there will be neither serfdom nor autocrats throughout all of Europe — take my word for it."

Such thoughts encouraged Shevchenko, and he returned from his hospitable friends, carrying under his arm a new book and, in his heart, a ray of hope that he would live to see better times and regain his freedom.

He almost never brought books into Lavrentiev's home so as not to bring a new disaster on his friends. Instead, he went into the steppe where he either read for a long time, wrote his verse, or else sat silently by the river, engrossed in his thoughts.

Sometimes he was accompanied by Fischer, because General Isaiev had been taken seriously ill, and after tutoring Lidia

Andreievna's boy, Fischer left discreetly, realizing that neither she nor Natalia were disposed to entertaining guests.

"Write! Write again! Remind them of your existence," Fischer advised the poet insistently. "But don't mention that you live in private quarters."

Shevchenko gave a sigh.

"I have written already — to Sazhin, Lizohub, Pletniov, Dahl, Grigorovich and Hrebinka, I was going to write to Zhukovsky, but Gern learned that he was abroad. I even wrote to Karl the Great, as we used to call Professor Brüllow. And nobody has written a word in reply. Just to think of it — nobody at all!"

"Damn them! And they are supposed to be friends!" Fischer cried angrily. "They're not friends but filthy people of the basest sort! Lackeys who don't know what honor is! Every decent person must — do you hear me? — he simply must extend you a hand of assistance, and in case such help is impossible for the time being, support you morally at least. What a time has come, when everyone trembles for his own hide like a wet dog!"

"From the Moldavian to the Finn all silent are in all their tongues, because such great contentment reigns!" Shevchenko quoted from his *The Caucasus* as he chewed on a dry grass stalk.

"All right, so don't wait for the letters! Don't expect any help! Help yourself then! Write to Dubelt! Write to Orlov! Fool them! Renounce your convictions in word, so as to preserve yourself for the struggle, for the future! Appeal for pardon! Repent!"

"Never!" Shevchenko snapped back. "I'd hate myself for doing that. I spent days writing a letter to Governor Funduklei in connection with my belongings having taken away from me during the search, and you cannot imagine how repulsive and difficult it was for me."

"I see!" Fischer said after a pause. "You are a terrible judge on history's behalf. You are an exposer, a witness of their black deeds! I shouldn't have advised you as I did. Please, do forgive me!"

Fischer fell silent, shamefaced.

During the golden evenings of early autumn Shevchenko frequently thought of his Ukraine, his heart was there on the banks of the old Dnieper River as he wandered by the ruins of the monastery at Trakhtemiriv, the refuge of the old, feeble Cossacks. He recalled the fearless swordsmen, crowned with the glory of the battles of long ago, who in their declining years retired to the monastery to atone for their sins by prayer. A Cossack retired from the secular world with noisy and pompous celebrations, but under the monk's cowl he now and then yearned for the past, recalling his merry, heady youth and the temptations of the sinful world in which he had known both glory and happiness as well as a lot of overwhelming, unforgettable grief.

In his mind's eye he also saw the steep bluffs of the Dnieper at Kaniv, Kiev and Tripillia. And he conceived an unborn dream of returning to his homeland and building himself a comfortable cottage on one of those bluffs.

But every time the sorrow of his recollections and contented dreams was ruthlessly invaded by something horrible and hateful: all too much had Shevchenko seen hideous scenes of serfdom, and the bitter fate of his serf brothers and sisters became an inseparable part of his soul. His eternal enemies, the lords and landowners — they stood before him, ready for the sake of their drunken orgies to take away from the poor peasant his last cow which fed his children.

Verse after verse, poem after poem was written down in his bootleg notebook, reviving the horrible truth of the epoch of serfdom. In the distant steppes beyond the river Ural he thus settled his lengthy account with all the serf owners and even with the czar himself.

But there were also moments when despair gripped him, and then his verse turned into laments and tears.

Summoning his will, he always got the better of himself: he had to preserve his life. Perhaps he'd live to see the day when he could fight for the freedom of his people in word and deed. That was his duty, his calling, the aim and purpose of his life. He had to fight, even when wounded, to the last drop of blood, to the last spark of life in his tortured body.

In early September, rains set in. It became instantly cold, and during this first spell of bad weather maneuvers were suddenly announced.

The company was moved from place to place. Though this was no parade ground, the men marched in goosestep, covering from twenty to forty *versts* in a day's march. The nights were spent in tents which were broken at dawn, and then the men moved on in their cumbrously heavy greatcoats drenched with rain to the last stitch and they slugged on through the slimy, sucking mud that stuck to their boots, turning them into veritable dumbbells. But the most difficult part of it all was to drop on the ground and shoot or crawl around in the mud. Previously, Shevchenko's legs were racked with rheumatism every autumn, and now the disease was rampant. In vain did he try not to lag behind the others to the torrent of foul cursing by the sergeant-major and noncoms. Once he dropped to the ground, he could not get up. At last the battalion medical attendant reported to the superiors that Private Shevchenko had to be hospitalized. Shevchenko was relieved of the marches, but for another two weeks he had to remain in the battalion train until the maneuvers were over and the battalion returned to Orsk.

On learning of Shevchenko's illness, Doctor Alexandriysky immediately visited him, found the patient to be ill with rheumatism and scurvy in its initial stage, prescribed him an ointment and alcohol compresses. The notion of vitamins did not exist in Shevchenko's time, but from experience it was known that a patient affected with scurvy got better when he ate fruit and vegetables. In Orsk, though, they were difficult to find. The physician turned to Isaiev for help.

First thing next morning Lidia Andreievna and Natalia sent Shevchenko a whole basketful of turnips, onions, and heads of cabbage, with the strict order that he eat the vegetables raw. The latter helped Shevchenko much more than the ointment, and the alcohol prescribed for the compresses Shevchenko drank up together with Lavrentiev to the health of Lidia Andreievna and Natalia.

Alexandriysky frequently called on Shevchenko. He always brought along a book and eagerly told him interesting events from the medical profession or from his personal experiences, to which Shevchenko liked to listen.

His Polish friends also made their calls, lavishing him with the best of tobaccos and once bringing him a new anthology of young Polish poets to read.

In two weeks Shevchenko had recuperated and had a good rest. When he got on his feet, the first thing he did was to go for an unsteady walk into the steppe. The autumnal skyline was perfectly straight like the horizon at sea. The wind swept the reddened balls of tumbleweed into the distance. Storks winged their way to the south in extended wedges, and their honking voices reverberated in the poet's heart with deadly sadness.

14. A VISIT TO THE BAI

In the evening, Lavrentiev gave Shevchenko a cunning wink, and said:

"Well, Grigorievich, let's go on a visit tomorrow."

"Where to?" Shevchenko wondered, not too keen about seeing Lavrentiev's friends: Sergeant-Major Laptev and the two dashing noncoms — the curly-headed Zlintsev and the pock-marked, taciturn Kunitsin.

"To the Kirghiz. They arrived yesterday and are staying by the Or for the winter. They come every year. The general told their *bai* several times to set up the *aul* at least forty *versts* from the fortress, because we in the fort, as well as the Cossacks and the people from the settlement need the pastures and hay for our own horses and cattle. As soon as I learned about their arrival I reported to the general, but he waved it off. 'Let them be,' he said. 'They'll stay just one more winter, but next year I'll chase them away. Djantemir can wander wherever he wishes, but we need the steppe around the fortress."

Shevchenko looked forward to the prospect of gaining some new experience.

They walked straight across the steppe to the distant bend of the Or where the indistinct outlines of the yurts looked like Asian skull caps scattered around the plain.

"The Kirghiz have their own customs," Lavrentiev explained, blind to Shevchenko's effort to keep up with the pace because of his ailing legs. "Their guests are not supposed to come up right to the yurt. They must stop some thirty paces away and wait until the host or someone of his family comes out. The guest is approached, asked his name, what business has brought him here, whether this is a friendly call for a pleasant chat, after which the dogs are chased back and leashed, and only then is the guest invited into the yurt. The dogs they've got are real beasts: whoever comes too foolishly near is torn to pieces."

"Oh-h!" Shevchenko let out a moan at last. "Just halt for a minute. I can't keep up with you. My legs are aching so much."

Lavrentiev slacked his pace, and then carried on his lecturing.

"Now mind you, they are outright savages and heathens at that. They must bow to us and submit. When you are inside, sit down in the depth of the yurt opposite the entrance on a white piece of felt, but not by the threshold where the dogs and falcons sit."

Lavrentiev's way of seeing things annoyed Shevchenko, but any careless comment on what the clerk said could be, even inadvertently, reported to his superiors, and so Shevchenko kept silent.

They were now approaching the *aul*. The first to take note of them were the dogs which rushed toward the uninvited guests with deafening barks.

"Company, halt!" Lavrentiev commanded in jest. "Stand at ease!"

Both stopped in their tracks.

Djantemir *Bai* was just then sitting in his reception yurt with the *akyn* Abdrahman, whom he had not seen since the wedding party, and was treating him to kumiss.

"It's a long time since I heard your songs, Abdrahman," Djantemir said, handing him a bowl filled to the brim with kumiss. "I have missed them, and a good chat too."

"There is not much of cheer in the world today to go with a song," the *akyn* said with a sigh. "The Russian czar is oppressing us more and more, making us pay the *yassak*, the ruble and a half for every yurt, for fishing, for wool, for the possession of flocks, for the *kerege* wood — to pay for everything, as a matter of fact."

"Oh yes, you are right," Djantemir gave a nod. "I, too, am being knocked about, sitting here and waiting every minute for Isai Pasha to chase me away from my winter pastures."

At that moment the *aul* dogs broke into a frenzied bark.

"Hey, people! Have a look what's going on out there?" Djantemir called, partly getting on his feet. "Iskhak, go and have a look what's the matter!"

Iskhak went out of the yurt and was back a moment later.

"Some Russians from the fortress are coming to us."

Shauken who had been sitting by the threshold instantly went into a bustle, hiding something away in the dark corners, and Djantemir went pale as he put on his gown.

"See, it's just what I said: they're after me," he mumbled. "Why are you standing here?!" he shouted suddenly, and, whip in hand, came up to Iskhak. "Run over there, and ask what they want and who they are."

In the meantime, Shauken was feverishly tearing the gold coins off her sleeveless jacket and hiding them in her pockets with trembling hands; then she grabbed the ivory-inlaid saddle hanging on the *kerege* and ran outdoors to hide it in one of the black yurts, while Kuljan and Kumish were pulling away a trunk holding the best clothes.

The shrewd Lavrentiev noticed immediately that his appearance had caused a stir, and smiled facetiously. At long last a tall young *jigit* emerged from the yurt and quickly walked toward the guest.

"*As'salam alaikum*," he said with a respectful bow. "What do the brave Russian *askars* wish?"

"Hello, Iskhak! Don't you recognize me?" Lavrentiev extended his hand. "Is your father at home?"

Iskhak's dazzling white teeth flashed on his swarthy face in recognition, and he shook the clerk's hands respectfully.

"He's home! He's too old and too fat. Can't run fast enough to meet his guests, so he sent me. Do come in, please. We have an *akyn* with us today. He's drinking kumiss and is about to sing us his songs. Will you listen to him?"

"Of course! Did you hear that?" the clerk turned to Shevchenko. "We've come just at the right moment to hear an *akyn* sing. And this is my friend," Lavrentiev pointed at Shevchenko. "Meet him and leash your dogs," he added cheerfully, anticipating a lavish treat.

Presently Djantemir came out of the yurt and saw the clerk from afar.

"Stop fussing around," he snapped at Shauken. "These are simple soldiers. There's no need to slaughter a second sheep. One is enough."

Turning to Abdrahman, he spread out his arms in exasperation, saying: "See, I have to kowtow to every cur. This soldier keeps company with Isai Pasha and the others and can put in an occasional word for the *aul*."

Wearing a false, sugary smile, Djantemir went to meet the guests.

"*Oi boi*, what a joy it is to me! Such fine guests have come!" he said, shaking Lavrentiev's hands with both of his. "Come into the yurt. There is an *akyn* inside who will sing for us," Djantemir carried on, as he shot sidelong glances at Shevchenko and could not pluck up his courage to ask Lavrentiev who he had brought along.

"This is a new man we've got," the cunning clerk intercepted the *bai*'s glance and understood his alarm. "He used to live in the capital, was a big chief, but then he quarreled with some general, for which he was sent here for some time. He's staying at my home," he put Djantemir's mind at rest finally.

Djantemir also shook hands with Shevchenko ceremoniously, saying that a guest was a blessing from Allah. Smiling as exaggeratedly as before, he invited both guests to sit in the place of honor behind the fire.

Shevchenko sat at Lavrentiev's side and looked around with interest. He had never been inside a yurt before.

Lavrentiev sat at Djantemir's side with the mien of an ambassador of the Russian Empire in the land of the Papuans. Djantemir still did not know the purpose of his visit and smiled ingratiatingly at him, trying to get a conversation going.

"How did you fare here throughout the summer?" he asked.

"Not bad," the clerk replied, twirling his mustache. "Yesterday I was told you arrived, so I reported to the general about it this morning."

At this point Lavrentiev made an eloquent pause to lend his words the greatest possible import and create the impression that it was not the general who decided the fate of the *aul*, but that it was he, Lavrentiev, who had told Isaicv what to do. For all his restraint, Djantemir involuntarily straightened up, trying in vain to conceal the alarm behind his mask of attentiveness and politeness.

"'Our Djantemir has arrived at his old winter encampment,' I said. 'So he probably has no other place to pass the winter. His cattle are many, and the steppe around is occupied by other *auls*. It's a pity,' I said, 'because he makes a good neighbor. Will he really have to leave this place?'"

Lavrentiev paused again, and Djantemir could not hold himself in check any longer and clasped the clerk's hand. Lavrentiev gave a smile and continued:

"The general just waved his hand and said, 'All right, Lavrentiev. If you're so concerned about the man, let him stay this time, but next year he must look for another place.'"

Djantemir breathed with relief: so he could quietly sit out the winter on the Or till spring. Djantemir bared his sparsely set yellow teeth in a smile of undisguised joy.

"*Oi boi*, how well you reported to Isai Pasha! A great many thanks to you. Visit me more frequently to eat mutton, listen to the *akyn*, drink kumiss, and have a pleasant chat."

"All right, we'll be visiting you now and then!" Lavrentiev grinned. "I've brought here a friend of mine. He's a good and learned man. He taught my boys to read and write in no time. They're reading books now so quickly you'd be surprised."

"My Iskhak is also a learned man, and Rahim has started to study too," the *bai* boasted. "I've sent him to a madrasah. He can read the Koran and other books."

From the moment the Russians appeared in the yurt, Abdrahman did not speak a single word. He did not like the way Lavrentiev bit crunchingly into the lump sugar, but Shevchenko caught his interest. What sort of man was he, why was he looking so intently around the yurt, at the people and the things that were so usual for every nomad?

Shevchenko sat with a bowl in his hand, forgetting to drink the tea he had been served: everything around him was so interesting. Suddenly the eagle on his perch roused himself from sleep and let out a shrill scream, spreading his huge wings.

"An eagle!" Shevchenko said, astonished. "What a beauty!"

"A golden eagle," Djantemir confirmed gravely. "He hunts wolves and fox. A good eagle — big and strong. Jaisak caught him."

The eagle got up on his strong tall feet with big hooked talons, stood like that for a minute, jangling the chain and settled on the *tugir* again, the thin films of his eyelids closing over his keen yellow eyes.

Shevchenko's heart gave a start: here was a mighty proud creature but — fettered, a perpetual prisoner.

It was only Abdrahman who noticed the bitter smile which

barely twitched Shevchenko's lips, and he understood the meaning of that smile.

"So you are the *akyn*?" Lavrentiev suddenly asked Abdrahman, putting down the empty bowl.

The *akyn* gave a nod, having understood only one word, *akyn*.

"Sing something for us then," the clerk went on with gracious consideration. "My friend here loves to sing, too. He's a *kobzar*, for short."

"*Kobyz*?" the old man became animated. "We don't play the *kobyz*. We play the *dombra*," he said clearly and touched his simple instrument.

On seeing that the *akyn* was about to sing, the women took away the samovar and dishes. Abdrahman tuned up the *dombra* and, after a moment's thought, addressed Shevchenko:

"I will tell you a *kyui*, my brother, because I see that the song is your soul."

Swaying rhythmically, he started to retell the message of he *kyui*.

"Wait a minute," Lavrentiev stopped him. "My friend does not understand a word of your tongue. Call the boy who knows Russian so well."

Abdrahman fell silent, and without stirring, dropped his yes, while Kuljan darted off like a whirlwind to Jaisak's new jurt; a minute later she was back with Jaisak, her face flushed from the run. Jaisak greeted Abdrahman politely, then he bowed to the Russian soldiers and sat down at the *akyn*'s side. Abdrahman again passed his fingers across the strings, and swaying in time to an inner rhythm, retold the message of his *kyui*: how a bird, on a motherly impulse, saved her nestling from a wiper and died from its poisonous sting. Jaisak diligently, but rather clumsily, interpreted the *kyui* into Russian. When he fell silent, tumbling over the last phrase, Abdrahman turned to Shevchenko.

"And now listen how the *dombra* sings it."

Shevchenko was deeply impressed and moved both by the

music and the message of the *kyui*, and the sound of the *dombra* proved to be much mellower than any other instrument he knew.

Lavrentiev, however, made a wry face and said:

"Such music is no good. We're not boys to listen to songs about little birdies. Better sing us a real song and with a voice, not with this soundless balalaika."

"Do sing, brother," Shevchenko asked, putting a hand on the old *akyn's* shoulder.

Abdrahman looked at him in indecision, realizing that he had failed. At that moment the women brought in a bowl with steaming meat and *manty* and placed it in front of Djantemir. He rolled up his sleeves and cut each guest a piece of meat. Then he gave Shauken an order, and a bottle of vodka and little china cups appeared before the guests.

"The Prophet has forbidden us to drink this," Djantemir said. "We buy it from the Russians. Drink, please, as much as you want!"

Lavrentiev imbibed the vodka liberally, glad that the whole bottle was his, and quickly became muddle-headed. After eating a second piece of mutton, Shevchenko turned to the *akyn* again.

"Sing something for me, brother. Sing about people, about the bitter lot of those who slave for the rich. You must have such songs, don't you?"

The *akyn* understood almost next to nothing of what he had been asked. The only thing that was clear to him was the guest was asking him to sing. After Jaisak interpreted the request, Abdrahman looked inquiringly at Shevchenko, and replied after a pause:

"I will sing. But first explain me why you, an *akyn*, became a soldier? Do you get pleasure from killing?"

For Shevchenko the question had the effect of a whip lash. Looking at the drunken clerk snoring by the empty bottle of vodka and at Djantemir whose senses had been blunted by the plenteous food and strong kumiss, Shevchenko suddenly replied frankly:

"It's because my homeland, Ukraine, is bathed in tears and blood under the heel of Czar Nicholas. It's because I composed songs about Cossack freedom and the bitter fate of the peasants. My songs spread across my native land. That is why the czar forced me into the army and prohibited me from composing songs. So here I walk with a sealed heart and with the frozen songs on my lips — a living corpse that has not been buried."

The old man was shocked. Jaisak looked fascinated at Shevchenko, while Kuljan, sitting in a far corner amid me carpets and cushions, furtively wiped away a tear.

Abdrahman sat silent for several minutes, then he seemed to have shaken off the burden of years, and plucking an unexpectedly vibrant chord, said:

"We, too have such *akyns*. They honestly serve their people, singing about those who rouse them against sultans, khans, the czar and such as him" — he motioned with his lead at the cozing Djantemir. "Have you heard anything about our Srym Datov? No? He called on the people to fight. Together with Pugachev he fought against your czarina. I will sing to you about him, about the unforgetable Srym, and you, Jaisak, interpret well to my brother *akyn* so that he knows that we, too, had heroic souls amongst us."

Shevchenko was all ears to every sound and every word of the song which Jaisak interpreted quickly and almost unhaltingly. He vividly imagined this whirlpool of the people's wrath, with *auls* ablaze, horses neighing, weapons clanging, and then shared with the legendary rebel the wholly familiar feeling of bitter exile, abuse and humiliation. When the *akyn* fell silent, Shevchenko clasped him in his embrace.

"How wonderful! My friend and brother, it's simply wonderful. But you must keep reminding the people about that. Reminding, rousing, kindling their yearning for freedom like a spark under the ashes of a dead fire," Shevchenko aid passionately.

Suddenly he saw that a crowd had gathered at the entrance to the yurt. Jaisak looked reverently at Abdrahman, and the people in the crowd whispered with enthusiasm and nodded approval of the *akyn's* singing, as they shot sidelong glances at Djantemir. The *bai* slept through almost all of the song and opened his eyes only when the *akyn* stopped singing and the last note of his accompaniment died away.

Shevchenko did not let the old *akyn* out of his embrace immediately. Touched by such a hearty response, the *akyn* bowed low to the poet.

"Thank you, Russian brother, for not mocking our songs." Then he handed him his *dombra*. "Now it is your turn. Let me, too, taste the sweet honey of your soul."

Shevchenko was perplexed.

"You see, I write my songs on paper, I do not sing them and I cannot play the *dombra*. If it were a *kobza*..."

"We have a *kobyz*!" Kuljan jumped to her feet and rushed to a trunk. "I'll find it right away."

"It seems there is nothing I can do but play and sing," Shevchenko said, accepting an old Kazakh *kobyz* from Kuljan. He still wavered, but in the back of his mind he was already choosing from the inexhaustible treasure trove of his nation's songs the one which by its rhythm and mood would fit the occasion. Then he plucked the first tentative chord on the *kobyz* and sang the verses from his *Testament* in a melodious recitative:

> *When I am dead, then bury me*
> *In my beloved Ukraine,*
> *My tomb upon a grave mound high*
> *Amid the spreading plain,*
> *So that the fields, the boundless steppe,*
> *The Dnieper's plunging shore*
> *My eyes could see, my ears could hear*
> *The mighty river roar.*
> *When from Ukraine the Dnieper bears*
> *Into the deep blue sea*
> *The blood of foes... then will I leave*

> *These hills and fertile fields —*
> *I'll leave them all and fly away*
> *To the abode of God,*
> *And then I'll pray... But till that day*
> *I nothing knew of God.*
> *Oh bury me, then rise ye up*
> *And break your heavy chains*
> *And water with the tyrant's blood*
> *The freedom you have gained.*
> *And in the great new family,*
> *The family of the free,*
> *With softly spoken, kindly word*
> *Remember also me.**

Some of the words he accentuated with chords, and so as to make Jaisak grasp and interpret the words the easier, he replaced the Ukrainian words with the Russian ones the young Kazakh knew.

When Shevchenko finished, a whisper went through the crowd, but the Kazakhs did not dare express their fascination openly, so accustomed had they become to the green Russian uniforms being associated only with trouble. But the way they clacked their tongues, smiled, and beat their alms against their thighs meant for Shevchenko more than any words or thunderous applause. Abdrahman got up and raised his arms to the skies. "Praised be Allah that the Russians, too, have such people!"

Djantemir considered himself a great connoisseur of singing, but now he sat morose and angry; only the fear of Lavrentiev's vengeance made him smile occasionally and clack his tongue in pretense of being fascinated by Shevchenko's verse. He was mad at Abdrahman for the song about Srym, and in Shevchenko's *Testament* he indistinctly sensed similar motifs about the people's

---

* Translated by John Weir

wrath and desire for revenge. For him, Shevchenko's voice was akin to the hostile voice of Istai Taijanov, the leader of the poor, the defender of the very people whom Djantemir worked so ruthlessly.

Both *akyns* sensed his mood.

"It's time I went back to the fortress," Shevchenko said, rising to his feet. "I don't know what to do with him, though."

He tried to jolt Lavrentiev out of his drunken sleep, but the clerk mumbled something incoherently in reply and continued snoring loudly.

"Let him stay here for the night," Iskhak suggested. "We'll take him to his home in the morning."

"All right," Shevchenko agreed and thanked his hosts for their hospitality.

Djantemir forced himself to put on a broad smile, politely shook the poet's hand, and ordered Jaisak to chase the dogs away and see the guest off.

"Where have you learned to speak Russian so well?" Shevchenko asked when they had walked some distance rom the *aul*.

"When I was a teenager, the *bai* drove his herd to Omsk for sale and had Iskhak sent to study at a madrasah. A merchant, Ovchinnikov by name, bought the horses, and the *bai* left me at the merchant's home for the winter. There I learned your tongue," Jaisak explained eagerly.

"Who were the people who gathered by the yurt when we were singing?"

Jaisak's face clouded.

"Those were the *jataks*, or as you would say, the *bai*'s servants and all sorts of poor people, distant relatives, menials and *tyulenguts*," he said with a sigh. "All of us are poor. Extremely poor. For old rags and offal from the *bai*'s board we work for him from sunrise to sunset. Did you notice Shauken gathering sheep bones into a bowl? That was the meal for those poor people. The Russians are much better off than we: your muzhik is clothed, has a warm house, a plot of land, garden, and some cattle. We can only dream of such a life!"

Shevchenko stopped in his tracks from bewilderment. Did there really exist such hapless souls who envied the serfs? They should have tasted then the serf's bread brined with the tears and blood of the muzhik.

15. THE SOUL OF THE STEPPE

For a number of days Shevchenko lived under the vivid impression of his visit to the *aul*. The Kazakhs had fascinated him, as had their slender figures, their unrestrained movements and their artless open-heartedness. They worked strenuously for Djantemir day and night but had preserved the proud bearing and light gait of a free people.

On parting, Jaisak asked Shevchenko to visit his yurt, and the poet promised to do so during the next holiday.

Shevchenko prepared himself for that visit with pent-up excitement for he had an unconquerable desire to draw some of the Kazakhs. He had no oil colors, but Lidia Andreievna had presented him with some drawing pencils, a bar of sepia, and an album of Whatman paper.

I am forging my own shackles, Shevchenko thought, preparing to go to the *aul*, but he could not force himself to leave the album and pencils behind.

Jaisak's yurt looked cramped and poor compared with Djantemir's yurts, but still a white piece of felt was produced for the guest and he was seated in the place of honor opposite the entrance: the poet immediately noticed the young eagle on the *tugir*.

On hearing human voices, the eagle roused himself from sleep and gave a shrill shriek as if he were greeting the guest. In three months the half-naked eaglet had grown into a mighty, formidable looking bird, and Jaisak was proud of him. Kumish brought in a samovar and treated Shevchenko to tea while Jaisak told him about the *akyn* Abdrahman.

"Our *bai* quarreled with Abdrahman. When you left, Djantemir reproached him for having sung about rebels, which made Abdrahman call him a vampire and drunkard, and then and there he composed a humorous song about the *bai* and sang it to the whole *aul*. Djantemir got so mad he chased Abdrahman out of the yurt and told him never to show up again."

Shevchenko burst into hearty laughter; then he opened his album.

"What are you going to do?" Jaisak asked. On seeing that it was neither a flute nor any other instrument but a large notebook of thick white paper, he added: "You are going to write....I thought it would be some music."

This was uttered with such unhappy disappointment that Shevchenko could not help but smile.

"I want .to draw your *aul*, yurts, the people near them, and all of this," he swept his hand across the scenery and the sky. "You, too, sit down, Jaisak, beyond the threshold by the fire," Shevchenko added. "I want to draw you too."

But Jaisak shook his head.

"No! I will sit behind you. I want to see how you do it: I've never seen it."

"All right, sit down and watch," the poet agreed. "But give me a little board to put under the album."

Jaisak hurried off to look for a board. He did not find one in the end. So he pushed his mother's trunk to the middle of the yurt, and Shevchenko put his album on top of the lid.

What Jaisak saw made him regard Shevchenko as a magician: his pencil created a different, motionless life on the paper. And when there appeared the figure of Kumish with pails near the smoking samovar, Jaisak gasped and frightenedly grasped Shevchenko by the hand.

"*Oi boi*! But that's *apa*! Don't make a little *apa* on the paper! I'm afraid: *apa* might fall ill."

"Don't be afraid," Shevchenko laughed. "Would I be doing anything bad to you? We're friends, aren't we?"

"Yes, we are, big friends," Jaisak got excited, misusing Russian words. "But won't that be dangerous for *apa?*" he asked seriously, still alarmed.

"No, it won't. Upon my word it won't. I've drawn myself a lot of times by looking into a mirror," Shevchenko put his mind at ease. "If you want, I can draw you, too, and when I'm dead, you can look at yourself and remember me. Do you want a picture of yourself?"

"No!" Jaisak almost shouted. "Don't die. You must live long! Long! Like Abdrahman and twice as much! Let Allah grant you a great life, Taras *Aga!*"

Presently they heard a young female voice, ringing and clear like the spring, coming from behind the wall of the yurt. It was Kuljan singing, as she delighted in the beautiful pattern she had managed to reproduce on the carpet she was weaving. Shevchenko carefully lifted the flap and looked outside. Illuminated by the sun, Kuljan stood several paces away from him, and Shevchenko froze, afraid to alarm her. He quickly took the album and pencils, but to draw her he'd have to go outside, which could have scared the girl.

"Oh damn it!" he muttered. "If there were only a tiny window or hole…"

"You'll have one right away," Jaisak said with determination, and before Shevchenko could stop him, he thrust his razor-sharp knife into the felt wall of the yurt and cut a hole in it.

"Sit down on the trunk, Taras *Aga*! Draw on the paper a little Kuljan," Jaisak said, choking with excitement. Then he recalled that Kumish had a board after all — a board she was kneading dough on — and brought it to Shevchenko.

Shevchenko did not hear nor see anything going on around him. He had not noticed how Kumish entered and clasped her hands in horror and despair on seeing a hole cut in the yurt, their only refuge from the terrible snowstorms. Jaisak took his old *apa* by the arm and told her something so seriously and kindly that it set her mind at ease immediately; she fell silent, gave a submissive and quiet smile, and disappeared somewhere.

His pencil had already sketched a young girl as slender as a cypress when Kuljan suddenly sat down, turning her back on him to cut out appliqués for the carpet.

"Oh-h! Shevchenko moaned. "Tell her, Jaisak, that she stay on her feet for a quarter of an hour at least. Just a little bit. I beg of you!"

"All right, I'll do it right away. You just go on drawing the little girl on the paper. I'll go and tell her."

"But don't scare her off. Be careful!" Shevchenko said, trembling with excitement.

Jaisak gave a nod and darted out of the yurt. What the two young people were talking about then Shevchenko did not hear, but he guessed that Jaisak asked the girl to show him the finer points of her work. The conversation by the carpet lasted for a long time. Kumish looked into the yurt several times, but Jaisak was not there yet; she tiptoed outside lest she interrupt Shevchenko's pursuit and did not even dare to steal a glance at his drawing.

"Well, that's enough for today," Shevchenko said at length. "I'll work on the details in the settlement or come here another time."

He hid the pencils in his pocket, looked out of the yurt and waved to Jaisak to come in. After inspecting the sketch, Jaisak said with a sigh:

"At the home of the merchant I told you about I saw the picture of a god in the corner, but I did not know how he was made. The way you did it is much better. You do things like Allah Himself."

Kumish brought in a bowl of *airan* to treat Shevchenko, but he was in a hurry to get back to Orsk. Jaisak apologized lengthily and with evident embarrassment for not having slaughtered a sheep for such an honorable guest. Shevchenko put his mind at rest by saying that he'd be very much saddened to know that Jaisak had wasted his property so carelessly.

"You are young and have an entire life ahead of you," he said. "It's time you got married, and for that you have to have money, or sheep as is your custom."

"That's true," Jaisak agreed. "You say, 'This costs thirty kopecks,' but we say, 'This is worth half or a quarter of a sheep.' Our *bais* have money because they sell wool and cattle, but we are poor people as you see yourself. Come and visit us on the Bairam holiday. That's when we always slaughter sheep for the occasion."

"That's just what I won't do," Shevchenko said in jest "I'll come on a usual day on purpose. Looking at you and that girl, I thought that you'd make a good pair. Both of you are slender, young and handsome. Don't you really take a fancy for her?"

"*Oi boi*, I do! She's like a houri from the gardens of paradise," Jaisak sighed, excited. "I would chop my hand off for a wife like her! I'd take out one eye just to admire her with the other! And what a kind heart she has! How she pitied my father and mother. But she isn't mine: she's engaged already."

Jaisak told him everything about Kuljan. Shevchenko listened attentively, occasionally interrupting him with a question. He realized that a great and pure love reigned in the heart of the young herder, and he had to help him somehow to achieve his happiness. But how could he help, if he himself was a poor exile deprived of the opportunity and right to earn a kopeck?

"I am sure you will achieve happiness," he said after some thought. "That betrothed of hers will hardly get well. I have seen a lot of such sick people: they lie in a plaster cast for five or six years and only one out of ten gets on his feet. He'll die and that'll be the end of the engagement."

"Still, Djantemir won't give her in marriage to a poor man. He loves money much more than his daughter," Jaisak said sadly. "Besides, her stepmother, Shauken, hates her. She's glued her lips now and does not dare chase Kuljan to do hard work, but her heart is that of a snake. She derives joy from our grief and waits for our separation like a big holiday."

"You must fight for your happiness," Shevchenko said sternly. "So you want to hunt with an eagle you say? That's a wonderful idea. If you get enough fox furs, I'll help you sell them to the general's daughters: they'll pay a good price."

Although they did not come up with any new ideas during the long conversation that followed, Jaisak's heart lightened and he looked on in awe as the artist was finishing drawing the landscape, because Kuljan was now sitting with her back to the yurt and sewing varicolored appliqués on her carpet.

A large caravan track, along which goods from Bukhara and Persia were carried to Russia, ran through the wild steppe near Orsk. Some five *versts* from the fortress a caravanserai, much smaller and poorer than its counterpart in Orenburg, was built for the merchants. It surrounded a bartering yard which occasionally turned into a real fair ground. But mostly the caravans did not stop there for long.

When a caravan appeared on a holiday, Shevchenko took his pencils and a piece of bread and left the fortress to wander through the bartering yard and admire the lush colors of Oriental dresses, camels, asses, and the wares. Or when the caravan passed by, he sat down in the tumble-weed or tall thistles somewhere in the steppe and sketched either a camel or the figure of the most colorful man he could find.

He had to sketch stealthily, because Muslim law prohibited the representation of animals and people, and if he had been caught at his work by some Bukharan fanatics, he might have been struck by a dagger or strangled. There was yet another danger he had to beware of — being caught by his superiors or the boon companions of Kozlovsky and Belobrovov, soldiers who were capable of denunciation or blackmail. Shevchenko kept out of harm's way so carefully that for a long time nobody at the fortress suspected that he had been violating the czar's order.

There was only one time he could not hold himself in check — when he came across the drunken sergeant-major Laptev and the noncom Zlintsev staggering down the road. He picked up a little piece of charcoal lying on the ground and drew such a lifelike caricature of the two characters on the white wall of the nearest house that passersby held their sides from laughter. General Isaiev was informed of the incident. He went to inspect the caricature himself, which drew his boisterous laughter as well.

"And you call that a painting?" he said to Globa then "It's just a joke to teach our drunkards, so they keep off the streets at least in such an indecent state. He's been forbidden to paint or to draw, of course, but this is no more than a trifle."

"And what if he draws your Excellency like that or, God forbid, some illustrious person?"

"He's got enough common sense not to do such a foolish thing, and if he does, he'll be punished severely," the general said. However, when the general met Shevchenko, he warned him of the denunciation by the vengeful sergeant-major and got the poet's promise not to "play with fire" anymore.

16. THE UPS AND DOWNS OF LIFE

While waiting for the occasional mail to arrive at Orsk, Shevchenko continued writing letters.

In vain did he persuade himself that it was not his friends who had faintheartedly forsaken him, but the post which had not delivered his first letters to the addressees — the bitterness of the insult he felt, and his disappointment in people, became ever deeper, and more and more often there recurred a sense of despair at the thought that he had been rejected by the whole world to the end of his days, and was doomed to the hopeless vegetation of a garrison soldier.

At times a withering contempt grew in his heart — contempt for people who in word seemed to hate czarism as well, but who had not the courage, even secretly expressed in a private letter, to show at least a little bit of sympathy with a fighter against czarism.

Clenching his teeth, he tried to think of something else — this contempt for his contemporaries stifled him, but after a moment of anger he would be overcome by fatigue. Everything became meaningless, infinitely remote for him. Later, however, the pain in his soul would recur, the unconquerable love of life and a keen yearning to save himself would flare up again.

Then Shevchenko would address his letters "to freedom" once more — to knock at the doors of people's hearts.

He also wrote to the painter Chernishov whom he had met briefly in Orenburg. On learning that Chernishov was preparing to leave for St. Petersburg in the autumn, Shevchenko had given him a number of letters which he had promised to pass on to the poet's friends in the capital. Now Shevchenko asked him about the fate of those letters and described the stupid drill and the stenchy barracks, the officer's fisticuffs, knocked out teeth, caning, and ceaseless abuse — everything that could harry him to his grave.

His letters to Lizohub were worded in a warmer and softer manner. He asked him to send books and paints "just to have a look at them and recall the past," complained of intellectual hunger, and described his adventures in an ironic vein. Lizohub, however, would not be able to read them without tears welling up in his eyes.

After sealing up the last letter, Shevchenko fell to thinking. He realized well enough that his friends were afraid of losing their offices for corresponding with a "state criminal," but what about his lady friends? When the shackled Decembrists were exiled to Siberia for penal servitude, Princess Volkonskaya and Princess Trubetskaya launched a challenge against the czar by forsaking high society, their habitual comforts and merry careless life in order to share their husbands' fates. And following them, a common French woman who was no more than the mistress of one of the convicts, enjoying no civil rights whatsoever, prepared to go on the distant journey to Siberia as well.

Shevchenko would not have accepted such sacrifice, of course. He wished no more than just two lines of affectionate greetings from the one he called his starlet and whom he recalled every time when the sun set and the mountains turned black.

For her sake he had alienated himself from Princess Varvara Repnina, who loved him. He did not accept her loyal heart, for he cared for another woman. And that other woman did not even answer his despairing letter from Orenburg. Had she forgotten him? No, she had not. She simply did not take all that as love; to her it had been no more than a caprice, an accidental, passing whim of a high-society lady.

He snatched the sealed letter addressed to Zakrewska from the table and tore it to pieces. It was only that he realized his blindness in regard to Repnina, and only now did he appreciate all the wisdom contained in the proverb: "A friend in need is a friend indeed." Nonetheless, there stood before his mind's eye the charming image of Zakrewska he had drawn last summer, trying to spiritualize her features as much as possible.

"It was not her I was drawing. I was just drawing my dream. I crowned her with the halo of a Madonna and did not see that she was a shop-window dummy," he told himself, pacing from corner to corner. "Enough! She is not worth my tears. And if I ever scramble out of this grave, I will never come to her. I shall reverently bow to Repnina for all the care she bestowed upon me, for her selfless pure affection, for every teardrop she shed because of my blindness and egotism."

He sat down at the table, took a fresh piece of paper, and wrote in his fine but clear handwriting:

"Dear Varvara Nikolaevna ..."

He stopped abruptly and threw the pen aside.

And what if she, too, wouldn't answer? What if she saw in him only an artist and poet who could exalt her image in verse and on canvas?

He abandoned this thought instantly. For didn't she find him the job of a drawing instructor at Kiev University? Didn't she herself knit him a warm woolen muffler on seeing that he had no fur collar on his winter coat? Didn't she subscribe to all the journals and bought all the books which could be of interest to him? Whoever else might ignore him, but Varvara Nikolaevna would undoubtedly respond to his letter. She was incapable of forgetting.

Shevchenko clutched his temples and sat still and frozen for a long time. Then he took up the pen and wrote in a simple, warm and serious manner like he would have written to an elder sister who understood everything, who felt that he had to be snatched out of here one way or another while his soul was alive, while his talent had not decayed, while the desire to live blazed in him.

How difficult, how contrary it was to his nature to ask and complain. He quickly changed to describing the local nature and the Kazakhs.

"...the Kirghiz are so colorful, so distinctive that you cannot help but take a pencil and draw them. Sometimes I visit the caravanserai and look at the Bukharans. What a slender built people they are! What wonderful heads they have. There is an inherent dignity about them without any haughtiness whatsoever. If I were permitted to draw, how many new and original drawings would I have sent you! But there is nothing I can do about it! To look and not to draw — what a torment it is for me.

"...It is over half a year now that I have been cut off from literature. Send me, if you please, Gogol's latest book *Selected Excerpts from Correspondence with Friends* and the *Studies of the Moscow Archeographic Society* published by Bodiansky."

He read what he had written with a lump in his throat. Again he had to beg, beg, beg...

That is my last attempt, he thought, sealing the letter. If there is no reply this time as well, then I'll...

A week later Shevchenko prepared to visit Jaisak again and took along the portrait of Kuljan he had finished drawing in the settlement.

"If you love her so much, let her always stay with you," he said to the young herder, and gave him the drawing. "It may help her become your wife one day."

Jaisak beamed with joy. The drawing did indeed seem to him to be a miraculous charm which would help him marry Kuljan in spite of all obstacles. He did not know how to thank, where to seat, and with what to treat the guest. That day, like almost every other day, he had nothing to offer but fresh *airan*. Trying to demonstrate his affection and gratitude to the poet, he saw him off right to the fortress.

It was a wonderful day, with a cloudless sky overhead. The sun was warm like in summer, and there was not a single ripple of wind in the air. Even the light balls of tumbleweed lay still in the places where the merry wind had left them when it had spent itself the day before. After parting with Jaisak, Shevchenko walked along the river for some time and then went to the settlement.

A man of about thirty-five, with a beard and a felt hat got to his feet to meet Shevchenko in his room.

"Let me introduce myself: Mikhailo Lazarevsky, the elder brother of your Orenburg friend. I have brought greetings from your friends and some letters."

At last! Beside himself for joy, Shevchenko embraced the welcome guest. All his anger and the wrongs his friends were supposed to have done him melted away.

The guest undid the leather straps of his grip and took out the letters, books and packages.

"Here is a letter from my brother Fedir and from Serhiy Levitsky," he said. "And this letter is from your homeland and one is from Karl Gern. I've brought you two issues of the *Sovremennik*, a new novel, *Notre Dame de Paris*, by Hugo, and some newspapers. There's also Ukrainian spiced *horilka* and home-made sausage. All this they received from their parents and asked me to pass it on to you."

Shevchenko's hands trembled from excitement when he tore

the envelopes open. Lazarevsky, pretending not to see the poet's excitement, continued as he put his empty grip on the floor:

"I live not far away from here, at Troitsk, and work as a trustee of the borderland Kirghiz. I'll be visiting this town on business about once every two or three months. My work also takes me to Orenburg, so I can pass to and from you whatever you wish and would be glad to help you."

"Thank you. Thank you ever so much," Shevchenko said, alternately reading the letters and rushing back and forth to ask the lady of the house to put on the samovar and fry the fresh fish Kuzmich had brought him.

Mikhailo Lazarevsky stayed up with Shevchenko late into the night, and when he left in the morning, parting with the poet as the best of friends, he gave him fifty rubles which his brother Fedir had supposedly asked him to pass on to Shevchenko.

Shevchenko read and reread the amiable letter from Lizohub — the first greeting from his homeland. This letter crossed the one he had sent only a week ago through Alexandriysky. He was no less gladdened by the ardent letter from his young friends in Orenburg.

It was Sunday. After seeing off his guest, Shevchenko stood for a long time at the last hut in Orsk and followed the black dot of the *tarantass* disappearing in the reddish distance. The gray feather grass shrouded the skyline, the sun blazed as it did before, but separate clouds shielded it now and then, casting gray shadows on the steppe like sorrowful recollections of the poet's past.

After sunset a cold spell suddenly set in. A sharp wind came blowing from the north, black clouds overcast the sky, a biting rain stalled to fall during the night, followed by' heavy snow. It snowed all night, at first wet and then large frost-bound quick-descending flakes. When Lavrentiev roused his lodger from sleep in the morning, the window panes were plastered with snow outside and covered with a frost film inside, while outdoors the wind swirled the snow and wailed wildly.

Winter whipped across the garrison unexpectedly. Although a transport had brought warm outfit, all the covering documents were drawn up incorrectly, so everything that had been brought was locked up in the storehouses; the soldiers were issued only last year's *bashlik* hoods, foot clouts of cloth, and ragged mittens.

It was fifteen degrees Centigrade below zero. The company was routinely ordered to march to the parade ground and lined up. The wind tore at the skirts of the greatcoats and *bashlik* ends sharply lashed across the men's faces, blew up into their sleeves, and chased the snow in whirls. The men stamped their cold numbed feet, but the command "Attention!" made them stand rigid. Captain Globa noticed right away that the alignment was disturbed: the foot of one soldier had slipped off a frozen earth clod and stuck slightly out of line, another man had his feet planted further apart than was provided for by regulations. Globa grew mad, and instead of issuing the command "At ease!" he went spitting out such volleys of curses that even the snow seemed to blush.

The men stood stock-still and scowled sullenly. Their numb hands barely held the rifles. Their legs had lost their litheness, and when at last Globa commanded, "Forward march " in a voice that had become gratingly hoarse from the cussing, many of the men could not swing their legs properly enough and bring them down with a uniform thump on the frozen ground

And again there was vile cursing, face slapping, and fisticuffs.

The snowstorm persisted for three days; all that time Globa tortured his inadequately dressed company. What made it still worse was that the men had no felt boots on, while the temperature had dropped to twenty-five degrees below zero with a strong north-westerly wind. A half of the men got their noses, ears and cheeks frostbitten, but most of all it was their feet which suffered greatly when festering wounds appeared on them. Many had to be admitted to hospital which lacked not only enough beds but even straw and hay for the mattresses to bed the sick on the floor. The first thing the soldiers would do in the morning was hurry to the windows to see whether the snowstorm was still raging. But outside an impenetrable curtain of white was hanging in the air, waves of snow swept over the ground like apparitions, and the orderly, each time he returned from the company headquarters and was asked whether there had been an order to have warm clothing issued, waved his hand hopelessly.

"Have you gone blind, or what? Don't you see what's going on outside? Who's going to drive into the steppe to his death? No order's come from Orenburg yet."

On the evening of the third day, Shevchenko went to Lidia Andreievna with the secret intention of telling the general what Globa was doing to the men. Lidia Andreievna met him in a sad and agitated state. Shevchenko noticed at once that she looked drawn.

"Father is feeling worse every day," she replied quietly to his alarmed inquiries, and her chin trembled. "The whole summer through I had been telling him to take a holiday, go to the Caucasus to take in the sun and warmth and mineral water. He caught a chill on his kidneys a long time ago. But you cannot persuade him. And now he's bad. He's got such swellings it's horrible to look at! His legs look like logs. The weather has made things even worse. There is no chance to get out of Orsk now. Oh my God, is he going to die here?"

Shevchenko comforted Lidia Andreievna and Natalia as best he could.

In the corner of the hall stood the dust-covered grand piano nobody had played on for so long. Natalia saw the dust on the lid, hurried off for a duster, and on returning started to clean the lid and the keyboard. The piano responded to her touch with a polyphonic hum, and the next moment the low voice of the general came from the depths of the house.

"Who is there?"

"It's Taras Grigorievich," Natalia replied.

"Who? I can't hear you! Let him come here!" Isaiev ordered.

Lidia Andreievna saw Shevchenko into the room of the sick man. The windows were tightly curtained. The stove in the room radiated generous heat, and a tall candle burned on a bedside table amid the apothecary jars with long prescription slips.

"Good evening, your Excellency!" Shevchenko snapped to attention.

"Good evening, my dear chap. Please be seated," he extended his hand to Shevchenko. "What's new?"

"Seems to be nothing except for the snowstorm."

"So why am I kept in the dark then?" the general said angrily. "Thank God my eyes can still see!"

"No, Daddy, the window cannot be opened," Lidia Andreievna got excited. "I have been calling on Meshkov three days now, asking him to send a glazier. We have to put in another set of windowpanes for the winter, but we don't have the glass for them. The cold is coming through the windows, and cold is bad for your health."

"What scoundrels! How they toadied when I was still in good shape. They must be thinking I'm a frail man and have spent my fires. But I am still alive, damn it! Take a piece of paper and write my order: have the glass issued and a glazier sent over immediately. They've got one in the third company... and write in the putty, too."

Lidia Andreievna quickly wrote the note; the general signed it, and gave it to Shevchenko.

"Do me a favor, dear chap. Go to our churl and get him to issue the glass right away."

And suddenly, on seeing Shevchenko's footwear, the general stopped him, surprised.

"Why aren't you wearing felt boots? It's cold outdoors after all."

"We've not been issued any yet, your Excellency. Indeed, it is very cold today: twenty-three below zero."

"The hell knows what's going on! Has drill been stopped then?"

"By no means; it's held on schedule. But..." Shevchenko fell silent for a moment, and then he plucked up enough courage to say, "... but about a half of our company's got frostbite. Many of them have been hospitalized. The men are almost dying with the pain."

"Well, well," the general drawled. "It's commendable, quite commendable on your part. You show us an example of Christian love for one's fellow man. Get me Meshkov and Globa, Sorokin!" he called to his batman. "On the double. And have the quartermaster-sergeant come, too. And you, dear chap, better go home. They should not be seeing you here! Otherwise they'll plague the life out of you, once I'm gone. And you, Sorokin, don't breathe a word about Shevchenko having seen me. Lidia dear, give Taras Grigorievich my felt boots. No, no, Taras Grigorievich, do not refuse them! I will be issued new boots, while you may show off in these for the time being."

The general was indeed getting worse every day. His daughters sat at his bedside round the clock, and Shevchenko came every evening to relieve the overtired Lidia Andreievna or Natalia. The physician Alexandriysky called every day as well, but his prescriptions could not help the sick man any more.

Once, after retiring from the general's bedrooms together with the physician, Shevchenko asked him:

"Is the situation really that hopeless?"

Alexandriysky shrugged his shoulders.

"He has chronic nephritis. Medicine is helpless in this case. In its initial stage, when the patient lives in a warm climate and eats a lot of vegetables, the disease is manageable, but now it is too late."

"How long will he live?"

"A couple of weeks — no more. He's been gravely ill for three years."

During the last days of his life Isaiev did not recognize anyone and was unconscious almost all the time, but late in the evening on the twenty-fifth of November his eyes suddenly opened as if he had come out of a deep sleep; they strayed around the room and then stopped on Lidia Andreievna.

"Where is your husband?" he asked. "He was here just now... visiting me," he added, a strange dull ring in his voice.

"Daddy... dear Daddy, that's Taras Grigorievich," Lidia Andreievna mumbled, frightened; Natalia bit into her handkerchief lest she cry out in horror.

Shevchenko put new ice on the sick man's head and carefully wiped off the sweat which had suddenly covered his face profusely. Isaiev fixed him with a long vacant look, and then dropped his eyelids. His breath came in gurgling and broken gasps as if his lungs were filled with water. His hands gradually started to turn cold.

Shevchenko realized what was coming. He took Natalia by the shoulder and quietly but insistently led her into the dining room where he sat her at his side on a sofa and gently pressed her fingers. Both of them were silent. What could they say anyway, when the great mystery of death was claiming the life of a human being in the adjoining room.

The death of General Isaiev stirred the whole of Orsk. Meshkov, on Lidia Andreievna's request, gave Shevchenko leave to help with the funeral arrangements.

Isaiev was buried with all the military honors befitting his rank. During the service in the church the soldiers sang with religious solemnity as the occasion required. The guns of the fortress rumbled when the coffin was slowly lowered into the grave on long slips of linen.

The Kazakhs huddled off to one side of the mourners. The entire *aul* had turned out for the funeral of Isai Pasha. They looked with interest at the church banners gleaming in the sun and the priest's funeral vestments of brocade, as they listened to the mournful chorus. On their way back to the *aul* the Kazakhs exchanged their impressions in whispers:

"*Oi boi*, the *askars* are in for a bad time if their new pasha will be as furious as the Meshka *Mayir* or the red-mugged Globa.

Then *akyn* Taras will never visit our *aul* to play on the *kobyz* and sing his songs to us."

"This calls for a tip, madame and mademoiselle," Kozlovsky rushed up to the Isaiev sisters. "For the repose of your daddy's soul in the abodes of paradise, so to speak."

"Oh yes, yes. Certainly," Natalia said, confused. "Here you are. That's for the men who dug the grave. Give it to them, please," she said, pushing some silver coins into Kozlovsky's hand.

"*Grand merci*," he said, clicking his heels, and made himself scarce on seeing Meshkov approach.

Shevchenko came up to the sisters, and since tears had exhausted Natalia and she stood infirmly on her feet, he carefully took her by the arm. Meshkov gave him an oblique glance, noticed the white non-regulation kid gloves on his hands but did not say anything and took Lidia Andreievna by the arm.

"Let me present my condolences to you once more and see you home."

She leaned on his arm without saying a word, and after staying at her father's grave for some minutes more, crossed herself and slowly walked away.

Globa quickly approached Natalia.

"Allow me, Mademoiselle... Natalia... Andreievna," he said and rudely shouldered Shevchenko aside.

Natalia was so smitten with grief that she only raised her eyes on Globa and remained standing by the grave, unaware that her sister had already left.

"Allow me," Globa repeated, and without waiting for a response, hooked her dejectedly drooping arm.

She walked off like a sleepwalker, totally indifferent to everything around her.

Shevchenko stood for a while among the dispersing crowd which commented in lively tones on the priest's graveside oration, on every movement of the orphaned sisters, and on the singing of the church chorus during the service. Then he walked silently to his quarters.

In the evening Lavrentiev brought him word of the commander's order "to confine Private Shevchenko for one day in the guardhouse for appearing on the street and in church in white gloves instead of the regulation mittens."

The night in the guardhouse refreshened and invigorated him after the three sleepless nights he had stayed at the bedside of the dying man. He instantly sunk into the deep, restful sleep of an utterly exhausted man and was roused when the noncom on duty Zlintsev rattled the bolt of the cell door and opened it in the morning.

"Go to the Isaievs right away," the noncom said. "The lady asked the major to have you for a week to help her pack. Of all the people to ask help of," he added maliciously, letting Shevchenko through the door. He could not forgive the poet the caricature he had drawn of him and of the sergeant-major.

The week passed like one day. From morning till night Shevchenko sawed and planed, knocked together crates or else packed and sewed up the sisters' belongings in bast mats. Meshkov, as temporary commandant of the fortress, provided the Isaiev sisters with horses. The luggage was loaded onto several paired sleighs, and the grand piano was put on a large sleigh hitched to a team of four. When the luggage sleighs left, the late general's covered wagon with sleigh runners on its wheels drew up to the porch. The first person to appear on the porch was Petya wearing a white sheepskin coat and fur hat. Then the two sisters came out. They took a last look around, shook hands with Shevchenko, and blushing with embarrassment, persuaded him to accept as a memento a clean sketch book with some ruble bills stuck in between the pages. The wagon moved off, its runners crunching through the deep snow.

Shevchenko remained standing on the porch, watching the retreating vehicle for a long time. Now he had no one to unburden his soul to and listen to music with.

Life is a continuance of endless partings with someone or something, he thought. You part with your parents when they pass away, with childhood, with your childhood playmates, and then with youth, with your first love, with shattered dreams and the dear places where you dwelled, with the graves of parents, with freedom, and, finally, even with I the hope of ever being a free man again.

Back home, he met a sad and agitated Lavrentiev.

"Things are going badly for you, Grigorievich," he said as soon as Shevchenko crossed the threshold and started taking off his sheepskin coat. "You're in a nasty mess. The major, you see, ordered you back to the barracks. I begged and pleaded: 'Permit him, your Excellency, to stay at my home some more. He's a quiet man, doesn't stir up any trouble, and he's taught my children the ABC and is now teaching them 'rithmetic' Well, I vouched for you, you see, saying you weren't a drunkard or a troublemaker, but he just hissed back at me: 'That rebel went against the emperor; he's an enemy who must be destroyed, so don't you dare stand up for him. If the general — God rest his soul — treated him with indulgence, he'd have to answer for the consequences himself, but I do not want to be kept responsible for the man's crimes. That's the whole story of it. Get your things ready, old chap, and I'll take you back to the barracks. Don't you be sad, though: by the grace of God we'll have another general assigned and I can ask him to let you stay in my house again."

The barracks met Shevchenko with the familiar stench and groans.

"After the feast comes the reckoning," the downgraded ensign Belobrovov laughed spitefully, rocking back and forth on a bench near the table. "We thought you'd fallen in with the general's daughter and made a break for Orenburg."

Shevchenko clenched his fists.

"The less you touch them, the less they'll stink," Kuzmich told him quietly. "They'll wag their tongues some more and stop. It's unhappiness that's turned them into such brutes."

"That's true," Shevchenko said, pulling himself together, and looked with respect at the old soldier.

His bunk was unoccupied, because in winter all the men sought the welcome proximity of the stove.

Taxing days of gloomy life in the barracks followed. Twilight descended early. The endless night brought him nothing but gray sorrow. Sleep had fled from him. He lay on the bunk and gazed into the darkness; he felt as if he had gone blind, and perpetual darkness gave him no hope for a glimmer of light.

In his thoughts, he wandered around Kirilivka, the village of his childhood, or through the streets of Kiev, clearly seeing every building in it, among them the dark-red university with its high pediments and the black Ionic capitals crowning its columns. He entered its long, resounding corridors with vaulted ceilings and gleaming pig-iron floor plates. From the university his memories carried him to the neat-looking Finishing School, where he had been with Professor Kostomarov at a commencement ball the previous spring. He admired the wonderful creations of Ukrainian baroque — the Raphail Zaborovsky Gate on the grounds of the Saint Sophia Cathedral and the matchless form of St. Andrew's Church which the inspired Bartolomeo Rastrelli had put like a toy on the crest of Old Kiev Hill overlooking the Podil district lying below. He also delighted in the extraordinary beauty of Johann Schädel's bell tower at the Cave Monastery and the snow-white St. Nicholas' Cathedral, an outstanding monument of Ukrainian baroque. Then he visited the unobtrusive St. George's Church, because in it was buried Ypsilanti, the leader of the Greeks who rose against the Ottoman oppression; under Ypsilanti's colors had fought Byron, a man who had reigned over human thought for two generations.

In his imagination, he also wandered along the Dnieper bluffs during those sleepless nights, and visited the homes of his Kiev friends who had betrayed him in his greatest grief.

At times he recalled Vilnius where he lived a year and a half when he was a youth. The city buzzed with excitement then, as it prepared for the insurrection of 1830. Every night anonymous hands left bold appeals for struggle on the walls, pasted up proclamations to peasants and townspeople, and drew cartoons of the czar and his officials. People made ardent speeches against censorship, calling for freedom of the press and equality of men and women before the law.

"Why aren't you sleeping, brother?" Kuzmich asked him once; the old soldier's foot had been frostbitten and now, with his sole operated on, he was temporarily relieved of garrison duty. "However much you'll be thinking, there'll be no end to it. If you've tramped around all day, better have a good sleep. It's good that the bed bugs have been done away with by the general, God rest his soul in His Kingdom for that. Life is a little more bearable now: they haven't returned yet."

"And why don't you sleep yourself?" Shevchenko responded quietly.

"I? While you're marching on the parade ground throughout the day, I stay alone in the barracks and sleep, and then I can't seal up my eyes at night, much as I try. Besides, the past always comes to my mind and troubles my heart."

Shevchenko looked closely at the old man, but with the dim light from the one and only wick lamp in the barracks he could not see his eyes.

"Still, I cannot understand, Kuzmich, how you came to be in this place. You're a quiet, God-fearing man. It seems strange."

"Oh, brother, don't touch my old wounds or else they'll hurt. There is only one thing I can say: woe to the peasant who rouses his lord's wrath, but he's worse off if the lord takes a liking to him. That liking brought me to a soldier's fate."

Shevchenko kept silent, understanding how the man felt.

Kuzmich became thoughtful, and then, groaning in his old man's way, he sat down at Shevchenko's side, and said:

"I come from around the town of Orsha, and was a serf of the landlord Kazanovich. When the French attacked our land, my father perished. Shortly after, my mother died too, and I was left a helpless child. I. was picked up by an old woman, and when I grew up, the lords took me into the manor and made me an assistant to the gardener. He taught me to grow trees and flowers and all kinds of shrubs. I gave him a hand in the greenhouses and hothouses. They also had a conservatory where lemons and peaches grew. The lords lived mostly abroad or in St. Petersburg, visiting the manor for a month or two and then leaving again.

"My lord was sick for a long time. People said that his bones were rotting in him — consumption they call it. At first he limped in one leg, then in the other, and in the end was laid up for good. They took him around all sorts of places for treatment, spent their money on it and even sold their house in the capital for his treatment. He died, and his wife came back to the manor. She was getting on in years, had a student son, and was quite good looking. Before the lord died he gave me permission to marry. I loved my wife Dunya dearly. She bore me a fine healthy boy. While I worked in the garden, I was in the habit of singing. Well, those songs of mine were the cause of my troubles. I caught the eye of the lady and she appointed me her valet. Now and then she treated me to a drink or gave me a new livery. I hadn't the slightest idea why she was so kind to me. Sometimes she let the girls have evenings off, called me to her study, ordered me to kindle the wood in the fireplace, and asked me this and that about my life. At first she spoke so kindly, and then suddenly fumed with rage: 'Go away, you fool, if you don't see happiness coming your way!' I went to my quarters under the stairway, and when she went to sleep, I ran off to the village to see my family. She had me tracked, and blazed with anger then: 'Where have you so-and-so been traipsing all night long?' 'I've only been to my home, seeing my lawful wife and baby son.' She didn't say anything, pressed her lips tightly, and went to her boudoir with black looks, for three days she didn't speak to me and then suddenly ordered Dunya to leave for a remote manorial farm some forty *versts* away. Dunya was to be sort of a stewardess there. She was given three girls to help her take care of the house, orchard, garden, to rear chickens and ducks and, generally, look after the whole farm. Well, being a stewardess is much better than reaping in a field, but our separation... One week passed, then another. On a holiday I asked the lady to give me leave for one day. She refused. Another week passed. She let all the servants go to a fair, and I was the only one left in the manor house. In the evening she rang for me to come to her bedroom. I went upstairs, knocked on the door as is proper, and entered. She was in bed. 'Come closer,' she said. 'I want to tell you something!' I went up closer, and she said: 'You're a fool not to see your happiness. I'll give you freedom, a plot of land, and build you a house. You'll be a human instead of a serf, but leave your Dunya. I'll set her free, too, and I won't forget your child either.' I was struck dumb, standing as if I were rooted to the ground. I just did not know what to say. Then she threw the blanket aside, and there she was lying in her birthday suit and beckoning to me. 'Lady, but I've got a lawful wife and was wed in church,' I said. 'The priest read us from the Scriptures that whoever God has united, man cannot separate.' Oh my..." Kuzmich started suddenly. "To cut a long story short, I was forced into the army, and my poor Dunya is now set to the hardest of work."

Kuzmich gritted his teeth and retreated into his corner.

After Shevchenko returned to the barracks, his illness recurred. His legs ached from rheumatism; however much medicine the medical attendant gave him it did not bring relief; nor did iodine, which he daubed on his joints. No other medicine was known to either the attendant or the physician Alexandriysky, and Shevchenko found it ever more difficult to march on the parade ground. He became short-winded and swellings appeared on his body.

When he had been a student at the Academy of Arts in St. Petersburg, Shevchenko contracted pleurisy, and a physician examining him also found him to have an organic heart disease. Now his heart gave him trouble with increasing frequency: when Shevchenko had to run or go through usual drill, he became short-winded. Globa, however, would not make things easier for the "state criminal."

Besides, scurvy attacked him again. The entire body became covered with sores and bruises. Now there were no Isaevs to provide him with vegetables, and only occasionally, when he was temporarily relieved of drill because of this illness, did the cook give him a turnip or onion.

One day Alexandriysky visited him and stealthily passed on a letter.

Breathless for joy and impatience, Shevchenko retired to the farthest corner of the hospital and tore the letter open with trembling hands. The letter was from Lizohub — warm-hearted, cordial lines that were filled with love and moved the poet deeply. It was the reply to Shevchenko's first letter. Although it warmed his heart, a sad thought still haunted him: why did Repnina not reply? Shevchenko knew her all too well to doubt her courage. What if she had left Yahotin for somewhere else or if the letter had not been passed on to her?

In preparation for the next occasional carriers who might be passing through Orsk, Shevchenko wrote a long letter to Lizohub, in which he sympathized profoundly for the death of Lizohub's little daughter, inquired about Repnina, and unable to restrain himself, wrote the following: "I wish my cruelest enemy would not be made to suffer as much as I am now."

"I have yet another request," he wrote. "Send me your little casket which has everything I need, a clean album, and at least one Charion brush to look at once in a while — it'll make me feel better."

In this way, by means of a transparent allusion, Shevchenko again asked Lizohub to send him oil paints, and then shedding all allegories, he asked for Homer's *Odyssey* in Zhukovsky's translation and Ketcher's translations of Shakespeare.

Shevchenko almost never left the barracks. In strict compliance with the garrison duty regulations, Meshkov did not permit the soldiers to go beyond the bounds of the fortress without a leave pass which was issued only once a week and for some three hours. Shevchenko's bootleg notebooks therefore had almost no new verse in them: in the barracks, he could have been denounced for violating the czar's prohibition; in the steppe, snowstorms raged all the time; and it was only occasionally that he visited his Polish friends and Alexandriysky's home, the only place where he could write poetry.

17. KOZLOVSKY'S ADVICE

The winter persisted unbearably long. Blizzard followed blizzard, and even during the brief spells of what oldtimers considered calm weather, there was such a gusty ground wind lashing across the steppe it buffeted against people's backs and made them move at a trot.

Shevchenko's illness made him ever weaker. He could barely bend his swollen joints and was racked by pain. When the medical attendant reported to Globa on the poet's condition, the company commander pounded his desk madly with his fist, and shouted:

"That's a lie, you bastard! I know those tricks! He must have given you a ruble for vodka, and here you stick up for him! One word about the lazybones from you — and I'll throw you into the guardhouse!"

"But, your Excellency, let the doctor have a look at him. You can do whatever you will to me, but the man is sick and that's all there is to it."

"Go to hell!"

The attendant fell silent, and Shevchenko was again chased to the parade ground for drill.

Every Sunday and holiday the soldiers were marched off to church.

Once Shevchenko bumped into Meshkov in church. As it was proper for a soldier, Shevchenko gave way to the commander and rapidly took his cap off.

"Three days in the guardhouse!" Meshkov's voice lashed Shevchenko like a whip. "It's time you knew, Shevchenko, that a cap is taken off a soldier's head with his left hand, not with his right."

Meshkov disappeared into the depths of the church, but Shevchenko remained standing in place, clutching his cap. The beggars around him snickered quietly, and a legless soldier long past his retirement age, boomed in a didactic way:

"Got yourself into a guardhouse, eh? Next time you'll know that a soldier has no right to look with only half an eye." On seeing several women in woolen kerchiefs coming out of the church just then, the cripple went off into a twangy lament:

"For the sake of God give a kopeck to a crippled soldier who's suffered for the faith, the czar and country... Give an old soldier for the repose of your parents' souls."

That is how I might end my days, begging, Shevchenko thought, and with a heavy heart went to report at the guardhouse.

Christmas was approaching. In Ukraine this holiday was associated with a multitude of customs, legends and rites which ran back to the pre-Christianity past.

On Christmas Eve the soldiers, instead of being marched out to drill, were ordered to clean and mop the barracks. Everyone, except for the noblemen Kozlovsky and Belobrovov, got down to work. The men refused to take the day meal, because they were fasting "up to the morning star." In the afternoon the company was led to the bathhouse where the barber diligently cropped and shaved the men and the quartermaster-sergeant issued them new underwear, uniforms and caps.

After the Christmas Eve supper in the unusually clean and aired barracks, the men refrained from singing drunken songs or cursing. Their faces became solemnly concentrated. Kozlovsky let his eyes wander along the bunks, made a wry face and shook his head.

"My God, it's so boring, like at a sumptuous funeral feast," he said and burst into raucous laughter.

None of the men, however, followed suit.

Shevchenko went to his bunk and lay down, facing the wall lest anyone see his tears. He recalled his cheerless childhood and that poignantly bitter Christmas Eve when his mother died and he had to go with his elder sister and take the evening meal to their old grandfather as custom dictated. On crossing the threshold, the boy had to say the customary: "Holy Evening to you. Father and Mother willed that we bring you the holy supper, Grandfather," but the orphan could not make himself utter these words after his mother, wasted away by misery and serf labor, had been confined to the grave. Tears gushed from his eyes, and his sister burst out crying as well. And now, recalling that evening far away from his homeland, he seemed to have been forgotten by the entire world, and just like during his childhood, he sharply felt his lot as an orphan.

"Don't be so sad, old chap. There's no need for it," Kuzmich suddenly said in a tender voice, putting a hand on his shoulder. "It's a sin to grieve so bitterly when there is peace the whole world over and goodwill amongst men."

Shevchenko did not say anything in reply, but this unexpected tenderness made him tremble the more with his silent tears, as Kuzmich was lightly stroking his shoulder and saying:

"There are a lot of us like you around here... and everyone has a wound in his heart. Let hope lighten it at least once a year. With God's grace, you, too, will get home some day."

"I'm all right... I just remembered my mother," Shevchenko said.

"Certainly. A man's heart withers without tenderness. Even in gray-haired old age it is difficult to be an orphan," Kuzmich said soothingly. "I grew up without a father. On Christmas Eve we used to get together and go around the houses glorifying Christ. Some gave us money, others a pie or a hunk of bread, and still others a sausage or a piece of fatback. We'd bring all that back to Mother, she'd cry at the sight of this charity, divide it between us children, but would not take a single bite herself. 'I've already eaten,' she said, while it never occurred to us that she was utterly hungry," Kuzmich concluded with a sigh, wiping away a tear.

Both of them lapsed into silence and became thoughtful. Suddenly, from the opposite corner where only vile curses and scurrilous songs originated every day, a strong voice started singing an ancient moving carol with a solemn ring:

... and strew some hay and put God's son into the crib...

Unwittingly, Shevchenko quietly joined in the carol, its words sounding the dearer to him, since he knew them since childhood. His voice gradually gained in strength and soon lead on the other voices. From the carols he switched over to Ukrainian folk songs. Minutes later all the men in the barracks crowded around him and supported his singing with a great deal of excitement.

"What the dickens! You are a remarkable singer!" Kozlovsky cried out when Shevchenko finished, and then added without his usual insolence: "Don't give me your oblique looks, Shevchenko! It's a cursed life that's crippled me. Grief is what made me take to drinking... et cetera... et cetera. Otherwise I'd have been a dead man long since..."

When the men had dispersed in silence, each retiring to his bunk, Kozlovsky came up to Shevchenko, sat down at his side, and said unexpectedly, a crooked smile curling his lips:

"I'm a villain, and I know it. There's nothing to be done about that. But I've still got principles. Yes, sir! I'll ne-ev-er fool you anymore or steal a thread from you. But... for Christ's sake, give me twenty kopecks, because I'll go crazy if I don't have a drink."

Grabbing the coin Shevchenko offered, Kozlovsky dashed out of the barracks.

For the three days of the Christmas holidays the men could leave the barracks without any leave passes. Shevchenko went to see his friends. First he went to convey his best Christmas wishes to Lavrentiev, and on the way dropped in to Chalhushian's grocery where he bought some fruitdrops for his former pupils Stepan and Vasiliy.

"Let's go see the *bai* in the *aul*," Shevchenko proposed after

Lavrentievhad treated him to a drink and some fatback and sausage.

"Impossible," the clerk said. "I've promised to visit the sergeant-major. His wife is celebrating her birthday today. Go to the *bai* alone, you know the way. The Kirghiz, though, have no holiday today: they are heathens and don't believe in Christ."

Shevchenko had to go alone. After the singing of the day before he had slept well and felt almost healthy. The long walk, however, made him tired and he barely reached the *aul*.

Jaisak was happy to see his dear guest and invited him to sit in the place of honor opposite the entrance. The other day he had bagged a couple of hares and was glad to treat Shevchenko to fresh hare roast.

"I hunted with him," Jaisak said and nodded at the eagle dozing in the corner on the *tugir*. "He's good at getting hare, fox and even wolves. Take a look, Taras *Aga*, how many furs I have already: seven silver fox, nine red fox, and three wolves. I hunt so many hares that *apa* and I have enough every day and our dogs have become sleeker for the hare meat," the young herder said merrily, flashing his pitch-black eyes. "Iskhak is also hunting with the *bat's* eagle, because there are so many wolves in the steppe now that six *jigits* guard the herd every night. This winter I'd be unable to handle a pack of wolves myself: they'd tear me up for certain."

"Do you know how to process furs?" the poet asked.

"I don't, but my friend Taijan knows how," Jaisak said, putting the furs into the trunk. "When I get together about half a hundred furs of silver fox and a lot of red fox, I'll go to Orenburg to sell them." Then he added with a sigh: "It's so difficult to scrape up money for the bride and the wedding. But I don't want to lose hope."

"Is there any news about Kuljan's intended husband?"

"Nothing new. He's lying in bed motionless. Next year we will see what happens."

Shevchenko noticed that the subject was unpleasant for Jaisak, so he asked:

"And where's Abdrahman?"

"He's going around the *auls*, singing his songs. Where else should he be? Right now a young *akyn*, Azat, is our *bai*'s guest. If you want, we can go there and listen to his songs."

When heavy frosts set in, Djantemir moved from his yurt into a little house on the bank of the Or. Its spacious but low-ceilinged rooms as well as the floors and walls were covered with carpets and wolf skins. The house was heated by a real stove. The double-framed windows had shutters on the outside with thick mats of hay hung for additional warmth when the frosts were viciously bitter. Trestle platforms were used to sit and sleep on, although Djantemir had bought for himself in Orsk a real bed with a spring mattress, of which he was very proud.

When Shevchenko entered the room with Jaisak, Azat was singing a merry song that sounded like a dance tune. Zeineb, Nurina and Shauken swayed their heads in time with the music, shrugging their shoulders and even snapping their fingers. On seeing the guest, the *bai* gave him a nod and gestured that he sit at his side, without interrupting the *akyn*. Since Djantemir did not get up this time and shake hands, Shevchenko understood that the *bai* had not forgiven him the *My Testament* he had recited during his first visit.

When Azat was resting after his songs, Djantemir turned to Shevchenko.

"Tell your *mayirs* to shoot the wolves, of which there are too many in the steppe. They must be destroyed. Every day they kill two sheep at least."

"You mean to say that a hunt should be staged?" Shevchenko asked to get the meaning of Djantemir's words right.

"Yes, yes! A hunt! It has to be a big hunt! Tell that to Meshka *Mayir*. I beg of you. A *jigit* asks you. Djantemir asks you."

"All right, I will tell him," Shevchenko said, deciding that he would pass the request on to the officers through Alexandriysky as a last resort.

"Don't forget it," Djantemir repeated. "I will give you a sheep as a present for that."

"I'll do it without a sheep," Shevchenko said and fell silent on seeing Azat reaching for his *dombra* again.

That instant a wind buffeted against the windows, and everyone turned round and saw that the sun was shrouded by a white mist.

Time to go back — a blizzard is building up, Shevchenko thought.

Nobody tried to talk him out of leaving. Pulling his cap deeper onto his head and tying the ends of the *bashlik* tighter around his neck, he quickly walked toward Orsk.

"Wait a minute, Taras *Aga*! I'll give you a horse and see you off," Jaisak said, rushing after him, but Shevchenko did not turn round — either the wind had stifled Jaisak's words, or Shevchenko did not want to heed him.

The wind grew stronger and changed direction all the time as if it were performing a wild dance over the snow. A ground wind lashed across the steppe, swirling snow at the height of Shevchenko's knees. Some twenty minutes later the snow was whipping around his waist. He seemed to be walking into a white river that was growing deeper and deeper. Far away on the horizon flashed the cross of the Orsk church, but it was quickly disappearing in the haze.

He quickened his pace, but the racking pain in his knees and feet made him slow down.

He plodded thus through the snow over an hour and suddenly noticed that dusk was falling and a gray mist had enveloped the sky. He summoned all the strength that was left in him, believing Orsk to be within a stone's throw, but through the dense curtain of snow he did not see a single light blinking, while the frost chilled his body more and more. Exhausted and gasping, he stopped to regain his breath.

This is the end, the thought flashed through his mind. But what I do not know yet is who will launch me into eternity: the wolves or the frost?

"Taras *Aga*! Where have you disappeared to?" he suddenly heard the voice of Jaisak from above. "Get on the horse. How could you have gone so far astray? It was only hounds which found you."

A horse's head and over it the shaggy *malakhai* of Jaisak appeared out of the blizzard. The hounds sniffed the poet suspiciously all over. Jaisak led another saddled horse by the bridle.

Shevchenko was short of words to thank his savior. He was so exhausted he could not get into the saddle. Jaisak slipped to the ground, helped Shevchenko up, hopped onto his own horse and urged it ahead at a trot, holding the poet's horse by the bridle as before.

"*Oi boi*, you just don't know what place you've come to. You walked right into the saxaul grove swarming with wolves," Jaisak said. "The shaitans must have led you astray. It was only your black cap I saw through the snow."

They had been riding at a trot for a good thirty minutes before they saw the first glimmering lights of Orsk. When they stopped at the barracks, Shevchenko barely slipped to the ground. His legs did not bend.

"Come in and warm yourself," Shevchenko invited Jaisak. "You saved my life. Come in and drink some hot tea, because you, too, are stiff with cold."

"I can't! There's still the herd to take care of. There are a lot of wolves around," Jaisak explained and jumped onto his horse. "So don't forget, Taras *Aga*, to tell your *mayirs* to shoot the wolves. Without the *mayirs* we won't be able to do it. Well, I'll be going!"

"Where have you been for so long, *mon cher*?" Kozlovsky said, on meeting Shevchenko. "At the clerk's home I presume?"

"I visited the Kirghiz, and went astray on my way back. One of their young men found me when I had wandered the hell knows where. I was already preparing myself for death," Shevchenko said, sipping the scalding hot tea Kuzmich had brought him. "I thought the wolves would tear me to pieces."

"Do wolves really attack people?"

"And what did you think?" Kuzmich retorted gruffly. "They're fierce and as big as a six-month-old calf."

"Djantemir asked me to talk with the officers about staging a battue. But I doubt whether our Meshkov will agree," Shevchenko said, concerned. "How can we make them interested in it?"

Kozlovsky suddenly became wildly excited.

"Thank God, *mon cher*, that there are wolves in this world! Don't you realize what a fantastic opportunity is dropping into our laps?"

Shevchenko looked at him, puzzled.

"Why can't you understand that this is our only chance to stop our betters picking on us for a long time to come?" Kozlovsky said angrily.

"What has picking on us have to do with the wolves?"

"Because it's 'You scratch my back, and I'll scratch yours.'" Kozlovsky exclaimed. "But you have to scratch delicately, cleverly, tactfully. A battue could simply be a fantastic thing! You go ahead and organize it. Our brother soldier who'll be flushing the game with a will, apart from the army grub, he'll get a shot of vodka, while the lord officers will get soaked with drink. Besides, every one of them will receive several wolf skins as hunting trophies, for a good half a year they'll leave us in complete peace, and the main thing" — here he raised his index finger meaningfully — "keep their eyes shut to everything. Do you understand me now?"

"First of all, I don't understand anything about hunting, and so I won't be able to organize the battue properly; secondly, where should I get the money to buy all that booze? With the officers vodka won't be enough: they are used to drinking rum and champagne."

"And what do you think Djantemir is for? It must be explained to him that such a service calls for a good treat for the officers and the beaters. The wolves gobble up two sheep every night. For the *bai* it'll be less expensive spending ten sheep than losing a hundred by spring. As for me, I am an experienced hunter and will help you. With no reward whatsoever, that is, of course, except for the treat of vodka you'll be offering everyone. In this case the chiefs will also leave me alone for a long time."

Shevchenko kept silent.

"Let's see Meshkov first thing tomorrow," Kozlovsky insisted. "We'll come to him not like soldiers but like messengers from Djantemir and make Meshkov agree. I swear he'll give his consent at once. From Meshkov we'll go to Djantemir. Meshkov will also give us a horse for the sake of the future spree; we'll appear at the *bai*'s as Meshkov's representatives, so to speak, and explain to that fat hog that, firstly, he must provide us with as many beaters from the Kirghiz as he can so that we won't have to chase the entire company out into the steppe, and secondly, he must provide enough food and drink for the officers and men. Then we'll take along that Jarabek, or whatever you call him, and have a good look at the place where the wolves slink around; the next few days we'll be busy preparing everything we need, buy the vodka, and take all that to Djantemir, because holding a boozing party in Orsk is out of the question. You'll be in charge of the money and all the other arrangements, while I'll be the chief huntsman."

"All right, I'll think it over and let you know tomorrow morning," the poet said at last, and when Kozlovsky walked away in his peculiar gait, Shevchenko took a pencil and a piece of candy paper out of his pocket, and got down to complex mathematical calculations.

Of the money he had received from Lazarevsky and Lidia Andreievna he had thirty rubles left. After lengthy calculations, hesitations, and talks with the former cook of the Isaievs, Shevchenko realized that the money would be enough to treat the officers and that Kozlovsky's scheme was really a splendid opportunity to get rid of drill for some time at least.

18. THE BATTUE

In the morning, Shevchenko went with Kozlovsky to Meshkov's home. The appearance of Shevchenko in the company of Kozlovsky surprised the major tremendously, and he ordered both of them to be called to his study.

"What is it you want to tell me?" he asked, coming out in a dressing gown to see them. "Why do you approach me, and not submit your report through proper channels?"

As he said this, he kept glancing at Shevchenko with undisguised curiosity.

"We've come here, your Excellency, not on private or the company's' business," Shevchenko replied, standing stiff at attention. "Yesterday evening I was at the *aul* visiting Djantemir to listen to the singing of their *akyn,* and Djantemir asked me to pass on to your Excellency a request on his and the entire *aul's* behalf that you help them do away with the wolves. The wolves are a real nuisance to the Kirghiz: every night they run down a horse, a couple of sheep or even more. They beg you to stage a big hunt, a battue... I gave it a thought with my comrade here," Shevchenko inclined his head toward Kozlovsky, "and decided to ask your Excellency's permission to put on a big battue after the feast of the Epiphany. Our Cossacks also suffer a great deal from the wolves, which steal up to the horses in broad daylight. We suggest detailing fifty infantry, and having the Cossacks provide a hundred men for beaters. The *aul* of the Kirghiz will turn out as one man for the hunt. We'll surround the valley in the saxaul grove where the wolves' dens are. For the officers this will be a pleasant diversion, and for the people a great benefit: we'd shoot the gray brutes, and then go to the *aul* for a rest, a meal and drink lest the men, God forbid, catch a cold from the frost. Everything necessary will be arranged ahead of time. For the beaters there'll be a meat pie and a shot of vodka, and Djantemir, for his part, will surely treat us to some mutton."

Meshkov's eyes flashed with excitement. An approving smile spread across his lips and hid under his mustache, but for appearance's sake he knit his brow, stood thoughtfully for a while, and replied indecisively:

"Yeah... killing wolves... is a very useful thing. I simply don't know what to tell you... When do you intend going to that ... what you call him... Djantemir again?"

"We might as well go now. It's a holiday. If only we have your permission, your Excellency."

Meshkov hesitated for a minute or so and then waved down his hand abruptly.

"All right, go ahead. Tell him I agree, and the officers are in agreement as well. I'll have a talk with them myself. Let Djantemir get everything ready together with you, and now go and see him in the *aul*... No, take a horse and ride there. You've got sick legs, haven't you, Shevchenko? Going on foot will make you tired," Meshkov added with a polite grin. "Tell Silantyev to have the stallion Rapid hitched to my sleigh for you."

"Well? Didn't I tell you that he'd take the bait!" Kozlovsky rejoiced on their way to the battalion stables. "He hasn't had a sniff of vodka yet, but remembered your illness. And he addressed you politely. Here's the first result of a clever venture."

Djantemir was overjoyed at the news. Shevchenko managed to achieve in one day what the *bai* had failed to do throughout the whole of last winter. He pressed the poet's hands in both of his and immediately started talking about what would be best to treat the hunters to. The number of hunters and beaters made him start from fright at first, but Shevchenko promised to bring along a sack of flour and three pailfuls of vodka.

"Good, good," Djantemir said. "That's for the soldiers, but we don't know what the *mayirs* will need. Tell us and we'll get it."

"Vodka is not enough for the officers. They'll have to have champagne," Kozlovsky said, anticipating a sumptuous banquet.

"Everything will be done. It will be a big *toi*," Djantemir said with an emphatic nod. "There will be the wine that burns in a spoon and smells so fine, and the one that shoots like a gun. We'll buy everything. Allah has prohibited us to drink such things, but for the *mayirs* we'll buy it. They will be pleased. For three days they will be so drunk they'll be lying around like logs. Here, take a look."

To support his point, he opened a trunk, in which stood bottles of rum, cognac, vodka and other alcoholic drinks the names of which he did not even know. Seeing the greedy glint in Kozlovsky's eyes, Djantemir brought out a bottle of vodka and ordered cooked lamb to be served.

Then he had Jaisak summoned so that he show Shevchenko and Kozlovsky the location of the wolves' den.

The men mounted the horses Djantemir had provided for the purpose and galloped off down the bank of the Or where the snow was covered with abundant fox and wolf tracks. Kozlovsky dismounted now and again and closely inspected the tracks. They rode round the valley along the edge of a cliff that dropped steeply as if it were diving under the ground, and then they rode back on its crest.

Shevchenko was silent for some time, reluctant to betray his complete ignorance of wolves' habits, but in the end he asked Jaisak:

"Can the wolves really scramble out of that gulch?"

"Oh no, Taras *Aga*," Jaisak replied with a smile. "Thanks be to Allah they have no wings yet, because if they did, we would be defenseless against them both in the yurts and on our horses."

"I thought there might be some sloping paths under the snow here."

"There is one, but it's a little further down where a brook falls into the river," Jaisak said with a wave of his hand in that direction.

Kozlovsky kept looking out for wolf tracks here as well, but there were almost none. The men realized that the wolves went on the prowl at the end of the valley where there were no steep cliffs.

Back at the *aul,* Shevchenko and Kozlovsky got into the sleigh to hurry off to Orsk before dusk.

"Tell Djantemir that we'll bring everything we have promised next week," Shevchenko said on parting with the group of Kirghiz who had gathered around the sleigh.

Half a *verst* away from the *aul* Kozlovsky reined in the horses and turned to Shevchenko.

"We'll have to set our brains to some good work now," he said, worried. "The scale of the chase is different from what it might be, say, in Belorussia or Polessie. To surround such a valley we'll need not fifty infantry but our entire company along with the Cossacks and Kirghiz, but in this case we'll be short of money for the vodka and meat pies. You can't leave a soldier out in the cold for the whole day without a shot of vodka."

"There is no way of backing out of it now," Shevchenko said with a sigh.

"That's true. No backing out. We'll have to use pennants."

"What kind of pennants?"

"Red ones, of course! Wolves shy away at the sight of red, believing it to be fire. We'll have to calculate how many pennants we'd need and get enough string and red calico. The cliff cuts off the wolves' route of retreat. That's where we won't need any people or pennants. But along the river and at the further end of the valley we'll have to station beaters or put up pennants. They are sewn one *arshin* from one another on a string which is stretched between bushes, pegs or reeds. We'll drop in to the store now and ask how much that red calico costs, and then cut the pennants."

The storekeeper threw a roll of red calico at five kopecks an *arshin* on the table, and hard as Kozlovsky bargained, the storekeeper sliced off only thirty kopecks for the entire roll of fifty-six *arshins,* charging two and a half rubles for it.

Shevchenko's face clouded.

"We've surely got ourselves into a mess, which I think we won't get out of."

"We'd better get out of it or else Meshkov will make it too hot for us. Fifteen rubles will buy us a sack of flour and three pailfuls of vodka. Let Meshkov give us their dry issues. That'll save us another fifteen rubles to buy string and red calico. If we cut the roll of calico in three parts lengthwise, we'll have one hundred and sixty-eight *arshins,* and out of each *arshin* we'll make four pennants, that is, six hundred and seventy-two pennants altogether. They'll have to be stretched over two *versts* along the river bank. One *verst* has five hundred *sazhens* or one thousand five hundred *arshins.* Consequently, we'll have to have three and a half thousand pennants, whereas we've got only six hundred and seventy-two so far. That means we'll have to buy another roll of calico…"

"But then we won't have anything left to buy the string with."

"I don't believe in hopeless situations," Kozlovsky said, shrugging his shoulders. "And my name won't be Andrei Kozlovsky if I don't find a way out."

Indeed, he roused himself into energetic activity. First he rushed off to the storekeeper, then he had lengthy confidential talks with the quartermaster-sergeant and the property clerk of the quartermaster supply unit, and when Shevchenko was about to hit his bunk with a heavy heart of imminent disaster, Kozlovsky suddenly came to him and, with his usual aplomb, declared peremptorily:

"The string is ours, and I got it for a song — half a bottle of vodka, and without as much as a pickled cucumber to go with it. But I surely had to toil to get it."

Shevchenko looked silently at Kozlovsky.

"That's it, *mon cher*! In the storehouse we have huge nets for catching herring. When our battalion was stationed at Guryev, they caught herring in the Caspian Sea. Then the nets were discarded. But if they're no good for holding loads of fish, they're good for holding our pennants. The quartermaster-sergeant gave them to me for half a bottle of vodka. It's a fantastic bargain! *Comprenez vous?* It's just a stroke of genius on my part! We'll grease our betters so they'll remember us for a long time, and drain a lavish cup with everything that goes with it!"

"Wait a minute," Shevchenko stopped him. "Nets are not string yet. It's a terribly difficult job untying the knots."

"And what about this dim rabble?" Kozlovsky said, pointing at the soldiers. "Instead of stinking and cursing the whole evening through, they might as well do some work. The quartermaster-sergeant showed me how the knots can be untied quickly with an awl of which he has as many as you could ask for."

"But the calico! The storekeeper said he had only one roll."

"Oh damn it! That's true," Kozlovsky said, the oversight making him slump on his bunk. He scratched his head, looking perplexed at Shevchenko.

"What about making the pennants out of the tattered underwear we cast off at the bathhouse?" Shevchenko suggested.

"A marvelous idea!" Kozlovsky jumped from the bunk and slapped his forehead. "*Mon cher*, you're beginning to show some signs of brightness. We'll just have to dye it red — and there you've got three thousand pennants!"

Kozlovsky disappeared abruptly again.

In the morning of the third day of the holidays, he dragged Shevchenko to the quartermaster-sergeant, and speaking in a voice choking with enthusiasm, told the sergeant about the "fantastic" plan of making pennants out of the tattered underwear.

"Well, the underwear is quite fit for that purpose, I should say," the sergeant confirmed gravely. "But I cannot give it to you without a proper write-off record. Let the major issue the order, and you'll have the whole lot. But I haven't got any dye-stuff for you."

"What about red ink?" Shevchenko said. "I have a big bottle of it. Lidia Andreievna gave it to me before she left."

"It's all right for the purpose, but one bottle is not enough, even if it is the size of a champagne bottle. Lavrentiev, though, has about twenty of them in his office. He might give you some."

So Lavrentiev had to be told about the details of the forthcoming battue.

All the preparations seemed to be going well, but Shevchenko and Kozlovsky failed to see Meshkov that day because he had left for the nearest fort some sixty *versts* away and would be back only the next morning — with the wolves being abroad, no one dared ride through the steppe at night.

"One — two! One — two!" the next morning the soldiers were going through the arduous drill on the parade ground as before.

Shevchenko's legs throbbed with pain, and in half an hour his heart was thumping wildly and he panted from lack of air. If only he could get out of the barracks for a week or two to take medical treatment. The hopes for a battue hung on a thread again. Everything depended on whether or not Meshkov would agree to write off the old underwear before the general annual inventory.

Back home, Meshkov learned from his batman that the day before he was again visited "by those two who were busy preparing the wolf hunt." Meshkov intentionally went to the parade ground to have a talk with "that odd Shevchenko" who evoked so much concern among Colonel Matveiev, General Fedyaev and other high officers from Orenburg. When at last Globa ordered "At ease!" and the men lit up, Meshkov crossed the parade ground and went up to Shevchenko.

On seeing the major, Shevchenko stiffened to attention.

"Good morning, Shevchenko," Meshkov said. "I was told you wanted to see me."

"Good morning, your Excellency! Yes, I was at your home together with Kozlovsky. It is our idea to regale the officers pleasingly and feed the men after the hunt. The more money we spare on the pennants the more we'll have for the drink and food," Shevchenko said, ironic sparks flickering in his eyes which he hid immediately by dropping his eyelids. Even the primitive-minded Meshkov could not help smiling.

"Oh, I see you two are quite some tricksters! I suppose that's not everything you want?"

"No, sir. We need a lot of other things too. Firstly, I beg your Excellency to let the late general's batman Private Gordeiev go to the *aul* two days before the hunt. As you know, your Excellency, he is a superb cook. Well, and we need a sleigh and horses to take the vodka, a sack of flour, crockery, and foodstuffs to the *aul* along with the pennants, rifles, shot and other hunting equipment. Besides, do us a gracious favor — give all the beaters their rations on the day of the hunt, and to that food we'll add vodka and other fare to make the men drink and eat their fill."

"You've thought that out wonderfully!" Meshkov said with a smile. "All right, everything will be done. I relieve you and Kozlovsky from drill up to the New Year so that you prepare all these things properly. Come to my office in the afternoon. I'll have the order ready, and you go ahead with the preparations. At times it's good to have some diversion in our dull life," be added, as he tipped Shevchenko a friendly nod and left the parade ground.

Rifle shots rent the quiet of the steppe for over an hour, after which twenty-three wolves and eleven red and silver fox fell a prey to the hunters. The *jigits* shot five wolves. The wolves were loaded on sleighs and taken to the *aul*. The entire *aul*, both young and old, gathered around the sleighs to have a close look at the animals which struck so much fear in man and beast.

The meal that followed was truly sumptuous and tasty: broth with meat pie, hare and lamb roast, Kazakh *mantys* and puff pastry with nuts and raisins. Vodka and wine appeared alternately on the table. Tea was served, each cup flavored with half a glassful of Jamaica rum Djantemir had bought from the Bukharan merchants back in the summer.

For the beaters a white, well-heated yurt was pitched near Djantemir's house. Shevchenko personally treated each beater to a glass of vodka, half a herring, and a big chunk of meat pie. Then Jaisak, whom Djantemir had put in charge of the yurt, brought in with Iskhak a huge pot of borshch and another pot of cooked mutton, and gave each soldier a big piece of cooked meat. The meal was so plenteous that the soldiers barely touched the liberally buttered buckwheat porridge; drowsy from drink and languid from the warmth and the fat and tasty food, they laughed merrily at Jaisak who categorically refused to have a drop of vodka.

In the meantime, a storm had gathered in the steppe again. When the soldiers were about to leave for the fortress at four in the afternoon, snow started to fall and a driving ground wind swept across the steppe. Sergeant-Major Laptev went out of the yurt, looked at the sky and steppe, and sent noncom Zlintsev to report to the major about the weather situation.

The major was so drunk by that time that he did not understand at first what Zlintsev was reporting to him about.

"What do you mean 'they won't make it?'" he asked with faltering tongue. "I won't have none of that! Let the men march off immediately!" he roared, bringing his fist down on the table.

"I'm afraid they might lose their way, your Excellency," Zlintsev explained carefully, afraid to arouse Meshkov's rage again. "Take a look what a blizzard there is outdoors. You can't see God's world, let alone the road. There isn't any road at all for that matter: we came here simply by crossing the steppe."

For a moment Meshkov looked dully at the noncom, then he got heavily to his feet, and went out onto the porch. Even from this vantage point the white yurt sheltering the beaters was almost invisible in the swirling snow.

"Damn it!" Meshkov said hoarsely, scratching his head. "Right you are. If at least they'd ring the bell in the church, then the men might follow its sound."

"I have a machine which will show you the way," Djantemir suddenly said behind his back. "I'll bring it to you right away."

A moment later Djantemir was back, holding on the palm of his hand a real mariner's compass.

Meshkov shook his head in confusion: he just did not know how to use this instrument with the flickering needle under a thick mirror glass, and the soldiers would not know how to use it either.

Shevchenko was just then coming out of the house with a heap of dirty dishes. He had seen how Djantemir took the compass out of his trunk, and now understood Meshkov's perplexity. The major was drunk and could very well send the men to certain death in the snow-swept steppe. Shevchenko put the dishes on the steps of the porch and addressed Meshkov quietly:

"Your Excellency, among the soldiers there's a fisherman from the Black Sea and he knows how to handle a compass. Request permission to have him called."

"Yes, yes, Shevchenko! Call him, of course. It's a good thing you happened to be around."

Shevchenko ran off to the yurt with the beaters.

"Hey, Sahadji! The CO is calling you!"

"Do you know how to handle this thing?" Meshkov asked, carefully taking the compass out of Djantemir's hands.

"Yes, sir. Without it a sailor is just like a priest without a cross," Sahadji said with a grin.

"Now look here, take it and lead the men to Orsk. And mind you get all of them there, to a man, without anyone lagging behind or being frostbitten. Take care to bring this thing in one piece to Orsk" — he motioned at the compass. "When the blizzard is over" — he slapped Djantemir on the shoulder — "you'll have it back immediately. Thanks a lot for helping us out."

The blizzard raged the whole night through, making the windowpanes in Djantemir's house rattle. The officers had no heart to leave the safety of their host's home. So mutton was cooked again, fresh *mantys* were kneaded, hares roasted, and samovars set to boil. The officers ate, drank strong tea and the still stronger liquor. Toward the evening of the next day the blizzard had spent itself, and however much Djantemir tried to make the guests stay, they ordered the horses to be hitched to the sleighs, loaded their rifles, lighted torches to ward off the wolves if any were to cross their path, and returned to the fortress without any mishap.

The next day it was drill as usual. But just before the midday meal an orderly arrived from the hospital to see Shevchenko.

"Hurry up! The doctor wants to examine you," he gasped out.

On crossing the threshold of the hospital, Shevchenko saw Alexandriysky, Meshkov, Stepanov and Globa sitting in the room, with the medical attendant reporting on the state of Shevchenko's health.

PART II

I. TO THE BLUE SEA

Pletniov was reclining in a deep armchair at the desk in his study, and seemed to have dozed off. He had just returned from the university after the annual gala meeting. As University Rector and Professor of Russian Philology, he had to deliver a long speech. He was of sturdy stature and all too corpulent for his fifty-five years, which made him look older at this particular moment. A vigorous well-clipped beard densely streaked with gray fell smoothly over his snow-white dickey and the lapels of a dark-blue tailcoat of the finest English cloth, on which gleamed the gold of two stars, while a red ribbon of the Order of St. Anne ran obliquely across his waistcoat.

Deep silence reigned in the house. Outdoors a dense St. Petersburg fog clung about the panes of the large windows.

Dusk was falling. The short winter day was imperceptibly turning into night. Pletniov remained sitting still in the armchair, either engrossed in thought or dozing after a sleepless night.

Suddenly the bronze clock on the mantelpiece struck four times. He sat upright, reached for the bell and rang it. A man servant entered the study noiselessly with a lighted candle.

"Light the candles!" Pletniov ordered. "Where is the lady?"

"The lady said to tell you that you should not await her for dinner. She was invited with the miss to General Lansky's for dinner."

While he reported, he lit three tall stearin candles standing under a dark-green lampshade of silk.

"Do you wish dinner to be served?"

"No. Where is the mail?"

The servant left the study just as noiselessly as he had entered it, but the next moment he was back, carrying a tray with several letters, newspapers, and the last issue of the *Reader's Library* which still smelled of fresh printing ink.

Pletniov started listlessly breaking the seals, and after reading quickly through the letters, threw them aside on the desk. There was an invitation to an evening party, a letter from his old aunt at the manor, with the usual complaints about poor health, a bad crop and a humble petition for monetary help. One more invitation, a letter from a colleague from Dorpat*, a prospectus of the latest Parisian magazines and journals, and an invitation to a meeting. Well, this one was not urgent at all. What else was there?

Among the mail there was a rough, cheap envelope with an address written by an unfamiliar, although intelligent and almost refined hand. Pletniov tore the envelope open. Orsk Fortress. He did not even know such a fortress existed in the world. Two pages of simple paper, and a signature: Shevchenko.

Pletniov raised his eyes for a moment, recalling. Could it be that talented Little-Russian poet whose book he had once reviewed? Certainly: a young natural painter, the former serf of the landowner Engelhardt. Then he got himself involved in a clandestine Slavic society together with Professor Kostomarov. Yes, yes, that was him! Where could he be now? What happened to him?

Pletniov put the candles closer to the letter and became absorbed in it. Terrible! The young man soldiering! He was forbidden to write and paint! And this was meted out to a poet and artist! It was tantamount to confining a living soul to a coffin! Life is anything but sweet for our writers! Pushkin was killed, Koltsov died of consumption, Bestuzhev was hanged, Rileyev too, Lermontov was killed, Odoievsky was forced into the army. There seemed to be no end to this list of martyrs.

---

* Currently the city of Tartu in Estonia

Pletniov jumped to his feet and rushed over to the window. Then he poured himself a glassful of water and drained it at one gulp.

What has made me so overexcited, like a schoolboy? he wondered, sinking back into his deep armchair. Of course the man should be pitied, but it is too risky to interfere in this affair. Let others do it — say, the Vehement Vissarion [Belinsky] from the *Otechestvenniye zapiski*. It is enough that I have been scowled at for so long because of my friendship with Pushkin. Now if others were to get interested in Shevchenko's fate, then...

Pletniov put the letter into the drawer of his desk and reached for the bell again, when another, muffled bell tinkled in the vestibule, and a moment later the servant entered with a visiting card on the tray.

"Alexei Philippovich Chernishov," Pletniov read aloud. "I do not recall anyone by that name. What does he want?"

"He has called several times, sir, but you were out. He is on some very important business from Orenburg, so he says."

"From Orenburg? All right, invite him in. Not to the sitting room, but here, into my study."

"Let me introduce myself: artist Chernishov. I have just returned from Orenburg and bring your Excellency a letter from the poet Taras Shevchenko who has been a friend of mine from the days when we were students at the Academy of Fine Arts."

"You mean the Shevchenko who was convicted because of his involvement in the Slavic society?"

"As a matter of fact, he was convicted not for that reason. The Third Department failed to prove his membership in the Society of Cyril and Methodius. But during the search at his quarters they found two dissident poems," Chernishov replied, and looked Pletniov in the face.

"Oh, I see. But how come you know about it?" Pletniov asked with suspicion, thinking: Dear God, if I were searched they'd find a few things, too — Rileyev's poems or Pushkin's epigrams.

"On his way to the place of exile, that is, to the army, he

stopped in Orenburg for several days," Chernishov explained. "There he came across some decent and influential people who took care of him, and he was permitted to live outside the barracks and go freely around the town in civilian clothes. I met him by chance on the street and invited him to my home. On learning that I was leaving for St. Petersburg, he asked that I pass on his letters to you, Brüllow, Dahl, Count Vielgorsky and some other persons. I have seen them, and they all gave their word of honor to help him by all possible means," Chernishov added, slightly exaggerating the real state of affairs.

"Oh, I see," Pletniov said, animated. "Well, with joint efforts we might achieve something in the end."

"Exactly,' Chernishov said. "Can you imagine the poor man finding himself at Orsk, the farthest fortress from Orenburg? The commandant of Orsk, General Isaiev, died not so long ago, and now there is a certain Meshkov, a primitive man who rose to his present position from the rank of noncom. The company commander is of the same type. For six hours a day they are forcing the man, tormented by rheumatism and scurvy, to march around the parade ground. A clerk from the border commission was there recently and he was shocked by the state of Shevchenko. The man is perishing, and so is his talent. I have come to you as to a cultural figure, as to a friend of the great Pushkin and to a decent man, and I know and believe that you will add your prestigious voice to the voices of those who want to save him."

The idea was stated so bluntly that Pletniov could not refuse, but venturing to do something definite right away was also impossible. He kept silent for a minute and then produced the letter he had just received.

"He has written to me already. Here is his letter. Read it! I thought something should be done for him, but I did not know in what direction to act, since he has not told me what he was accused of."

While Chernishov was reading the first letter, Pletniov opened the envelope his guest had brought him, and became absorbed in the second letter. It did not jar on his nerves that much. There was nothing about the accusation and trial in it, but it carried such an implication of contempt for the fainthearted and the petty egotism of "cultured philistines" that color flooded Pletniov's face as if he had been slapped.

What power and will to live the man possessed, he thought, and reproving his own cowardice, he said:

"Here, too, he does not say what he was accused of. But can you, young man, confirm by your word of honor that apart from writing those poems, he was not involved in anything else?"

"Yes! Upon my word of honor, I swear by the art I serve like a deity."

"Well then, I will try to help. I will have a talk with Orlov and Dubelt."

Chernishov knew that Pletniov was a man of his word. He thanked the professor heartily and was about to leave when the bell tinkled again in the vestibule.

"Lieutenant Butakov," the servant announced, pushing aside the heavy *portiere*.

"Invite him in, please." Pletniov regained his animation.

The servant stepped aside, and a swarthy naval officer of medium height, with a round face, dense dark hair and clever black eyes, entered the study.

"I've come to say farewell to you," Butakov said in a loud and merry voice. "You can congratulate me: I got what I went after in the end. The expedition has been authorized, the funds allotted, and I am leaving for Orenburg."

"Congratulations!" Pletniov said joyously and shook Butakov's hand. "It seems to me that you are not acquainted, are you? This is the artist Chernishov, recently from Orenburg. Lieutenant Butakov, our famous mariner. Let us go to the fireplace," he said, suddenly turning from an amiable aristocrat to a hospitable host. "Tell me everything in detail: what kind of an expedition will it be, how long will it take, and what is your mission all about?"

"The mission is not too complex," Butakov said. "For a long time now I've lost sleep over the white blot on the geographic map to the east of the Caspian Sea. Neither Herodotus nor Pliny ever mentioned a sea existing in the desert there. But on the map from the times of Boris Goduov and on another one of 1627 there is a mysterious Blue Sea. Now we know that the Kirghiz call it the Aral Sea. So I must trek through the desert and steppe, locate the mouth of the Syr Darya, and explore that sea in detail on a schooner, put it on the map for future mariners, describe the islands, sound the depths, reveal currents, reefs, sand banks — in short, collect as much information about it as possible."

"Will you be staying there long?"

"For about two years. Now I am fitting out the expedition with topographers, navigators, hydrologists and geoloists — the whole crew. I want to bring together a well-organized body of men so I won't have to deal with our naval bureaucrats, embezzlers and eye-washers. It seems to me I have chosen some good men. But so far I have failed to find an artist. The famous ones from the capital have turned down my invitation, and I don't need any inept ones. Are you returning to those parts again by any chance?" he asked Chernishov suddenly. "What if you join us?"

"No, I have just come from Orenburg, but ... if a diploma of the Imperial Academy of Fine Arts is all right with you, I can recommend you a real artist who will thank God and fate if you snatch him out of the place he is in now."

Butakov raised his brows in surprise. "Oh! Who is he?"

"You yourself, Alexei Ivanovich, are something of a literateur," Pletniov intervened. "The artist our young friend has in mind is not only an artist, but an extraordinarily talented poet. He is Taras Shevchenko, the author of a collection of Little-Russian poetry entitled *Kobzar*. I think it was published in eighteen forty, and a year later there was a second edition of the book."

"*Kobzar?* Shevchenko? Oh yes, I remember! But how did he find himself in Orenburg?"

"Not in Orenburg, but in Orsk Fortress," Chernishov specified. "Last year he was arrested and sent to serve in a line battalion of the Orenburg Military District."

"You can save him from the horrors of soldiery, drill, the officers' fisticuffs and caning." Pletniov added.

Butakov took out a notebook.

"Wait a minute, gentlemen. I have to put down his name, all of his particulars, and then find out who to deal with — the war minister or the Orenburg Military District authorities. I hope I may wrest at least one talented man from the Third Department."

"Here are his letters. Read them, Alexei Ivanovich," Pletniov said, taking both letters out the drawer. "Read them and you will see what formidable power this man has to live, create, write, paint, and struggle."

"And to struggle not for himself but for his people,' Butakov said reflectively, handing back to Pletniov the letters after he had read them. "It could be that we have read the letters of one of the most famous of our contemporaries. Who knows…"

"Well, that is a bit far-fetched," the professor said with a smile. "He is simply a talented man from the people. You could not really compare with with, say Baratinsky or Zhukovsky, could you? Or the more so with Pushkin in whose verse the Russian language has been elevated to the level of one of the first languages in the world? Nobody will be able to outmatch Pushkin even in five hundred years from now."

And Pletniov started to air his lengthy, wise and dull reflections he was so fond of.

But not all of Shevchenko's acquaintances were equally responsive to his pleas for help. The only thing Karl Brüllow did when approached by Chernishov and Lazarevsky was shrug his shoulders.

Lazarevsky could not restrain himself at such a reaction, and said:

"I should say you are lapsing into sin, Karl Pavlovich, by being so indifferent to one of your best students! Why then did you have to keep him in your home and feed him for several years, and then renounce him at a time when he is perishing?"

"Who gave you the right to judge my actions in such a manner?!" Brüllow flared up. "If the emperor himself is angry with Shevchenko, nobody's pleas will make him change his mind, but, on the contrary, they might only worsen the fate of the unfortunate Shevchenko. The emperor regards him as a person who dared offend the imperial family. In this case you have to do only one thing: keep quiet. Let the emperor forget about Shevchenko, and in about two years, at a suitable moment, he'll be given a pardon to sign. For the time being any reminder about Shevchenko will only prolong his exile."

"But he will perish by that time!" Chernishov exclaimed. "He is at the end of his tether."

"Talk with Orlov and Dubelt then, if you don't believe me," Brüllow cut him short angrily and left the room.

Chernishov and Lazarevsky went out into the street in a downcast and sorrowful mood, not knowing what to do next. Brüllow had been their greatest hope.

After saying goodbye to Lazarevsky, Chernishov stood at the corner in indecision for some time, then he hailed a carriage and went to Vasilevsky Island to Dahl.

The famous ethnographer and collector of folk songs, riddles and sayings did not receive him immediately. He was ill, and Chernishov had to wait for a long time in his study piled with papers, thick notebooks, files and file boxes. The sight of this seeming disorder, which actually had a system of its own, evoked bitter thoughts in Chernishov. He doubted whether he would be able to elicit sympathy for Shevchenko's fate.

"Excuse me for having made you wait so long," he suddenly heard the voice of Dahl.

Dahl entered in a dressing gown and with a hot compress on his neck.

"Be seated, please. I have been taken extremely ill because

of our city's permanent dampness," Dahl said. "What can I do for you?"

"I have brought you a letter from Taras Shevchenko. He has been exiled, or rather forced into a line battalion in the Orenburg Military District. He is ill and pleads for help. Here is his letter."

Dahl read the letter lengthily and attentively, then he folded it neatly and put it back into the envelope.

"You must have already seen some of his acquaintances, I suppose?" Dahl looked searchingly at the artist.

"I have," Chernishov replied. "Brüllow said it was too early to intercede. But Shevchenko might perish in the meantime."

Dahl slowly paced the room, then he sat down opposite Chernishov, and took a snuff box out of his pocket.

"Tell me please everything about Shevchenko's case and everything you have heard from Brüllow and the others. Then I'll think what can be done."

Chernishov told in detail about his meeting with the poet in Orenburg, as well as his conversation with Pletniov and Brüllow. Dahl listened so attentively that he even forgot to open his snuff box.

"Brüllow is right," he said after Chernishov had finished the story. "It is too early yet to talk about pardon, but to intercede for Shevchenko to have his fate alleviated is something which can and must be done. Try to be granted an audience with Dubelt or Orlov. Ask them to help the sick man. In the meantime I will write him a letter promptly and send some money and books. Money makes even a soldier's life easier: for half a bottle of vodka any noncom can excuse him from fatigue. Unfortunately, I cannot give much now, but here is my little share," he concluded, taking twenty-five rubles out of an old secretaire.

The other of the poet's acquaintances, apart from sincere sympathy and a little money, could not offer anything else, and that same day Lazarevsky and Chernishov sent Shevchenko the seventy-five rubles they had thus collected and a parcel with warm underwear, medicines and books. They wanted to send oil paints as well, but then decided against it, since it would be fraught with trouble for Shevchenko.

Officially Alexandriysky was not a medical officer, but since Orsk had no other doctor available, he was invited to treat the gravely ill officers and men and sat on the military medical commissions. For this effort he received a meager fee.

He treated Shevchenko, considering it his public duty. He liked the poet for his talent, inquisitive mind and extraordinary honesty. He delighted in talking with Shevchenko and deeply sympathized with his fate. Almost every day Alexandriysky visited him, occasionally bringing him last year's magazines, and tried by all possible means to entertain him and dispel his sullen mood.

Shevchenko slept his fill in the pleasantly warm hospital, and rested from the battue which had worried his nerves considerably. But, on the other hand, there was much more time for his sullen moods.

Alexandriysky understood everything without any explanations, and it was with a particular feeling of joy that he brought him a total of three letters the poet had been waiting for so anxiously from Repnina, Lizohub, and Mikhailo Lazarevsky. On the morning of the next day he received a parcel from Ukraine, and then another one and money from St. Petersburg.

Shevchenko felt as if a stream of sunlight and warmth had flushed his sore heart, he read and reread the letters that were replete with warm sympathy, taking in their every word like healing balm, and with tears of gratitude he now and again took up the paints, albums, books, pencils, brushes, note paper, and warm underwear out of the caskets, and then put them back again accurately and carefully. He had been sent everything he had written and asked for: two volumes of Lermontov's poetry, Shakespeare, Koltsov, Gogol, and *The Papers of the Moscow Archeographic Society*. Only the *Odyssey* in Zhukovsky's translation was lacking, because it had not appeared in print yet.

The books heightened his days at the hospital for a long time. He repeated with rapture the charmingly beautiful verse of Lermontov, delighting in their music, and clenched his fists every time he recalled the poet's tragic death. He read them out loud to Fischer and Alexandriysky, and during his sleepless nights he recited from memory the verse from the incomparable *Mtsyri* which echoed his mood so much at that time.

Shakespeare's tragedies moved him deeply as well. Fischer and Shevchenko argued at length about Hamlet and Othello. They were captivated by the immediacy of Romeo and Juliet's love and the power with which Shakespeare exposed to the reader the dark souls of Iago and Shylock.

But Gogol's book evoked in Shevchenko a feeling that bordered on despair. There was nothing left of the former satirist who wrote *The Inspector-General* and *Dead Souls*. The great master and artist of the written word, whose keen eye did not miss a single dark feature of serf-bound Russia, had practically buried himself alive. Seized by dark mystic visions and hypocrisy, Gogol was now extinguishing the light he himself had kindled.

Shevchenko's health was getting better. Alexandriysky was glad to see his patient convalesce, but he realized with sadness that the time was approaching when he would have to discharge him from hospital. He wanted to continue the treatment until spring when it would be warmer, but his patient could not force himself to moan and complain of an unexisting illness.

An unexpected letter from Orenburg excited the physician: Lazarevsky wrote to tell him that a naval officer, Butakov, had arrived in Orenburg and started building a two-masted schooner to explore the Aral Sea. Further on he informed him that Colonel Matveiev and Gern, together with General Fedyaev, had talked Butakov into including Shevchenko in the expedition party.

Alexandriysky hurried to Shevchenko with the news, but the poet, instead of being overjoyed, was horrified.

"What? To a place still further away from here? Into the boundless steppe where wolves prowl in winter and every crack swarms with snakes in summer?"

"For God's sake, come to your senses, old chap! This is a happy chance! It's a way to freedom!" the physician argued. "Hear me out attentively. Firstly, you will be relieved from drill for a year and a half, or maybe two. Everyone refers to Butakov as a clever, decent and learned man. There is an officer from the general headquarters with him and several junior naval officers not assigned to the expedition by the war ministry but picked by Butakov himself. Of course, every geographic expedition has its difficulties to reckon with: lack of food, exposure to heat and cold and the like. Such an expedition is likely to win you a citation. And your very first citation might be a good investment for the future: you'll be officially permitted to paint. Do you understand? To paint! In this way the first part of your verdict will be null and void, and then you will be granted permission to write. Thus your talent will not decay, and you will not lose the art of working with pen, brush and pencil."

At first Shevchenko listened like a distrustful child being told a fairy tale, but when he heard Alexandriysky's last argument and then read the letter from Orenburg, his heart was filled with joy.

In the barracks no one knew about the future expedition. Alexandriysky advised Shevchenko to keep silent about it as well.

After thinking the news over, the poet decided that these were no more than his friends' dreams, and his Orenburg betters would never permit him to join the expedition. The "most august monarch" himself had given orders to keep him under strictest surveillance, and what kind of strictest surveillance could there be in an empty steppe or on some island in a sea, the existence of which was known only from rumors?

On discharging Shevchenko from the hospital, Alexandriysky ordered the medical attendant to relieve the poet from drill for a couple of days. The commanding officers had nothing against it, since they remembered the drinking spree at the *aul:* now they regarded Shevchenko differently, addressed him politely, and did not shove a hairy fist under his nose whenever the raised tip of his boot trembled in formation from the rheumatic pain he still felt in his legs.

"You just follow my example of how to feast on reason, *mon cher*," Kozlovsky once said to Shevchenko approaching him with his peculiarly wobbly gait. "When they forget about the battue, and it is 'overgrown with the grass of oblivion,' as Eugene Sue put it, treat them to booze and make them remember you. For the time being, lend me twenty kopecks, because if I don't down at least a thimbleful of vodka today, my soul will turn into vapor and disappear altogether."

In the evening, the older and more level-headed soldiers frequently asked Shevchenko to sing something: "Your songs are very beautiful. They make our souls warmer, and then life doesn't seem to be so dull."

Shevchenko responded with a song in which two or three voices would join by and by — and thus an impromptu chorus appeared. Imperceptibly, the cussing ceased; standing in a tight circle around the singers, the men listened quietly after which they went to sleep silently, soothed by the beauty of folk songs.

In his letters to Lizohub and Repnina, Shevchenko wrote that he would probably be included on an expedition to the Aral Sea in spring, although he himself did not believe it as much as before.

One day he met Meshkov near the barracks. Shevchenko snapped to attention and took off his cap with his left hand.

Meshkov smiled, came up closer to him, and said: "Well, Shevchenko, we've been sparing you for over six weeks. You've received medical treatment and been given the chance to rest. It's time you got down to soldiering."

Three days later Shevchenko marched off to the parade ground.

"What makes our precentor and soloist look so despondent?" Kozlovsky asked him one evening in the barracks.

"I'm plagued by a toothache which gives me no sleep, and I can't eat because of it. Meshkov, though, is making me stump around the parade ground without any letup."

"That's his way of planting a seemingly stray thought in your head."

"Unfortunately, I can't stage another battue," Shevchenko said with a sigh.

"Oh, *mon cher*! Apart from hunting, there are birthdays, nameday parties, official holidays when all loyal subjects have to drink to the health of the czar and other most august persons. You could think up such pretexts by the dozens. The only thing is to find them. *Comprenez?*"

"So you suggest holding a binge right here in the barracks?" Shevchenko remarked angrily, annoyed by Kozlovsky's rudely condescending tone.

"As if there didn't exist married clerks, Cossacks and noncoms," Kozlovsky sniffed scornfully. "Go to hell, Shevchenko! I'm sick of teaching you!" He shuffled off into the corner where Belobrovov and Schultz were beating two recruits at cards.

Shevchenko lay down on his bunk and covered himself with a greatcoat, under which he slipped his head as well, pretending he was asleep. The next day he intercepted Lavrentiev by the porch of the company office. The clerk responded to his new troubles with sincere sympathy, and when Shevchenko told him of the conversation with Kozlovsky, the clerk immediately grasped the underlying idea.

"You know what — you just find a pretext and lay up some money, and Oxana and I will throw you a fitting party, with pies, roasted geese, sausages, and home-brewed beer. As for blackthorn brandy, we've always got some at home. We'll also buy the vodka, which will cost you three times less than before. Then I'll invite the officers, telling them that you were feeling awkward to do so yourself. They'll become kinder to you again, and probably let you lodge at my home. That'll make things easier for the other soldiers, too. They say that in the barracks the men just pray to God for you. What about it?"

The only reasonable pretext Shevchenko could find was his own birthday. In two days Lavrentiev's wife had bought everything that was needed and prepared such appetizers for the party it amazed Shevchenko. Apart from the officers, he had to invite the medical attendant, the sergeant-major, the company's noncom, and a blind accordion player who had been a former soldier and lived at the settlement. He alternately played marches and folk songs, and before the officers were at the stage of babbling drunkenness, he played a bouncy Russian folk dance. Globa and Stepanov went through its steps with gusto, and then Meshkov came mincing into the circle, waving a handkerchief as he enacted the part of a bashful girl. Then there was drinking, singing, and drinking again. Shevchenko was congratulated on his birthday, wished the best of luck in getting a commission as fast as possible, and being granted pardon. Then Meshkov, barely standing on his legs, dragged the poet into a corner and releasing stenchy vodka-laden breath in his face, whispered with a faltering tongue:

"You, Shevchenko, will be leaving u-ush s-shoon. There is-sh an order. You'll go to Raīm with s-shome mar-riners. But s-sho far thish ish a s-shecret."

Shevchenko's heart fluttered like a bird's. So what his friends had told him was true, after all. But to Meshkov he said:

"Now who would need such a sick man as me, your Excellency? A limping weakling? My legs are hurting me again. You cannot possibly recommend such a man as me to anyone."

"Don't worry, old chap. W-we'll help you out," Meshkov uttered, and when the accordion player struck up a dance tune, he went off in a dance on his unsteady legs, tripped in the process, plopped on the floor and burst into laughter. Shevchenko went up to the table, poured himself a full glass of wine, and emptied it in one gulp.

A new page had opened in his life.

2. FROM ORSK TO RAÏM

In February all of Orenburg was abuzz with the news of the future expedition. New people showed up in the streets and offices, and the uniforms of the mariners stood out among them. Lieutenant Butakov was appointed head of the expedition on the recommendation of the famous seafarer Admiral Belingshausen, and in March construction work on the two-masted schooner *Constantine* commenced. A large vacant plot of land on the bank of the Ural was fenced off, and there two sheds were built — from sunup till sunset axes hacked away merrily, sharp-toothed saws whizzed, planes and drawshaves swished and scraped, and steel chisels tapped steadily at the fresh bright yellow timber like so many woodpeckers. But in vain did the passersby peep into the chinks in the fence: they did not see any schooner but only logs and planks, around which huge mounds of splinters and bark accumulated every day.

The mystery was easily explained: the schooner was intended for a distant sea to which no river or any other body of water had access. That was why only sections of the future schooner were built in Orenburg; they had to be transported thousands of *versts* to the unknown sea, and then assembled into a schooner which would be launched for a long and hazardous voyage.

Butakov had to shoulder all the burden of preparing the expedition that was to last two years. At the same time while parts of the schooner were being built, he had to procure the food, clothing, all the equipment for the schooner, navigation instruments, sails, ropes, crockery, bedding, paper, tools, paints — everything to the last nail which would be needed throughout the winters and summers of the voyage. Some of the things he needed were available in Orenburg, but most of the gear was arriving from St. Petersburg and Sevastopol, and all this tremendous load, along with parts of the schooner, had to be transported somehow to the banks of the Syr Darya.

For all his worries of preparation, Butakov did not forget Shevchenko. He was overwhelmed by the horrible fate of the poet. Butakov was not personally acquainted with him, but knew him only as a poet: his collection *Kobzar* and his personality had been frequently commented on at the editorial offices of the magazine *Otechestvenniye zapiski* which, in 1843 and 1844, carried Butakov's skillfully written essays about his round-the-world voyage on board the supply ship *Abo*.

But it proved not that easy to snatch Shevchenko out of Orsk Fortress.

First of all, Butakov handed in a report to the military governor Obruchev. The latter refused to grant Butakov's request, arguing that Czar Nicholas had categorically prohibited Shevchenko from writing and painting.

Butakov was not cast down by the refusal, however after consulting Gern and Matveiev, he wrote another report to Obruchev, in which he referred to Shevchenko not as an artist, but simply requested that Private Shevchenko be included in the expedition force. Obruchev refused him again. The second failure disheartened Butakov, but Gern and Matveiev advised him to approach General Fedyaev.

The general received him courteously and affably. After a short conversation, Butakov told him straight out the reason of the visit, saying that he could not manage without an artist.

"I know the poor chap," the general replied, treating Butakov to a cigarette. "I wanted him to stay in Orenburg, but the gendarmes added to the verdict their own instruction to keep him at the farthest fortress. And I had to retreat. But today when the case has lost its initial acute-ness, the man can be helped."

Butakov gave a contended smile and extended to the general the report written beforehand.

"I feel a bit guilty in regard to him," the general continued, looking for his spectacles. "When we failed to keep him at Orenburg, Gern and I wrote a letter to Meshkov at Orsk, asking that he help Shevchenko, but that moron of a martinet did not understand us properly and started to torment him with drill. He almost plagued the life out of the poor chap. But you must understand my position as well: I just could not write Meshkov bluntly what I had in mind."

Fedyaev found his spectacles at long last.

"Why do you address your report to me and not to the military governor?" he asked.

Butakov had to tell him about the two failures he had gone through. Fedyaev fell to thinking: "Oh well, what will be, will be. I'll have a talk with Obruchev, and if he does not relent, I will assume all the responsibility."

The general had to argue with Obruchev for a long time: Obruchev was afraid of deviating from the letter of the czar's prohibition.

"All right, write the resolution as follows: 'At the discretion of Brigadier-General Fedyaev.' In this way, you will relieve me of any responsibility whatsoever, and untie my hands," Fedyaev said. "You see, I could not have known anything about what the czar and the gendarmes added to the verdict. But destroy all the previous reports from Butakov."

Obruchev wrote the necessary resolution, and the next day Fedyaev informed Butakov that everything was done as he had requested.

In early April the building of the schooner sections was completed, and caravans of wagons from St. Petersburg, Bryansk, Tula, Sevastopol and other towns trekked through the spring mire to Orenburg to bring the equipment for the expedition.

To transport all this load from Orenburg to Raïm called for over fifteen hundred wagons and six hundred camels with camaleers and numerous guard troops, all under the command of General Schreiber. Late in April the expedition set off.

Two days earlier Djantemir's *aul* had left its camping site, the *bai* being intent on conclusively deciding Kuljan's destiny.

Jaisak came to Shevchenko to say his farewell. Throughout the winter the poet had frequently thought about him, but he did not have the courage to see him again.

"We won't come here anymore," Jaisak said sadly. "Meshkov

told our *bai* he must look for another winter ground. The steppe is big, so big, and the people in it so small: we'll probably never meet again," he said with a sigh and hung his head.

"I won't be here, either," Shevchenko said. "I'm going to Raïm. My betters are sending me there."

"To Raïm? The one on Syr Darya?" Jaisak's face brightened suddenly. "But that is where we are bound for. Maybe I will see you there. *Oi boi*, how happy I shall be then!" the young man added with fire, and even laughed for joy.

"Good luck to you, Jaisak. I wish that Kuljan becomes your wife," Shevchenko said and clasped the young man in a strong embrace.

"Are you out of your mind, Shevchenko, to embrace a Kirghiz? Fie!" Lavrentiev spat with disgust on seeing the two men part as he passed by.

After the party at the clerk's home, Meshkov told his fellow officers that Shevchenko had been included on a scientific expedition to the Aral Sea, and before the caravans were to appear near Orsk, his health had to be improved somehow. The poet was relieved of drill and appointed assistant to the battalion's quartermaster-sergeant. The things at the storehouse had to be put into order, for an inspection commission was expected.

From that day on Shevchenko did not march around the parade ground to the deafening roll of the drums, but hung linen and musty felt boots in the sun to dry, destroyed rats, counted heaps of linen, and lugged bundles of rags to the battalion tailor. For Shevchenko it was tantamount to a good rest and he became noticeably stronger and merrier.

Shevchenko wrote to Lizohub and asked him for paints and brushes. Lizohub sent him everything right away, and the poet took all these treasures to Alexandriysky.

The caravan with supplies reached Orsk on the ninth of May and pitched camp for a day on the far bank of the Ural to give the tired people, horses and camels a respite.

Orsk became astir at such an unexpected sight. The people from the settlement and the Cossacks rushed to the Ural with pails of milk, boiled eggs, roast, fish, fowl, and pots of borshch and porridge. The hungry wagon drivers and cameleers bought up the food in no time, and the housewives hurried back to their homes to bring more food. Now and then Shevchenko walked beyond the ramparts to the bank of the Ural to have a look at the noisy camp and then returned to the barracks lest he miss the moment when his betters would summon him. All the time he had a feeling they had forgotten him, but he did not dare remind them, waiting instead by the porch of the office until Lavrentiev would notice him through the window. When the latter came out onto the porch for a smoke at last, Shevchenko ran over to him. But the clerk only shrugged his shoulders and replied quietly:

"There hasn't been a single word about you. Better get yourself scarce before Globa sees you. You know the captain doesn't like the men hanging around the headquarters."

In the evening the poet was racked with despair. He must have been fooled! So it would be drill again — for weeks, months, years. He lay on his bunk drained of strength, unable either to stir or utter a word.

A deep sleep abruptly cut short his sad flow of thoughts, and the next day, before breakfast, he was summoned by Meshkov and officially informed that he was appointed to the Aral expedition and was to report immediately to his new commander Lieutenant Butakov.

For the first few moments Shevchenko was at a loss. A sharp pain stabbed his sick heart like a hot needle, and his hands trembled helplessly. He stood there and did not understand what Meshkov was telling him. He saluted automatically to his tormentor, and only outside on the porch did he realize that he had not asked where he could find Butakov.

"Shevchenko! Hey, Shevchenko!" Lavrentiev came running after him. "The lieutenant is here in the office of the company CO. He's calling for you."

Shevchenko stood for a while as if he had not understood the clerk, and then he hurried inside. On entering the office, he bellowed with an unexpectedly joyous boldness:

"Good morning, your Excellency! Private Shevchenko reporting on your orders!"

"Good morning, Taras Grigorievich," Butakov said, walked up to him and shook his right hand which was still pressed to his side "at attention." "I am very glad to meet you, and the more glad to have had the fortune to snatch you from Orsk. Be seated please. I want to have a talk with you."

Butakov understood what Shevchenko was going through at this minute, and to give him a chance to regain his self-control, he kept on talking as he sat down.

"They would not let you go as an artist, nor as a soldier. You have been detached to my expedition force as a sailor. But whatever your status may be, the main thing is that you have been released. You will share the same cabin as we, the officers. You will be our artist, and if you like" — he gave his lively black eyes a cunning squint — "our comrade and companion."

"I ... I don't know how to thank you. I..." Shevchenko managed to say something at last, and then fell silent, with a lump in his throat. "Thank you!"

"Still, I think it's me who should thank fortune for having acquired such an assistant and comrade," Butakov responded warmly. "This expedition is the main purpose of my life. I have been obsessed with its idea for years. Throughout many sleepless nights I have been thinking about it, dreaming about it, and then started pushing it through. If you only knew how difficult it is to overcome our indifference to everything new, our bureaucracy. Man's soul yearns for the new and unknown..." the excited Butakov lapsed into silence. "Well, we'll have enough time yet to talk about all that." A minute later he spoke up again: "After all, we'll be seeing each other for a year and a half or even two years and will probably get tired of each other within that time. But right now I ask your magnanimous apology — I have work up to my neck: a number of our wagons have broken down and have to be repaired immediately. We are setting off tomorrow morning, Taras Grigorievich. Pack your things in crates or suitcases and take them to my tent. I shall order Tikhon, my batman, to put them together with my personal belongings and navigation instruments which are the most valuable cargo we have. You can now change into civvies."

The men were getting ready to break camp: tents were taken down, the horses were hitched to the wagons, the camels loaded, the men took up march formation, and at ten o'clock after the parting prayer, the caravan marched out.

The first to gallop off were the guides, accompanied by half a dozen Cossacks, to reconnoiter the trek. Half a *verst* behind them followed a company of infantry troops with two cannons, and after them came the rattling bulk of the main caravan. It moved in three files at a distance of more than a *verst* from one another. The wagons were followed by baggage camels, behind which plodded the flock of sheep intended partially for the needs of the Raïm Fort and partially to feed the huge mass of people who pushed through the steppe like a horde from the times of the Great Migration. A hundred Cossacks and an infantry company with two more guns brought up the rear, and yet another hundred Cossacks armed with lances, swords and rifles moved on the left and right of the caravan to protect its flanks.

Shevchenko went of foot in the forward company detailed from the Orsk garrison. He wore the canvas suit Levitsky had given him and his old summer coat; all of his things, carefully tied and tightly covered with cloth, were riding in a wagon in the caravan. He was in a wonderful mood, the company moved on easily, and he exchanged banter with the right flankmen now and then.

After two hours' march toward the south-east, the caravan passed not far from the camping site of Djantemir's *aul*. Through the dense cloud of dust it was difficult to see the gray-yellow adobe walls of the *bai*'s house, but Shevchenko noticed right away that the campsite had been abandoned, all of its traces obliterated by the winds, rains, snow, and sandstorms.

"Our *bat's* left for good," the soldiers remarked.

"That's certain! The major's chased him from his old haunt," Kuzmich said with a sigh.

The dust scratched the men's throats, grated between their teeth, and made their nostrils dry.

Shevchenko turned round: a dense impenetrable curtain shut off the steppe behind the caravan, while ahead it was clear. He quickened his pace and outdistanced the wagons by about a hundred paces.

They were now passing the cliff rising over the valley where the battue was staged the previous winter. Shevchenko stopped, dumbfounded: instead of the dry barren branches of the saxaul he saw a pleasantly rosy haze someone seemed to have thrown like a transparent veil on the dry scrub, through which glittered the sunlit River Or swollen with the thawed snow and the recent April rains.

Shevchenko hurried toward the cliff, not believing his own eyes.

The dry and dead scrub of the saxaul had come to life. The branches were clustered with green succulent offshoots, each bearing a blooming tassel of tiny rosy flowers.

"A beautiful sight, isn't it?" a horseman remarked, leaning down from his saddle.

Shevchenko started at the unexpected voice, but on seeing the gilded buttons of a uniform showing from under a cape, he snapped to attention.

"Yes, sir! A very beautiful and interesting sight. It's a pity my oil paints are packed away; I would have put all that on canvas at once."

"Oh, so that's what you are!" the horseman said with a drawl and jumped from the horse. "Let me introduce myself: Junior Captain Maksheiev, Alexei Ivanovich. You must be the artist Shevchenko? So we'll be sailing the Aral Sea together."

225

"Yes, sir," Shevchenko repeated, not knowing how to conduct himself in the presence of this smart looking officer.

"Would you please drop those formalities, dear Taras..." the officer faltered, shaking the poet's hand.

"... Grigorievich," the poet prompted.

"What are these strange trees or shrubs called?" Maksheiev asked, looking back at the cliff.

"That is saxaul. They say the trees do not bear any leaves. I thought it was a dry stand — and here..." Shevchenko made a sweeping movement of his hand.

"Remarkable! I'd like to break off a twig and have a closer look, but here's such a steep..."

"There ought to be a little gully with a brook somewhere here. You can walk down it, but I've forgotten where it is." Shevchenko said, looking around. "I think it's farther ahead."

"Get on my horse with me," Maksheiev said, jumping into the saddle. "Otherwise we won't catch up with our troop."

"No, thank you kindly. I'll make it on foot."

Maksheiev galloped ahead, but Shevchenko walked on along the cliff, now and then shooting sidelong glances at the caravan which was passing him at quite a distance now. When he had reached the gulch where a cold, limpid brook gurgled over rounded pebbles, Maksheiev was already returning with a bouquet in his hand.

"They don't smell. What a pity! I thought they would smell like lilac."

"I believed they smelled like almonds. How tiny these flowers are! They're not as pretty as I thought they were; from above their beauty quite struck me."

Farther on Maksheiev walked, leading the horse by the halter.

"You know, we have a lot of common acquaintances," he said. "I am a friend of Mombelli. He often told me about you, and even showed me your book. Unfortunately, I do not understand Ukrainian, and so could not read your poetry. In Orenburg I learned of your fate, and decided to get acquainted with you by all means. Butakov was fortunate to get you out of Orsk. It's an abominable town! Even the Kirghiz call it Jaman Kala, which means 'bad place.'"

"You know their tongue?"

"Only separate words. But I am very interested in it."

The conversation flowed back to their St. Petersburg acquaintances. Then Maksheiev told him what was new in the literature of the past winter season, how he had made the acquaintance of Petrashevsky and the talented writer Dostoyevsky and the poet Pleshcheyev and the latest news from the theater world. Shevchenko listened with rapt attention. His soul was starved from lack of intellectual sustenance, and he greedily took in the scanty news. With the conversation neither of them noticed how two hours had passed. It became cold. The cloud of dust stirred up by the caravan was spreading more and more over the steppe. Thirst started to plague the men.

"Look how our infantry kicks up the dust," Maksheiev remarked, wiping his sweaty dirt-grimed forehead.

"I just cannot understand why we have such a large guard troop in the desert: two companies of infantry, guns, three hundred Cossacks," Shevchenko said with a shrug. "Looks like we are out for a fight."

"It's something like it," Maksheiev said with a smile. "Legally, our border runs along the River Ural. Orsk Fortress stands right on the border, while the steppe beyond the Ural is not ours."

"Does that mean that Meshkov chased Djantemir's *aul* out of its own land?"

"If only they could call it their own land. The British are stealing up to Central Asia from the south. In diplomatic language, this is called expanding the sphere of influence. So our expedition is a sort of reconnaissance mission. We'll try to lay our hands on the sea which the Kirghiz call Taniz Aral."

The caravan stopped only once to graze the horses and cattle.

Next morning when the caravan set off, the whole steppe glistened with profuse dew, as if it were spangled with diamonds.

To evade the dust, Shevchenko left the camp half an hour before the departure of the guides and scouts, and throughout the whole morning he breathed fresh, clean air, delighting in the quiet of the boundless steppe. The day was bright, but at midday Shevchenko saw way ahead, on the very horizon, white cloudlets which now and then appeared and moments later seemed to melt, without rising any higher.

"The steppe is burning! The Kirghiz have set it on fire!" one of the guides cried out. "What for?"

"So that last year's feather grass doesn't get in the way of the young grass. The old grass burns away, leaving ahes, and ashes are the best fertilizer. For the Kirghiz grass is the first thing that counts, because they live off cattle breeding," Maksheiev explained as he rode up to the poet.

"I wonder what will happen to us?" Shevchenko reasoned out loud. "We are heading in that direction, after all."

"We won't perish, don't you worry," a Cossack guide laughed, flashing his dazzlingly white teeth. "Right now the river makes a turn. The fire is beyond it."

He had spoken the truth. An hour before sunset separate fiery dots appeared ahead. They grew in number, and when twilight was falling, the dots gradually merged into one glittering band which glowed in a twisting stream of fire, growing brighter and broader with every minute. But now the glittering ribbon of the River Or stretched between the fire and the caravan. A light breeze rippled the river, and the burning steppe was reflected on the water in golden scales. Just at that moment a Bukharan caravan appeared by the water's edge. The camels walked one after the other in a long file and seemed to be carved out of black wood against the backdrop of the burning steppe. The sight of this beauty held Shevchenko spellbound, and he rushed to the wagons. He simply had to paint the river, the golden scales of the rippling water, and the camels. He ran around between the wagons, looking in vain for the only conveyance with the inscription "Personal Baggage of the Expedition Chief, Wagon No. 301" until he came across Butakov's batman. Together they quickly located the wagon. Shevchenko took out his oil paints and album, but by the time he returned to Maksheiev, the Bukharan caravan had already disappeared in the thickening dusk.

The steppe fire raged the whole night through. Maksheiev sat at Shevchenko's side and admired the elemental force of the flames, but then fatigue overcame him and he went to sleep. Shevchenko, oblivious of sleep, remained sitting outdoors till morning. It was too dark to paint, but when dawn colored the fleecy clouds purple and the last fountains of fire still spurted beyond the river, Shevchenko feverishly dashed off a watercolor — his first work of art after a year of military bondage.

Walking around the camp that morning, General Schreiber came across Shevchenko. He stopped by the artist, took the watercolor in his hands, and after regarding it for a long time, gave it back to Shevchenko with an expression of pity on his face. Shevchenko caught the hint. What could he do?

"Your Excellency," he said, embarrassed, "I see you like my work. May I present the watercolor to you in memory of this fire?"

Throughout the next day the caravan trekked along the right bank of the river, but on the fourteenth of May Schreiber gave the order to cross it. The water was still at its spring high, so a bridge had to be built. Maksheiev was charged with the construction of the bridge, for which the ship building timber and thick rope were used. It was forbidden to hew or saw the timber, which complicated the work immensely. For all that, the bridge was built in a couple of hours; at first the guns and then the wagons rolled across the bridge. The camels forded the river.

Further on the caravan moved through a fire-ravaged steppe. The smell of burning and ashes made the dust denser and the more stifling, while the sight of the black ground cast a somber gloom on the troops. Man and beast quickly succumbed to exhaustion, but Shevchenko walked on in good spirits.

The journey continued for another week. Though tired from the trek by now, Shevchenko remained cheerful and even-tempered, and if anyone were to have asked him what he had experienced and thought over these days, he could have said sincerely: "It was easy to breathe and I was almost happy."

Daylong halts were sounded ever more frequently to give the exhausted men and beasts a rest. Shevchenko used every halt to draw. He had drawn the rivers Kara Butak and Irghiz with the forts of the same names, and felt that he was gradually regaining precision of draughtsmanship and a feeling for color.

During one such halt, when he had walked far into the steppe to sketch a half-dry nameless stream, Królikiewicz came to see him.

"Hello!" Shevchenko greeted him joyfully. "Sit down, and let's have a chat while we have the time."

"That's just why I was looking for you," Kloiikiewicz said. "I have to tell you some fantastic news I recently heard from a compatriot from the Orenburg unit. Ho, too, is an exile, but came from my country only two mouths ago. Just imagine: there's a revolution on in Paris! All the people have revolted. Louis Philippe ordered the national guard to crush the insurgents, but it sided with the people. So he abdicated and fled, and the people seized the Tuileries, took his throne to a square, and burned it in front of a huge crowd. Well, a provisional government was formed, with two representatives from the workers and not a single aristocrat. The bankers and financiers fell into panic. I'd love to know what our autocrat thinks on that point. He's probably..."

"For God's sake, tell me what is happening in France in greater detail!" Shevchenko exclaimed impatiently.

"All right then. A republic was proclaimed. Everything is buzzing and seething in Paris. It almost came to a fist fight when they tried to decide what color the republic's state flag should be: red, or tricolor like it had been during the first revolution. The poet Lamartine and a certain Dupont de l'Eureare are at the head of the provisional government. My compatriot does not know anything more, because he had been arrested by then, and even what I am telling you now was learned from his wife during their last meeting before he was taken to Warsaw."

"And what's going on in Ukraine? What's happening in Poland? In Russia? In Galicia? Does everyone keep silent there as well?"

"Oh no! Although the Cracow Republic does not exist anymore, there is no peace there either, just as throughout all of Poland. That unfortunate man was not arrested for nothing."

Królikiewicz looked around, although the place was so barren that even a little gopher would have hardly found himself a hideout. Then he continued nervously, tugging at Shevchenko's sleeve:

"Throughout the past year the peasants in Warsaw, Radom, Lublin and Augustów provinces refused en masse to pay taxes to the landowners. Quite a few manors were set on fire. Many village elders and even more stewards were killed. The authorities got scared of the peasant movement, and Grand Duke Constantine issued an order prohibiting the landowners to levy any taxes, except for the usual ones, on the serfs. Clandestine societies and circles are springing up everywhere, fiery appeals are being written, and small-scale peasant rebellions flared up in Galicia last summer. They had been preparing to rise in one body, but the treachery of a number of landowners thwarted the general uprising, because the Austrians arrested the peasant leaders. In Poznań something of the sort is being prepared now. You must know that our suffering is the worst under the Prussian heel. The Prussian rulers not only plunder and ruin our country, but have started Germanizing us: Polish schools have been closed down, Polish newspapers and journals prohibited, Polish officials are not permitted to speak in their native tongue at the offices where they work, and they are forced to study German. Is it really possible to tolerate such horrible humiliation? The very ground there is ready to burst into flames: you just give them a slogan, and everybody will rise as one man — from magnate to the most piteous beggar!"

"The lords as one with the rabble?" Shevchenko said with a laugh. "That would be a curious sight!"

"For the first battle the lords' sword will come in very handy, and eventually we will sort things out. As a matter of fact, there is bitter unrest everywhere: the Russian muzhiks are rebelling too. Hungary also seems to have come to a stir. The trouble is that the people are scattered over large territories in small groups, without an independent postal system or such a wonderful new means of communication as the telegraph. So it is difficult for the peasants to unite. For the workers it is much easier: they work all together and have better opportunities to organize..."

"What else did you hear?" Shevchenko hurried him impatiently.

"Isn't this enough for you, my colleague? Well, if you like, there is also bad news. Such as the epidemic of cholera in Russia. There are even rumors that a plague has broken out. If that is so, quarantine will be set up everywhere. Don't expect any letters from home then. So far it is a rumor and, more likely, a lie."

Though really out of the ordinary, the news was all too brief and fragmentary. The sun had sunk considerably in the east by then, and because of the scanty light it was impossible to paint any more. Shevchenko gathered his painting tools, and both men, hungry and excited, walked back to the camp.

That night Shevchenko could not sleep. He tried to draw in his imagination the atmosphere of an imminent uprising: passionate speeches and arguments, clandestine circles, ardent proclamations, and the maneuvering of the lordlings in their attempts to exploit these sentiments for their own ends.

Once, while looking through Shevchenko's album which had quite a few sketches in it, Maksheiev remarked:

"It's a pity you gave Schreiber your first watercolor of the fire in the steppe. You did it quite well."

"I gave it away because it did not come out as I wanted it to be," Shevchenko said with a laugh. "I had not held a pencil in my hands for a year and a half and could not master the coloring of the scene right away. But I remembered well all the shades of the fire, the smoke and the glow, and the beautiful way in which they reflected in the water. One of these days I will renew all that in my memory, and you will see: it will be much better, livelier than the first attempt at painting from nature."

The caravan had covered almost a half of the trek, but the steppe was as monotonous as before. Then the terrain became rocky, with splinters of quartz, over which it was impossible to walk barefoot. The drivers wound pieces of sheepskin and rags round their feet or else climbed onto the wagons which the exhausted horses pulled laboriously along with the excessive loads.

The caravan forded the half-dry Irghiz River and moved along its left bank, leaving behind to the right a hill with the graves of *batyrs*. A halt was about to be called at the grave of *Batyr* Dustan when the scouts suddenly came galloping back and reported something to the general in great excitement.

The report must have been very alarming, because General Schreiber immediately called an officers' council, and then everyone was stunned by the news that there had been a skirmish about three *versts* away the day before: the little caravan which had left Orenburg two days earlier was attacked by a troop of Khivans, and although the escort beat off the attack, quite a few wagons were plundered. A score of drivers were taken prisoners, many of the men were killed or wounded, and the beheaded corpses were still lying in the steppe unburied.

An augmented reconnaissance force was sent out in all directions. The wounded were given first aid, and the corpses were brought together. Off to one side the men were already digging a communal grave. Shevchenko looked with horror at the beheaded corpses of soldiers whose fate he could have shared just as easily.

"But where are their heads? Why were they taken away?" he asked.

"The heads are with the attackers, who will bring them to the chieftains. Each head is rewarded with money or something valuable, and the chieftain will order the heads to be stacked in a pyramid by his tent or take them to his camp as a military trophy," Maksheiev explained. After a minute he added: "Do you understand now why we cannot do without an armed escort? Here you can be attacked by men from Khiva, Kokand, and the insurgent Kirghiz from Kenessary's band."

The rest of the daytime halt was filled with sadness.

Whoever needs this blood and sacrifice? Shevchenko reflected as he sketched the **grave of Dustan** *Batyr*.

The troops slept through the night without undressing, their arms at the ready. The guards were relieved every hour, but the night passed without an unpleasant event, and the next day the caravan reached Uralsk toward the evening. **Uralsk**, a wretched settlement of adobe houses and mud-and-straw huts surrounded by a low wall, looked more like a cattle pen and produced an oppressive impression on Shevchenko and the sailors.

Beyond Uralsk, the caravan twice pitched camp on the banks of a steppe lake; by the third night they reached the fetid river Djalolli, behind which started the Karakum Desert. Old soldiers told such horrors about the desert it made the men's skin creep and they prepared themselves for the worst.

Two hours before sunup the wagons were additionally greased, the tents taken down, and the loaded camels set forth so as to cover the first stretch of the way in the morning cool. Fortunately, a northern wind rose and it became so cold that the men had to put on their greatcoats.

The sharp north wind persisted for three days. The men started to make fun of the oldtimers when the wind suddenly stopped blowing, and within an hour, instead of the cold, there came such a heat that Butakov's thermometer registered forty degrees Reaumur*. An egg buried in the sand would be fried within five minutes. The men were drenched with sweat and overcome by a savage thirst. The scouts could not locate the usual wells which must have been buried by the last sandstorm. Another ten *versts* had to be covered to the nearest wells and this stretch proved to be much more difficult than the previous three-day trek. The water in the wells they reached was bitterly salty.

The thirst-plagued men drank it with abhorence. Shevchenko took it like medicine, flavoring it with some lemons Maksheyov had given him.

The caravan moved on again before dawn the next day. The trek ran across the bottom of a dried-up lake covered with a layer of snow-white salt. In the morning sunlight it seemed to be of a pleasantly rosy hue, but when the sun climbed higher it turned so dazzling white it hurt the eyes.

"Don't look at it," Butakov warned Shevchenko. "You will be blinded and miss a lot of interesting things on the way."

Shevchenko looked distrustfully at Butakov.

"Be so kind, my friend, as to take your orders," Butakov reprimanded him in a friendly way. "I've been sailing in the southern seas for a long time. People there suffer from snow blindness, and this salt sparkles just like real snow."

Indeed, everything started to get mixed up and tremble before Shevchenko's eyes shortly after. So he walked on, his eyes fixed on the haunches of Maksheiev's horse.

At long last the salt-strewn plain was left behind, and the caravan again moved across gray-yellow dunes which were getting lower with every *verst*. Clusters of saxaul appeared here and there; they had already shed their blossoms, and on the sharp tips of the young shoots there were tiny seed capsules. One day later a narrow strip of blue showed far off to the south.

"Hello, you welcome Blue Sea. We've reached you, after all!"

---

* 50° Centigrade.– *Tr.*

Butakov said, strongly excited, and taking off his cap, he crossed himself.

The men were instantly buoyed up with animation. Even the horses quickened their pace without having to be whipped on. At noon the next day the caravan approached one of the northern bays of the Aral Sea. The soldiers, drivers, cameleers and Cossacks — all as one rushed to the warm curling waves which rolled onto the sandy beach with a rustle. The soldiers unbuckled their belts, threw off their uniforms and shirts on the run, and jumped into the waves with boyish laughter, but once they were out of the water, they spat with disgust, complaining: "Oh God, there's water up to the horizon, but nothing to drink!"

There remained another two days' march to Raïm, but the men, after having a good rest, covered the distance much faster. The arduous fifty-day trek had come to an end. Walking almost all of the distance on foot, Shevchenko had become haggard and suntanned; though physically exhausted, he remained in high spirits.

For the first three days he, like all the other men, slept or lounged on the soft sandy bank of the Syr Darya, chatting with the soldiers from the Orsk garrison.

Then General Schreiber ordered the troop of infantry and Cossacks to get ready for the march back home, leaving in Raïm two platoons from the Fifth Battalion under Lieutenant Bogomolov and fifty Cossacks to winter on Kosaral Island together with the sailors.

Shevchenko parted sadly with Kuzmich and many other soldiers. One of them, embracing the poet, wiped a tear from his cheek with his fist. Even the heart of the thievish Kozlovsky gave a start when he shook the poet's hand for the last time:

"*Au revoir*," he said with unexpected sadness. "I regret very much parting with you, *mon cher ami*. At times I had a feeling I was turning into a decent man again in your company. But now..."

He waved his hand in a gesture of hopelessness and quickly went away.

3. THE SCHOONER CONSTANTINE

Fort Raïm stood on the crest of a hill dominating a green valley. Luxurious meadows down below passed gradually into stands of reed through which the sunlit ripples of the full-fed Syr Darya glittered now and then. In the middle of a square inside the fort stood a tall monument of stone at the grave of **Raïm** *Batyr* who died a hundred years earlier and after whom the fort was named.

At the end of a three-day rest, the Orenburg carpenters and Baltic sailors started assembling the schooner with a will on a level bank of the Syr Darya where no shrubs or reeds grew.

Shevchenko sat on the sand under a shed where sail cloth and rings of rope were stacked, and delighted in drawing the light fleecy cloudlets on the horizon.

But his thoughts were far away from the place where he was now.

He recalled his last week at Orsk, shortly before the arrival of Butakov's caravan. As he usually did every holiday, he had walked beyond the ramparts — remnants of fortifications from the times of Czarine Catherine — where the building of the town of Orenburg was started on the site of Orsk, sat down on the steep bank of the Ural and drifted into gloomy reverie. He had not noticed then how an old man had come up to him. The man served his long sentence in exile and was now living out his days near his prison. He could not work anymore and the wardens, whom he helped by distributing the food to the prisoners or tending the stoves when blizzards raged outdoors, fed him with the offal from the prison kitchen, and even the supervisor of the prison turned a blind eye to his existence, since the almost hundred-year-old man had nowhere else to go.

It was not the first time Shevchenko talked with him, listening to his sad life story and telling him about his own. They had a lot of things in common.

The old man had once been a serf, an orphan and beggar among beggars. The lord he belonged to had two boys growing up. The orphan was taken into the lord's household as a playmate for the boys. Like wolflings they often hit him painfully and beat him while playing. The lordlings grew up, tutors were invited to teach them, and the orphan whiled away his time during the lessons. He, too, memorized the letters, forming them into words and reading and writing no worse than the lordlings by and by. After two years of private tutoring, the lordlings were taken to school in town, while the boy was made to work in the fields. He walked behind the plowmen, harrowing and tilling fields, but did not forget what he had learned. When he grew up and became a young man, he fell in love and became engaged to his sweetheart. The day of the wedding had been set, preparations for it were already underway, when suddenly the lordlings came home, took away his bride to be, disgraced her and she bore a child out of wedlock. The young man was outraged by the monstrous insult and started seeking likeminded men to avenge the wrong done to him. The lordlings finished school, returned to the manor, and found themselves brides. On the day of their wedding when the newlyweds were returning from the local Roman Catholic church, the avengers attacked them and killed the entire train to the last man, after which they took refuge in a forest and brought ruin and destruction on the lords for many years. But in time their chieftain got weary of the bloodshed in his futile struggle against serfdom. He got, weary because man is not created to kill only. So he gave himself up.

Shevchenko recalled with particular vividness the sorrowful and harrowing story of the old man. He put away his brushes, took the notebook out of his bootleg, and started writing. In a day **he wrote an entire poem**, in which he gave vent to the feelings bursting from his agitated soul; in the morning next day he came to the same place to finish painting the landscape.

Shevchenko had a strange sensation during those days, as if someone had opened a locked door in his heart and let in a whiff of free air which was just as fresh and vital as the subtle sea breeze gently tousling his hair and softly caressing his suntanned cheeks.

While painting, he recalled the fire in the steppe, the vast expanse of scorched ground it left behind, and the Karakum Desert — strange and fantastic images resurfaced in his mind. Life must have once teemed in this boundless steppe, with blooming orchards and noisy towns and hamlets. But then a thoughtless man stole an ax from God and started hacking down the orchards and destroying the shadowy groves. The forest giants toppled to the ground, sending splinters and twigs flying. A rainstorm broke out, and lightning started a fire. Man, bird and beast perished in the flames, and the once blooming land turned into a black barren desert with only one tree miraculously surviving in it; to this day the tree grows and flowers to the wonder and joy of the rare passersby.

His brush was softly putting dab on dab. The painting seemed to have come alive with the vivid colors, while in his head there rang the first line of the poem **"Behind God's Door There Lay an Ax…"**

Two weeks had passed. Shevchenko's album had in it five landscapes with the Raïm Fort, a landscape with the improvised dockyard on the Syr Darya, and a scene of the "assembly of the schooner."

The *Constantine* was ready to be launched. The slipway of planks was extended into the river and sunk to the depth of some two meters. The wedges were knocked out from under the hull, about a dozen men gave her a mighty push from the stern, the schooner started slipping slowly down the oily planks, and several minutes later she was rocking on the waves.

On the twenty-fifth of July the commanding personnel of the expedition and two privates, **Werner** and Shevchenko, went on board and took up quarters in the only well furnished cabin, which they formally called wardroom. The rest of the crew occupied the bunk room.

After a litany of gratitude, the broad pennant of the expedition chief, Lieutenant Butakov, fluttered atop the main mast. On the stern a St. Andrew's flag was run up. Then the smoke of a salute fired from seven guns enveloped the sides of the *Constantine*. In response, seven guns boomed from Fort Raïm, and the *Constantine* started slowly sailing down the Syr Darya.

The schooner was going adrift all the time, as the wind pushed her to low waters and the left bank. For a long time she could not head out for the open sea. An anchor had to be thrown out for the night. This went on for several days. During one such evening of forced anchorage, the navigator Pospelov and the medical attendant Istomin asked Butakov to tell them what was known about the Blue Sea at that time.

"I looked through old geographical treatises and other sources for a long time, but I found very little. Almost nothing," Butakov eagerly started the story. "The authors of antiquity did not even suspect its existence. On the map of Ptolemy, from the second century A. D., which was published only in 1590, both the Syr Darya and Amu Darya flow into the Caspian Sea. We see the same thing on all the European maps to the end of the seventeenth century. The Russians learned of the sea when our merchants started to penetrate into the Caspian and trade with Persia. In 1552, Ivan the Terrible ordered his officials 'to measure the land anew and make a draught' of the Russian state. This 'draught' was supplemented during the reign of Czar Bori's Godunov, and in 1632 there was added to it *The Book Called the Big Draught*, in which there was the Blue Sea.

"Then Peter I sent to the eastern shores of the Caspian Sea an expedition under Bikovich-Cherkassky who was the first to reveal that the Syr Darya and Amu Darya emptied not into the Caspian but into the Aral Sea. The first topographical data on the northern shores of the Aral Sea were furnished in 1733 when Russia embraced the Kirghiz in its empire. Then the surveyor Muravin drafted the map of the route from Orenburg to Khiva through the steppe and along the eastern shore of the Aral Sea, and, at last, separate sections of its northern coast were surveyed during the past few years with the participation of our esteemed **Artemiy Anikievich**" — Butakov made a bow to Ensign **Akishev** — "and that is why I was so interested in him joining us. But all the previous explorations were conducted in an uncoordinated way, while the sea itself, the center of its water surface, has remained unexplored to this day."

"What does the word *aral* mean?" Istomin asked.

"In Kirghiz *aral* means island, but they call the sea Aral Teniz, and what the word *teniz* means I do not know."

On the fourth day the wind changed course, and the *Constantine* sailed into the mouth of the river.

The sails billowed. There was a heavy swell as the *Constantine* bore through the deep blue of the Aral Sea. Behind the stern the propeller of the log dragged by a thin chain rotated quickly, measuring the schooner's speed. Everything here was unknown and unexplored, so Butakov gave the order to go at half speed.

On the bow stood a sailor who took the soundings and kept calling over his shoulder:

"Twenty-eight! Forty-two! Thirty! Twenty-five! Thirty-nine!"

Akishev wrote down the soundings. The helmsman froze with every call, while Butakov did not take the binoculars away from his eyes and frequently looked at his watch. The fishermen had told him that sailing before the wind he could reach the nearest island Kugaral in two hours, but the wind kept changing direction. Butakov had to tack. The craft went into a roll. The sailors did not notice it, since they had been used to the roll "since the cradle," as they put it. But Maksheiev turned pallid, then his face became a ghastly green and he retired to his cabin, feeling the onset of sea sickness.

From the moment he appeared on board the *Constantine*, Shevchenko had a feeling he was absolutely out of place and of no use here.

At first he could not understand the underlying source of this feeling. Everyone treated him in a friendly way. He was respected and appreciated as an artist, poet and a person, but everybody was in the mad grip of one desire, one scientific purpose, carried away as they were by a common cause and dream. Even during off-duty hours their conversation revolved around astronomical, geological, geodetic and topographical topics as well as soundings and hydrography. Only these subjects excited them and provoked heated arguments. Shevchenko, however, had to keep silent, because he did not understand such things.

His heart was filled with a desire to share the thoughts and work of these heroes and martyrs of knowledge.

In his mind, Shevchenko compared his fellow travelers with his former acquaintances of the recent past — the merrily garrulous and carefree hussars and uhlans who were lusty carousers, the big landowners and masters of crofts from the so-called "lovers of native antiquity" who in word did nothing but think about the common people, hinting over a drink about the need for reforms and abolition of serfdom, while in deed...

These comparisons gave birth to caustically worded, wrathful verse about those "friends of the people" who dressed in peasant coats and embroidered shirts, while in reality they were wolves in sheep's clothing.

All these thoughts deprived him of sleep and mental equilibrium.

Butakov and the other officers noticed that the poet was behaving strangely — either because he missed his homeland or was ill.

Shevchenko moved around taciturn, his bushy brows bristled into a frown, or else fled to the crew deck to the sailors. With them he regained his animation, joked, sang, listened to their stories about distant seas and lands, and reluctantly returned to the wardroom when it was time for meals and sleep.

It was only with **Tomasz Werner** that he felt at ease, probably because he was also an exile and a private, whose acquaintance he had made at the Gems'.

One day the *Constantine* rode at anchor off a little island. Butakov, Maksheiev and Akishev went ashore to make a survey, the navigator Pospelov and Istomin took their hunting rifles and left to add some game to the crew's usual fare, and Shevchenko and Werner remained alone. Werner was sorting out samples of rocks and fossils he had collected on Kuraral and other islands for a geological collection, while Shevchenko was biting at a pencil as he thought over a verse. Suddenly he crossed out what he had written, tore the page into little bits and pieces, and threw the shreds into the sea through an open porthole.

"Nothing coming out?" Werner asked with sympathy, raising his eyes from a fossilized shell-fish.

"The hell with it!" Shevchenko cursed.

"I, too, cannot identify this dratted shell," Werner sighed with disappointment, and looking round at the door, added: "I have been keeping at it so long I suppose I have to air my brains somehow. For a long time it's been on my mind to ask you Taras, to tell me a bit about painting. I'm already in my thirties but I don't know anything about it — it's simply a shame to confess it. At times Maksheiev and you get into a conversation, mentioning all sorts of artists, while I sit there and only blink my eyes like a savage, without understanding anything you are talking about."

"How come, if you studied at a Gymnasium?! You are a nobleman, aren't you?"

"If you only knew how I grew up and studied!" Werner winced at the very recollection. "My Polish comrades don't know anything about my past. Though they consider themselves revolutionaries, most of them are really... Oh well, to hell with them! My father was so poor he had to serve as a coachman with a count, and he could barely sign his name. I was the eldest of eight children. At the age of ten I was taken to work at the lord's stables. My father dreamed of making me an educated man, but he had no means for that. Unexpectedly, luck singled me out. One day my father was digging holes for pillars in the park where a new arbor had to be built. As he dug away, his spade hit against something hard. He dug some more and threw a pot out of the hole. The pot had money in it: copper, silver, and several coins of gold. My father thought a lot whether to surrender the money to the count or leave it for himself. Mother burst into tears: 'It was the Lord God who sent it to us so that Thomas would amount to something. Don't give it away!' After some thinking, my father offered up a prayer to God and kept the money for himself. My parents bought me a pair of boots — the first in my life, dressed me in new clothes, got textbooks for me, and sent me to school. But nothing much came out of it. The money lasted only two years, and I had to go back to work in the stables again, although I did not stop studying. Up at the crack of dawn, I had to take out the dung of twenty horses, bed the stalls with fresh straw, curry the horses, plait their manes and tails, give them oats and hay, and water them. I was in a real hurry not to be late for school. But after school I had so much work on my hands I did not know what to do first: run to the stables or get down to do my homework. At first I passed the examinations for three grades, then for five. I barely got through modern school and enrolled in a technical college. And here I was in trouble again: while studying, I had to help my younger brothers and sisters. Father had passed away by then.

"Friends taught me to love my country. I have not done much for her — almost next to nothing, but even that was enough to have me convicted. I am only afraid of one thing: I'll never ever become an engineer," Werner gritted his teeth and turned away to hide the tears of despair growing in his eyes. "I have read too little, and have been to a theater only once in Warsaw," he added and started nervously shifting the rocks he had laid out on the table, without noticing that he had again mixed up what he had already sorted out.

Shevchenko came up to him and put a hand round his shoulder.

"Forgive me, brother, for any bad word you might have heard from me. Of course, I will tell you about art and about everything else I know. Oh, how I understand you! When all of you sit there at the table and talk about magnetic deviations, a certain Mesozoic Era, and isobars, I listen to all that like an outright fool. Teach me your geology a little bit at least. Maybe I might be helpful to you with something and won't feel myself out of place here."

"I will teach you, of course!" Werner said. "We can start right away! All right?"

After the talk with Werner, Shevchenko cheered up. Thomas gave him a book on geology to read, and Shevchenko almost learned it by heart. In Orsk his brain had been famished for lack of spiritual nourishment and he greedily absorbed every drop of knowledge like the parched soil receives an unexpected rain. But however much he delved into the subject, some of the questions remained unclear to him and he frequently asked Werner things for which the latter could not always provide the answers.

Whenever Werner went ashore, Shevchenko always accompanied him, and if there was no interesting landscape to paint, eo took a most lively part in collecting rocks for the mineralogical collection.

Thus in good cheer he returned to the schooner, and in the evening he and Werner inspected the finds at length.

"We have three chests with books on board," Butakov told the poet one day. "There is not much poetry, though: apart from Lermontov and Pushkin, there is nothing else. But if you're interested in, say, sea, voyages, botany or geography, the books are at your disposal."

Shevchenko greedily jumped at the chance to read whatever he could get hold of. In the ship's chests he found the works of Humboldt and the famous French travelers Arago and Dumont d'Urville, the reminiscences of Krusenstern and others. They presented in an engaging way the nature of distant continents and islands, the life of their people, customs and cultures. Had the people there cast off their shackles or did they still share the bitter fate of the Russian, Ukrainian and Polish peasants? Shevchenko asked himself every time he opened a new book. The horrible lot of the Africans who were sold into slavery in the United States of America shocked him the most. He could not forgive the geographer and traveler Humboldt who was so passionately vocal in sympathizing with the Africans and other slaves beyond the Atlantic, while at the same time speaking out his mind indecisively and half-heartedly when it came to serfdom in his native Germany, in Austria, and in the Russian Empire, too, which he had had a good opportunity to study during his travels throughout the Urals, Altai, along the Caspian coast, and in many other regions.

Under the influence of Humboldt's works, Shevchenko became interested in botany, and now helped Werner in collecting plants for the expedition's herbarium. But, however fascinating his new occupation was, the horror of the barracks could not escape his memory. At such moments he was oblivious of both an interesting plant and an unknown piece of rock.

Once he and medical attendant Istomin asked Butakov to give them a lecture on astronomy.

Butakov gave the lecture on the evening of a dead calm. At first he told them in detail about the solar system. Shevchenko listened spellbound. It was the first time he was being given a glimpse into the universe, and when Butakov, his voice grown hoarse after speaking for an hour and a half, fell silent, the oppressed Shevchenko went on deck, smoked silently for a long time, looked at the stars, and suddenly burst into a roar of laughter: "And the bible says that 'the creation of the world' occurred six thousand years ago and lasted for six days!"

4. LIEUTENANT BUTAKOV

The *Constantine* had been confidently plying the blue waters of the Aral Sea for many days now. The sea was choppy, and the schooner was mercilessly tossed from wave to wave even in a light wind. To make her a little more stable, Butakov gave the order to have her ballasted with rocks which made her sink by four feet at the stern and three and a half feet at the bow.

Whenever she came to anchor off some island or in a bay, Butakov went ashore for astronomical observations, and Maksheiev for topographical surveys. After each such trip the pieces of white Whatman paper in the navigator's cabin were covered with new grids, in between which were the wavy outlines of land and the dark or brighter blue of the sea. But Butakov did more than draw outlines of coasts and islands on the map; he carefully studied their geological structure, climbed up and down the gullies and gulches to see the sequence of rock layers, dug prospecting shafts — or holes, as he called them simply — and returned with sacks of mussels, pieces of rock, fossilized and live plants. And every time he said with chagrin, as he threw his cap on the desk:

"There's no trace of stone coal!"

"Why are you so set on finding stone coal?" Shevchenko asked him once.

"What else should I be looking for then?" he said, throwing up his arms from emotion. "For thousands of *versts* around this sea there is nothing that might be called a real forest — only shrubs. Where will you get the fuel for steamships when the sea is to be explored?"

"Oh, nobody has heard about steamships in this place yet," Maksheiev said, smiling. "People are scarce here. To the Kirghiz our *Constatine* and *Nicholas* must seem like some weird birds."

"We are lagging behind all of Europe and even Turkey which, thanks to the Britons, has steamships already. The era of sailboats is receding into the past."

"But still, why do you keep on hoping so persistently to find coal here?" Istomiv wondered.

"Because our esteemed Artemiy Anikievich" — Butakov nodded in Akishev's direction — "found pieces of it on the western coast this spring. Today I landed three miles from the Izendiaral Cape and ordered the sailors to dig holes one and a half *sazhen* deep right on the shore. At the depth of one *sazhen* the clay was so hard it had to be hacked with axes, and then the holes started to fill with water. The men suffered, working in ice-cold water up to their knees. The water had to be scooped out with pails all the time. They suffered, and so did I together with them. And the main thing — all our work was in vain: there is no coal."

Akishev was sitting there confused and embarrassed.

"I could have made a mistake. We did not try to find out whether it burns... and anyway ...I am neither a geologist nor an engineer... The men said it was coal, and I took them at their word," he justified himself lamely.

"Well, so we'll be looking again and again," Butakov said.

The next morning Butakov sailed the *Constantine* to Barsakelmes Island in the central part of the sea. Maksheiev, Akishev, one noncom and six sailors went ashore to make a full topographical survey. Butakov also ordered the party to clean the wells to replenish the ship's water supply; he himself returned to Cape Izendiaral and sent ashore Werner with a party of armed sailors to look for the elusive coal. Only Shevchenko remained in the ship's boat to draw the imposing grandeur of the cape.

The elevation of the Kulandy Peninsula was high; its shores did not rise over the surf in a single rocky wall but descended to the sea in several terraces half a *verst* wide each. Butakov went into the depth of the peninsula to make astronomical observations, Werner and his party climbed the first terrace and turned to the south.

After walking for about five *versts*, they stopped on a plain which seemed to be colored with soot. Sparse blades of grass and little grass tufts stuck out of the ground here and there. Werner stopped, picked up a handful of the black soil, ground it in his palms, and ordered the men to dig.

Everybody was silent. The sailors dug deep and narrow prospecting holes in two places simultaneously. Werner chewed on a dry grass blade with excitement, silently going up to one hole, then to the other, while noncom Abizarov alternately watched the surroundings both with naked eye and through a telescope, since anything unexpected could happen in this strange and unknown country.

The holes were quickly increasing in depth. The sailors were throwing clods of blue-white clay over the top when suddenly the shovel of one of them slipped across the bottom of the hole with a clatter and, scraping up the blue clay, left a deeply black trace behind.

"Coal!" his neighbor cried out, shoving the clay aside.

Werner rushed over to the hole, the sailors quickly cleaned the layer of coal of the last clay clods, and then started hacking pieces of coal with a pick and handing it up to Werner.

The coal layer was half an *arshin* thick, but the coal was of good quality. It did not give off a bright silvery glimmer at the fracture points like anthracite, but neither did it crumble: it was hard like stone and of a richly black color.

"There's coal here, too!" a sailor called from the second hole.

Werner compared the pieces of coal from both holes. There was no doubt: this was real coal. The sailors gathered brush twigs and tumbleweed, built a fire, stacked the pieces of coal in a loose pyramid, and joyously showed Werner how the coal was turning red, glowed ruddily, then resembled heated red metal radiating real burning heat."

"Dig! Dig deeper!" Werner ordered.

The sailors took to digging again. The first layer was followed by gray saline clay, then came greasy clay reeking of petroleum, and at last there was a layer of coal over a foot thick. This coal also burned well as did the petroleum-saturated clay, but the sailors dug on and on. They dug to a third layer from two to three fingers thick, and stopped.

In the meantime, Butakov had established the position of the island and returned, looking for Werner. On seeing the lieutenant, Werner started waving his cap from afar. Butakov quickened his pace, descended from the upper terrace, and hurried to the prospecting holes.

"Coal! It's wonderful coal!" Werner said. "Our work has not been in vain after all."

Butakov examined the pieces of coal attentively, ordered another few holes to be dug in different parts of the plateau farther inland and, when layers of coal were found there too, he gave a bright and happy smile. The dying fire was rekindled, and when the coal in it had burned out, everybody saw that it left only a small amount of ashes. This, too, was a feature of the coal's good quality Butakov's face beamed. So in the future, shipping on the Aral Sea and the first forts and settlements on its shores would be provided with fuel.

The sun was setting in the west. Butakov was in a hurry to get back to the schooner.

"Your Excellency," a sailor stopped him. "Request permission to hack some coal for the galley. We're running out of firewood, and everyone loves a cup of hot tea."

"Go ahead!" Butakov agreed cheerfully.

In half an hour all the pails and sacks they had brought along were filled with coal. Groaning under the burden, the sailors made for the boats. Werner and Butakov followed behind, discussing the future of the deposit they had discovered. No one cared that their hands and faces were grimed with coal which made them look like real miners just out of a pit.

The *Constantine* lay in a bay shielded from the eastern wind by Cape Izendiaral. The cape was high and white all over, and in some places, fallow pale from the limestone and clay strata of the Mesozoic. Washed out at its foot by the surf, the cape hung dangerously over the seething waves in a broad vault which seemed about to hurtle into the sea any moment. In quiet weather a boat could skim under that vault.

The barometer had dropped in the meantime. The wind changed direction, and a storm broke out toward the evening. Now the bay, instead of being a refuge from the wind and waves, became a trap for the schooner. Sailing out of it along the chain of submerged cliffs enclosing three quarters of the bay was out of the question. The churning water and savage wind rebounding from the cliffs chased the waves into the sea. They hurtled against the cliffs, reared in boiling geysers, and rumbled like a hundred cannons. The *Constantine* shuddered from bow to stern, and with every blow of a wave everything droned in the cabins and the hold.

Butakov ordered a second anchor to be dropped and to pay out 70 *sazhens* of one anchor rope and 45 of the other. The schooner jerked helplessly and every minute she could break adrift and smash against the cliffs.

Butakov realized that the *Constantine* was on the verge of destruction. Gritting his teeth, he stood on the bridge, snapping terse orders. The hungry, soaked and frozen sailors wordlessly complied with the orders with automatic precision. They were aware of the danger, but trusting in their captain, his experience and knowledge, they worked fast and effectually.

The night dragged on unbearably long. The schooner was alternately tossed upward, then she topsided, or dipped into the frothy abyss, throwing her stern high up. The waves rolled over the deck, and the sailors clung to the lifelines lest they be washed overboard. The yards stripped of running rigging swayed frenziedly over the men's heads as if they were intent on wiping out the background of cliffs and the ragged clouds racing across the sky from the northwest.

Despair settled in Butakov's heart.

"They'll die of hunger," he repeated again and again, thinking about the topographers he had left on Barsakelmes; he was completely oblivious of the immediate danger staring into his own eyes at that moment. There was nothing more he could do to save the schooner, but he had to hide his presentiment from the crew. So passing command on to navigator Pospelov, Butakov retired to his cabin, sat down at his desk, and clutched his head.

They'll die of hunger on the island, the thought haunted him. The island had an ill-omened name: the Kirghiz explained the meaning of Barsakelmes as "once you go there, you won't return."

When the sun rose, the storm started to wear out a little, but the sea still raged in wild abandon the whole day through; only toward the evening did the waves become flat and wide, without the flaring, frothy manes on their sharp crests, and the ship rolled much more smoothly than before.

Butakov had a glassful of vodka issued to each member of the crew, except for the watch, and ordered everyone to have a rest. Tacking slowly, the *Constantine* sailed out of the treacherous bay.

The topographers met the schooner with exultant joy. They, too, had lived through a sleepless and alarming night after the storm had toppled their tent. Drenched and exhausted, they spent the rest of the day collecting the equipment and gear the wind had scattered, which prevented them from completing the survey. Butakov left Akishev and three sailors behind on the island, and Maksheiev and the others were taken on board. The *Constantine* replenished her supply of fresh water and, joined by the fishing schooner *Mikhail* exploring the fish shoals, returned to the Kulandy Peninsula to plot its position to the end, after which Butakov sailed to the south along the western coast of Kosaral.

Now the weather was really calm and sunny. The sea rippled like blue satin and silvery trails scattered across its expanse as far as the eye could see. Since the calm endured, the wardroom again became a gathering point for conversations and arguments.

Shevchenko gave a talk to the sailors and topographers about the painting, architecture and sculpture of the Italian Renaissance, as well as on his favorite sculptor and carver Verrocchio, on the master of the three arts Leonardo da Vinci, and on the tender representation and beauty of Murillo and Rafael's madonnas. Since there was not a single book plate of their paintings or engravings on board, Shevchenko either drew a rough sketch, such as of Leonardo's *Last Supper*, or described the works of art as vividly as possible so that his listeners would get a much deeper idea than a bad reproduction could have communicated to them.

For his part, he asked Butakov to read a lecture on seafaring. Butakov eagerly devoted an entire evening to the subject.

Shevchenko's friendship with Butakov grew stronger with the days. After the poet became keen on botany, he helped Butakov collect plants for the herbarium and learned to use a field guide in determining the family, genus and species of every flower, grass and shrub twig he dried. They also prepared fish, crabs, snakes and lizards, made collections of butterflies, beetles, scolopendra, even poisonous tarantulas and black widows, but Butakov categorically forbade the taking of live samples on board the ship. Geography, however, remained Shevchenko's favorite science. He had learned Humboldt's books almost by heart. By and by he identified himself with the members of the expedition, shared their interests, rejoiced at their successes, and often caught himself thinking that he had started to delight in the beauty of the Aral Sea and to like it, although initially he had called it a good-for-nothing pond. Now he was equally curious about its greatest depth, its fish resources, and the remarkable blueness of its crystal clear waves, and when a depth of 68 *sazhens* was sounded half a mile off Cape Bai Gubek, he was next to being happy.

As the *Constantine* sailed farther south, the crew noticed that the water was becoming sweeter and more turbid, and occasional shoals and tufts of reed appeared along the schooner's course. Butakov realized that the *Constantine* was approaching the delta of the Amu Darya. He had a boat lowered to sound the depth which proved to be no more than one *sazhen* in some places. When the boat returned, Butakov headed east and dropped anchor off **Tokmak Ata Island**.

And here he had to do some serious thinking.

In the instructions he had received from the war ministry, there was a separate clause added on the insistence of Karl Nesselrode, Minister for Foreign Affairs: the expedition was specifically forbidden to approach the southern Khiva shore, let alone enter Khiva's territorial waters. Violating that clause would mean inducing international complications, exchange of diplomatic notes and the like. But being so close and not conducting the exploration to the end... The energetic lieutenant was not used to going off on another tack once he had set his mind on something.

From the top of the main mast he scanned the island covered with sandy knolls and dense shrubbery. It was a wonderful place for building a fort or trading station. On the island he also saw yurts, camels, cattle, and clusters of people who were curiously gawking at the ship they were seeing for the first time in their lives. But there were no boats in sight.

The wind died down, and by evening a dead calm set in. The sea spread in a rippleless mirror of blue, reflecting the coastal stands of reed and the cumulus clouds resembling a huge snow-clad mountain range rising over the horizon; from the north a deep swell was building up as if the sea were drawing its breath from the depths as it softly and evenly swayed the undulating surface of its shimmering expanse. The schooner drifted toward the northern shore, her sails drooping helplessly from the yards. Even the broad pennant, always fluttering in the faintest whiff of air, hung limply down the main mast like a dead bird.

"Wonderful," Butakov said, rubbing his hands with glee. "In such a dead calm, I have a legal enough reason to be here: without a steam engine I cannot make the schooner budge an inch."

The *Constantine* stayed in the bay with drooping sails the whole day through, and in the night Butakov sent Ensign Akishev with navigator Pospelov in a boat to sound the depth to the north off Tokmak Ala Island. He gave them a dark lantern, enough fire arms and cold steel, and ordered the sailors to bind rags round the oarlocks.

When it became completely dark, the boat pulled off the Jacob's ladder. Butakov stayed behind on the schooner, which he ordered to remain on the alert. The guns were charged with grapeshot, and carbines, hunting rifles, officer's pistols, cutlasses, pikes and dirks were brought on deck to be ready at hand. The crew slipped into their hammocks without undressing, while the schooner, her lights doused, melted into the heavy mist of the moonless, cloud-hung night.

Maksheiev and Butakov sat on deck, listening alertly to every sound, while the rest of the crew, except for the watch, were below deck lest they break the silence by any chance.

Time trickled away slowly. Half an hour before dawn, the boat slipped lightly and quietly like a bat alongside the schooner and pulled up to the ladder.

Pospelov reported that after rounding the island from the south, he came across water that was no more than two to three feet deep at half a *verst* off the mainland.

Butakov realized that Tokmak Ata was thus linked to the mainland by a sand bar, to the west of which there was no estuary. No wonder the sea water there was much clearer and saltier than to the east to the island.

The dead calm persisted. On the third day a faint breeze wafted from the northwest, making first the broad pennant flutter, then the canvas, and the schooner started to beat with effort. However, the breeze soon died, as on the days before, a long swell came from the north, making the craft drift to the Khiva shore again.

Butakov scaled to the top of the main mast and saw through his telescope a huge river spilling into the sea in several branches to the east, while Akishev established the compass points between which spread the fan-shaped plain of the delta.

At midday Butakov plotted the schooner's position by the Greenwich meridian, then calculated the precise place of the Amu Darya delta. In the evening they ordered the boat to be ready again.

The depth of the river's mouth had to be sounded to establish whether it was navigable.

In view of the risks involved, Butakov decided to do everything himself. He took along Ensign Pospelov and picked for the mission the strongest oarsmen who could swim well. Butakov and Pospelov were also wonderful swimmers. The oarlocks were wrapped in rags again, the schooner was placed on the alert, and the two daredevils equipped with a compass and dark lantern climbed down the Jacob's ladder into the boat. The lights on the schooner were doused. The thin crescent of the moon had dipped into the sea a long time ago, the sky was overcast with dense clouds, and a black velvety night enveloped sky and land with a profound murk and silence.

Shevchenko sat on the deck among the sailors, who did not dare so much as light a cigarette. Everyone was silent and listened intently, but not even the sound of drops falling off the oars reached their ears. The watch stood stock still at their posts. Their tense figures were charged with alarm. The topman scanned the horizon, but he could not detect any movement or a glimmer of light anywhere. As before, the long swell slowly rocked the schooner.

A barely perceptible chill was penetrating the soft warmth of the night. The watch, their ears pricked up to every rustle, glanced alarmingly at the stars: Butakov should have been back a long time ago.

Suddenly a quiet, familiar voice sounded by the board:

"The *Constantine*, ahoy!"

Moments later Butakov, followed by Pospelov, came up the ladder.

"How did it go?" Maksheiev asked.

"Wonderful! But let me get to the cabin first: I'm as wet as a muskrat."

In the cabin Butakov quickly changed his clothes, leaving a big puddle on the floor. He rubbed himself with a towel and put on a dry uniform.

"It'd be good to have a cup of hot tea or a shot of vodka now. I'm drenched like a stray dog."

"Come on, pour out the story!" Maksheiev said impatiently. "Where did you get so wet?"

"On our way back we had completed the soundings. The boat was going along the reeds, our sounding rods got caught in them and were pulled into the water. The current there is very swift. Another moment and the rods would have disappeared in the impenetrable darkness. So I dived into the water in my clothes, because we could not leave the Khivans such material evidence: all the markings on the sounding rods are in Russian."

"Did you really manage to take all soundings?" Akishev exclaimed with enthusiasm.

"Of course! We went round Tokmak Ata and headed for the nearest arm of the Syr Darya. It's where we stripped and waded across the arm with those ill-fated sounding rods. The current there is slow, but now and then we came across springs with ice-cold water; the depth is a foot or two everywhere. Then, without getting out of the water, we waded round the island between the first and second channel and continued the soundings. They had to be recorded later on in the boat to the light of the dark lantern. We also waded round the second island. The third arm is much deeper and has such a strong current you cannot stop for a single moment, because it sweeps you off your feet; here and there the water is ice-cold and froze us to the marrow. Then we had to grope for our boat. But now the job is done. When the wind gets up, we can quietly sail out of here and not annoy the Khivans, and Nesselrode for that matter. Though low on food supplies, we are prohibited from trading with the natives: that would be a conscious violation of instructions," Butakov added, sitting down at the table on which a samovar was already boiling.

The dead calm endured for several days more.

All this time Shevchenko painted. When he was put ashore, he first of all sought picturesque landscapes and immediately took up his brushes. Each such outing lasted two or three hours. So he just sketched the outlines, marked the shades, and took to brushing on the paints to capture the distinctions of the landscape's color scheme and natural lighting, leaving all the details for later.

At that time his heart also gave birth to poetry. He finished writing his poem *The Kings*, in which he pictured the monarchs from the Old Testament with withering sarcasm. He could have added to this gallery the predators of later vintage, but other themes and other images fired his vision.

... The young village girl Marina glowed with loveliness. But one day a licentious landlord had her fiancé impressed into the army, took the girl into his chambers at the manor-house, and locked her in to crush her resistance to his advances all the faster. The girl could not stand the humiliation, went out of her mind, and set fire to the manor, where she herself perished in the flames. How many such stories had he heard during his childhood and, later on, in the barracks!

A host of characters, grief-ridden, horrible or moving, haunted his mind. And all of them from real life. They passed before his mind's eye in an endless line, shedding heartbroken tears, with deep and festering wounds in their hearts — all their dreams shattered, their hopes betrayed. And what about him? Had he ever experienced the simple happiness of shared love or the warmth of a family nest?

He did not know where his Oxana — his first pure love — had disappeared to. For a fleeting moment the tender and sensitive Polish girl surfaced in his memory. Then there was the beauty Hanna, a married woman he met when he, already a famous artist and poet, returned to his homeland. She had not responded to his letter which he wrote with blood dripping from his heart. Had she forgotten him? She must have never loved him, while her ardent words and kisses had been nothing but a game. And still her charming image haunted the poet as she seemed to look at him with eyes as blue as this sea, this strange and hostile but wonderful Aral Sea which had helped him escape the barracks and saved him from the abominable drill and horrible mental starvation.

Would she have recognized him if they were to meet again? he asked himself. During those days he dedicated his second poem to the treacherous but still dear Hanna.

The *Constantine* rode at anchor in Taldy Kultuk Bay for another week, and then sailed eastward. But a choppy sea kept pressing her to the southern shore all the time; only on the second of September a fresh breeze made it possible for her to move away from the Khiva shore.

The sailors welcomed the wind, because the schooner's supply of water and food was running low. When she sailed out of the mouth of the Syr Darya, the crew switched over to naval rations and it turned out that the rye rusks had become green with mould, the groats had molded as well, becoming musty and bitter to the taste, and the butter was so salty it could not be added to the porridge. Only the peas had remained fresh and tasty, but their supply was meager and so had to be cooked only twice a week. During anchorage the men angled for fish. But the sea was not always generous, because the fish sought deeper waters during storms and even during a fresh breeze.

For all that, Butakov did not hear a single word of complaint. The men understood that he was not to blame, the more so since he and the officers ate from the same mess as the crew and he never permitted a single piece of better food to be served for himself. The medical attendant Istomin watched strictly that the rusks and groats he roasted well, and there was not a single recorded incidence of illness on board.

But then the rations dwindled alarmingly and had to be cut to last to the end of the navigation, that is, to the first of October.

The schooner moved slowly along her course, and on the seventh of September she came upon an unknown low island overgrown with reeds, avens and saxaul. In recognition and gratitude for the effort the military governor of Orenburg had put into organizing the caravan, Butakov named the island in his honor.

Then a storm raged for a week. The waves tossed the schooner from crest to crest like a splinter of wood, and the crew went out of its way to keep her seaworthy. Butakov had to postpone the survey of the eastern, newly discovered island till spring.

Heading then to the north east, he decided to cross the sea diagonally.

The decision was extraordinarily bold, because to the south off Barsakelmes Island the fishermen sailed only along the shores, never daring to venture into the central and widest part of the sea.

The schooner raced through the night like a huge black bird over the desolate and choppy sea, and at dawn the crew saw on port a hilly island which everyone took for Barsakelmes at first, but on checking the reading of the towed log against the time of day, Butakov realized that this was yet another unidentified island.

He wanted to drop anchor, because the schooner had run out of fresh water, but since there could not be any water on the island, he decided to return to **Barsakelmes**, replenish the supply of water and firewood, and then return to the island.

During the night a storm broke out again. The schooner had to change course and hide behind Cape Uzinkair. During the forced two-day anchorage, the supplies of firewood and fresh water were replenished. The crew bathed, washed their clothes, because while at sea they had to save on fuel and wash only in cold water.

On the third day, with the waves still high, the *Constantine* sailed to the newly discovered island. Butakov named it in honor of Czar Nicholas.

In the morning a boat took Akishev and three sailors ashore to make a topographical survey, Butakov and Pospelov went to plot the position of the island, and Shevchenko joined them in order to draw the landscapes.

Here they made an unexpected discovery. The island, which no human being seemed to have set his foot on, was inhabited by saigas, steppe antelopes. With naïve curiosity they came very close to the sailors. Pospelov aimed his rifle and brought down three saigas with a number of well aimed shots. For a minute or so the herd looked with horror and incomprehension at the men, and then fled headlong in panic.

The crew was extraordinarily happy at the discovery Not counting the several birds Pospelov had bagged, the men had not tasted fresh meat for two months.

Toward the evening a storm gathered unexpectedly. The *Constantine* rode at two anchors in a wide deep bay sheltered from the wind, but the storm made it impossible to sound the depth around the island and explore its coast. Shevchenko, for his part, was satisfied to have made a number of wonderful watercolors on sea and land.

The storm thundered for a whole week, during which time the crew had their fill of fresh meat and stocked up firewood and fresh water which was much better than the water from Barsakelmes. It was only on the seventeenth of September that the *Constantine* ventured into the open sea; to the north off Nicholas Island she came upon a low island which Butakov named the Island of the Heir; a little to the south there was yet another island which he named after the schooner.

Autumn set in. Butakov had learned from a salesman marketing the catch of a fishermen's gang that the mouth of the Syr Darya was shallow in the autumn. The schooner changed course, going from Constantine Island to the south of the Syr Darya, but in order to negotiate the shallows in its delta, she had to be unloaded and towed to the river. After making fast in a little inlet off Kosaral Island opposite Fort Kosaral where the current of the Syr Darya was subtle, Butakov hauled down the St. Andrew's flag and broad pennant, and on the thirtieth of September the schooner prepared for winter.

5. ON KOSARAL

Within the sixty days at sea Shevchenko got used to the life of the mariners. They had fired him with their enthusiasm and spirit of storm-tossed travelers dreaming of unknown islands and countries, and introduced him to their circle of interests. The dangers and cruel storms, which made them gamble with death every minute, had hardened their nature. He realized that he'd always have a warm feeling for these men.

But when they were on shore, this continuity of interests and the friendship began to crumble. At first they still slept on the ship, but from morning till sunset each was occupied with his own work. The meals were taken on shore near the field kitchen, the men never appearing for their meals in one body.

Loneliness and homesickness overcame the poet again. The year before the burning hatred of army drill had aggravated his loss of homeland. Now this pain merged with the quiet sadness of his recollections. Forced idleness made him feel useless.

Butakov, Pospelov and Akishev quartered in their felt tent, Maksheiev, Shevchenko and Werner shared another such tent, while medical attendant Istomin occupied the partly built headquarters and office of Fort Kosaral together with its commandant, Lieutenant Bogomolov, who had been transferred there from Orsk.

Throughout the whole day Butakov, Pospelov and Akishev occupied themselves on a high promontory jutting far out into the sea.

During the previous winter, the foundation of the fort had been laid there to provide winter quarters for fifty Ural Cossacks and a detachment of infantry troops from Orsk. Everybody — sailors, Cossacks, and infantry troops — took a hand in building the fort. They put up a large barracks for one hundred men, two storehouses, a bakery, stables, a sheepfold, a barn, a dwelling house and the headquarters; they erected ramparts, dug earth houses, built stoves, made adobe and bricks, and kneaded dung into fuel bricks. Both the Orsk soldiers and Cossacks noticed with wonder that none of the officers ever used bad language or bawled them out, threatening to bring fists or canes into play, but were doing their job thoroughly and conscientiously, and this made the men work without any abusive prodding.

Shevchenko made an attempt to join in this tense team work, but Butakov strictly forbade him to do so.

"Don't chill your hands, sir," he told him sternly. "Help Werner get his collections in order, write poetry, paint whatever you want, and read. We've got enough hands as it is."

In early October the mail arrived at Raïm. This event occurred three to four times a year and was expected with particular impatience. From Raïm the mail was taken to Kosaral by fishermen who heaped the letters and parcels right on the desk in the future office of the fort. Moments later the room was packed with people and Lieutenant Bogomolov started reading aloud the names of the addressees. Those who stood nearest to Bogomolov passed the letters to the recipient over the heads of the others, and he immediately elbowed his way back to the door to read with pleasure the warm lines addressed to him, experience joy from their message, or else heave a sigh if the news was sad.

Shevchenko and Werner stood in a corner and watched with excitement and hope as Bogomolov picked up letter after letter. They were expecting to hear their names called any minute, but the heap was melting before their eyes, and in the end they saw that there was nothing for them. The room became empty just as fast as it had filled. Both men made silently for the door. Werner's lips trembled and he barely held back his tears. Shevchenko was more composed than his friend. Dusk was falling. Silently they lay down on their cots, without looking al each other. From outdoors came the dry rustle of reeds. The sky dimmed in the tent's smoke outlet overhead.

"It's difficult to be alone,' Shevchenko said on impulse. "You wait so anxiously for those letters, but people do not, they simply cannot understand how necessary any mail is in captivity! Homesickness gnaws at your heart like thirst in the Karakum Desert. If I had a mother or a wife, they would have understood and written to me…"

"They would, my foot!" Werner said with a bitter smile. "I, for one, have a mother and a wife and a sister… and even a child I haven't seen yet. And no letters. This is the third year they haven't written. It would have been better if they had not existed at all! I wouldn't have waited in vain then. I'd be at peace with myself and be hard as a rock."

Werner turned round to the wall abruptly.

Shevchenko kept silent, then he got up, sat down at the table, struck fire with a flint, lit the wick lamp, and started to write.

The steppe bordering on the Aral Sea was much poorer in vegetation and more desolate than the plains around Orsk. Everything here indicated the proximity of the deserts — the Karakum and Barsuk. Here and there the clay or rock rises were covered with thorny bushes and sparse patches of feather grass, and the eye grew tired of the dazzling white depressions of saline land — mostly the bowls of long dried-up lakes. Except for the thick stands of reed crackling dryly in the wind, the only thing Shevchenko saw as he wandered around Kosaral were barren skeletal shrubs of saxaul and balls of tumbleweed which the winds had swept here unbeknownst from where. And over this entire dreary scene hung a low cold sky of yellow.

> *Thick, torpid waves, skies dull and sightless....*
> *On shores that wear a veil of haze,*
> *Tall reeds, though no wind with them plays,*
> *Sway as if drunk. O God Almighty!*
> *Beside this wretched sea and far,*
> *In this lone prison without bars,*
> *Am I intended long to languish*
> *In endless pain and endless anguish?...*
> *As if alive, the parched and dry*
> *Grass stirs, but, mute, makes no reply...*
> *'Twill not disclose the truth, alas,*
> *And there is no one else to ask!**

---

* Translated by Irina Zheleznova

That is how Shevchenko reflected his mood in verse five days after the arrival of the mail, when he roamed across the dunes, between which the muddy waters of the Syr Darya laboriously negotiated a barely water-covered shallow reaching into the sea in a long tongue. On one such day he spied Królikiewicz who waved his cap from afar. The encounter was so unexpected that Shevchenko stopped in his tracks and spread his arms in wonder.

"By what miracle have you appeared here, colleague? I was sure you had returned to Orsk with the party under General Schreiber," Shevchenko said, shaking hands with Królikiewicz.

"That's how it should have been. But during a halt for the night I was stung by a snake. They put me on a wagon, brought me to the nearest fort, and dumped me into the lap of the medical assistant. It was not him who got me back on my feet, but an Ural Cossack and his herbs. Now the supply train has brought me to Kosaral. I'll be probably staying here for the winter, if the train won't take me back to Orenburg," Królikiewicz said, looking close at the poet. "Though you've grown leaner, you seem to be looking pretty chipper. And you've got a wonderful suntan, a real gypsy, I'd say. I see right away that you've been fanned by all the sea winds. Well, how was the seafaring? What did you see and discover?"

"We've seen storms, even met death several times, but it did not notice us," Shevchenko said with a smile. "As for the news, it's you who have always been my reliable source. Tell me, what is going on now in the wide world?"

"Any spring of water dries up in the desert from heat. I, too, dried up throughout the summer. If it were not for a scrap of a Polish newspaper my friends passed on to me from Orenburg, I would not be able to tell you anything. The local blockheads tore that paper into four parts for rolling cigarettes. There were only two paragraphs about France, where there is a famine now, with the peasants going hungry and the city dwellers dying from lack of food and work. In May a constituent assembly was convened. The people demanded a law ensuring the right to work, and insisted on having work and bread. To pen up the sentiments of the jobless, state workshops have been set up, but they are but a drop in the ocean for the needy! A demonstration burst into the session hall of the assembly with a petition. The frightened deputies took to their heels.

So the people proclaimed the assembly dismissed and the deputies' mandates void, but the soldiers dispersed the demonstration, arrested its leaders, and the assembly continued its work. What happened then — I do not know, because the paper was torn off."

"And what did the men escorting the supply train say?"

"Nothing. I did not even dare ask, because there were none of our exiles on that escort, and asking a stranger was too risky. Some of us landed in Siberia just for that. But in Raïm there is a physician, Kilkiewicz, who comes from Lithuania. He occasionally receives mail from his homeland, and his good friends tell him a thing or two. I advise you make his acquaintance because he, too, was once brought to book when he talked too much to a patient who denounced him to the police. The poor chap barely got himself out of the fix. Now once bitten, he's twice shy."

They chatted some more, and Krolikiewicz left. He hurried to get to Raïm, which was about six *versts* away from Kosaral; besides, he had to cross a shallow tributary of the Syr Darya on his way.

Shevchenko had a prolific spell of writing at that time. Again and again he drew sad pictures in verse of the peasants' plight, when the beauty of a serf woman was a bane, not happiness. Ever more often his poetry dealt with a serf whom the landlord forced into the army in order to gain possession of his wife or bride-to-be. He also wrote of the tragic fate of a widow, a feeble mother whose son, her only breadwinner, was conscripted into the army, or of an unmarried mother who, after begging alms in church, immediately surrendered the few coppers to buy a candle to light in front of God's image for the health of her child.

Throughout that autumn he also wrote quite a few lyrics to songs, merry and sad, most of them written in the third person feminine: of a poor servant girl going barefoot and dreaming of a pair of morocco leather boots to dance in once at least in the company of rich women; of a rich man's daughter whose parents forbade her to go outdoors lest she meet with her sweetheart, a poor orphan, and she remained lonely to the end of her life, her fading youth and beauty needed by no one.

But he put the greatest passion of his heart into the poetry in which he appealed for protest against the injustices of life.

With the first autumn frosts, the winterers moved into the earth house and took to processing the astronomical data and systematizing their collections. Reading the newly received books and journals was a favorite pastime.

Once in the morning several Kazakh horsemen came galloping into Kosaral.

"Where do your *mayirs* live here?" one of the oldest and most dignified of them asked.

"We haven't got any," an Ural Cossack answered with a contemptuous grin.

"Well, if you haven't any *mayirs* around, take us to a general," the *axakal* insisted. "We've come on important business."

"How do you like that! He wants a general," the Cossack jeered back. "Go to the mariners," he pointed to Butakov's earth house.

"We've come on important business to you," the *axakal* repeated, on entering the Lieutenant's quarters. "Good morning, Russian chief! Help us, please!"

"Good morning. Be seated," Butakov replied affably, motioning the guest to a bench as he settled back in his favored armchair. "What trouble has brought you to me?"

"*Oi boi*, there is big trouble!" the old man said, shaking his head. There is a tiger living in the reeds here. A big tiger. Our *jigits* wanted to kill him, they looked for him everywhere, but he is hiding. In the night he kills our sheep, horses" — the *axakal* was bending his fingers, counting — "and even a child he did kill."

"Where is his den?"

"We don't know. Our men are afraid to go into the reeds which we need very much. We just don't know where his den is."

Butakov fell to thinking. Hunting a tiger on foot would end in nothing. He had to have a talk with Cavalry Captain Chortorogov.

"Would you please see me again the day after tomorrow," the lieutenant said. "By that time we'll think of something."

When the Kazakhs left, Butakov immediately had a talk with the Cossack officers, because the presence of a tiger near the camp did not promise anything pleasant.

Butakov could not have come at a better time. The day before a number of soldiers and Cossacks hunted wild boar, and a fortunate hunt it was: apart from three small pigs, they brought down a huge boar. The men barely managed to drag the dead boar out of the sucking marsh onto hard ground, and left him there to pick him up with a wagon the next morning. When they arrived at the place, they saw that a half of the carcass had been devoured and there were tiger tracks on the ground all around. Any minute the tiger could come hack to continue his interrupted meal. Being of two minds what to do, the men returned to their commander for advice and met Butakov there.

The opinions on the further course of action differed. Some suggested hitching the horses into a wagon and leaving immediately for the remainder of the boar, others proposed laying an ambush and waiting for the tiger near the carcass, and still others simply laughed the idea off:

"A tiger has a much more sensitive scent than we. It will be a useless ambush and we'll just freeze for nothing throughout the night, while the tiger, once he sniffs humans in the air, will stay away and go gobble up sheep or calves instead, or he might even get to our horses."

Shevchenko stood silently behind Butakov, smiling into his mustache, and after everybody had talked himself hoarse and fell silent, he said:

"What if we put up charged shotguns aimed at the carcass, tie a string or wire to the triggers, and fix the ends to the carcass. As soon as the tiger pulls at the carcass, the shotguns will go off and he'll be either shot dead or gravely wounded."

Shevchenko's suggestion brought peace to the arguing party, and the conversation centered now only on how and in what place it would be best to install the shotguns.

Two fast-working carpenters got down to the job, and about three hours later the charged shotguns were pointing in the dense stand of reed at the unfinished boar carcass, while Shevchenko, Butakov and Lieutenant Bogomolov were carefully tying fast to the boar's ribs and tusks the ends if the strings running from the cocked triggers. In order to efface the human scent they dragged the carcass of a dead pig behind their retreating tracks and left for Kosaral.

The next morning the hunters hurried to the trap The remainder of the boar carcass had not been touched but only turned on another side. Around it were two pools of blood and a large number of tiger tracks.

The hunters did not dare venture into the dense reeds after the bloody tracks. Everybody knew that a wounded tiger was the first to attack. Only after twenty well armed men had been brought together did they dare follow the wounded animal in pursuit. Some half a *verst* from the trap they came upon the dead tiger lying in a pool of blood: all the six bullets had pierced him, and it was a sheer wonder how the will to live had made the deadly wounded, blood-dripping animal slink away so far.

Everybody congratulated Shevchenko on his wonderful idea, but he was in a hurry to put the savage strength and beauty of the huge tiger on paper in pencil and water colors.

"Taras *Aga*! Is that you really, my friend?" the excited voice of Jaisak suddenly rang out. "*Oi boi*, how glad I am to see you again!"

269

"Jaisak!" Shevchenko cried out joyously, and getting to his feet, he almost got his water colors smeared.

"We are wintering not far away from here," Jaisak said, jumped off his horse, and strongly embraced the poet. "And how did you get here, Taras *Aga?*"

"Unlike you I sailed across the Taniz Aral. And these are my chiefs or *mayirs,* as you call them," Shevchenko explained, gesturing at Butakov and Bogomolov with a broad sweep of his hand.

"I know! I saw it! A large boat, a very large boat with wings and canvas. Good morning, Russian chiefs," he suddenly checked his emotions and respectfully shook Butakov and Bogomolov's hands with both of his. "Do come and visit us. We are finely settled now in a big *aul.* Djantemir became a very rich *bai,* with white yurts and a lot of sheep. He built himself a house just like the one in Orsk. We will treat you to *bishbarmak,* Russian vodka, cured and fried fish. We catch a lot of fish here and cure them, too. Djantemir is even glad that Meshka *Mayir* chased him away from Jaman-Kala. Here it's better and warmer. It's only the tiger we were afraid of, but now he is dead. Who killed him?" he asked, his eyes shifting from Butakov and Shevchenko to the others.

"It was Taras Grigorievich's idea to put up shotguns against the tiger," Butakov replied, laughing.

Jaisak did not understand to the end what he was told, but he did not dare ask questions and only said to Shevchenko:

"Show me where you live, Taras *Aga.* I will visit you another time; there is much I want to talk about with you. Right now I have no time."

Shevchenko showed him his earth house from-afar. Jaisak jumped into the saddle, lashed at his horse, and galloped off, while Shevchenko took up his brushes again.

The tiger was unusually huge, with terrible, seemingly polished fangs and a rich yellow coat with black velvety stripes. While he was finishing the **watercolor,** the Ural Cossacks skinned the animal. Eventually the skin was acquired by Butakov for three pailfuls of vodka and three cans of tinned meat.

Before snow and blizzards set in, Shevchenko made quite a few pictures in water colors, sepia, and red and colored pencils. He did a number of landscapes with Fort Kosaral viewed from land and sea, the sea inlet at the mouth of the Syr Darya, and a wonderful oil painting, *Moonlit Night*. When snow started to fall, he painted portraits of his expedition friends and the interior of their quarters. Pospelov had a wonderful figure and Shevchenko eagerly drew him naked to the waist and involuntarily admired the handsomness of his sitter.

Maksheiev frequently engaged Shevchenko in arguments about art. Theoretically, both of them stood for truth in art, but Maksheiev believed that Shevcheuko's words and deeds were at variance. He criticized Shevchenko for his early paintings, in which human features were rendered inaccurately by prettying the sitter, lengthening his face, and lending him artificial postures.

"I never did that," Shevchenko countered angrily.

"Oh no, my dear fellow: you have sinned against the truth of life on many occasions. It's a pity I don't have your pictures here. I'd prove that I have a reason to judge so. Every year I visited the exhibitions at the Academy of Arts, and didn't miss a single one. I saw and remember pretty well your *Katerina*. That's no grief-stricken serf girl for you, but a manorial lady dressed in peasant garb. She has tender, well-groomed hands unaccustomed to menial work; neither is her face touched by the winds and the scorching rays of your blazing Ukrainian sun. She never saw the plight of serfdom, your Lady Katerina. And believe me, her image would have been the more touching, if you had not beautified her. I am also acquainted with the Keikuatova, and saw your oil portait of Mademoiselle Keikuatova at their home. No doubt she is like a well cared for hothouse flower, but at the same time she is a healthy person, while in your portrait you have made her an almost incorporeal and anemic creature that seems to be mortally ill with consumption. No denying it, the portrait is a wonderful work of art, but it is what you imagined Mademoiselle Keikuatova to be and not what she really is."

Such arguments would make Shevchenko angry and excited: he would fall silent, offended, and go out of the earth house.

"An argument must be honest, without imputing to the opponent what he did not do, what he does not have and never will," he repeated again and again.

But still, doubts gradually started to stir somewhere deep in his mind. What if there was a grain of truth in Maksheiev's words? Without noticing it, his new drawings showed, like never before, how carefully and thoroughly he conveyed the truth of life, profound and unfathomable in its beauty and horror.

Frequently Shevchenko recalled his great teacher Brüllow. At the Academy Brüllow was considered a progressive man who determinedly went against the pseudo-classicist trend in art, and instead of making his students copy only the great masters of Italian, Spanish and Dutch painting he demanded that they draw people and landscapes from nature.

But Brüllow's demands for lifelikeness and truth in art did not go beyond a certain limit: he studiously evaded everything that seemed mundane, dull and commonplace to him. In the latter category he included a lot of things, considering worthy of art only the beauty of the human figure, inspired or classic faces, and even in his best painting, *The Last Day of Pompeii*, which won him acclaim throughout Europe, there was not a single ugly or even slightly insignificant face nor a single feature devoid of grace in the entire crowd of horror-stricken people fleeing from Vesuvius spewing forth its lava and ashes. It represented not the tragedy of an entire city doomed to death, but an affectedly pompous theatrical scenery to a tragedy. That was how the life he could not grasp was taking revenge on the artist.

A year before his arrest, Shevchenko heard rumors that Brüllow was living through an inner crisis, a sort of reevaluation of his former esthehic standards. It was said that he had started on a new painting based on Russian life, in which there was neither the glaring Italian sun nor the effects of a volcano's glow and fiery streams of lava, or lightning. But what Brillow produced in the end Shevchenko was not destined to find out on the shores of the distant Aral Sea. He was independently seeking his own way in art.

The days were growing shorter. Shevchenko devoted ever more time to reading the books from the library which the *Constantine* had brought to Kosaral. What he liked most was to compare the occasionally fantastic and at times remarkably accurate statements of the geographers of the past with the explorations of the latest expeditions throughout the jungles and deserts of Asia, Africa, South America, and on the islands of the Indian Ocean and the Pacific.

Maksheiev brought along a suitcase of books. A part of them were devoted to topography and the military sciences, and the rest mostly dealt with philosophy of the most contrastingly opposite schools of thinking.

Shevchenko lived in miserable penury that winter. Frequently he did not have a copper to buy himself tobacco, an envelope or postage stamp, a cake of soap or sugar for his tea. So he had to look for some earnings. He wrote letters for the illiterate soldiers and Cossacks, but they, too, had nothing to pay for his services. At times he proposed that the officers have their portraits made in pencil or water colors, for which he was paid ten rubles. But in Raïm there were no more than ten and in Kosaral three officers, and they were not that well off to afford such a luxury as a portrait. As to the local civilian population, there was none as yet, except for a priest two clerks and two physicians with their families. Shevchenko frequently had to go about with the bitter thought of where to get himself some shag for a cigarette. Even such a trifle proved to be a difficult problem, because almost all of the Cossacks were Old Believers and did not smoke, while the soldiers were always short or their shag ration and he just could not make himself beg from them.

Occasionally the sutler helped him out, but for a pack of shag Shevchenko had to write out an application for him or make a fair copy of an account, and when there was nothing to write, the sutler did not give him anything on credit.

The days passed by, but no mail arrived.

That year cholera raged throughout Russira, and the bubonic plague, brought from India, swept across the land. Quarantine was enforced everywhere; any parcel coming from the infected areas remained unhandled and the letters were fumed with sulphur smoke. The newly arrived officers told about entire villages dying out,

What if his friends, too, had died of the horrible disease in Ukraine, and he was wailing for a message from them in vain?

The thought about the plague visited the poet again and again, inspiring him to write a semi-fantastic ballad, "The Plague": Black Death stalks the towns and villages, mowing down the horror-stricken people and hurtling them into graves it digs for them; they lock themselves up in their homes, but there is no lock or key that can save them from inevitable Fate; hungry cattle roam from yard to yard; gardens and streets are overrun by weeds and nettles, the ponds get muddy and overgrown with reeds, and the last to die are the grave diggers who drag the deceased with chains into the communal graves; a year later new people arrive at the village and set fire to the horrible hotbed of death, obliterating thus every trace and memory of the old village.

To chase away boredom, Butakov suggested a visit to Djantemir's *aul* one gloomy day: "Taras Grigorievich here says that Djantemir is incredibly rich. I think we ought to visit him, get acquainted, have a look how he lives, and then invite him to our place."

Butakov's idea was to everybody's liking, but only five people went on the visit: Butakov, Maksheiev, Shevchenko, Bogomolov — who as the commandant of Kosaral had to get officially acquainted with his new neighbors — and Ensign Nudatov, who was exiled to Raïm for two years, because several

Polish exiles had escaped with a Bukharan caravan when he was on duty.

"Don't forget the water colors and pencils," Butakov advised Shevchenko. "Every one of us will surely want to have a memento of this visit."

The horses were already snorting near the earth houses. Knowing that Shevchenko was a bad rider, Bogomolov ordered that the poet be given a tractable mare.

Shevchenko's spirits buoyed at the thought of a good treat and, most importantly, of the fragrant Persian tobacco and he jogged along on his Rosinante (as he had immediately nicknamed the mare) if not in a dashing so at least in a lively manner. They forced two sea inlets, rounded several estuaries, and galloped along the Syr Darya upstream; an hour later they saw white and black yurts in the distance.

The group was met by a wild barking of dogs.

"Stop here, Alexei Ivanovich," Shevchenko said as he rode up to Butakov. "Let us wait until the hosts show up and chase the dogs away, because those wolfhounds have such fangs we'll hardly escape once we make a move."

On learning about the appearance of some chiefs, Djantemir, heavier and much fatter than he had been the year before, hurried to meet the guests halfway.

"Glory be to Allah for having sent me such good and respected guests," he said solemnly, a sugary, sleepily insinuating smile freezing on his puffed-up round face.

By custom, he led the guests to his yurt, while Iskhak and Rahim took care of the horses.

Inside the yurt, the guests were immediately served tea, while a sheep was being skinned by the threshold. Butakov and Maksheiev regarded the interior of the yurt with curiosity and involuntarily were lost in admiration of the proud giant of a golden eagle dozing on its perch. When a bowl with the steaming mutton was brought in, Iskhak id Rahim offered the guests water to wash their hands and some towels.

"Don't shake the water off your hands onto the floor. Wipe them on the towels or with your handkerchiefs, because otherwise you'll offend the hosts," Shevchenko said to the officers in a whisper.

In the meantime, Djantemir had taken a bottle of vodka out of a trunk and poured the drinks into bowls up to the rim, saying:

"Oh, how wonderful the *mayirs* did to have killed the tiger. He destroyed many of our sheep and did us great harm. The women were afraid to let their children outdoors, because he gobbled up one child. They say he liked children's meat."

"It was Taras Grigorievich's idea to kill him the way we did," Butakov said.

"Taras *Aga* is a good man," Djantemir confirmed with a nod. "Back in Jaman Kala he arranged the wolf chase. The *mayirs* killed a lot of wolves then. A good man he is indeed!"

Shauken was busy setting the fare. Dressed in her holiday sleeveless jacket of velvet, she waddled back and forth among the guests like a duck. Soon she was to bear a child, her pregnancy making her look like a huge ball with a smaller one attached in front of her. Her face beamed with such solemn self-satisfaction that Butakov barely held back his laughter.

Nudatov found himself in such an exotic environment for the first time and admired everything with rapture. The yurt, the golden eagle, the patterned pieces of felt along the *kerege*, the drinking bowls, and the hosts in their striped garb — everything was so new and distinctive for him.

"It's a pity I won't take in and remember all of it," he said with a sigh. "Memories always lose their freshness with the passage of time. I wish I had at least a souvenir to remind me of this visit."

"That's where I can help you out," Shevchenko responded cheerfully. "I will draw you in this setting. It's a good thing Alexei Ivanovich advised me to take the water colors along."

"Everything would be fine, my dear Taras Grigorievich, if the ten rubles I gave you for your work last lime were expended for something useful. You'll just squander them on drink, and tomorrow you'll be going around cadging for a pinch of tobacco from good people."

Shevchenko hung his head. Nudatov's words had stabbed him painfully.

Nudatov felt ashamed at what he had said. The officers shrugged their shoulders, indignant, and turned away from him.

"Oh well," Nudatov stammered on, "I understand how it is. At times you just blurt things out. But please do me a favor — make a drawing."

Shevchenko reluctantly picked up his brush. In the drawing he did, Nudatov was half reclining on a carpet with a drinking bowl in his hand. Opposite him sat the grave and corpulent Djantemir, his legs crossed like a Buddha's. In the depth of the yurt dozed the golden eagle, and a saddle and huge empty *saba* hung on a wall. Shauken disappeared from the yurt, frightened that the Russian *akyn* would make a drawing of her.

Everybody liked the drawing, but Shevchenko flatly refused to take any money for it however much Nudatov and the others insisted. When a new round of fare was being served, Shevchenko slipped out of the yurt unnoticed.

Jaisak had just returned to the *aul* and was eating millet porridge with *airan* when the poet entered his yurt.

"Be seated, Taras *Aga*," the young herder said joyfully, spreading under the guest the only piece of white felt he had. "How is life?"

"Not much to be happy about," Shevchenko replied with a sigh. "Although it is far easier than last year, bondage remains bondage. Better tell me what's new with you and how are your affairs with Kuljan?"

"Nothing has changed. I bagged a lot of fox. The eagle I have is a good hunter. As to Kuljan… Zulkarnai came to the *jailiaou* and said that his son was still laid up in that … how do you call it?"

"Plaster cast, you mean?"

"Yes, plaster cast."

"So what did they decide?"

Jaisak waved his hand in a gesture of hopelessness.

"The poor girl's tears don't dry. Before that her only grief was that she would have to marry Ibrai, but now there is new, much worse trouble in store for her. Zulkarnai did not come alone, but with his relatives to strengthen the friendship with Djantemir. Among the relatives was Zulkarnai's uncle Moldabai. He's over seventy years old, toothless, hunchbacked, and can barely sit on a horse. As soon as he saw Kuljan he seemed to have gone out of his mind: he said that if Ibrai were to die, he would marry her. There is nothing you can do about it: *amenger* is a law."

"What a loathsome thing to do!" Shevchenko could not hold his tongue. "Well, and how did Djantemir take it? Will he really agree to that?"

"Djantemir realizes that Moldabai is very rich and an imam besides."

Both lapsed into a long silence.

"I got a lot of fox furs," Jaisak said, breaking the silence. "But I have nowhere to sell them. It takes three days to get from Jaman Kala to Orenburg, and from here it's five times that much. How can I get there all by myself?"

"If anything unexpected happens to you, let me know.

Come and see me anyway. I like talking with you," Shevchenko said, getting to his feet.

Jaisak saw him to Djantemir's yurt where the officers' horses were already snorting and jangling their bridles as the guests were taking leave of the *bai*.

"Where is my Rosinante?" Shevchenko asked with comic surprise.

"She limps in one leg," Iskhak explained. "Get on our horse. Rahim will go with you and bring it back."

"But it's evening already. What if wolves attack him on his way back?" Shevchenko said, worried.

"They won't. It is not full winter now. The wolves are not hungry yet," Iskhak said with a smile. "But if you fear for his life, let him stay the night with you and return to the *aul* in the morning. You agree, *ata*?"

"Let him, if he wants," Djantemir replied and went on thanking the officers for their visit.

Rahim, dressed in a fine striped gown he was given to wear only on holidays, rode at Shevchenko's side. When they were passing the black yurts and a gang of boys came running out of them, he called out something loud and derisive to them.

"What did you say to them?" Shevchenko asked when the boys had fallen behind.

"I told them that I was going on a visit to your place where you feed your guests well," Rahim burst into laughter. "They are always hungry and think only of food. So I just teased them."

On hearing such a reply, Butakov said, "So why don't you help them? They are your relatives after all."

"Father said that if we were to feed all the hungry, there would be nothing left for ourselves," he said, and his face colored. "In the summer they got the idea of separating from us. They were attacked by the Khivans and plundered. Now they have turned into real *baigushes*, but I am friends with Ismagul and Izgut and always give them mutton," he added, lashed his horse, and dashed ahead.

"Now here is what you tell those boys the next time you meet them," Butakov said sternly when Rahim was level with him again. "Let them come to us at Kosaral every day. We have our meals at midday — that is when the sun stands the highest in the sky. We will feed them."

"You will feed them?" he asked incredulously.

"Yes, we will feed them every day. Do you understand? Will you tell them?"

"*Oi boi!*" Rahim jumped up in his saddle. "They'll come for sure, because they all are hungry!"

Suddenly his face beamed with such sincere joy it made Butakov smile as well.

It was cold in the earth house. The fire in the little iron

stove had died long ago. Shevchenko brought in an armful of brushwood, a bundle of tumbleweed and several pieces of dung, made a fire in the stove and put on it the evening meal to warm.

Rahim was not used to sitting on a stool, so he made himself comfortable on the floor by the stove.

"Let me make up the fire, Taras *Aga*," he said and started deftly feeding the fire with pieces of tumbleweed and dung.

Maksheiev stayed at the commandant's home in Raïm for the night. Werner had also disappeared somewhere, and Shevchenko was left alone with the boy. He served him a plate of puffy buckwheat porridge. By custom Rahim ate with his fingers at first, but then he followed his host's example and picked up a spoon.

"Tomorrow morning I will draw you," the poet said after the meal, and gave the boy a sheepskin coat. "Spread this on the floor and cover yourself with the other half."

The boy obediently put his "bedding" on the floor and was fast asleep a moment later.

Shevchenko, however, stayed awake for a long time, the words of Nudatov gnawing at his heart. More than once he had blamed himself for his susceptibility to vodka or strong tea flavored with Jamaica rum which deadened the pain in his grief-stricken heart now and then. He had sincerely made friends with all the members of the expedition and taken a liking to them, but he could not forget that he was a bondsman and they were but temporary companions along his endless path of suffering. Any minute cruel life could throw him back into the filthy cesspool of the penal army barracks.

The morning was bright and sunny. Hoar frost glittered on the reeds and shrubs. Pearly smoke rose over the stacks of the barracks, headquarters and the earth houses. In the sky a caravan of similar pearly white clouds drifted by high up.

Shevchenko worked with inspiration. Rahim sat motionless, which made the artist's work much easier. The narrow, black eyes of Rahim looked at him thoughtfully and sadly. What the boy was thinking about Shevchenko could not know, but it seemed that the very soul of Asia was looking out of the eyes of its son.

"It's finished!" Shevchenko said at last and almost fell down on his cot: he had been working on the drawing for three hours without stopping.

Rahim jumped to his feet, put on his striped gown, felt stockings and boots, girded himself, then he bowed deeply to Shevchenko and ran off to the stable for his horse.

Shevchenko remained sitting in his earth house his eyes fixed on the drawing.

Maksheiev would not find any conventionality or embellishment in this picture now, he thought. There it was — the real truth of life.

Thus unwittingly Shevchenko embarked on a new period in his work as a realist artist.

6. THE WINTERERS

Every day, about an hour and a half before the midday meal, Fort Kosaral was visited by a crowd of Kazakh children ranging in age from six — who barely minced along in their worn felt stockings — to lanky awkward teenagers of fourteen in tattered boots and sorry-looking short *chapans*, out of which their arms, red-blue from the cold, protruded almost from the elbows. They wore shaggy caps of fox or wolf fur which cast weird shadows on the snow. Each of them carried a wooden or earthenware bowl.

On seeing them in the distance, the cook would say with a smile:

"Here comes the horde in the raw. It's amazing how they can tramp such a distance for a spoonful of porridge."

The distance from Kosaral to the *aul* by sleigh trail was quite long — about twelve *versts*, but the children did not go round the lakes or the big bend in the river: they just tramped across the ice-bound floodlands, stands of reed and inlets, making a considerable shortcut.

While waiting for the meal, they huddled up to one another like frozen chicks, and to feel warmer burrowed themselves in the haystacks standing behind the mess and stable. But no sooner would they get a little bit warm than they started larking about, kicking and tumbling until a Cossack would shout at them, his eyes bulging with mock severity:

"Hush, you naked panhandlers! Why do you fuss around in that hay? Or do you think it was cut specially for you?"

The children would calm down at once and look at him either frightened or roguishly out of their slitty eyes, pressing closer to one another to show how cold they were. When the frosts were bitter, the Cossacks occasionally invited them into the barracks. But mostly the children just sat in the hay, waiting until the "Rus aga," that is, the Russian father, would open the door of the galley, as the men persistently called the mess, and ladle out the food. At such moments they instantly flew across the yard like a flock of sparrows, and falling silent abruptly, modestly and almost piously lined up in front of the field kitchen. The cook poured each a full ladle of borshch into their bowls and added a hunk of cooked meal. They went to the wall, sat down on the ground, and scalding their lips and tongues, slurped the hot soup out of the bowls, after which they picked the meal and vegetables with their fingers and returned to the cook. He gave each a big serving of porridge. The children went again to the wall. When they finished eating the porridge, they thoroughly licked their bowls, hands and fingers.

The sailors stood to one side, patiently waiting for their turn, as some with a look of sadness, and others, with a kind smile, watched the children eating their food with a serious mien. In many of the men the scene awakened the yearning for a family nest and warm parental feelings which nature plants in the heart of every human.

During withering frosts and blizzards the children did not show up. The sailors would then go beyond the rampart and look intently into the dense veil of swirling snow, alarm stealing over them: "What if they left the *aul* and the blizzard has overtaken them? The poor mites will freeze to death out there!"

But the children proved to be keen-witted: several times they brought along their dogs from the *aul* and never ventured into the steppe without them in bad weather; the dogs remembered well the tasty bones the cook treated them to and led the children to the fort by the shortest route, and after a good meal, they guided the children back to the *aul*.

The *aul's* poor had met with disaster at the time the *Constantine* was drifting off Khiva's shores. Offended and deceived by Djantemir, they decided to strike it out on their own and left the terrible *bai*. In vain did Jaisak and Taijan try and persuade them to put up with the situation till spring and then wander to the Ishma or Irtysh where the Khiva plunderers did not roam. The hotheads would not listen to the good advice, believing that Jaisak was quite well off as Djantemir's chief herder and so his advice did not come from a sincere enough heart. They took down their yurts, left the *aul* with their cattle, and were plundered by the Khivans several days later. Three men were killed and a dozen or so wounded in the fierce skirmish. They failed to retake their cattle, and having lost everything they could call their own, returned to Djantemir, begging his forgiveness and help.

Djantemir did not accept them immediately and gave them paltry crumbs as alms, and on credit at that. The poor people had to submit to the harshest and most humiliating terms to save their lives. Butakov's help at that moment came as a real godsend which saved the children from death.

The mariners helped the Kazakhs as much as they could, sharing their last shirt with them or giving them a hand in fishing and hunting. Twice a week Istomin visited the *aul* to treat the sick, and prepared and administered the medicines himself.

Butakov made the following entry in his diary during those days:

"It is amazing how these hapless Kirghiz still exist. They dwell in wretched tents in which chilling winds freeze a man to the marrow. They go around in rags through which their naked bodies show, and in footwear which gets filled with snow. All our assistance will be but a drop in the sea unless a really strong power capable of defending them from the Khivans is established here."

Christmas was approaching. Everybody succumbed to a dolorous mood, recalling their childhood, the merry time of Christmas caroling, Christmas trees, and their kith and kin. And everyone wanted to share the recollections with his friends.

Shevchenko keenly sensed the mood of the men, and even his personal anguish troubled him less than the air of sadness which clung about him like a mist. So when Butakov proposed to stage a play, Shevchenko supported him wholeheartedly.

Werner and Shevchenko volunteered to stage the show and soon were carried away by the preparations for it. The experience Shevchenko gained in organizing the wolf chase the year before stood him in good stead now. First of all he and Werner devised a program for the show and then wrote a list of all the things they had to make themselves or, as Werner put it, "make from scratch," after which they started seeking the "scratch." Butakov immediately agreed to have them issued the old underwear and linen for the costumes and stage curtains. Bogomolov dug up some red and blue ink in his office. Istomin was so generous as to give them six white hare furs. The quartermaster-sergeant found some cardboard boxes and pieces of gold and silver braid. Maksheiev gave them a bottle of shoe lacquer. The cook came up with skins of an astrakhan sheep and of a black shaggy long-fleeced sheep. Chortorogov contributed a bear's skin, and Shevchenko asked Jaisak for eagle's feathers and Kumish's old sleeveless jacket of velvet. In this way they also procured thread and glue — and plunged into work.

Knowing that the mail would arrive soon, Shevchenko snatched some minutes from his hectic holiday preparations to write a letter to Lizohub, in which he frankly described his mood: "I cannot say that I am exactly happy, but I am cheerful at least now, and that means a lot to me: thus, gloomy sadness and despair have withered in me."

Shevchenko's energy fired everybody. The "actors" dutifully rehearsed their parts and perfected them to make their performance the more distinctive. In the meantime, Shevchenko had made a fantastic headdress out of the eagle's feathers, and persuaded Istomin to perform an Indian dance to a weird melody which noncom Abizarov played on his guitar, assuring everybody that it was really an Indian dance tune. Of course, nobody succeeded in making him change his mind. Nonetheless, the number was a tremendous success.

Two days before Christmas a dress rehearsal was held in Kosaral but without any makeup, because there was none really and Butakov had forbidden the deficient stock of water colors to be squandered for the rehearsal.

A horseman was sent to Fort Raïm to say that the Kosaral garrison would descend on Raïm in a body with the show on the first day of Christmas.

At midday the men set forth in four big paired sleighs, without waiting for the Cossacks who decided to take part in the performance at the last minute.

Both the program of the show and the performers were a tremendous success with the audience. There was no end to the congratulations and thanks which Shevchenko and Butakov received for the interesting entertainment. The merry, though short spectacle, was followed up by a grand ball.

The ball lasted to the third hour in the morning. Nobody dared return to Kosaral because of the wolves, so the residents of Raïm took the officers into their homes, while the sailors and Cossacks slept the rest of the night in the barracks.

On the third day of the holiday Raïm paid a return call to Kosaral with a group of musicians. The visit was followed by dinner, dances, and supper. Again there was merriment, laughter, a lot of drinking, and with all the bustle neither Shevchenko nor Werner or the other members of the expedition had any time to be sad.

New Year was celebrated in a calm and modest way at Butakov's quarters. The guests downed a goblet of champagne, wished one another all the best in the New Year, and quietly retired to their quarters an hour later.

Shevchenko marked this New Year by another little poem in which he noted that two years after he had been forbidden to write he was still writing and embarked on the third year of his creativity at a happy moment.

7. TWO SCHEMES

Just at that time Djantemir unexpectedly summoned Jaisak.

"Now listen," he said to the young herder, after making sure that nobody was eavesdropping on them. "In a month or a month and a half Shauken will bear me a child. If it is a son, I will hold a big *toi* and *baiga*. Pick the best two-and three-year-old horses out of the herd and start breaking them, and then train them to run long quick races. I pin my hopes upon you. But mind you — let not a single soul guess that you are preparing the horses for a *baiga*. We will announce it not months but just weeks before it starts. Everybody will enter his mount just like it is, while we ...he-he-he! Then my horses will be the first to finish, and my fame will again spread across the whole steppe."

"All right, I will do it," Jaisak said laconically. "But I'll need a strong helper. Besides, give me one of your sons for an assistant. And we'd need also arms in case we run into the Khivans."

"Take Taijan and Rahim, but mind they don't wag their tongues," Djantemir added sternly, and called Rahim.

"Did you call me, *ata*?" the boy asked, slightly alarmed, because his father mostly called his children to punish rather than say a kind word to them.

"Yes, I called you. Enough of you traipsing around and doing nothing. You'll be breaking horses together with Jaisak. But

I warn you: if you say a word about it to anyone, I'll skin you alive! Understand?" He raised his fist. "Keep your mouth shut like a sheep's head cooked in rice. If Shauken bears a son, there'll be a big *toi* and *baiga.*"

A light flashed in Rahim's eyes but faded the next instant.

"And what if it will be a girl?" he asked. "*Baibishe* says that there are more girls being born now than boys."

"If it will be a girl, there'll be a *baiga* anyway, but not now — a little later during Kuljan's wedding. It's high time we got over that accursed affair." Djantemir grew angry suddenly.

Jaisak and Taijan saw through Djantemir's scheme.

"In this case, too, that jackal wants to fill his pockets," Jaisak cursed. "He'll fool the poor folk again."

"No doubt about it! Other *bais*, at the joy of a son being born to them, invite the entire steppe to a *baiga*, and even if their horses win, they give away a flock of sheep as a prize," Taijan said with a wry smile.

"He'll arrange things so that everyone will have to pay for the right to enter a horse in the race," Jaisak said, spitting with disgust. "And the prizes he'll take away for himself. The only good thing is that he allowed me to try my luck."

"We'll outtrick that crook," Taijan said with a guffaw. "Hush! Don't rejoice ahead of time," the superstitious Jaisak stopped him and changed the subject of the conversation on seeing Rahim in the distance.

But the boy knew more than Jaisak realized. When he was alone with Jaisak, Rahim spoke out bluntly:

"Don't hide anything from me, Jaisak. I know everything. Kuljan has already wept a lot because of that dratted wedding. If Ibrai dies, she will wither completely with that ugly old man Moldabai for a husband. You must get rich by all means. Your horses must be the first to finish the race. One thing will add up to another. She loves you, Jaisak. And I, too, want her to be your wife and not leave our *aul* forever, because I cannot, do you hear — I just cannot part with her!"

Jaisak only heaved a desolate sigh. Rahim had spoken so sincerely and passionately that Jaisak realized that Kuljan had become a second mother to the boy, and moved, he silently embraced him.

"Good, I'll help you," Rahim whispered with ardor. "You must know that I am also a brother to you and a real friend."

Jaisak and Taijan started breaking in the future racers. They were skillfully experienced and exceptionally good horsemen, but for all his strength and agility, the heavy Taijan was twice thrown out of the saddle on the very first day. Fortunately for him, he tumbled both times into a snow pile which had become slightly compressed after a recent thaw. The snow cushioned the blow, and he did not break any bones. Jaisak was much lighter and lither than Taijan. He was thrown out of the saddle only once and did not hurt himself, falling into a ditch filled with snow. But on impact the shock registered in his shoulder which the wolves had mauled the year before, and he had to ride to the *aul* and stay there for three days.

"Go to the Russians, son. They have a doctor there," Kumish advised.

"Never mind, *apa*!" the young herder waved off the advice. "Heat me a bundle with sand. I'll put it to the shoulder and everything will be all right."

During one of his regular visits to the *aul* Istomin learned of Jaisak's accident and went to his yurt. After examining Jaisak's arm and shoulder, he daubed them with iodine, massaged them, and approved of the poultice.

While Jaisak was away, Taijan broke five horses with the help of the younger herders.

A week later Jaisak and Taijan armed themselves with rifles and sharp yatagans, and without explaining anything to the herders, saddled two colts, and galloped far off into the steppe. Rahim followed behind on his Karaigir, holding by the halter another two of Jaisak's stallions.

After several trial races the men let the horses rest and

returned to the camping site of the herd. In the afternoon they saddled another two pairs of horses, covered the same distance as they had in the morning, and returned when dusk was already falling.

Thus during the first day they had tried out four pairs of colts for the *baiga*.

"We need one more rider," Taijan said to Jaisak. "Otherwise we'll fail."

"But we don't know who Djantemir will decide to let in on the secret."

"That'll blast our scheme," Rahim cut in. "I know what we have to do: my friend Ismagul can keep his mouth shut, and he's older than me by one year. Also, he knows everything about Shauken and Kuljan and can be trusted completely."

The *jigits* fell to thinking. Ismagul was a good boy, brave and honest, but still the venture was too serious: how could they entrust such vicious, half-wild colts to the boy's care?

The events that followed erased their uncertainty.

Back at the *aul*, the *jigits* found the family of Djantemir in an extraordinarily agitated state: shortly before dusk several horsemen came galloping into the *aul* with loud shrieks and shouts.

"Oh, our dear Ibrai! Our dear Ibrai!" they carried on, dashing past the *bai*'s house and the white yurts to the ear-splitting barking of the dogs.

After riding in between the yurts in two large circles, they stopped at the white yurts of Djantemir. They were the messengers from Zulkarnai, bringing the news of Ibrai's death.

Djantemir himself received them. He asked in great detail about the last days of the young man who died of tuberculosis of the spine, treated the guests to a lavish meal, put them to bed, and in the morning the messengers set out on their homeward journey, accompanied by Iskhak and Djantemir's two younger brothers, who went to attend the funeral of Ibrai.

Kuljan was seized with despair. Her future rose before her in the ugly image of Moldabai, an old, toothless, trembling libertine.

No sooner had the messengers left than Rahim rushed to his sister, but Zeineb blocked his way.

"Let her be, Rahim. She is smitten with grief. The poor thing wept all night and morning and has only now fallen asleep. Don't wake her. When somebody is in distress, sleep helps a lot."

Rahim disagreed with the kindly *baibishe*, but kept silent, and when the women went into the adjacent room, he sneaked into Kuljan's room and roused her. The girl woke and extended her hands to him with a tender and joyous smile, but the next moment a cold knife seemed to have slashed her heart, the cheerful smile vanished on her lips, and a grimace of soul-racking pain contorted her face. She wanted to say something, but Rahim put his hand across her lips and whispered in her ear, his words running into each other from excitement:

"Don't cry, Kuljan *Djan*. I will tell you a great secret, but promise you will not breathe a word about it to anyone. Soon there will be a *baiga*. Jaisak's horses will win; he will get a lot of sheep as a prize and become rich. Ibrai will be mourned for a whole year, during which no one can marry you off. Then Jaisak will propose and you will become his wife and never leave our *aul*."

She looked at her brother with eyes big from surprise, certainly not understanding what he was talking about. Rahim had to repeat three times everything he knew about the *baiga* and Jaisak's racers. At last a smile flashed across her face, pallid after the sleepless night, but then the smile faded as rapidly as it had appeared.

"I have no luck in life. Kish *Ata* will probably bear a girl and then there will be no *baiga* at all."

"No, there will be," Rahim insisted passionately. "Some days ago I could not fall asleep and heard how *baibishe* and Kumish said to Shauken that she will have a boy by all means. And then…"

He stammered into silence, and not knowing how else to console his sister, Rahim suddenly blurted out:

"And then Taras *Aga* and the *mayirs* promised to help Jaisak, if he gets into trouble. The Russians can do everything, and they will make *ata* marry you off to Jaisak." Again she looked at her brother with big misty eyes, while Rahim told her in a voice choked with emotion how they had been breaking the best horses from the herd, what wonderful stallions Jaisak had, and how rich the *mayirs* from Kosaral were. For the third month now they were feeding all the poor children of the *aul* with borshch and porridge, and Taras *Aga* had drawn him when he was staying in his earth house.

All this Kuljan had heard before, but now every word of her brother's was somehow merging in her heart into one string of events, the end of which glimmered in a light of great hope.

After the departure of Zulkarnai's messenger, Djantemir prepared to ride into the steppe at long last to have a look at the racers that had been picked for the *baiga*.

The first trial races lasted from morning till midday. In the afternoon the rest of the horses were saddled, and it was off into the steppe again.

"Who do you wish to ride the third pair of horses, *aga*?" Jaisak asked. "Rahim is still a boy. I permit him to ride only the gray ones you have seen in the morning. The rest are so vicious and strong Rahim won't stay in the saddle for long, and the day is short now: the third race will fall for the night, and wolves roam in the steppe."

"Why didn't you tell me right away that you needed one more rider?" Djantemir grew angry abruptly.

"I suggested Ismagul to them, *ata*, but they did not dare take him without your permission," Rahim cut in resolutely. "We've been expecting you any day. Although Tsmagul is only one year my senior, he's the strongest among the boys of the *aul*. And he knows how to keep his mouth shut. Jaisak here does not permit me to mount any other horses, as if I were a woman," he added cautiously.

"What do you think, Jaisak? Will Ismagul cope with the task or not? He seems not a bad horseman to me."

"I think he's all right," Jaisak said, seeing Rahim's desperate gestures behind his father's back. "He's quite a good horseman."

"All right, I agree. But if Ismagul breaks his neck or starts wagging his tongue, you'll be responsible to me for that," Djantemir concluded. "Now let me have a look at your stallions and let this little devil have a ride."

Djantemir was pleased with Jaisak's job, praised Taijan, and slapped his son's shoulder, calling him a *jigit* for the first time. But when he left, Rahim confided to Jaisak:

"You and Taijan galloped at hot haste, but I kept back your horses so they wouldn't outrun my father's. I swear by my honor, Jaisak, that there are no racers to equal yours."

8. THE RAFFLE

The supply train arrived at the end of January.

This time it was not a little caravan with two field guns or fifty Cossacks and two guard companies, but a thousand-strong troop with a huge flock of sheep and three hundred sleighs carrying food, men, their belongings, mail, and assorted freight of a military and civilian nature.

Butakov's expedition received a sizable part of the supplies, along with fresh news.

All the men congratulated Butakov on receiving the rank of captain-lieutenant. The expedition also learned that he was elected to full membership of the Russian Geographic Society. This was recognition of his merits as a scholarly researcher, traveler and explorer.

Werner was also radiant with joy: he had been promoted to the rank of warrant officer, which was the first step on his road to freedom. He ardently thanked Butakov for the recommendation and wonderful reference.

Shevchenko had his share of pleasant news too. He received

a long and amiable letter from Lizohub, a parcel with warm underwear, a set of oil paints, medicines, and various small personal items. There was also a letter from Lazarevsky and Chernishov mailed from St. Petersburg. They had sent him some money and informed him that they had been to Orlov who at first did not want to hear anything about him, but on reading his letters and learning of his illness, he promised to forward an inquiry to Orenburg and Orsk on the poet's conduct and attitude "with the object of alleviating his fate."

All these letters had been written in spring and had been lying at Orsk throughout the summer and autumn, but for Shevchenko the most important thing was that his friends remembered him and were doing everything they could to have him freed. Repnina's letter was also filled with warm sincere words of sympathy; she prayed for him every day and promised to intercede for him with Orlov and others as soon as she went to St. Petersburg.

He reread these lines with tears of gratitude, and in his heart there mounted a hope he was still afraid to cling to — the hope of a bright future.

Maksheiev was in an excited mood, because he was being recalled to Orenburg. He quickly took to processing his surveys and sketching the maps of the islands and parts of the shorelines he had plotted. One copy of the maps had to remain in the files of the expedition, and the other was to go to the headquarters of the Orenburg Military District where work on a military-topographical map was underway.

The days were extremely short, Maksheiev worked only in the daytime; he got up at dawn, while Shevchenko left the earth house lest he interfere with his friend's work.

Fort Raïm was the farthest point the supply train had to reach. On arrival, the people, horses and even camels were usually so exhausted by the long trek that they had to rest three weeks before returning to Orenburg.

But this time the respite had been doubled, because a general came with the train to make an inspection and a full audit of the fort. Accompanying him was a tax inspector who had to impose the *yassak* on the *auls* in the area and levy it. A full infantry battalion arrived as well to relieve the one that had been there for the past two years.

The tax inspector **Korsakov** was a clear-eyed man. Concerned with the interests of the state though he was, he did not forget his own interests either. The covered wagon he rode in was followed by two pairs of sleighs loaded with pig-iron and bronze cauldrons, samovars, basins and drinking bowls, sacks with flour and sugar, crates with rolls of calico, cheap silk, velveteen, knives, lace, large glittering buttons the Kazakh women used to adorn their sleeveless jackets, needles and other small wares. This cargo was under the charge of his serf, lackey and steward Trokhimovich.

On seeing that Raïm was full of Orenburg officials in whose presence it was awkward to ply his trade, Korsakov at first traveled to the most outlying *auls* and only after two weeks did return to the outskirts of Raïm.

Maksheiev stretched himself wearily. Midday was nearing, and from eight o'clock in the morning he had been keeping his shoulder to the collar on an elaborately detailed military-topographical map of **Barsa Kelmes Island**.

Suddenly heavy footfalls came from behind the door of the earth house; he heard a voice he did not recognize, and the next moment Korsakov, in a coat of wolf fur and a cap, literally tumbled through the open door, followed by Trokhimovich with two suitcases.

Maksheiev looked at him in surprise.

"Hallo, *mon cher*! Don't you recognize me? I'm Alexandr Ivanovich Korsakov. From St. Petersburg. I met you many a time at the home of Baroness Pritwitz."

"Oh, do excuse me! But you've come so unexpectedly... and we met such a long time ago," Maksheiev said and extended his hand, showing no particular joy at such an intrusion.

The guest threw off his coat and cap and applied his handkerchief to his mustache, eyelashes and brows turned gray with rime.

"Shove those suitcases under the table and come here," he ordered Trokhimovich and sat down opposite Maksheiev without ceremony. "It's my third day back from the *auls*. I have been wandering about Raïm... Abominable conditions of life here for sure! I have been sleeping on floors, with hay for bedding. I just could not stand it and ran away! On learning that you were here I was overjoyed. An old acquaintance would not refuse to take me in."

"I am afraid you will suffer discomfort here too. I do not live alone here, but with two comrades from the expedition."

"Well, well, I have been told you have let some soldiery into your place. They won't be worse off living in the barracks. After all, I am here only temporarily and on official business at that. I am no longer with the Board of Guardians in St. Petersburg. Now I am a tax inspector, guarding the interests of the state, so to speak."

Maksheiev felt a wave of rage rising in him at the words and tone of Korsakov, but he checked himself and asked just for the sake of propriety:

"You seemed to want to marry the daughter of the baroness. How are they — alive and healthy?"

"The marriage did not materialize. We fell out on business matters. As it proved, her estate was a majorat, and the exclusive right of its inheritance belonged to her eldest son. I am not a rich man, though. Why should I be counting coppers for the rest of my life? My wife is a Muscovite, born Solodnikova. She is pretty, studied at a finishing school, and has considerable money. Of course, every girl coming from a merchant's family finds it pleasant to become a noblewoman. I'll suffer in Orenburg for a year or two and then return to the capital again. I am sick of the provinces."

Maksheiev realized that it would be not that easy to get

rid of Korsakov. He removed the drawing board from table, and on seeing Shevchenko entering just at that moment, made a sweeping gesture in his direction, and said: 'Let me introduce you to Mr. Shevchenko, Professor of Painting at the University of Kiev and currently artist with the Aral scientific expedition."

Such an unexpected introduction confused Shevchenko, and he silently bowed to the guest.

"I am very pleased to meet you. Korsakov is my name, and I am an old friend of Alexei Ivanovich," Korsakov said, flashing his jagged, nicotine-stained teeth. "Dear Taras Grigorievich," Maksheiev addressed Shevenko with exaggerated politeness. "You are still in your coat, so would you please do me a favor: make arrangements to have lunch served as quickly as possible. Our guest must be very hungry after the journey, and I, frankly speaking, am too tired after this drafting business. During the meal I'll have some rest — and then it's back to the drawing pen again. You see, I am being recalled to Orenburg," he explained to Korsakov. "So I am in a hurry to have the drawings done, because otherwise I won't be able leave. Time flies and I have a good month to work yet."

In fifteen minutes a rich naval borshch and a tin of marinated fish appeared on the table, and Maksheiev poured out strong *starka* vodka. The guest did not leave the gesture unanswered and produced a bottle of *zubrovka* vodka. A conversation began. Korsakov told how a pack of wolves had shadowed the supply train along its trek. Maksheiev recalled the tiger hunt. The borshch was followed by a roasted hare Istomin had bagged the day before, then a boiling samovar was put on the table, and Shevchenko solemnly produced a bottle of real Jamaica rum.

"Where did you get that?" Maksheiev asked, surprised.

"I earned it. I did a portrait of one of the newly arrived officers, and apart from the agreed fee, he gave me this bottle and a wonderful frame for watercolors."

After the meal Shevchenko sat aside to finish his landscape

of the bay with the ice-bound schooner on a sandbank, while Maksheiev continued the conversation with Korsakov.

"My office is a really nasty one, *mon cher*," Korsakov complained, sipping his tea flavored with rum. "Here I've been wandering about the steppe for a whole year, levying taxes on the local savages. I'm slaving away, with no hope of earning any gratitude. And the main thing: I cannot make them pay the taxes in full. That's what I got from listening to my dear father-in-law. 'You go into the civil service,' he said, 'and rise to the rank of councilor of state, so that my daughter becomes the wife of a general. Then I'll load you with money!' And that's what he has a lot of, being a millionaire. But how can I achieve that rank when those Kirghiz devils never get out of debt? I've already gone so far as to have the debts cut almost by half, for which his Excellency recommended me for the Order of St. Anne.'

"Oh? But how did you achieve such brilliant results?" Maksheiev asked, pouring some more rum into the guest's cup of tea.

Korsakov had one cup too many during the meal and was talking too much.

"Very simply: by applying the whip. Imagine, there are such scoundrels that are prepared to die under the whip rather than pay taxes."

Shevchenko sat upright, blood gushed to his head, his fists balled against his will, but he restrained himself with great effort and picked up a brush again.

"Don't you really understand that no whip can wrest out of the beggars something they don't have?" Maksheiev asked.

"Oh, my dear chap, that's where you are wrong! All of them just pretend to be beggars. Believe me, my office is really a nasty one: I am sick of hearing their complaints, screams and the like. That's not what you officers have to deal with! You return from a military raid as rich men, whereas I have to live on my salary alone."

Maksheiev raised his eyebrows in surprise.

"What has a military raid got to do with levying taxes?"

Korsakov screwed up his eyes ironically.

"Have you really never taken part in such an operation?"

"No. I am a military engineer-topographer by education. In the Caucasus I saw some chance action. But here?"

"Oh, now I understand. Such a raid is not simply a punitive expedition against rebels. It's a campaign ... well, how should I put it...not so much to frighten as, above all, to... well, improve your business at the expense of those ... aliens."

"In other words, it's a marauding raid, or a *barimta*, as they call it here?" Maksheiev specified. "Why put it so bluntly?"

"And that's what you do in regard to beggars who live in tattered yurts, and who, as well as being naked, graze their hungry cattle in the snow-covered steppe? What baseness!"

Maksheiev jumped to his feet and paced quickly up and down the narrow earth house, bumping into bundles, his drawing board, and the suitcases of the uninvited guest. Korsakov smiled indulgently at the sight.

"What an idealist you are! I could have understood you, if you were sixteen years old or in your first year at university, but at the age of thirty it's — I beg your pardon — simply a quixotic way of seeing things!"

At that moment the door was opened silently, and Trokhmovich appeared on the threshold.

"Do you wish me to go to the Kirghiz to trade, sir?" he asked quietly, darting an uneasy glance at Maksheiev and Shevchenko. "They say there is an *aul* not far away from here."

"Of course, of course!" Korsakov answered with a smile. "You know yourself, so why ask about it? And don't forget about the furs."

"Who's that?" Maksheiev asked casually when Trokhimovich left.

Korsakov answered confusedly: "Well, let this be between you and me, *mon cher*. I am neither an officer nor a Cossack, and so I cannot get rich from a military raid. My wife holds her capital firmly in her grip, and I cannot get my teeth into it. The man you saw is my serf. He buys up sugar, flour, calico, cauldrons and other trifles in Irbit and then sells them to the Kirghiz. He accompanies me as a sort of outsider, so that I am not officially involved, so to speak."

"And what about the money he gets from those sales? Who gets it?" Maksheiev asked in a chilly tone.

"Oh, it comes to me," Korsakov answered merrily and with shameless candor.

That moment somebody pulled at the door hesitantly.

"Who is there? Come in!" Maksheiev called out.

Jaisak entered. He made a low bow to Maksheiev and Shevchenko and stopped silently at the threshold.

"What can I do for you, old chap?" Korsakov asked, carelessly crossing his legs.

"People say you need fox furs, *yassak* chief. I have some. I was in Raïm. You were not there and came here."

"I see. Yes, we take furs, if they are worth it. Show them to me!" Korsakov carried on idly as before.

Jaisak pulled two wonderful silver-fox furs out of his bosom, Korsakov's eyes flashed with a greedy glint. He took a fur, huffed at it, stroked it up and down, and then asked with affected indifference:

"How much do you ask for them?"

"I don't know. As much as you will give me, *yassak* chief. I have to pay the *yassak* and for the *baiga*... I need a lot of money."

"How many furs have you got?" Korsakov interrupted him disdainfully. He was not interested in Jaisak's affairs in the least.

"I have a lot of them. Maybe two times ten or three times that much. I have to count them."

"Thirty? All right then, I'll give you fifty kopecks for each."

"*Oi*, chief!" Jaisak gave a small scream. "A Bukhara merchant gives three rubles for a small fur, but these... They are big winter fox."

"Go to your Bukhara merchants then." Korsakov calmly turned away from Jaisak and sipped from his cup which had more rum in it than tea.

Maksheiev exchanged angry glances with Shevchenko, while Jaisak shifted from foot to foot and looked with despair at his wonderful fox furs.

"I beg your pardon… but the furs are of large fox and of excellent quality," Maksheiev broke into the conversation, trying to maintain a proper tone.

"You can have them if you like them that much," Korsakov replied in French lest Jaisak understand him. "But I'm not that rich as to squander money."

Maksheiev wanted to buy a fur or two at first and even readied for his pocket, but then he remembered that he had a long, almost two-month journey ahead of him and his hand stopped halfway. The gesture was not lost on Korsakov.

"After all, in Moscow you'll get no less than sixty rubles for them," Maksheiev remarked.

In the meantime, Shevchenko had inconspicuously pulled at Jaisak's sleeve and gestured him to take back the fox furs. But something extremely serious must have happened to Jaisak, because he did not heed Shevchenko, heaved a sigh of hopelessness and shook his head in disagreement. He listened intently to the foreign tongue, his eyes straying from Korsakov to Maksheiev and from Maksheiev to the *yassak* chief, and then he suddenly turned to Maksheiev:

"Take it, *mayir*! I'll give it away for two rubles a piece. I need the money badly."

Everyone was silent. Maksheiev did not have the heart to accept the furs for such a minute price, and he really did not have more money to pay. Korsakov smiled ironically.

"All right!" he broke the silence abruptly. "The chief is taking pity on you: I offer two rubles for each piece of fur."

With the mien of a benefactor he extended Jaisak four rubles — not in silver, but in bills, which was considerably cheaper than in silver. Jaisak heaved a sigh again, took the money, and left with a hanging head. Shevchenko picked up his coat and rushed out to catch up with Jaisak. When the door slammed shut behind Shevchenko, Korsakov slapped his knee and roared with laughter.

"That's a truly sensational bargain. In Moscow I'll get not sixty but one hundred rubles in silver for each fur. Take a look what beauties they are. What rate of profit does that make?"

"It's dishonest!" Maksheiev cried.

"But I've just dealt with a savage! God himself decreed that these savages serve us as a source of profit. What makes you blow up like that, *mon ami*?"

"It's a shame, sir! Instead of us becoming a source of enlightenment, an example of honor, duty and justice, you…"

Korsakov burst into a roar of laughter: "Ha-ha-ha, my dear friend. They don't even understand such words. These are primitive people out of the Stone Age! Just travel around the steppe and go into their camps — you won't find a single cesspit or outhouse anywhere. Even a bird does not soil its nest like these savages their own yurts…"

"Did you see many lavatories and cesspits in our villages?" Maksheiev interrupted him sharply. "It's precisely you and the likes of you who are to be blamed for that. We must teach and be an example for them, not plunder them and bring them to their graves with whips, bribes and fraud, my dear sir!"

Korsakov jumped to his feet.

"Wh-at? Just repeat what you said?" he screamed in a piercing falsetto.

Maksheiev grew pale from rage.

"I will do so with pleasure!" he rapped out the words pointedly. "You swindle and engage in the dirtiest and basest speculation and trading which sullies the honor of a nobleman and the uniform you wear!"

Unexpectedly for himself, Maksheiev took the empty bottle of rum standing on the table, and swinging it like a cudgel, shouted at the top of his voice:

"Get out! Get out of here, you scoundrel!"

Korsakov's arrogance and brash self-confidence vanished in a trice. He recoiled with fright, his mouth gaping for air, snatched his coat and cap off the nail, and made himself scarce, forgetting the fox furs.

After regaining his breath, Maksheiev put the bottle back on the table, threw Korsakov's suitcases outdoors, drank his by now cold tea at one gulp, placed his drawing board on the table again, picked up his drawing pen, and bent over his work.

Shevchenko caught up with Jaisak a long way beyond the barracks.

"Jaisak, wait a minute! What's happened?" Shevchenko shouted, grabbing the young herder by the shoulder. "Why did you give the furs away to that swindler? I pulled at your sleeve, winked at you, but…"

Jaisak stopped and, jarred back to reality.

"There's trouble, Taras *Aga*! Ibrai died. We had his father's messengers at our *aul* yesterday evening. Iskhak and the others left for his funeral, and Shauken bore a boy during the night."

"What's so horrible about that?" the poet asked, surprised. "Ibrai died — so God rest his soul, but there'll be the *baiga* you have been dreaming about all the time. You must be happy, not sad."

Jaisak gave Shevchenko a sorrowful look.

"And Moldabai?"

"What Moldabai?"

"Ibrai's relative. That old man who wants to marry Kuljan. He'll ruin her life. But it makes no difference to Djantemir, because he does not want to give away the advance he got as part of the bride money."

"Oh damn it!" Shevchenko cursed. "And when will that Moldabai show up?"

"By law, only when the year of tears ends after Ibrai's death, that is, after the funeral rites, but …"

"That's great!" Shevchenko almost shouted for joy. "First of all, nobody can engage her, since she is in mourning, and during that time the old fiancé might kick the bucket forty times over.

Secondly, within this time you can make a lot of money and grow rich."

"Grow rich?" the young man questioned with a bitter smile. "I need the money now. A lot of money. But where can I get it? Did you see how much the *yassak* chief paid me for the furs? Back at Jaman Kala, Isai Pasha and Meshka *Mayir* and even the bald *mayir* always paid me a red bill.* In Orenburg they give you even more. But how can I reach that place? From Jaman Kala it was a three-day journey, but from here…"

Jaisak waved his hand in hopelessness, and added:

"Besides, our laws are not always abided by. Moldabai is an imam. It's enough for him to say, 'This is permitted!' and nobody will utter a word against him. Even now he can come here, without waiting for the end of the year of mourning. So there is no one to stand up for Kuljan. Even three years won't be enough for me to acquire the sheep for the bride money, for the wedding, and to support my mother and wife. Oh, Taras *Aga*, there's no place where a poor man can be happy!"

Shevchenko took sincere pity on the young herder. He had to cheer up Jaisak somehow.

"What an impatient character you are!" Shevchenko said. "Better half an egg than an empty shell. Don't carry on like a woman. It's no sweeter for me either, but I don't shed tears all the time. That is, I did cry once and a lot at that, but my tears have already dried. Now I'm angry, and that takes the load off my chest. If you want me to help you, I will. Don't sell any more furs to that scoundrel! Bring me twenty furs tomorrow. I'll try to gain for them much more than you: I won't sell them for less than ten rubles a piece, that's for sure."

When Shevchenko returned to the earth house, he did not see either Korsakov or his suitcases there anymore.

"Where is our guest?" he asked.

"I've chucked him out," Maksheiev answered, and his temper

---

* Ten-ruble bill. — *Tr.*

flaring up again, he said with agitation: "Jaisak is thrashing like a bird in a cage, and here this swashbuckler grows rich on his sweat! I was short of throwing a bottle at him."

"To tell you the truth my hands itched as well to kick him out into the cold," the poet said with a laugh. "All right, the hell with him! We must really help Jaisak. The money I've been sent is not much, but nonetheless I'll give him ten rubles of what I have."

"I'm in no better position before leaving," Maksheiev confessed. "Still, we've got to do something for him."

"That's exactly how my friends once broke their heads over how to buy me from my landowner Engelhardt," Shevchenko said with a grim smile. "Brüllow did a portrait of Zhukovsky and it was raffled off. The proceeds were enough to buy my freedom and keep me going for some time at the beginning."

"A raffle?" Maksheiev said. "Why, that's a wonderful idea. But what could *we* raffle off?"

He looked at the wall and his eyes stopped at the hunting rifle Pospelov and Istomin had glanced at with envy many a time. Was it really worth taking back to Orenburg? He would not need it either on his journey or at his former place of service. And what kind of a hunter was he anyway?

"We'll raffle off this rifle to make Jaisak happy!" Maksheiev exclaimed. "Just to spite that scoundrel Korsakov! The rifle is absolutely new, and I paid exactly two hundred rubles for it. The only thing I don't know is how such lotteries are held. So please help me, since you're such an experienced hand at it."

"That's very simple. Write a list of all the acquaintances you know at Kosaral and Raïm. Let everyone pay you the price of the ticket right away and put his signature opposite his name. Then we'll make the tickets. All of them will be blank, except for one which will have the inscription: hunting rifle. Let everyone get together during the next holiday we have on the calendar and draw the tickets out of the basket or bag. Someone will draw the lucky ticket."

"Wonderful," Maksheiev said merrily and immediately got

down to compiling the list of the avid hunters from among the expedition members and the Ural Cossacks.

The next morning, taking his hunting rifle as a good bait, Maksheiev went round the men written in the list. Pospelov and Istomin bought three tickets each at once, from among the sailors there were only two who were tempted by the rifle, whereas the Ural Cossacks were filled with admiration at the sight of the piece, and the tickets sold like hot cakes.

"The reeds around here are a real paradise for hunters," the Cossacks said as they paid for the tickets.

Altogether there were eighty tickets priced at five rubles each. After the midday meal Maksheiev ordered his horse saddled and galloped off to Raim to tempt its garrison with the prize. Here the hunting rifle had the same success, while the story of the recent tiger hunt produced such a tremendous impression that Maksheiev returned to Kosaral with only two tickets left.

Shevchenko did not waste his time either. In the morning Jaisak brought him twenty furs, and the first thing the poet did was to go round all the homes of the married couples in Raim. The wife of the newly appointed commandant Damis paid twenty-five rubles for two furs to make herself a coat collar and a muff. At another home he sold two more furs. Even the Armenian sutler bought one big fur for his incredibly corpulent wife Annush.

The twelve furs he still had were sold off to the ardent admirers of the dark-complexioned local belle, Liudochka Tsibisova.

Shevchenko went about his trade in a subtle and diplomatic way. On learning that Liudochka was to celebrate her eighteenth birthday in a week, he met every one of her suitors as if by chance, and once he was alone with the beau, he engaged him in approximately the following conversation, hiding a cunning glint in his eyes:

"My dear young man, you and I live in such a wild, out-of-the-way nook where you cannot buy a decent present for a young lady. Liudochka will be eighteen in a couple of days, and here there's no delicate perfume, expensive candy or live flowers to get by. I got hold of a wonderful thing by chance: a Kirghiz I know has to pay taxes without delay, but he hasn't the money. So he brought me this wonderful fur. He's giving it away for a song. It's grand fur, I tell you! Buy it: it'll be simply a godsend for you."

At that he would produce the silver-fox fur, and the beau swallowed the bait without fail.

"But please do not so much as utter a word about it," Shevchenko warned. "Someone might get the same idea, and the effect of the present will be lost on Liudochka."

In this way all the furs were sold, and at the last moment even Maksheiev bought one as a present for his wife.

On Liudochka's birthday every one of her loyal wooers gave her a fur as a present. There was a lot of laughter and banter on that point, but neither the beaus nor Liudochka or her parents had anything against such a miraculous influx of lavish furs. The parents realized at once that the furs would be a real treasure in a big city and thanked Shevchenko from the bottom of their hearts, after which, having treated the furs with tobacco against moths, they left two pieces for Liudochka's collar and muff and hid the rest in a hope chest where they were gathering a dowry of their "princess."

The next Sunday the raffle was held. The winning ticket was drawn by a sailor who, then and there, sold the rifle for fifty rubles to Pospelov, and on Monday, as it had been agreed upon, Jaisak arrived from Kosaral.

He was in a state of dazed torpor at the sight of the heap of bills, silver, gold and copper coins lying on the table. Tongue-tied, he looked now at Maksheiev, then at Shevchenko.

"How much of the *yassak* do you have to pay?" Shevchenko asked, delighting in the impression all that money had produced on the young man.

"A ruble and a half," Jaisak forced the answer in a choked voice. "Father paid only a half of that last year."

"But you don't have to pay taxes for the dead," Maksheiev remarked.

Jaisak nodded in agreement.

"The *yassak* chief demands it right away, and threatens to whip me, if I don't pay on time. He gave me three days to think it over."

"To hell with the dratted scoundrel! Let him have your father's share of the tax. That'll be two rubles and a quarter. And another fifty kopecks as a fine on the tax. In all, it comes out to three rubles. How much would you have to pay to enter the *baigai*?"

"I don't know yet. The *baiga* will be held after the child is one month old," Jaisak answered falteringly as before, as if joy still had not penetrated to the depths of his heart.

"All that money is yours," Maksheiev said. "We'll count it now, and you can take it with you. Do you have anywhere to hide it well?"

"I'll give it to *apa*. We have no other place to hide it."

"It's better if it stays with us. Take three rubles to pay the *yassak* and some more to buy sheep at once. They say that people are now selling sheep throughout all the *auls* to pay the tax. You can buy two or three hundred if you want."

It was only now that Jaisak sensed with his heart that fortune had visited him at long last. It would bring him freedom and win him the girl he loved so passionately.

"*Oi, Mayir* Maksi! *Oi*, Taras *Aga*. You are like two great magicians," his words ran into each other from excitement.

Something constricted his throat, tears grew in his eyes, and his heart throbbed like that of a lark hovering over its nest.

"You two did as much to me as only Allah could have done!"

He clenched his fists and pressed them to his chest, as if afraid lest his heart jump out of the chest. Excitement robbed him of speech, and he looked wordlessly at his friends. To hide and contain their emotions, Maksheiev and Shevchenko started counting the money. Maksheiev wound every one hundred-ruble bill with a thread, while Shevchenko sorted the coins and arranged them in neat stacks starting with the bright yellow imperials and half-imperials of gold and the white silver one-ruble coins to the heavy, dark five-kopeck pieces of copper.

Jaisak took only three rubles to pay the tax and fifty to buy the sheep; the rest — a fortune of six hundred rubles — was buried under the floor, and its existence would be the knowledge only of the dwellers of the earth house from now on.

"Mind you don't tell anybody how much money you have and where it is, because the Khivans might attack, kill us, and plunder you," Shevchenko and Maksheiev frightened him intentionally. "If anyone in the *aul* asks you where you got the money to buy the sheep, tell them that the *mayirs* bought your fox furs for five rubles a piece, and that's what made you rich."

Jaisak rushed back to the *aul* on wings to share his joy with his mother and, of course, with Kuljan too.

Kuljan had been weeping for days at the thought of her marriage to Moldabai. But on learning of Jaisak's good fortune, she smiled for the first time in days and at once started praying for the health of Taras *Aga* and the "Mayir Golden Mustache," as Maksheiev was called by the Kirghiz.

9. THE BIG TOI

For Djantemir the birth of a son was a great joy. When the infant was three weeks old, Djantemir sent out his *jigits* to all the near and outlying *auls* to broadcast the news and invite the people to the big *toi*, while the women, relatives and servants were ordered to make preparations to receive the guests.

Djantemir wavered for a long time in his choice of a messenger to the Russian chiefs in Raïm and Kosaral. Out of respect for them he'd have to send *axakals* or one of his sons, but Iskhak had left for Ibrai's funeral, while Baisali and Undasin did not know the Russian language and the *axakals* did not know it either. To send Rahim he did not dare, since the *mayirs* might take offense on seeing such a young courier.

"Send me, *ata*!" Rahim insisted relentlessly. "They invited me to their place the last time. They are not as haughty as our *bais*. I'll take along only Jaisak who is so liked by Taras *Aga*."

Without finding any better alternative, Djantemir agreed in the end.

The first thing Rahim and Jaisak did when they arrived in Kosaral was to see Butakov. They found him in his earth house with all the former dwellers of the wardroom. Rahim took off his shaggy cap and made a ceremonious bow like a real envoy.

"Glorious and highly respected chiefs and *mayirs*," he began in a solemn mien, but the next moment he faltered and blurted out, mixing Kazakh and Russian words: "Let's go, *mayirs*, to our *aul* for a big *tol*. There'll be a big *ait*, too. Very lavish. *Akyns* will come. A *baiga* will be! My *ata* Djantemir invites all of you! I ask you very much — let's go! *Ata* ordered me to bow real low to you and ask you very much! Let's go to the *aul*!"

Butakov smiled unwittingly, but lest he offend the boy, he quenched his smile and answered in a serious tone:

"Tell your father Djantemir that we are very grateful for his invitation and will come by all means, the more so since Alexei Ivanovich" — he motioned toward Maksheiev — "likes fine horses and has a good knowledge of horse breeding. For him a *baiga* is the best type of entertainment. On behalf of all of us I thank you and your father for the invitation and say, 'Rahmet!' as you do in your tongue!"

The guests started arriving in the morning. Baisali, Undasin and Iskhak met them in the steppe, a hundred *sazhens* from the yurts, and after exchanging greetings, saw them to the house of Djantemir. The other guests arriving from afar were first invited into a yurt where they could have a rest after the journey, and only then did they go and see Djantemir.

The *aul* soon turned into a noisy and merry place. Camp-fires were on everywhere as the women cooked mutton and *manty*, and boiled water for tea. The young people walked around in groups, making the acquaintance of their peers from the other *auls*. Here and there they jostled or started playing games.

At midday the men from Kosaral arrived, followed almost immediately by the guests from Raïm. Djantemir himself went out to meet the *mayirs* and solemnly saw them to his house.

The army and naval officers were in dress uniform, and the officials wore their civil servants' uniforms and decorations. Even Werner, on Butakov's permission, wore his student's uniform from the Warsaw Technological College, while Shevchenko donned his old coat tail.

The guests merrily greeted Djantemir and Shauken who after a long pause waddled out of her room with the infant in her arms. The mariners presented the happy parents a beautifully polished cradle made by the ship's carpenter and a big veil of curtain lace against mosquitoes.

In the delta of the Syr Darya, with its placid inlets, numerous lakes and impenetrable thickets of reeds, mosquitoes were a prodigious nuisance, which made children suffer most. Realizing what an amazingly useful present he had received, Djantemir thanked Butakov and all the mariners profusely.

The guests were invited to the table for a lavish and tasty treat. Apart from the traditional mutton, there were also veal, game, and fish in gravy. This was followed by Oriental sweets, nuts, dried apricots, sultanas and almonds. For the officers and the other Russians there was wine, vodka, cognac and rum.

The *axakals* remained silent for a long time, as they sipped their tea, until a *bai* from the Irghiz clan spoke up, placing his empty drinking bowl on the table:

"In my opinion, Kudaibergen knows horses best of all and will be an honest and impartial judge."

"Wonderful!" Djantemir remarked. "But we need not one but three judges. Whom will you bestow your trust upon, *axakals?*"

The old men exchanged whispers. Some wanted to elect Djantemir, but others disagreed: since his horses were to take part in the *baiga*, he could not be an impartial judge. A number of names were proposed, but each was immediately met with one objection or another. In the end, a gaunt old man in a dazzling yellow gown of heavy Persian silk decisively cut short the whispers and low-voiced arguments.

"Choose Djangirbai and Kaskarbai. They are honest people and have a good understanding of horses!" he declared.

At first the proposition came as a surprise. Everybody raised their heads and sat silently for a minute or so, then they laughed with their toothless mouths and nodded agreement.

"That's right! They are good people! How didn't it come to our minds earlier?"

Both Kaskarbai and Djangirbai were elected unanimously.

The three judges got to their feet of one accord and went to the adjoining room to hold counsel. They had to decide on the procedure of the *baiga*. Occasionally not separate horses but the best racers from each clan's herd were entered in a *baiga*. In such cases the prize went to the clan which owned the herd. There were also free competitions when every Kazakh even a servant, *tyulengut* or semi-slave, could enter his horse with the hope of falling into luck. The influential *bais* did not favor such independent contestants and sedulously protected the fame of their herds, but today, after passing by the long horse lines, the judges had seen a great multitude of wonderful racers of unknown ownership, and barring them from the competition went against the judges' compunction as real connoisseurs of good horses.

Besides, the judges had to determine the entry price in the *baiga*, and agree on the division of the prize and the number of racers each owner could enter.

In the meantime, a big crowd had gathered by the windows of Djanteniir's house, eagerly waiting for the final decision of the judges.

Kaskerbai came from a poor family. Throughout the entire steppe from the Ural to Alatau he had gained fame as the best herder and horseman of Kazakhstan. He never asked whose horse it was that flew the first over the furrow of the finish line, but always looked whether it was a fine horse and whether it could rival the best of the best mounts of the Big Steppe. When Kudaibergen and Djangirbai proposed to double the entry price for the *baiga*, Kaskerbai immediately stopped them with a convincing objection:

"A *baiga* is a trial for a horse, not the horseman. Let more light-footed horses take part in the *baiga*, and the pockets of their owners will become heavy without our assistance."

In respect of his experience, the *axakals* did not argue, and the three judges went out onto the porch to announce their decision. The crowd froze and then surged ahead like a sea wave.

As the oldest, Kudaibergen had to speak first. He stepped forth and announced in a voice that was unusually ringing for his age:

"It is not clan with clan, but horse with horse that compete in this *baiga* for the joy and glory of those who reared it, because this *baiga* is held on the occasion of a joyous event — the birth of man. So let the life of the newly born be joyous, satisfied, and merry as today's *toi*."

A noise of approval rolled through the crowd which again lapsed into tense silence when Kudaibergen stepped back and Djangirbai came forward.

"For each horse the owner pays fourteen sheep or two cows: if he has not sheep or cows, he pays one bull camel or one cow camel. Those who do not want to pay in cattle, can do so with money: five rubles in silver or seven rubles in bills."

As soon as he finished he stepped back, and Kaskerbai continued loudly:

"The horses of one age accepted to the *baiga* form up in one line. On the sign of the master of ceremonies they will race to the *aul* along one and the same course, without deviating from it or impeding the progress of the others. The race course must be straight as a taut string, marked with pegs, without any obstacles whatsoever, and twenty *versts* long. The two- and three-year-old colts run in the first heat during the first half of the day. Horses that are four or more years old run in the afternoon."

After Kaskerbai, Kudaibergen announced the final conditions of the race:

"Nobody has the right to enter more than a pair of horses in the *baiga* — only one pair to each heat."

The crowd droned either with approval or displeasure — it was difficult to tell. That instant a young ringing, excited voice asked:

"And how will the prizes be distributed?"

The judges raised their arms, demanding silence, and Kudaibergen announced:

"The horse that comes first will be awarded half of the cattle paid as the entry price. The horse that finishes second gets a half of the cattle that remain from the prize of the first horse, that is, a quarter of all the cattle. The third horse gets a half of what remains after the prizes for the first two horses are paid out, that is, one eighth part, while the last eighth part will be distributed between the fourth and the fifth horse — not in equal parts, but two sheep out of every three for the fourth horse, and the last sheep for the fifth.

"And now, *jigits* and *axakals,* take your horses to the review ground and herd the cattle to the *baiga!*"

The horses were lined up like at a cavalry parade. Not completely broken yet, the steppe racers had barely grown accustomed to bridle and saddle and could not stand still beside their neighbors, which they tried either to bite or kick. Their saddles were straddled mostly by teenagers who kept their mounts in check with effort. It was only Jaisak's horses that stood still — the snow-white, thin-legged Akbozad and his younger brother Karkerat which was black all over as if he were chiseled out of black marble. They were used to each other and had frequently stood in the steppe with crossed necks; their neighbor, Djantemir's beauty Whiteleg, was also well known to them. He was not picking on Jaisak's favorites but only bobbed his head, irritated by his neighbor, a red-pelted colt which time and again pushed or tried to kick him.

To their right and left stood clusters of onlookers. They all rode horses which were barred from the *baiga* for one reason or another. But most of the guests had already galloped ahead and disappeared beyond the horizon. It was much more interesting to stop far off in the steppe near the racing course and watch the passing hoofed avalanche in which the potential winners could already be discerned. Of the judges there was only Kaskarbai on this stretch of the course. He, too, was on horseback, while Djangirbai and Kudaibergen were waiting for the winners at the *aul*. Rahim kept his eyes glued on Kaskarbai. Presently he raised his pistol. A cracking shot ripped the air — and the line of horses immediately dashed forward; only one horse reared, trying to throw off the rider, but he did not get confused, whipped his mount which then seemed to tear itself loose from the ground in one big bound and joined the others in a thunderous gallop.

The straight line broke up at once. At first the horses raced in one bunch similar to a shower of meteorites gradually stretching in a long tail like a comet, out of which Akbozad broke quickly, followed by someone's silvery dapple-gray, Whiteleg, and two red-pelted racers from Ishimbai's kin.

Rahim was riding Akbozad.

"Giddap! Giddap!" the mounted rooters shouted frenziedly and whipped their horses lest they lag behind the *baiga*.

Kaskarbai was racing outside the peg line, watching that none of the guests stray onto the broad race course. From behind the horizon appeared the horsemen from the *aul* to meet the *baiga*.

But where had Ismagul with his Karkerat disappeared to? Oh, there he was! Ismagul was slowly gaining on Rahim. That was a good development! If not one, so the other would be the winner! Rahim was already hearing the loud pit-a-pat of Karkerat's spleen, and then came Ismagul's voice:

"Drive him on, Rahim! We'll win!"

Suddenly Akbozad slipped on a heap of thawed clay; he did not hit the ground but went down for a moment like a dog on his haunches. Rahim tumbled over the horse's head and landed in the snow covered with a prickly frozen crust, badly bruising his hands and face. Slightly stunned, he nonetheless made himself jump to his feet with superhuman effort. He ran up to Akbozad standing a dozen paces away from him.

That was the end!

Whiteleg, Karkerat, and the dapple-gray shot past him. Ismagul shouted something and waved his hand. Never mind! Rahim was again in the saddle. And again the wind was whistling sharply in his ears. As before, Akbozad was flying ahead. Presently Red flashed by on the left and disappeared somewhere behind. Then the dapple-gray was racing alongside and started slowly falling behind. Rahim did not spare his snow-white beauty. He kept whipping away at its sides, while his voice, faltering and filled with despair, implored:

"My dearest dear! Make it faster! Faster! Save my sister! Save her!"

The horse did not understand the words, but in the boy's pleadingly insistent voice Akbozad discerned both torment and despair — and the wind whistled the sharper in Rahim's ears.

From behind his back he heard shouts, cursing, and the furious lashes of whips. Never mind! Forward! Forward! At any price forward!

Red had been behind just moments ago. Now he was galloping side by side with Akbozad. Presently he started falling behind. There were only Whiteleg and Ismagul on his Karkerat up front. Suddenly Ismagul turned round and lashed Whiteleg across the muzzle. The suddenness of the blow made Whiteleg jump aside, and the road was open. Now there was only Ismagul in the front, but Karkerat also belonged to Jaisak after all.

The white yurts of the *aul* came into sight. Akbozad was losing breath but did not slacken his speed. Whiteleg again showed up slightly behind on the right. One of his eyes was bloodshot; he shook his head from pain but could not outdistance Akbozad, much as he tried. Karkerat still held his leading position.

At the same moment Whieleg managed to overtake Rahim's racer. Ahead was the black furrow dug the day before.

Karkerat was the first to fly over the finish line, then came Whiteleg and Akbozad.

Deafening shouts hailed the winners, behind which came the rest of the contestants to which nobody was paying any attention by now.

Bruised, offended, his cap lost somewhere along the race course, Rahim jumped to the ground.

Rahim came in third. But Karkerat was first — so this was a victory for their cause after all. Jaisak came running to him and Ismagul. His face was of a bloodless pallor, but a happy smile touched the corners of his pale lips when the judges went up the porch of the *bai*'s house after a brief counsel and announced the names of the winners — the horses and their masters.

"Wonderful," Maksheiev said, counting up quickly in his mind. "Jaisak earned about one hundred and fifty sheep, that's half the bride money."

The *toi* unfolded by the rules of a custom developed throughout centuries. The carefree young people danced and made merry. Musicians strummed their *dombras*. Merry banter and pert jokes evoked unbridled roars of laughter. A heavy *jamba* of pure gold was fixed to a pole and archers shot at it with long arrows fletched with eagle feathers. *Jigits* grappled in wrestling bouts, demonstrating their strength and agility, matched their skills in wielding yatagans in mock fencing, and the rest of the time pursued the girls and women with attention.

When the songs died away, there followed fantastic fairy tales or heroic lays about the glorious *batyrs* of long ago.

There was no end to tea drinking, and the *jigits* tirelessly carried deep bowls with cooked mutton back and forth among the guests. In the yurt that had been converted into kitchen, the women worked night and day. The poor people were especially happy for the occasion to still their perpetual pangs of hunger for three days in a row. They ate everything that was served and could be eaten, even gnawing at the tendons that remained on the bones and sucking out the marrow, throwing away to the dogs only what the strongest teeth could not cut.

Abdrahman, Azat and another two *akyns* from the outlying *auls* arrived at the *toi* on the afternoon of its very first day. Afraid lest Abdrahman recall old offenses and take revenge through scathing satire, Djantemir himself went to meet the famed *akyn*, helped him down from his horse, deferentially held the bridle, and seated him in his house opposite the door together with the *mayirs* and the most respected guests.

On seeing Abdrahman, Shevchenko greeted him with joy. Since the day Shevchenko met him outside Orsk, he had developed a great liking for the old *akyn*, and this liking grew the more after Jaisak's story of the famous *akyn* having quarreled with Djantemir and composed a satirical song about the fat *bai*. Shevchenko wanted Abdrahman to sing him the famous songs of Utemisov which fired and called on all the tribes of the boundless Kazakh steppe to struggle for freedom. These songs, as Shevchenko had heard from former participants in the crushing of Isatai Taimanov's movement, were fiery appeals of wrath and hymns of struggle for freedom.

Leading the *akyn* into such a conversation in the presence of the Raïm officers was impossible. They had a chance to talk a little in the farthest room of the *bai*'s house where they were left eye to eye, but for Iskhak it proved difficult to find the proper Russian words when the conversation drifted beyond the notions of everyday life. Because of this handicap Shevchenko and Abdrahman almost did not understand each other. Besides, Iskhak could not be completely trusted.

The conversation took on a turn for the better when Jaisak arrived. Distressed for some reason and nervous, he invited both men to his yurt, and there, far away from any treacherous ears, started to complain bitterly:

"Djantemir's gone mad. He pounced on me, stamped his feet, and bawled me out for letting Rahim ride my horse. I kept my mouth shut: I could not possibly tell him that his son was saving Kuljan from Moldabai."

"Help us understand each other," Shevchenko asked and, after Jaisak had regained his calm, explained what songs he would like to hear from Abdrahman.

"Yes, such songs once resounded in our land," the old *akyn* said with a sigh. "But our freedom was crushed, and with the songs of Utemisov's great soul. And now it is only here" — he brought a palm against his chest — "that those half-forgotten songs still live. I will sing them to you and tell you about the secret dreams of our steppe."

The three of them stayed in Jaisak's yurt for a long Lime, forgetting about the heady merriment outside, the sumptuous midday meal that had been consumed without their presence, and the wine and cognac Djantemir had not begrudged to enhance his friendship with the Russian authorities.

At Abdrahman's request, Shevchenko recited some of his poems in a melodious recitative imitating his favorite Ukrainian folk tunes.

None of them knew that both Butakov and Maksheiev were looking everywhere for Shevchenko to tell him of their imminent departure.

An hour earlier a messenger from Raïm had galloped in to inform the officers that an urgent order had been received to despatch the supply train back to Orenburg immediately, because armed units of Khivans had appeared in the steppe. Both Maksheiev and Akishev had to leave for Orenburg with the train. The officers asked the Kazakhs to find their horses which were grazing by the herders' camp.

"*Ai*, but you cannot leave like that, *mayirs*! You must stay for the *toi* to the end," Djantemir said, shaking his lead offended. "Tomorrow the *akyns* will be singing, the *dombras* playing, and the *kyui* will be recited. It will be also a *baiga* of *akyns*, and the best song will be awarded with a gown, saddle or carpet — all sorts of presents. *Ai*, you cannot go to Kosaral! Don't go to Raïm either!"

The *mayirs* jingled with their spurs, thanked for the treat and hospitable reception, but orders wee orders — they had to be complied with immediately.

"You may stay here, if you want, Taras Grigorievich" Butakov proposed politely, seeing how the poet met the news of the sudden departure with bitter chagrin. "I know how interesting it would be for you to attend a competition if *akyns*. A *kobzar* is a friend and brother to an *akyn*, isn't that so? You may return tomorrow or even the day after tomorrow if that will be convenient for you."

The permission to stay was irresistibly tempting, but his conscience could not go against his moral obligation to see off Maksheiev. He sadly took leave of Abdrahman and walked after the sleigh, in which Butakov and Pospelov had arrived.

Djantemir's sons accompanied the *mayirs*, but halfway they turned back to the *aul*, and it was only Jaisak who rode with the Russians to Kosaral. Maksheiev invited him to his earth house and gave him all his money, out of which Jaisak had spent but fifty rubles.

"Today you earned two hundred sheep at the *baiga*," Maksheiev said. "Buy yourself another hundred, and Kuljan will be yours. How much does one sheep cost now?"

"Without the Bukharan caravan around, two sheep cost one ruble. When the caravan arrives and the Bukharans ask for food, the price will be one ruble for one sheep."

"So do the buying while there are no caravans," Maksheiev advised. "It'll he enough for you and your wife to live, without misery. So help you God. But mind you hide your money well. You've got so much money it can buy five times as many sheep as you earned today."

"*Oi, mayir! Oi,* Taras *Aga!*" Jaisak exclaimed, realizing at last that his fate was taking a good turn. "How happy I shall be now!"

He shook their hands with sincere ardor. Maksheiev laughed, slapping him on his shoulder, while Shevchenko embraced the young man and kissed him on parting.

10. THOUGHTS, CONVERSATIONS AND ARGUMENTS

On the last evening before his departure Maksheiev had a lengthy talk with Shevchenko. Werner had gone to bed early and fallen fast asleep at once. They, too, were about to go to bed when Maksheiev suddenly changed his mind: "Taras Grigorievich, I've almost forgotten the main thing. Many a time I wanted to ask you to recite your poetry to me. You know, somehow it's even strange: we've been living together for over a year now, but I still don't know what you have written. Why haven't you ever recited anything to me?"

"I was sure you were not interested in my poetry," Shevchenko replied simply. "You never mentioned you were." Maksheiev felt embarrassed.

"On the contrary, it interests me very much, but I was under the impression you had certain reasons to keep silent about it.

Well, if things have happened as they did, let's remove our mutual misunderstanding. Recite something from your poetry, please."

Shevchenko was silent for a while, choosing in his mind what poem would be the best to recite in this case, and then he recited "The mighty Dnieper roars and groans..."

"Fantastically written. It's a bold, strikingly measured poem," Maksheiev praised him, sincerely surprised at the force and expressiveness of the poem's images. "What about reciting another poem?"

Shevchenko recited him the dialogue of the guards from the cycle *In Prison*, an excerpt from *Haidamaks*, the recently written *The Churchwarden's Daughter* and some smaller poems. Maksheiev listened with keen attention.

"Some more!" he asked every time Shevchenko stopped. "Wonderful," he said at last with conviction. "You have a broad range of themes, a distinctive way of treating them, and a lot of dramatic elements in the plots. There is one thing, though, which annoys me: why do you, a person who respects Pushkin and Lermontov so markedly, depart from the classical trochee and iambus and slip into folk song or syllabic verse?"

Shevchenko screwed up his eyes wearily: This man does not understand me, he thought. Why, the *akyn* understands me, and so does Kuzmich.

"I write the way my people sing and create. Above all, I am a poet of the people and must — do you hear me? — I must speak with them in a language and verse they understand and with which they can be stirred most," Shevchenko answered reluctantly.

"All right, you are really a poet of the people, and this cannot be denied you. But each nation has people of different... er... levels, and for each of such levels there exist other forms of language and versification."

Shevchenko did not say anything in reply and started undressing. When both of them lay down on their cots, Maksheiev suddenly said:

"I'm very glad to have heard your poems on departure at least. I deem it my duty to tell you that you are a poet by the grace of God, and well... by the will of the people."

Maksheiev left in the morning. The members of the expedition saw him off to Raïm and returned to Kosaral. Now the earth house was shared only by Werner and Shevchenko. They had missed having a long and sincere conversation, because throughout the past month Maksheiev had worked persistently and never left the drawing pen out of his fingers, or else was engrossed in his topographical calculations, which made his fellow lodgers read silently so as not to interfere with his work. Throughout that winter Werner and Shevchenko had, apart from making good friends with each other, developed what they both called an "exile's feeling," which did not allow them to speak openly of their hopes and mental wounds in the presence of a free person.

The first thing they did was jump at the chance of reading Maksheiev's newspapers, which they had read previously many a time but in snatches. As before, they sought answers to hundreds of questions and, in particular, to the further development of the French Revolution and the events in Poland. But in the pages of the St. Petersburg press it was difficult to find a sensible article, let alone a bare listing of facts: everything was slashed by the ever wakeful and unrelenting censors. Moreover, the newspapers were of very old date: the supply train that reached them in January had left Orenburg in November; now it was March, and so they discussed the events of last year and autumn.

Lizohub's letter contained hints of some extraordinary events, but the hints were so unintelligible that Shevchenko understood their meaning only after his conversation with Królikiewicz. "There is a lot of news," Lizohub wrote, "but since it concerns distant foreign lands, I will not write about them in detail. The only thing I can say is that everybody hopes for something better, although it all does not occur silently but to the accompaniment of twenty-four-pound cannon balls."

The last phrase suggested that skirmishes had started in Paris, because the cannons were silent during the February coup. One of the issues of the monarchist newspaper *Severnaya pchela*[*] buzzed away with malicious glee that it was time to commend the wisdom of statesman, in particular Cavaignac, who had finally bridled "the insolent rabble."

"That means defeat for the people," Shevchenko said. "But who is this Cavaignac? Have you heard that name before?"

Werner shrugged his shoulders.

"I wonder what is going on there?" he reasoned aloud. "They have established a republic, introduced universal suffrage, done away with censorship. What else do they want then?"

---

[*] *Severnaya pchela* (Rus.) — lit. Northern Bee — *Tr.*

"I heard last year that they had a horrible crop failure and famine. It could be that the storekeepers and landowners are withholding the grain, waiting for the prices to jump up, while the hungry people smash their storehouses. If only I could see Królikiewicz," Shevchenko said with a sigh. "He always knows all the news and could explain a lot of things."

But to meet Królikiewicz was not as simple as it had been in winter, because now that the thaw had set in, the ice on the Syr Darya became unsafe to walk on, and Raïm could be reached only before dawn, when the ice froze up during the night. At nights, however, no one dared travel because of the wolves.

They met only in April when the inlet was free of ice and Królikiewicz arrived at Bogomolov's office with a message from the Raïm commandant. He came by boat, and while the lieutenant wrote the reply, Królikiewicz went to see his friends.

Shevchenko and Werner were glad to see the unexpected guest and bombarded him with questions almost the very moment he appeared.

"We're waiting for the new supply train, and before it arrives there is nothing I can tell you, because homing pigeons do not fly to us and the telegraph has not been installed yet," Królikiewicz said. "We've got hard drinking bouts — that's the only news I can relay to you from Raïm. Although the new commandant locked up all of the vodka in the powder magazine and sealed up all the sutlers' barrels, the officers can barely keep themselves on their feet from booze as before."

"Where do they get the vodka then?" Werner wondered.

"From the soldiers. The ones who're not incorrigible drunkards do not swallow their share of vodka they get as rations, but carry it in their mouths and then spit in out into a small keg, from which the vodka is then sold to the officers," Królikiewicz said with a laugh.

"Taras Grigorievich received a letter from Ukraine in January," Werner said. "It mentions some twenty-four-pound cannon balls. We think it's a hint about the events in Paris, but we are not sure."

"Let me have a look," Królikiewicz asked, and after reading through the letter, he confirmed their supposition: "It's clear enough that Lizohub had the street battles in Paris of last June in mind. It was bloody and heroic fighting.

"The physician Kiłkicwicz received a letter from abroad through reliable people who wrote that after the May demonstrations I told you about last time, the Provisional Government and Constituent Assembly adopted an openly reactionary policy and started attacking the workers. At first, entry into the workshops was made difficult, and then its newly arrived out-of-town members were expelled. The workers bad no choice: either die of hunger or fight the bourgeoisie sitting on the Provisional Government. On the twenty-second of June the workers of the national workshops and all those who had been expelled from them staged a demonstration. They were joined by the workers of other industrial enterprises, and marched through the Paris streets, chanting slogans: 'Down with the Government of Lamartine!', 'Work and Bread!' In the evening they started erecting barricades, of which there were over six hundred by next morning.

"So the Constituent Assembly entrusted the war minister General Cavaignac with extraordinary powers.

"And the carnage broke loose. Guns, cavalry, infantry were thrown against the unarmed people. The workers had no commanders, no plan of defense, no weapons, gun powder or bullets — only cobblestones. But they fought with unmatched heroism and staunchness. Among them was a former hussar officer, who was an ardent advocate of the republic. He developed a plan of defense and directed its course. The hopeless struggle on the barricades lasted four days, and the workers, who were hungry and without so much as a weapon to resist, lay down their lives. In the meantime, the well-fed petty-bourgeois shopkeepers watched the bloodshed with blind fury and glee.

"What happened next was no more than a whole-scale massacre. The workers were hunted down, executed, drowned in the Seine or thrown into prison where they were shot at through the cell bars and left to lie dead for several days. The rest of the prisoners died of hunger, because they were not fed at all."

Królikiewicz fell silent. Always calm and stiffly reserved, he could not restrain his emotions now as if something was suffocating him.

Werner moved his lips wordlessly like in a prayer. Shevchenko clenched his fists.

"Beasts!" he uttered at last. "I thought that only our landowners are capable of such things."

"Just imagine what they had reduced the worker to! If he does not pay the rent for his dark and damp basement — out he goes into the street with his children. If he loses his job — he must die of hunger. He slaves up to sixteen hours a day. Now he's lost everything he gained in the winter. All progressive newspapers have been banned and their publishers imprisoned. People are thrown into prison for debts again, while the taxes have not been eliminated — on the contrary, new and additional taxes have been authorized. There is no harvest to speak of neither is there any work. Hunger, epidemics, death," Królikiewicz concluded sadly.

"But all of this took place in the summer. What about now? What is happening now in Paris?" Werner asked. "There are so many of our émigrés living there. What has happened to them?"

Królikiewicz did not say anything in reply to this sorrowful question, picked up his military cap and rose to his feet.

"Well, and what about Poland?" Werner rushed after Królikiewicz. "Are things there just as bad? And — "

Without concluding his thought, Werner tore at his shirt, Królikiewicz silently put one arm around him like he would do to a son to comfort him, and with the other he stroked his shoulder.

"Brace yourself, old chap!" he said with an unexpected tenderness. "We must steel ourselves. Tragic and sad as these events might have been, the blood did not flow in vain. By this example people will learn to fight the capitalists just they learned to fight the landowners. The workers won't go out on a demonstration empty-handed next time. And they'll find arms and will explain to the soldiers that the workers and peasants are their brothers. It is rumored not without reason that in our 'czardom of silence' as well the authorities have started tightening the screws. Our Czar Nicholas must be sleeping uneasily in his gorgeous palace when he recalls Louis Philippe and the barricades in Paris. Nothing new seems to be happening in Russia, but there is probably unrest in many countries now. People have been roused from their sleep, because the echo from the guns in Paris has resounded everywhere."

When Królikiewicz left, Shevchenko and Werner diligently resumed reading the yellowed newspapers. Quite a few of the hints in the progressive press and even in the buzzing of the *Severnaya pchela* now gained a new meaning for them.

They counted the days and hours until the supply train would bring them new letters, newspapers and journals. In the end, they lapsed into silence, oppressed by their horrible isolation from the rest of the world.

Werner frequently disappeared, because in the earth house there was little room for the geological collection which he had not put in order yet. For Shevchenko it was a period of prolific writing. Under the influence of the events on the banks of the Seine perhaps, the *koliïvshchina* peasant uprising resurfaced in his memory and ho wrote the ballad "Shvachka" portraying one of the leaders of the uprising.

One thought succeeded another. Spring was arriving. In Poznan and Galicia dramatic events were in the offing. The poet's heart yearned to be there, and unwittingly he recalled his years of youth in Vilnius where he, a Ukrainian, had fallen in love with a Polish girl. Under the influence of these memories he wrote a ballad about the love of a Jewish beauty and a young Lithuanian count.

Then he recalled the treacherous Hanna Zakrewska, nonetheless devoting yet another sad poem to her and hiding her true identity behind the initials H. Z. Shevchenko also wrote songs which have been sung by his people for over a hundred years now, although many Ukrainians, at times, do not know that the lyrics were created by their great Bard.

Occasionally he was so engrossed in his thoughts that he forgot where he had intended to go when he emerged from his earth house. There were enough serious reasons to make him so thoughtful. He realized that the *Constantine* would soon weigh anchor and embark on her second scientific voyage. Till autumn she would be tossed on the choppy Aral Sea and then....

Would he really have to return to the cursed barracks in the Orsk Fortress, to the stupid, cruel Globa, and the drunkard and martinet Meshkov? There would not even be Djantemir's *aul* where he could occasionally take refuge during holidays to see Jaisak and listen to the *akyns* and the soft tremolo of their *dombras*.

These thoughts unsettled him so much that he lost sleep, and after a seemingly endless night without a proper rest, he would get up with a headache and sore red eyes in the morning. Butakov did not see much of his artist now. But he, too, noticed that Shevchenko was not his own self anymore. At first he thought that this was an occasional mood, but then he understood the reason. Shevchenko's future had to be given a good thought. But the press of difficult and urgent affairs did not provide the captain-lieutenant with the opportunity to find time for the poet.

The expedition was planned to last for two navigations and end on the first of October 1849. The expenditures, materials, food supplies and everything else had been reckoned for such a period. The only thing that was not allowed for was that the one-thousand-*verst* trek from Orenburg to Raim and the assembly of the *Constantine* had cut the first voyage by three and a half months, which had made it possible to survey and explore in detail only the western coast of the Aral Sea and without its northern bays at that, while the entire eastern coast, the countless islands off it, and the incredibly twisted northern shoreline would remain unexplored. The expedition also failed to take the soundings of the central part of the sea.

After lengthy calculations Butakov realized that he would be unable to carry out the tremendous volume of work with just the *Constantine* alone throughout the summer of 1849, the more so since he had been deprived of such experienced topographers as Maksheiev and Akishev.

To save the situation, Butakov started preparing the navigator Pospelov to take on the duties of both topographer and captain of the schooner *Nicholas* which had been the expedition's auxiliary craft last year. Apart from navigating the ship on the open sea, Pospelov also had to carry out topographic surveys of the islands and shores.

"I will give you a boatswain as help and the best of the sailors who made the voyage round the world with me."

"And where will you get your own sailors from?" Pospelov asked, surprised.

"I will take about a dozen men from Bogomolov's infantry, and Istomin and Werner will be instructed to be officers of the deck."

"From the infantry? But it is very dangerous to sail on an unknown and rough sea with infantrymen instead of sailors!"

"Now what kind of a mariner would I be if I were afraid of danger?" came Butakov's calm and simple reply. "Our people are keen-witted, they'll learn on the job and by my personal example. Of course, I will have to show them a lot, but I don't see why I should be ashamed of it."

Pospelov sailed as navigator not for the first time, and so Butakov's idea did not surprise him. He decided to get down to studying seriously, realizing what great responsibility he would have to bear on the open sea.

Butakov coached his assistants for the forthcoming voyage like a patient, persistent and energetic teacher would instruct his class for a severe examination. Every day he spent several hours instructing Pospelov, then without taking a rest, he worked with

Werner and Istomin, after which he finished processing and systematizing last year's surveys and astronomical observations and diligently drawing the finally processed sections of the sea coast and islands. Thus, bit by bit, he drew the first scientific map of the Aral Sea which, right up to the mid-twentieth century, remained the best and only faultless source for navigators and students of the Aral Sea.

For all the complex and difficult work he was engaged in, Butakov kept thinking how to save Shevchenko from soldiering.

One day, when he was free, he went to the earth house which everyone in Kosaral, by force of habit, still called Makshev's.

After a sleepless night Shevchenko was in a gloomily depressed mood. He sat with his back to the door, clutching his head and rocking back and forth as if he suffered from a violent headache.

"Taras Grigorievich, what is the matter?" Butakov asked, coming up to him. "Have you been taken ill? Or do you have a head or toothache?"

Shevchenko started as if he had been roused from a hideous nightmare, and he looked at Butakov uncomprehendingly for a minute; then he got up and offered the guest a chair.

"Still, what is the matter with you, old chap?" Butakov repeated, alarmed. "Has anything unpleasant happened?"

"I've just been thinking," Shevchenko replied. "A soldier of a penal line battalion has a lot of things to think about."

"Yes, of course. That's just the reason I came to see you."

Shevchenko looked silently at Butakov; outwardly calm, his fingers pulling at a shred of newspaper.

"First of all, I will recommend you as a noncommissioned officer for your wonderful work as an artist. Secondly, we will soon go out to sea on our second and last voyage, as you know. Back from the voyage, we will go immediately to Orenburg. Neither here nor at sea on board the *Constantine* will you have the opportunity to finish and process in every detail your sepias and watercolors. That is why I have sent a report through the proper channels of command to have you and me go to Orenburg in order to process your drawings and copy all the sketches onto a hydrographic map after it is drafted. Then we'll make an album or even two albums with your drawings and present it to the czar. I believe they will furnish the grounds for your return to your homeland…"

Shevchenko kept silent. A sharp pain pierced his heart like a hot needle. Sick as his heart was, it trembled in his chest like water in a decanter during a swell at sea. Something buzzed thinly at his ear like a spring mosquito, and two transparent drops — as blue as the Aral Sea on a cloudless summer day — dimmed his eyes for a moment.

Butakov understood everything. So as not to put him out of countenance any longer, he quickly got to his feet, vigorously shook the poet's limp hand resting on the table, picked up his cap and left.

II. AN UNEXPECTED ROLE

The steppe along the Syr Darya turned green tenderly and inconspicuously. The shattering noise of countless flocks of ducks, geese, swans and all sorts of other small waterfowl filled the rustling thickets of scrub and reeds, where the birds built their nests, while high up in the sky wedge after wedge of swans drifted toward the north. In the evening the frogs croaked in a clamorous chorus in the boggy lakes. Everything sang of spring and the joy of nature's resurrection after the winter sleep.

The expedition members were preparing to head out to sea.

The *Constantine* was lying on her right side on the river bank. The sailors examined her bilge and sides, tarring and caulking her before the voyage. The tar bubbled in a cauldron over a fire.

Just like last year, Shevchenko sat on the sand under a shed roof and painted, trying to capture as best he could the vivid color scheme of the sunny spring day.

The short talk he had had with Butakov left a deep mark on him. Now he realized why the sailors trusted their captain so much and relied so faithfully on his experience and knowledge, taking his word as something far more reliable than any official commitment.

He was so engrossed in his work that he did not notice the appearance of Jaisak.

"Oh, that's you! Hello, my friend!" Shevchenko replied to the greeting of the young herder. "Sit down! What's new?"

"I'm in trouble again, Taras *Aga*! Help me one more time. I swear by the beard of the Prophet that I will never ever bother you with my affairs anymore... only save Kuljan ... and me!"

"What's the matter? Tell me about it, and then we'll think what to do to get you out of trouble."

"Yesterday I visited the farthest herd, when some strangers arrived there. 'Where is Djantemir?' they asked. 'We've come to see him from Imam Moldabai.' My heart nearly jumped out of my *chapan* like a rabbit. 'Djantemir is away now, but I will see him in a couple of days. What do you want me to pass on to him?' 'And who are you?' they asked. What was I to do? I went and lied, telling them I was his son. 'Tell me everything and I will let him know, because my father left with the *axakels* and kin for the funeral repast of his uncle Kamisbai. There is no one in the *aul* now.' They thought a little, exchanged whispers, and said, 'Tell your father that Moldabai will come and see him on the new moon to propose to his daughter who was Ibrai's betrothed.' 'All right, I will tell him,' I said, and the steppe swayed before my eyes like the waves of Teniz Aral. They took my word of honor that I would pass on the message. I invited them to the herders' camp, butchered a sheep, and treated them to a lavish meal. How I could stand all that is something that is beyond me. They kept looking at me closely all the time. 'You must be ill?' they asked. To which I said, 'Yes, I am; a cursed fever in devouring me and I cannot do anything about it.' They left today in the morning, and I came to you right away. Oh, what will happen now and what am I to do, Taras *Aga*! It will bring Kuljan and me to ruin."

Jaisak clutched his knees in utter despair.

"First of all calm down, and let us think it over," Shevchenko said.

On seeing Werner in the distance, Shevchenko waved to him.

"Hey, Thomas, come over here, old chap! The two of us are in such a mess we cannot get out of it by ourselves."

After hearing out Jaisak's excited story, Werner shrugged his shoulders, and said:

"I don't see what's so unclear to you about this whole affair. Kuljan must be proposed to right away and the wedding held just as fast so as to give Moldabai the run-around."

Jaisak looked at Werner with wide-open eyes, surprised how simply he had dealt with the problem, but his moment of joy passed just as quickly as it had appeared.

"Djantemir won't give Kuljan in marriage — Moldabai is much richer than I am!" he exclaimed in despair.

"Oh damn it!" Shevchenko rapped out.

"How many sheep do you have now?"

"*Oi*, a lot! At the *baiga* I got one hundred and fifty for Karkerat. My horse won me..." he started adding up his flock with his fingers, and got mixed up.

"We know how many," Werner interrupted him. "At the *baiga* you took two hundred and four sheep. How many are there left of your father's sheep?"

"After I gave some to enter the *baiga*, I had half a hundred left without one hand," Jaisak said, raising five spread-out fingers and stumbling falteringly through the Russian language as he usually did when he was excited.

"That makes it forty-five, and in all, you have two hundred and fifty. Then you bought another hundred before I he *baiga*," Shevchenko reminded him.

"Yes, and there are some left from Father's flock," Jaisak started again.

"We've counted them already," Werner cut him short. "So you have two hundred and fifty and the four hundred you bought. That makes it a total of six hundred and fifty sheep. And how much money do you have?"

"A lot of money. There are three big bills on which you see a fat woman against the light. She wears an iron skull cap with a cross on her head. And there are a lot of other bills, too."

"Three hundred," Werner made a guess. "And how much of the other bills are there?"

"*Oi*, I don't know. There is one hand of red ones… five," he corrected himself, recalling the proper numeral. "And ten… well, the color of this here young grass… There is one hand of blue ones, two or three larger bills, and silver coins. *Oi*, I don't know… also there is…" Jaisak tried to recall.

"So why do you keep sitting on your pants, you chicken-heart? Go to Djantemir and propose to Kuljan right away. What you have will be enough for the bride money, the wedding party, presents, and for your life."

"*Oi*, but he is as angry as a tiger after the *baiga*. And Shauken is always setting him against me. So she, too, is very, very angry with me."

"What for?"

Jaisak had to tell them how she tried to seduce him in the Alatau mountains. Shevchenko and Werner exploded in a gusty and long laughter on hearing the story, but for Jaisak it was no laughing matter, and when both men stopped, he frankly voiced what had been flickering in his heart as a last hope all this time: "*Oi*, Taras *Aga*! Ask the *mayirs* to see our *bai*. Djantemir is afraid of the Russian chiefs like of hell and will do anything they tell him, because without the *mayirs* he is nothing: if the Khivans attack — the *mayirs* kill them; should the *jataks* or *tyulenguts* refuse to work — the *mayirs* punish them for rebellion; if there are a lot of wolves — the *mayirs* shoot them. If the *mayirs* order, 'Give Kuljan in marriage to Jaisak,' he will do as they say."

Shevchenko realized that for Jaisak this was really his last and only hope.

"Well, we'll try," he said. "We will go to Butakov, Bogomolov and Chortorogov, and, hopefully, the commandant of Raïm will join us."

"*Oi*, but make it faster I beg of you," Jaisak said with a moan. "The new moon will be in three times my hand. And what if Moldabai arrives earlier?"

"Forget about Moldabai. When the *bai* accepts your bride money and sets the day of the wedding, send one of your reliable friends to Moldabai and tell that old fiend that he is late and Kuljan is married off already. Nobody will find out about your lie, if you keep your mouth shut."

Jaisak was so excited he only kept repeating: "*Oi*, Taras *Aga*, go see the *mayirs* as fast as you can! They won't listen to me. Ask them yourself. Djantemir has to be told many words... different words... clever words... which I do not know."

They were met by a merry and jaunty Butakov. Shevchenko told him without much ado what had brought them here at such an unusual hour.

"I don't see why we shouldn't help a good man," the captain-lieutenant said. "To tell you the truth, I'm a matchmaker without experience, but your idea is remarkably timely: I have to see Djantemir to buy some sheep to feed up my crew before the voyage. So let's combine the pleasant with the useful. All of us will go there and take Bogomolov along. But for such a ceremonial occasion as matchmaking dress uniforms and decorations must he worn. I advise you to spruce yourselves up, gentlemen, because for such a person as Djantemir every medal, every toy on a guest's chest means a lot and gains particular significance. By the way, I've received a badge for being a member of the Geographic Society. So I will pin it on, too. And you, Jaisak, don't worry. With God's blessing, everything will be all right. Taras Grigorievich, go to Bogomolov and Chortorogov and invite them to take part in this distinctive expedition."

In less than an hour, the Kosaral authorities, with Bogomolov and Chortorogov in the lead, as well as Werner and Shevchenko, crossed by boat the vernally brimming arm of the Syr Darya and made merrily for Raïm. Butakov dropped in on Commandant Damis and asked for any kind of carriage to get to the *aul*. Damis immediately gave orders to provide the "glorious mariners" two *tarantasses*, and on learning of the distinct purpose of their unexpected trip, he himself joined the group together with Lieutenant Eismont and Ensign Nudatov. They, too, put on their dress uniforms and all the decorations and regalia that went with them.

After seeing Butakov and the others as far as the fort, Jaisak raced off to the *aul* by the shortest route, cursing himself for going to Shevchenko on foot instead of on horseback. Still, he managed to arrive earlier than the suite of matchmakers and tell Kuljan that today his and her fate would probably be worked out. The news made Kuljan excited. He, too, was not his own self but advised that she dress in her holiday best and go out to meet the guests, and if her father or the matchmakers were to ask what she wanted, she should tell frankly what she dreamed of and what she wished with all her heart.

The wild barking of the dogs indicated that the matchmakers were approaching.

Djantemir was frightened out of his wits when he was informed that almost all of the officers were coming to his *aul*. He concluded that the Russians had decided to drive him away from his new wintering site, levy some new tax, or do some other nasty things to him.

They took offense... got angry with me... didn't stay to the end of the *toi*... and didn't listen to the *akyns*. Now they've come to take vengeance on me, the thoughts raced through his bewildered mind. I'll have to set things right — receive them in the best way, solemnly and respectfully.

"*Oi boi*, woe is me!" he mumbled over and over again, his hands missing the sleeves of his holiday robe.

Undasin, Baisali and Iskhak went out to meet the three horsemen and the mariners in the two *tarantasses*. A short-winded Djantemir hurried behind his sons.

"Guests are a blessing of Allah," Djantemir said, stretching his lips in a sweet and adulatory smile. "A big holiday, a big *toi* will be today because of your arrival at my modest *aul*. Be blessed the purpose of your visit," he went on, shaking Butakov's hand with both of his.

"I pray to God that this visit really becomes a holiday for two people at least," Butakov replied, trying to sustain the tenor of his host's behavior.

Djantemir shook hands with the other visitors just as solemnly and invited them to his home.

"I regretted so much for the unconquerable Russian *mayirs* having left before the end of the *toi*. I scolded my sons: they must have attended to the dear and respected guests badly if the most honorable of the guests go home so early," the *bai* fawned upon the officers.

"On the contrary," they argued, interrupting one another. "We were very much pleased, and regretted deeply our early departure, but there was nothing we could do: orders are orders."

In the largest guest yurt, tea was already being prepared. Kumish whipped up the day's first kumiss for the guests. While Djantemir's face was all sweet smiles, Shauken wobbled over to the big trunk and produced bottles of cognac and rum which, she knew, the *mayirs* preferred drinking with hot tea.

All this time Djantemir was breaking his head over the reason for the officers' visit to his *aul*. He darted sidelong glances at their dress uniforms and glittering golden buttons, orders and medals with colorful silk ribbons, and at the strange oval badges on the chest of Butakov and Eismont. These regalia lent the guests a particularly festive and solemn appearance, but it was a regular weekday when all the Russian chiefs should have been working. A mute alarm stole over the *bai*'s mind. He was also confused by Butakov's mysterious remark about the happiness of two people.

Djantemir invited the guests to be seated on the white piece of felt spread in the place of honor, while he settled to one side almost right near the *kerege*, where he diligently filled the drinking bowls with tea, cognac or rum. As the guests sipped their tea, Butakov exchanged glances with Damis, not knowing whether it was seemly to speak his mind right away or engage in small talk first and only then divulge the purpose of his visit. But neither Butakov nor Damis found any miscellaneous subjects to talk about with the *bai*.

"So who of the *akyns* were the winners?" Shevchenko suddenly came to the rescue of his superiors, since he was really interested in the outcome of the balladeers' competition.

Djantemir's face broke into a sweet smile.

"Now what *akyn* is better than Abdrahman?" Djantemir replied. "He captured the biggest prize: a horse and saddle inlaid with ivory."

"And what about Azat?"

"He sang well, too. His prize was a robe of Bukhara silk, and Koklai won a carpet, a good, beautiful carpet my daughter had woven."

"You have a beautiful daughter. It's time to think about her happiness in earnest," Butakov jumped at the chance to direct the conversation into the necessary channel.

"I will think about it. She must be sold and a wedding celebrated," Djantemir said, shaking his hand at a loss: did the officers really come just on an ordinary visit to talk and drink expensive wines or kumiss? "I'll hold another *toi* then."

"That's the reason why we have come to you today," Damis said suddenly, reluctant to surrender the role of chief matchmaker to Butakov. "We have a suitable party for her. He's an honest, industrious man, who will pay you good bride money and will be a true son to you."

"Who is that?" Djantemir asked warily. "Where does he wander?"

"He is right here, sitting at your side. He even comes from a *bai*'s kin. Once he was poor, but now he is rich."

"We don't want anyone poor," Djantemir said, alarmed. "I'll sell her to a rich man, so that she won't go hungry. He has to have a big warm yurt, sheep, camels, and horses."

Seeing that the conversation was taking an undesirable turn, Butakov gave Damis a sign and interfered determinedly:

"This man has done you quite a few services: he saved your flock during a snowstorm; he also saved Kuljan in the Karakum Desert. The wolves almost made him a cripple when they attacked your herd. He also caught a wonderful golden eagle for you. Don't you appreciate such a man, and wouldn't you want him to be your son and see your own sons as able and brave as Jaisak, the son of Shakir?"

"My daughter is not intended for a *baigush*," Djantemir said, blood flooding his face. "She'll be wed to a rich man. We don't want a beggar."

"How much do you ask for Kuljan?" Damis interrupted him abruptly.

"She is engaged already," Djantemir said with an irritated shrug. "I made a down payment when she was that tall," he stretched out his hand about an *arshin* from the ground.

"Yes, but her intended is dead. According to the *shariat*, the down payment remains with the parents of the future bride when her intended dies, and nobody has the right to demand it back."

This was something Djantemir did not know. His eyes flashed with greed.

"*Oi*, how does the chief know about that?" Djantemir asked, his suspicion aroused.

"I know! I served in Orenburg where the would-be son-in-law of a Tatar I knew died. He turned to a mufti, and the latter explained to him the law in this manner."

"That's a good law," Djantemir said, clucking his tongue. "But Ibrai's uncle wants to wed her. He is very rich, and lives in a white yurt. And that means eating pilau every day, letting others do the work for you, and lounging on carpets."

"She is almost a child, whereas he could very well be your father. It's a shame even to think about such an ugly arrangement!" Shevchenko blurted out.

"For a *bai* it is a shame to give his daughter in marriage to a servant," Djantemir snapped back, but immediately checked his tongue, remembering that the matchmakers were "big chiefs."

"He is not your servant, but the son of Shakir, who had been your father's friend and a *bai* just like you," an *axakal* suddenly cut in.

The *axakal* had inconspicuously approached the yurt during the conversation and had been standing silently by the entrance.

"On the night of Shakir's death," the old man continued, addressing the officers in rather good Russian, "he called all of us to his yurt. He also called Djantemir and told us how he had been friends with old Undasin, Djantemir's father, and had turned from a rich *bai* into a beggar when there was *jut*. You yourself, Djantemir, swore in the presence of all the *axakals* of your kin that Shakir was telling the truth. You should be ashamed not so much of giving Kuljan to a man who is poorer than his father as of receiving the friend of your father and, instead of helping him, turning him almost into a slave. And to this day you make his decent widow, the hapless Kumish, do hard work for you!" he raised his voice in anger. "That is a shame indeed! That is a disgrace! It is a black spot on the honor of all your kin! And now, when Jaisak *Aga* has become the best herder and does not want to leave your *aul* but desires to be your loyal son for whom the big Russian chiefs have come to intercede, you have the effrontery to offend a decent *jigit*, just for him being poorer than yourself."

"How much do you ask for your daughter?" Damis asked bluntly again, motioning the angry *axakal* to silence.

"Zulkarnai had to give me one hundred rubles and three hundred sheep," Djantemir mumbled reluctantly as he trembled from shame and anger, not daring, though, to assail the *axakal* with words in the presence of the Russian officers.

He realized that if he were to offend the old man, the entire *aul* might go against their *bai*. His hand nervously clutched the whip handle, while blood flooded his face, and even his neck, to the point of them turning blue.

"And how much of the down payment did you receive?" Damis persisted relentlessly.

"When Ibrai was alive, we received three red ten-ruble bills and a hundred sheep," Zeineb said; she had been sitting silently to one side, and the *bai* only nodded his head in agreement to what she had said.

"So how much do you want from Jaisak?"

"He's got no money, and I won't give her to him for less than Zulkarnai offered," Djantemir hissed through his teeth.

"Have Jaisak and the girl called," Damis ordered, realizing that he had to avail himself of Djantemir's temporary indecision.

The sweethearts must have been close by, because they entered the yurt a moment later. Kuljan bashfully bowed to the *mayirs* and stopped by the threshold, feeling her legs were trembling. Although her face was of a waxen pallor, she looked remarkably beautiful in her best holiday dress. Jaisak, too, had changed into a new dark-red *chapan* of cloth and a large white *malakhai* with split brims. He held a glittering gown of golden brocade on which lay an unfolded one-hundred-ruble bill. Bowing low to Djantemir, he extended the money to him.

"Accept from me, Djantemir *Aga*, the bride money and robe as a gift from your new son," he said in a solemn way. "And have someone accept three hundred of the choicest sheep from me as well."

Djantemir kept silent, his eyes shifting back and forth from the Russians to Jaisak. His lips moved wordlessly — he was either gasping for air or trying to utter something, which in the end he failed to do. Rage, shame and greed struggled within him, depriving him of the ability to think, speak and even decide anything.

"Tell me, beauty, do you want to be the wife of the old man

Moldabai or do you wish to be wed to Jaisak?" Butakov asked with a kindly smile.

Kuljan did not understand anything: she raised her dense lashes, and in the deep darkness of her eyes he discerned such sadness, torment of expectation, and such a tense inquiring alarm, that he instantly pulled at the hand of Rahim, who seemed to have grown out of the ground, and ordered him:

"Interpret to your sister what I have said."

Her swarthy face flushed red, she pressed palm to palm, and gave a faint scream as she threw herself at her father's feet: "Don't bring me to ruin! Marry me to Jaisak! He is my happiness! He alone!"

"Djantemir, if you really want us to be your friends, accept the bride money and set the date of the wedding; then send a messenger to Zulmoldai, or whatever his name is, to inform him that Kuljan is being married to another man, that is, to Jaisak."

"Who will be my chief herder then?" Djantemir suddenly uttered the first thing that came to his mind.

"I don't intend leaving you, Djantemir *Aga*. We will live and wander together, when Kuljan becomes ray wife," Jaisak replied. "I will breed you such racers that will bring fame to your herd and kin throughout the entire Big Steppe. I give my word of a *bai*."

Djantemir's eyes shifted alternately from the one-hundred-ruble bill to the gown of brocade he had dreamed of for so long in order to be dressed like a Russian mullah during festive occasions. His anger was gradually subsiding, but he still did not dare make up his mind.

"You will make a lot of money on your daughter," Damis said. "From Zulkarnai's kin you retain the thirty rubles and a hundred sheep, and here you have another one hundred rubles and not the remaining two hundred sheep as you might have received from Zulkarnai but three hundred, which makes it four hundred in all. I know of no girl who would have received so much money and cattle for her hand. Anyway, hers is a beauty no money should be spared for."

This argument swept away all of Djantemir's doubts. he grabbed the one hundred-ruble bill, turned it in his fingers to see whether it was counterfeit, then he raised it against the light: the watermark portrait of Czarina Catherine smiled at him with all the dimples in her puffy cheeks and on her curly head was a little crown resembling a skull cap — everything was in order.

"All right, I agree!" Djantemir waved down his hand with finality. "If it were not for the *mayirs,* you wouldn't have my daughter to the end of your days!"

Djantemir carefully folded the one-hundred-ruble bill, bosomed it, and then pushed Kuljan up with a foot: "Get up, and take your 'happiness!'"

She got to her feet as if she had woken after a horrible nightmare, and then swayed suddenly and her face turned ghastly pale. Jaisak and Shevchenko took her by her arms and sat her against the *kerege;* the happy Kumish offered her a bowlful of kumiss, while Zeineb moved up quietly to Djantemir and whispered something reproachfully and confusedly in his ear. He gave her a reluctant nod. Zeineb went out of the yurt for a while, and on returning with a bale, handed it to Djantemir. He unwrapped it and beckoned to Jaisak: "*Kyuit*! Take the *kyuit*! And thank Allah that everything has turned out that way."

It was a fine hunting rifle a father-in-law traditionally presented to his future son-in-law on the day of betrothal.

Djantemir did not let the guests leave without a good treat.

Next morning, after counting up what he had gained, he was wholly satisfied, and when Shauken tried to reproach him for cringing to the *mayirs,* he laid the handle of his whip across her back without much ado.

Kuljan was overwhelmingly happy, but her fear of the fickleness of fate kept her in a state of superstitious alarm. In the morning, Rahim and Taijan, accompanied by a band of well armed *tyulenguts,* rode off to the banks of Balkhash in order to break the news to Moldabai that his idea had been obliterated. Rahim decided to employ a boyish prank: instead of informing the old libertine about the refusal, he would extend to him a polite invitation to attend the wedding of his sister with a young and handsome herder she was passionately in love with. By such an unkind trick he would gain revenge on the old man for wanting to ruin Kuljan and causing her to weep so bitterly.

Kumish, too, heaved a sigh of relief. The very next day Zeineb told her that she would not have to do any work around the *bai*'s household anymore. After her son's wedding she would live in the white yurt of the newlyweds, and in the meantime, she could rest and prepare for the wedding.

12. KULJAN'S WEDDING

By the request of the *mayirs*, the wedding was set for the first day of Easter, when they could attend it without any detriment to their military duties.

After the engagement Jaisak settled at the herders' camp so as not to disturb the usual course of the wedding ceremony which had to take place alternately at the bride's and groom's place of residence. The last, seventh part of the wedding ritual was to be performed at Djantemir's *aul*, in the white yurt Kuljan had received with her dowry; in it the newlyweds would live from then on.

The day before the neighbors started arriving at the *aul* to help with the preparations for the wedding. Jaisak, in the meantime, had left the herders' camp with a retinue of friends, and according to custom made a halt half a *verst* from the *aul* to which he sent a *jigit* to announce to his betrothed about his arrival. The messenger was met, cheered merrily and immediately regaled with food while the young women and girls set off to meet Jaisak.

Jaisak made three low bows to them, as custom demanded, and Baisali's wife Zaruza proposed to build him a tent or yurt for the duration of the wedding party.

"But you won't get it just for nothing," she warned, playing with her tinkling necklace of silver coins and pendants of heavy one-ruble pieces.

"I have no money," Jaisak replied by custom, without raising his eyes. "See Taijan on that matter — he will pay you."

On receiving the ransom of several silken kerchiefs, the girls and young women set to work. The bridegroom's yurt was ready an hour later. In it he had to remain a captive of the women, almost unceasingly, to the end of the wedding ceremony. The women played tricks on him by sewing his *chapan* to the piece of felt or carpet he was sitting on without him noticing it, tried to soil his cleanly shaven head with charcoal or gravy, or stuck a live frog or beetle behind his collar; but most of them defended him and kept running back and forth from the *aul*, bringing him hot tea, kumiss, nuts, or various sweets to make his life just as sweet as the delights served at the wedding party.

Kuljan was sitting in her father's yurt in the meantime. On learning of the bridegroom's arrival, she, in conformity with an ancient custom, sat with her back to the entrance, her face turned to the *kerege*, and dropped the ends of her bridal veil on her breast while the bridesmaids around her started singing one of the main wedding songs called "Zhar-Zhar." This word denoted a *friend* or *a man*. The girls struck up the first stanza and at the end of every line a chorus of *jigits* responded with the refrain "Zhar-Zhar." This was to remind the bride that from now on her husband would replace her parents, relatives and girl friends, and she would have to rely on him alone.

For thousands upon thousands of Kazakh girls this song had sounded like a funeral dirge, but for Kuljan it was an exulting hymn of love.

The *baiga* that followed was noisy and full of excitement. But Jaisak still remained sitting outside the *aul*, in his temporary yurt under the watchful eyes of the women. Kuljan, too, stayed in her father's semi-dark yurt as the girls sang her sad songs of her passing maidenhood.

Rahim and Ismagul, however, felt themselves like heroes after they had won first and second place in two horse races.

In a display of designing generosity, Djantemir announced for all the *bais* and *axakals* to hear that he was surrendering the prize to Jaisak, since he had reared and trained not only the winning horses but also all of the *bai*'s racers, and accepting him for his son now, he considered him a participant in his victories. This cost Djantemir only twenty-eight of his sheep, but it gave an additional boost to his fame throughout the Great Steppe.

While the guests competed in fencing and marksmanship, danced and sang, the bridesmaids led the bride outdoors so that she bid farewell to the *aul*. She entered every yurt, bowed low to its occupants, uttered sad words of farewell or accepted greetings and the best wishes as her eyes beamed with happiness. The ceremonial round of the bridesmaids chanting sad songs of farewell lasted over two hours until they took her back to her father's yurt.

Zeineb, who performed the role of the bride's mother, threw the flaps of the yurt wide open and the men turned back the patterned white *koshma* bounding the yurt on all sides so that the guests and *aul* dwellers could see Kuljan through the lattice framework, while the young people sang in chorus a song lauding her beauty, kind heart and virtue, and praising her parents for having reared and brought up such a wonderful girl.

As the night was drawing on, the *aul* blossomed out with golden bushes of campfires. The sumptuous wedding party continued, and with the advent of night there also came the time for other ancient rituals, dating from the times when there had not been either marriages by contract or by buying and selling women, but rather the girls had been abducted to outlying *auls* never to see the homes of their parents again.

In Taijan's yurt a party for girls was in preparation; it had to be attended by the bride as well, while the bridegroom was to stay in his yurt beyond the *aul*.

When everything was ready, one of the girls, Marjan, went to invite the bride.

"Come to us, Kuljan *Djan*," she said.

"Why should I leave my parents' nest? Let me stay the last night in my yurt," Kuljan said, following the ancient custom.

"Wipe off your tears, bride! We will have a merry party. Dispel your sorrow among true friends."

But Kuljan only shook her head in response to the invitation.

"Bring her to us. We'll have a jolly time," the girl turned to the bridesmaids, but they, too, refused to take Kuljan to the inviting yurt of Taijan. Marjan left the yurt for a moment, cried out something into the darkness — and suddenly she came running into Djantemir's yurt with her girl friends to take Kuljan out by force.

"Help!" Kuljan cried according to custom, as she tried to break loose.

The bridesmaids surrounded her in a tight circle and started defending her, while Marjan's girl friends gradually became hot-tempered. What was initially a make-believe pushing and shoving started to take on a nature of a real scuffle. The girls fought with pillows and everything else they could lay their hands on. Someone caught on the oil lamp hanging on the *shangarak* and knocked it to the ground. Someone else ripped a cloth apart, a drinking bowl went flying to the ground, and another bowl was trampled under the shuffling feet. The women tore at each other's hair and broke crockery in the darkness. The *kerege* snapped. Still, the bridesmaids got the upper hand, and Marjan had to retreat. The oil lamp was relit, the pieces of broken crockery were swept up, but the girls had not yet cleaned up when Marjan broke into the yurt again — this time with the men. They fell on the girls who defended themselves with shrieks and laughter. Kuljan shouted at the top of her voice, calling her brothers for help, but the men tied her hands behind her back, wrapped her up in a carpet, and carried her off to Taijan.

In Taijan's yurt she was unwrapped and seated in the place of honor, after which followed a merry party. The bride, however, as was the custom, did not dance or joke but sat there silently and even tried not to laugh when all the young people almost rocked with laughter at a particularly witty or pert joke.

The young people made merry till midnight. After midnight the bride got to her feet, threw her fur *chapon* on her shoulders and made for her parents' *yurt*. Her bridesmaids, along with Marjan and her friends, accompanied her in a crowd. Suddenly they were attacked by a band of *jigits*. The excitement of it all turned the noisy scuffle into an outright fight, for which some paid with a blue eye, others with a scratched face. *Chapans* and veils were ripped, some of the girls had several gold and silver coins on their sleeveless jackets missing in the morning, still others did not know how to conceal the bruises and scratches on their faces. Getting the better of Kuljan, the men wrapped her up in a carpet and carried her off in an indefinite direction, but they, too, were intercepted by another group of guests who recaptured the bride. This group was rewarded with a sizable ransom, and at long last the bride was escorted to her parents' yurt

Exhausted, Kuljan lay down on a heap of quilted rugs and pillows. The two days of the unceasing wedding party had drained her strength. The noisy goings-on in the *aul* overwhelmed her with a lot of new impressions. She dozed off but started some minutes later when the elder female matchmaker entered with Jaisak, and immediately disappeared again.

Without uttering a word, Jaisak pressed Kuljan's fingers in his hand and settled at her side. They did not want to say anything, for words would have sounded awkward anyway in describing what they felt in their hearts. They looked at each other, their eyes conveying greater meaning than spoken words.

Kuljan and Jaisak did not notice how the black-blue sky in the *tunduk* flooded with a blue glow that had swallowed up the stars. The night passed like a fleeting moment.

Jaisak raised his head.

"Till we meet tomorrow, my rainbow," he said and left the yurt.

The following day the *aul* throbbed with merriment. Jaisak remained under the watchful eyes of the women as before. They replaced one another frequently, each being eager to dance, partake of the rich food and have some fun, or else cloud the reason of some of the visiting *jigits*.

The noise of the party died away toward midnight, and this time the elder matchmaker brought Kuljan to Jaisak.

Again the two of them sat alone till dawn, exchanging only a few words, happy at the thought of the approaching moment, after which nothing but implacable death would separate them.

Kuljan left one hour before dawn. Jaisak could barely wait for his female guard; he paid her a ransom in order to be free, jumped into the saddle of the horse Taijan had brought him, and galloped off to the herders' camp.

While Jaisak was away to fetch the presents for his father-in-law and bride, the *aul* dwellers started building a white yurt which rich parents customarily gave as a dowry to their daughters. To the yurt they brought also Kuljan's hopechest with her clothes and some of the things her mother had left her.

Jaisak and his friends arrived on horseback in the latter half of the day. He presented Djantemir with a dagger and five luxurious silver-fox furs, Kuljan received two necklaces and a length of velvet for a dress, Zeineb, a Persian shawl, and four of Kuljan's brothers, a wolfhound pup and a pistol each. After staying for some time with his future father-in-law and discussing various household matters, Jaisak, as custom demanded, returned to his lonely steppe dwelling to stay there under the strict eyes of his female guards.

In the evening Marjan came again to invite the bride to the party, and as the day before the bride was carried away after a brief scuffle.

At midnight Taijan's yurt was visited by all the relatives of the bride and the groom's only kin — his mother Kumish, who for the first time in many years, instead of her beggar's rags, wore a decent dress which Kuljan had made for her in secret.

The mullah from Irghiz-Kala had also been invited to the *aul* for the wedding, and when the *bai* ordered the young people, "Call the mullah so that he bestow the blessing of Allah on our children!" the mullah promptly appeared in Taijan's yurt.

At this point in the ritual, Iskhak and Taijan enacted a merry comedy: one of them played the part of the groom's father, and the other the bride's father. They haggled over the bride money, interspersing their bargaining with jokes, witticisms, proverbs and hints which sent the guests into roars of laughter.

"No, I can't agree the sheep having their tails bobbed off!" cried Iskhak who played the part of Djantemir. "They're not sheep, but sheep skins with bones and meat inside."

"But I can't have it otherwise, because all the nails on the fingers and toes of the bride were bobbed off yesterday. That's no girl anymore if she hasn't any long nails. So I'm asking the sheep tails for the nails."

The guests roared from the fun, while the two "actors" emulated each other in thinking up ever new reasons to pursue the argument. In the end, the mullah stopped them with an imperious gesture: "Enough! Now ask the bride whether she agrees to be wed to Jaisak, the son of Shakir?"

Taijan and Iskhak got to their feet and went over to Kuljan.

"Tell us, Kuljan: do you agree to become the wife of Jaisak, the son of Shakir?"

Kuljan remembered the instructions of the elder women and pretended not to have heard the question. The young men waited for another minute, and then repeated the same question. This time, too, she kept silent, although she wanted to shout for the whole world to hear: "Yes! I agree!" But custom bade her to keep silent, for a Muslim woman had no say in deciding her own destiny. Taijan and Iskhak asked her the third time Only now was a woman permitted either to utter the cherished *yes* or remain silent again. By that time Kuljan was so excited she only moved her lips, unable to utter the cherished word. So the bridesmaid sitting at her side said:

"Yes, she agrees."

"And now go and ask the groom whether he agrees," the mullah said.

Jaisak had by then left his temporary dwelling and was standing near the entrance to Taijan's yurt. Iskhak and Taijan returned and informed the mullah about the positive reply of the bridegroom.

The mullah placed in front of him a bowlful of water, blessed it, took a drink of the water, handed the bowl to the bride and groom for them to take a sip and pass it on to all those present. Then he went out of the yurt with the men. If there had been a mosque in the *aul*, the mullah would have offered a wedding prayer in it. He made for the guest yurt of Djantemir, while the women fell on the bride and carried her off to one of her father's yurt, despite all the attempts of her bridesmaids to defend her.

From there the elder female matchmaker, who had prepared the bed for the newlyweds in the white yurt, took the bride to her new home and then went to bring Jaisak.

Only now did Jaisak and Kuljan feel that all barriers had been overcome at last and they would belong to each other to their deaths.

In the morning the young couple went to Djantemir for the customary blessing. After he had blessed them and treated them to a sumptuous meal, he immediately started discussing with Jaisak the forthcoming *toi* and *baiga* at Irghiz, for which his son-in-law had to prepare several racers.

The *aul* emptied as the merry guests left for their homes. In the kitchen yurt the women were still busy preparing the farewell meal for the guests. The conversation of the *axakals* and *jigits* revolved around the imminent departure to the summer pastures.

13. THE SAILORS' SONG

In early May the *Constantine* and *Nicholas* put to sea. In parting, the *Nicholas* saluted Butakov's broad pennant with seven gun shots. The *Constantine* responded with the same salute — and the ships passed clear of each other, the *Nicholas* heading along the eastern coast to chart it in detail, and the *Constantine* to the north, skirting from the west the numerous islands stretching off the eastern coast.

Though difficult and dangerous, the voyage was in other respects boring and monotonous. The eastern shores offered no colorful islands, cliffs or inlets whatsoever. The islands were low and sandy, at times only slightly showing above the water. Extremely dangerous sandbanks surrounded them on all sides and stretched far out into the sea in long treacherous tongues barely covered by water.

"What am I to paint here?" Shevchenko complained. "How the sun is reflected in the sea? Or the reeds? People simply won't believe that this is the Aral Sea and not Lake Ladoga. There is nothing marine about it! Or am I to paint those dunes? I did only one watercolor on Chikanaral Island."

"Don't be upset," Butakov comforted him. "There will be some interesting landscapes yet. We won't be sailing through these tiny sounds forever. Once we are in the open sea, you will be missing those dunes and sandbanks."

"An open sea is all right with me: I don't know what sea sickness is," Shevchenko said with a laugh.

"He who hasn't been out at sea, doesn't know what fear is," Butakov replied with an old proverb.

The day was sunny and utterly quiet. While the topographer Rybin was finishing his survey, Shevchenko closed his album and went for a walk around the island together with Werner to add new plants to his botanical collection.

The schooner rode at anchor off Chikanaral Island throughout the night. In the morning a boat was sent with topographers to the island when suddenly a high wind rose. Butakov ordered the boat turn back with a gun shot, but the waves had already become so rugged the sailors could not come alongside the ship. The boat was hauled ashore, while the *Constantine* had to cast a second anchor, since the wind had reached gale force.

The sea in this place being shallow, the furious waves raked up the water right down to the bottom in long frothy rollers. Every time the *Constantine* flew up a crest, a roller threw her down a deep gulch between two watery hills and was about to smash her against the bared bottom.

During one of the strongest gusts the rope of the heavy bow anchor snapped and the schooner whirled the more helplessly at her smaller anchor.

"All hands on deck!" Butakov ordered from the captain's bridge.

Shevchenko and Istomin scrambled out on deck together with the entire crew.

"Bend the kedge!" Butakov ordered. Everyone rushed to the ropes. "Drop the kedge!"

The deck roared, turning into a steep slope which the sailors hung on to by some miracle. Foam, spray, and sometimes a roller covered the men. During one of the heaviest lists a sail boom from the mainmast was torn away and started swinging with destructive force over the deck. Every of its swing could knock off the head of anyone in its path. No sooner had Butakov issued orders than Shevchenko rushed toward the boom, took hold of it, and hung onto it, pushing it to the side to secure it with a boom sheet.

"Secure the boom!" Butakov shouted.

A sailor ran to the daredevil to give him a helping hand.

The white-crested waves lashed the tiny ship with u roar, threatening to destroy her any minute like a toy. The wind howled and scourged the men with cold rain and a no less cold briny spray. It whipped the manes off the waves and swept them over the savage sea like a thin mist which rained on the dreadfully chilled sailors.

"Dog down the hatches." Butakov ordered.

He realized that every roller, every gust could spell doom to his ship. But he had to keep the crew's spirits high — so without a single twitch on his facial muscles, he issued loud, terse orders to inspire confidence in the crew.

The shore was no more than half a mile away. The booming surf broke against the low dunes. After deluging a sandbank, the waves rolled back, their frothy paws raking up gravel and sand. The schooner had to be kept head to sea, while the wind tried strenuously to push her to one side all the time.

"Two points over the starboard bow!" the captain's voice rang out.

Their tooth clenched, the crew carried out the orders with faultless precision, realizing that survival depended on their efficiency.

After midnight the wind started to shift, and by ten o'clock in the morning had spent its force to an extent which enabled Butakov to send orders to the topographers to return to the schooner. An hour later he ordered all hands, except for the watch, to take a rest; he himself went into the wardroom and asked Tikhon to give him dry clothes and a cup of hot tea.

"You did a good job," he said to Shevchenko who was worriedly looking through his albums to see whether the sea waves had ruined them. "I see you managed to learn handling the wheel as well. Honest to God, you really did a good job," Butakov repeated, wearily sitting down on his bunk.

The *Constantine* had been at sea for seventeen days. Her supply of fresh water had dwindled alarmingly and had to be replenished at once. The schooner was sailing southward all the time, and soon Butakov made a new geographical discovery: two little islands. The **first of them he named for Menshikov, and the second for Tolmachov**. Rybin charted them on a map, and the sailors took to digging wells, but the water on both islands proved to be bitterly salty and unfit for drinking. Instead they came across some wonderful snow water that had gathered in a depression, but managed to take only six pails of it, because a strong wind got up suddenly and the schooner had to run to the safety of the opposite shore to evade another gale. The *Constantine* sailed further south, and soon approached the eastern estuary of the Amu Darya in the Djalpak Inlet. Butakov and Rybin went down in a boat and entered an arm of the river, but found to their great surprise that the water in the arm was salty.

A fresh wind kept the schooner hugging the Khivan shore for several days, and only a week later did it spend its force and Butakov was able to start sounding the Djalpak Inlet and continue looking for fresh water.

The schooner's water supply had run out completely by then. There was an unbearable heat wave. The desert all around was baked by the sun so much that the waters of the Aral Sea could neither relieve the heat nor moisten the air. People suffered from the blistering heat and from thirst, and the suffering could not be alleviated by bathing or ablutions. They drank the sea water with disgust; an hour later an unbearable pain would rack their stomachs and result in diarrhea. However, the crew did not complain, and only torment and pleading showed in the eyes of the sick. Utterly sick himself, Butakov realized that he had to put all matters aside and seek water as fast as he could.

He and Rybin had waded around the entire Djalpak Inlet and found out that the river had previously spilled freely into the sea, but the northern head winds and the sea current had gradually filled the estuary with sand which the Amu Darya was carrying out to sea, and during a great spring flood the river must have breached itself another outlet into the sea.

Butakov's Kazakh guide also recalled that there was yet another, fifth estuary to the east of this one in the **Bishkum Inlet**. Butakov decided to look for it at once, but another gale whipped up the sea and the schooner was tossed around at anchor for several days, after which she sailed into an inextricable labyrinth of sandbanks. The *Constantine* got out of it in the end, but the torments and thirst were beyond endurance by that time. There was no fresh water either on Tolmachov Island or on its eastern shore. Half of the crew was laid up, and the rest barely stirred their arms and legs. Istomin warned Butakov that the sick were on the verge of dying. The captain contravened all instructions and orders of the war ministry, headed for **Tokmak Island**, and cast anchor two miles off the western estuaries of the Amu Darya. Here on the leeward side of the island, the water was almost fresh. The feverishly thirsty crew could not have their fill of the water. A day later the pain in the men's stomachs subsided, and on the fourth day all of them without exception were on their feet.

Finding himself in the place he had visited the year before, Butakov decided to explore again the third brimming arm or the Amu Darya. During the night he and Rybin waded across the arm, sounding its depth. After checking the soundings with those of the previous year, Butakov concluded that this was the only navigable arm in the Amu Darya estuary which could be freely entered by flat-bottomed ships with a light draught.

The Kazakh guide told Butakov that there was the grave of a saint on Tokmak Ata Island. People held the saint in high respect, but the khan prohibited them from making pilgrimages to the island until the harvest of strawberries growing there was over. The khan, however, visited the island to pray in the winter.

With a small supply of fresh water, Butakov sailed forth in search of the *Nicholas* whose crew must have also been suffering from thirst.

The two schooners met at last toward the evening of the twenty-first of June. Pospelov immediately saw Butakov to report. He had managed to chart almost the entire eastern seashore, except for the last thirty miles, after a voyage that was much more perilous than the *Constantine's*.

"I've brought you water, sensing at a distance how difficult it was for you without it. Order the men to haul it on board," Butakov said, going into a bustle of activity. "Tikhon! Boatswain!"

"Boatswain here!" Kryukov responded as he rushed into the wardroom like a whirl.

"Issue the *Nicholas* one steel barrel of water and about seventy pails. And you, Tikhon, treat us to hot tea with lemons."

"And with some delicious berries," Tikhon added, laying the table. "I've been on the island with the topographers today, and picked a pailful of wild strawberries."

Since it was dead calm, the schooners stood alongside, as though at the pier of a large haven. Both crews took to hauling the water with a will, within an hour sixty-five pails of fresh water were transferred to the *Nicholas* and her thirst-plagued crew drank with delight the tea which the thoughtful cook had brewed for them.

In the wardroom tea was served as well, accompanied by a lively conversation.

Suddenly the tender sounds of a mandolin came from the upper deck, then a guitar joined the melody and someone started singing in a muffled voice as if hesitating whether to raise it, the guitar was strummed again, and a loud, affirmative chorus broke out. Shevchenko went on deck and after several minutes he returned to the wardroom and snapped to attention before Butakov with an uncommonly solemn and excited look.

"Your Excellency, the crew of the first naval Aral flotilla entrusted to your command humbly asks your Excellency to come on deck and listen to the song composed by the crew of the aforementioned flotilla in honor of the First Aral Survey Expedition and its gallant captain-lieutenant, discoverer of new lands and seas."

"Enough of making fun of mo, Taras Grigorievich!" Butakov said with an embarrassed smile. "Better sit down and have some strawberries. We haven't seen such a wonder of a dessert for so long."

"But I'm not making fun of you," Shevchenko said, this time seriously. "The crew has really composed a song in your honor.

Parfenov and Zabrodin come from a family of North Russian balladeers!"

"All right, let's go and listen to them, Alexei Ivanovich."

"The song sounds quite good," Pospelov said as he got up and let Butakov walk ahead.

The sailors were sitting around on coils of rope, on a bench, others on a spare anchor, bulwark, or right on the deck planks. Two of them played mandolins, and Parfenov the guitar. When the officers had settled on folding chairs, Parfenov strummed a ringing chord and Zabrodin sang in a high lyric tenor:

"When 'cross the sea…"

"When 'cross the sea, the Aral Sea," the men joined in.

The sailors sang in a masterly fashion. The melody was austere, brave in its purport, and distinctive in its own way. It conjured up pictures of the mariners' hard and heroic toil amid the perpetual roar of the choppy sea.

Butakov was deeply moved and excited. Embarrassed, he kept fingering the cap in his hands, while a faint breeze gently ruffled his dense black hair.

"Thank you, men. Thank you from the bottom of my heart," he said at length, his voice quavering against his will. "But you should have added that without such brave and good sailors as you no captain could have achieved anything. It's our common job and our common purpose."

"If only we could sail under you all our lives!" the excited sailors said.

"What other captain would have crisscrossed the sea to get fresh water for us?"

Butakov motioned to Tikhon, ordered something in a whisper, and a moment later the sailor was back with a flask of vodka and glasses.

"Men, let our voyage end well, and fortune bring us together on the seas again!" Butakov said, raising his glass.

During the night the schooners parted: the *Nicholas* sailed to the south-east to finish surveying and sounding the depths of her last leg of thirty miles, while Butakov, measuring the depths in the open sea, headed northward to the mouth of the Syr Darya, where he had to take food supplies on board, repair the masting, and test the chronometers. All this took up much time, and the *Constantine* put to sea again only after a month.

At that time the *Nicholas,* carrying quite a few sick men, approached the estuary of the Syr Darya. Butakov ordered Pospelov to have the sick hospitalized at Raïm and let the *Nicholas* lie in the Syr Darya no less than two weeks to let everyone have a good rest and regain their strength, after which they were to start sounding and surveying the northern part of the sea. Butakov then sailed into the **Perovsky Inlet where, in Chubar Tarauz Bay,** he found a wonderful haven protected from all winds. Besides, the haven was three hundred *versts* closer to Orenburg than Raïm and Kosaral, and deep enough even for large-keeled steamships and sailers.

From the Perovsky Inlet Butakov headed for **Cape Kara Tiube**. On the way Shevchenko admired the white **Aulye Cliff** resembling a huge marble sarcophagus rising high over the sea. Then the schooner sailed to the **Kulandi Peninsula** where coal had been found the year before. Butakov went ashore, ordered wood to be chopped and coal to be hewn to augment the galley's fuel supply, and with Rybin made a detailed survey of the site of a future coal mine. After rounding **Cape Uzinkair**, the *Constantine* entered the inlet on the far side of the Kulandi Peninsula and Butakov named the inlet in honor of Chernishov.

Further on they sailed to the north along the steep shores of the **Ustyurt**. Butakov kept sounding the depth, while Rybin went ashore to chart the land now and then. The *Constantine* ran into a furious gale which raged for two days, after which the mariners reached the **Kara Tamak** boundary line; six *versts* to the south of it, by a spring of bitter water, Werner discovered yet another deposit of coal, this time an outcrop seam.

Butakov was happy at the discovery. After Rybin had gone ashore the next morning, Butakov suddenly saw a caravan of several camels and a large flock of sheep moving across the coastal hills. His Kazakh guide put Butakov's mind at ease. Those were just traders heading for a bartering bazaar, but Butakov was nonetheless afraid they might take captive Rybin's survey group and sell it in Khiva, where a Russian seized in Khivan territory would fetch a good price on the slave market. The schooner was riding at anchor. Butakov ordered to have a blank cannon shot fired to call Rybin back on board, but the caravan took fright and hastily retreated behind the nearest uplands.

Rybin did not go ashore anymore, and only on the seventh of August did Butakov go ashore to establish the longitude and latitude of the schooner's position and have some wood chopped. The operation was in itself risky because a large *aul* was pitched in the uplands nearby.

A number of *axakals* rode up to Butakov on the shore and asked:

"Who are you and why have you come here?"

"We catch fish, cure them, and hunt game," Butakov replied calmly. "We have come here to chop some wood to cook mutton and brew tea, and hold out the hand of friendship to you. I have a present for you here: two mats, tobacco and needles."

The old men looked at one another, accepted the presents with words of gratitude, but shot wary glances at the weapons of Butakov's companions.

"Besides," Butakov continued, "we wanted to buy several sheep from you or barter them for various things you might need — axes, saws, knives and such like."

The *axakals* took counsel with one another in low voices, and then the oldest of them said with a nod:

"All right. Tomorrow morning we will drive the sheep here."

After the *axakals* left, Butakov walked up a neighboring hill and got down to work.

He had just finished his astronomical observations when a fresh breeze swept down again. The waves grew higher with every minute and tumbled on the narrow strip of beach at the foot of the hill with a wild roar, raising yellow mud from the bottom. The boat had to be pulled onto the beach, and Butakov had to stay on Khivan territory for the night. This was very dangerous, since it could have resulted in diplomatic complications, and he regretted having gone ashore in the first place. Fortunately, the night passed without any mishap, and in the morning he waited in vain for the promised sheep.

Nor did the men find any brushwood, and instead of wood they cut tumbleweed.

"It's all right," Butakov said to the sailors. "Porridge can be cooked on tumbleweed too; we'll find wood in another place."

The schooner continued sailing along the southern coast from Kin Kamish to Takmak Ata. The tumbleweed went for kindling as did the deck benches and even spare boat oars, but Butakov did not dare go ashore again and the *Constantine* had to chart the southern coastline "by eye." On the twentieth of August a cold wind started to blow, and the *Constantine* bore to sea at last in the direction of the colorful, densely wooded islands discovered the year before.

On the way Butakov unexpectedly came across yet another little rocky island and beside it a second, level island. The first he named for Admiral Lazarev and the second for the glorious Russian mariner Bellingshausen. Here the sailors chopped trees and brush for fuel. Rybin charted the whole island, while Butakov sounded the depths between the islands as well as the inlets and bays of Nicholas Island.

The strong wind suddenly changed to a dead calm, with only a gentle swell rhythmically rocking the schooner on the sheet of sea water. Then the cherished wind rose again, wiping the mirror-like glitter off the tenderly warm sea, and the *Constantine* sailed eastward across the sea to Menshikov Island where Butakov once again tried to locate the fifth, most easterly estuary of the Amu Darya in the **Bish Kum Inlet**.

This time he entered Bish Kum from the east, from behind an island which protected the inlet from the northern wind and open sea; there he found a wonderful anchoring place and named the island for Yermolov. The water in Bish Kum was sweet and teemed with very tasty and immensely valuable species of fish: the island itself was overgrown with a good forest, and the sailors immediately lay in a supply of firewood, water and fresh fish. The beach in this place was deserted, but during the night feeble lights glimmered in the distance — it was a camp of Karakalpaks who, as the old Kazakh guide explained to Butakov, came here to pick the strawberries which grew abundantly on the island.

For three days the *Constantine* lay at anchor in Bish Kum until a southerly wind got up. She scudded to the north, sounding the depths in the open sea for the last time; on the tenth of September she entered the estuary of the Syr Darya where she encountered the *Nicholas* again.

Both crews rested five days, then Butakov and Pospelov sailed into the Perovsky Inlet, established its position and, specifically, the site of the wonderful haven at **Chubar Tarauz**; then they returned to Kosaral where they had both schooners unloaded and their flags hauled down.

The expedition was over, but its members had still a lot of work to do. Butakov hastily put the finishing touches to his geographical, hydrographical and nautical charts of the Aral Sea, and systematized his astronomical observations. Istomin kept his calculator clicking from morning till night as he counted up the expenditures that went into acquiring food, medicines, clothes and the like. Rybin checked his topographical data and drew a topographical chart of the islands and coastlines.

Werner and Shevchenko also had a considerable share of work to take care of. They had to systematize, number and catalog every rock, clod of clay, and fossil, and put them into flat, numbered boxes. After the mineralogical collection they started work on the botanical collection and tended the potted plants which were gathered as samples of rare desert flora.

"If only the frost doesn't set in on our way back. It'll ruin my plants," Werner kept repeating again and again as he took the readings of the barometer and thermometer with great alarm every morning.

Both Shevchenko and Werner were in high spirits. Werner was sure that since he had become a noncom on Butakov's recommendation last year, he would certainly be promoted to ensign, that is, automatically be relieved of his status as an exile in recognition of his scientific contributions to botany, geology, and, above all, for having discovered yet another deposit of coal.

"I'll have myself discharged at once," he dreamed out loud, "and enroll in one of the technological colleges to the east of the Dnieper. In three to four years I will be an engineer."

"Why to the east of the Dnieper?" Shevchenko asked, surprised.

"Have you really forgotten, Taras, that we Poles have recently been prohibited from going into the civil service or studying at universities and colleges to the west of the Pulkov Meridian?"

"Oh, damn it! Again I'm forgetting where I live and in what times," the poet exclaimed.

Shevchenko wanted very much to see Jaisak and Kuljan to learn how they fared, but the *aul* had left Raïm almost simultaneously with the departure of the *Constantine*, without telling anyone where they would be wandering until winter.

Shevchenko rode to Djantemir's empty house, but the *jataks* guarding the winter quarters of the terrible *bai* did not understand any Russian; they greeted Taras *Aga* joyously, bowed to him, and talked away in their tongue, repeating the names of Djantemir, Kuljan and Jaisak. So Shevchenko had to return to Raïm without having found out anything in the end. He left Jaisak a written message with a *jatak*, in which he said that he was going to Orenburg where he could always be inquired about at the home of Fedir Lazarevsky.

Raïm was full of new arrivals that summer: soldiers' wives, merchants, officials, craftsmen. They had built themselves a lot of yellow-gray adobe houses with flat clay roofs and enclosures of clay as well. Little sheepfolds, cowsheds and tall haystacks huddled around the houses, and hens and chicks scratched in the dirt. Nothing here was of interest to Shevchenko anymore: his heart was far away.

And even the supply caravan not having brought him any letter almost failed to upset him.

He carelessly leafed through the newspapers of the past few months, showing Werner only a report from Paris about President Louis Napoleon Bonaparte reviewing a parade of the *Guarde Nationale*.

"You just give him an inch and he'll take an ell! Mind my word, that president will become a king yet. Just to think that all this happens in Paris, the cradle of the Republic! They write that the peasants greeted him!"

"That's because the late Napoleon gave them land, while all the others just wait for the moment when the land can be taken away from the peasant. Well, we have to hurry up with our work," Werner changed the subject of the conversation. "After the caravan has its rest, we'll have to join it on the way back to Orenburg."

During the last night at Raïm Shevchenko could not fall asleep. All his and Werner's things had been packed long ago, except for the bedding and the collapsible cots. Werner sat silently at the table, staring into the air, as Shevchenko pulled out his cherished bootleg notebook and started to write. Suddenly he became sad that thoughtlessness and even contempt had at times overcome him in regard to this blue sea, the grandeur of the brimming Syr Darya, and Raïm and Kosaral where he had lived much better than in Orsk. He had been treated with consideration and respect not only as a person, but as an artist and poet, and this sadness was involuntarily reflected in his parting verse.

Then an abrupt pain gripped his heart — either because of the imminent parting, or because of the indefinable forebodings of new woe.

The sailors suggested going by longboat to the Perovsky Inlet and then joining the supply caravan, but the caravan's chief refused to keep an eye on the expedition's goods on this stretch of the trek. So the crew had to join the caravan from the outset. In the morning the inhabitants of Raïm came out to see the mariners off. The day before, the officers had invited Shevchenko, Werner, Istomin and Pospelov to a farewell supper and had so much drink that they could barely stand on their feet. The sailors, Ural Cossacks and infantrymen also downed a shot or two of vodka, which they had honestly earned for their cruel struggle with the merciless winds and gales on the small but choppy Blue Sea.

And when the forward guard detachment with two field guns set forth, followed by the creaking wagons of the caravan and several old soldiers who had gotten tickets of discharge for long service, Boatswain Parfenov took his guitar, struck a ringing chord, and young low voices struck up the Butakov Song.

It rolled in a mighty wave along the Syr Darya right to the charted shores of this already explored but so far desolate churning Blue Sea.

14. AMONG FRIENDS

"Taras Grigorievich, my dear fellow! Can it really be you? I can't believe my eyes!" Serhiy Levitsky exclaimed enthusiastically, not letting his dear poet out of his embrace.

"It's me; honest to God it's me," Shevchenko said cheerfully, screwing up his eyes. "It took us over a month to get here."

"Take your coat off. You can't imagine how glad I am to see you again!" Levitsky rushed over, helped him out of a flimsy coat, and took his broad-brimmed hat of wool felt which the poet had acquired in Raïm. "You must be frozen? Sit down here by the stove."

"Wait a minute, old chap," Shevchenko stopped him. "First of all let me introduce you to my friend Ksenofont Yegorovich

Pospelov, navigator and sailing master of the schooner *Nicholas*, and this," he turned to Pospelov, "is the Serhiy Levitsky I have been telling you so much about."

Levitsky shook hands with the handsome young mariner: "It is a pleasure to meet you! Be seated please. Excuse me for the mess in the room. My landlady calls it a 'typical bachelor's den.'" He bustled around, trying to impart some semblance of order to the "den."

Levitsky picked up a heap of newspapers from a chair, threw them into a wardrobe, pushed two chairs toward the guests, cleared the table of dirty glasses, wine bottles and an ashtray filled with cigarette butts, shoved all that behind the door into Axinia's hands, exclaiming now and again: "Oh my, I couldn't have thought you'd be here today. All right, tell me how you sailed."

"And where is Fedir?" Shevchenko asked, looking around the room and noticing at once that Lazarevsky's bed was all too accurately made up.

"He is away on business. I waited for him from morning till late into the night yesterday. Maybe he will arrive today. The Kirghiz are getting into quarrels and squabbles, looting and stealing sheep, and we have to fuss with their complaints. So where did you spend last night?"

"At the fortress together with the sailors, and the first thing we did in the morning was shave, have our hair clipped, go to the bathhouse — and then directly to you," Shevchenko said. "The town's become a strange place. I was asked for my passport at the traveler's inn, and what kind of passport can a soldier have! So we came to you, if you won't chase me out."

"Wonderful! Great! It's good you've come!" Levitsky said, jumping to his feet. "Axinia! Bring the samovar! And something to eat, too!"

He quickly shoved some copper coins into her hand and sat down opposite the guests again.

"Our room, as you see, is big and warm. Recently the landlady agreed at last to let us the adjoining room as well. The door to it is over there behind the sofa. I was just waiting for Fedir to move in. I must have decent quarters now: no more am I an assistant, but an administrator with the rank of collegiate assessor."

"That's fine! Accept my congratulations. And what about Fedir?"

Levitsky faltered abruptly. He could not tell Shevchenko outrightly that Lazarevsky's name had been struck off the promotion list because of his "inordinately and tactlessly emphasized friendship with the political exile Private Taras Shevchenko," as the supervisor of the border commission had put it in his report.

"Fedir holds his old office so far, but we hope that fortune will also be kind to him before the year is out. But tell me at last about your voyage and wanderings. Have you come across anything interesting? What are your plans for the future?"

"We still don't believe we are alive after that voyage. We went hungry, suffered immensely from thirst and lack of firewood, chewed musty rusks with cold wafer, ate maggot-infested corned beef and porridge of moldy millet," Shevchenko said, knitting his shaggy brows, a cunning smile sparkling in his narrowed eyes.

"Oh, my God!" Levitsky gasped from horror. "Was that really so?"

He believed, and at the same time was reluctant to believe what he was told, his eyes straying confusedly from Shevchenko to Pospelov and back.

"All sorts of things happened," Pospelov said with a smile. "A sea voyage without them **is** just impossible."

"But we had wonderful moments, too," Shevchenko continued, "when we suddenly came across unknown islands with mountains and forests, cozy inlets and springs with fresh, cool water, didn't we? Oh yes, we did! Ksenofont Yegorovich, remember the night during the calm off the Khivan shore, when the moon rose out of the sea like some magic flower out of the primordial chaos."

"Indeed, the moon was of a weirdly orange hue," Pospelov added. "You'll see for yourself how beautifully Taras Grigorievich conveyed it in his painting *The Moonrise!* It's a wonderful canvas! But in it the sky is cloudless; when it is a little bit misty the moon turns into something really fabulous."

In the meantime Axinia had served breakfast, and the hungry travelers made their jaws work diligently. Once his hunger had abated, Shevchenko pushed his plate aside and asked:

"Are there any letters for me?" On hearing that there were none, he grew sad. "How come? Hasn't there really been anything since spring?"

"There were two letters from Sedniv, one from Yahotin, and another from St. Petersburg."

"So where are they?"

"Fedir sent them immediately to Alexandriysky in Orsk as you asked him."

"On my way to Orsk I dropped in to his place, but he was away on business somewhere. So where might those letters be?" Shevchenko reflected bitterly. "What if he sent them to Raïm?"

Levitsky shrugged his shoulders, upset.

"I'd be glad to tell you, but I don't know anything. Don't be so nervous about it. Since you are here, a thousand *versts* closer to your homeland, write everyone a letter and you will get an answer within a month. Better tell me about your personal problems, if that's no secret."

At this Levitsky imperceptibly gestured with his eyes at Pospelov, as if asking whether the guest could be trusted.

Shevchenko waved his hand in the affirmative.

"Mine is a roamer's fate," he replied with a bitter smile. "Butakov recommended me for a noncom rank for my work on his expedition, but I still have to finish all the drawings I did. All of them will be sent to St. Petersburg to the czar. My friends hope that I will be pardoned then. So far I'll have to work persistently. Today is Sunday. I'll have a rest, and tomorrow

I report to Butakov. Oh, if you only knew what a wonderful person he is! Isn't he, Ksenofont Yegorovich?"

"Indeed, a person of rare modesty, industry and feeling," Pospelov concurred.

"Well, if you have to get up early in the morning, go to bed and have a good sleep after the journey," Levitsky suggested. "I have to go to town for a while. Make yourself comfortable. Both beds are at your disposal, and when I'm back we'll move into the second room."

"Go to sleep, Ksenofont Yegorovich, while I read the newspapers; I've missed the news horribly!" Shevchenko said. "Tell me briefly at least what's going on in France!" he stopped Levitsky. "Lizohub wrote to me about the revolution there, but it was back in spring. What's happening in Paris now?"

"They've got a republic, and everything's cooled down. But you won't find a single word about it in our press, except for the trials and death sentences dealt out to the leaders of the June uprising. Anyway, I haven't kept track of those events."

"And what's up in Hungary?"

"They had an uprising there, too, in the spring. It was quickly quashed, though. Our troops under Paskevich were thrown in to help the Austrian Emperor, the Hungarians were surrounded and forced to capitulate."

"Damn!" Shevchenko said. "It's dire news!"

Then he glanced at the clock and reached for his cap.

"I'm off to the Gerns. The hell with the newspapers. I'll have my fill of reading them yet. Tomorrow it's down to work, and today I have to call on my friends."

"I'm really going to bed," Pospelov said. "Don't be away too long, because I'll feel uneasy being alone in another man's home," he added, taking off his uniform.

Gern himself opened the door.

"So here you are at last, our famous seafarer!" he greeted the poet cheerfully. "I had been expecting you yesterday. Butakov told me that you were to arrive with the supply train," Gern said, inviting the guest to his study. "Zosia is out shopping, and I'm alone at home. Well, let me have a look at you."

His keen eye immediately saw the bags below the poet's eyes, the thinned hair over his lofty "socratic" forehead, and the wrinkles above the jaws.

"Time flies by and leaves its traces on man," he said seriously. "On the whole, you don't look bad. I'm satisfied."

Gern had also changed throughout these two years. The first streaks of gray showed on his temples. Two deep wrinkles furrowed the bridge of his nose.

"You don't seem to be in a good mood," Shevchenko remarked with alarm.

"Oh, my friend, it's because of intrigues, gossip and scheming against me," Gern said with disgust. "I'm simply sick of it all! If, apart from this house, I were to have any other property, I wouldn't have given a straw for my service and got myself discharged."

"Scheming against you?" Shevchenko asked sincerely surprised. "What for? For what ridiculous reason?"

"It's an old and nasty story! Putting it briefly, prior to Obruchev we had Perovsky as governor. He was a great friend of our current monarch and thus carved out a spectacular career for himself. They say that he advised the czarina to roll the guns out into Senate Square on the fourteenth of December. Perovsky was then transferred to Orenburg. The rebellion of the Kirghiz under Isatai Taimanov was repressed by him with steel and blood — rivers of blood, as a matter of fact. Quite a few of our soldiers met their death running the gauntlet when he was around. On the whole, torturers, embezzlers, and all sorts of shady characters lived in clover under his rule, whereas honest, intelligent and humane officers stayed cooped up in the guardhouse for weeks on end. He surrounded himself with people of his own ilk. He was forced to leave because of the infamous Khivan campaign which took the lives of many of our men, and in place of this typical satrap, Obruchev was appointed governor. For all the outward signs of respect, Perovsky's former associates hate Obruchev and scheme against him in every way possible. But it is very difficult to discredit him. First of all, Obruchev is an honest, decent and modest man. He sensed right away that he lacked support here, and that led to a reshuffle: some he relieved, others he had court-martialed, and still others promoted to win them over to his side. And like every administrator who finds himself in a surrounding he does not know well, he started staffing his office with his people — so now there is fierce and uncompromising contention between the people of Obruchev and Perovsky. On the face of it, everything looks wonderful: polite greetings, amicable smiles, visits, congratulations, but deep in their hearts these people are ready to cut each other's throats. Pretexts for the contention are galore. War is waged for every office, every decoration and rank, every promotion; even for invitations to a ball, stately banquets, or a reception. Those who are richer behave independently, but for us whose service is the only source of livelihood it is incredibly difficult. As an aide responsible for special missions, I have to be in the thick of this brawl all the time. What makes it especially difficult for me is that Obruchev can be easily swayed by the first influence he is subjected to. He is too soft and doesn't have one determined policy, which makes it difficult to guess how this or that case I take up might end. Oh, let them all go to hell!" Gern concluded. "You have enough of your own troubles to take care of. Better tell me how you fared in Orsk and on Butakov's expedition."

Shevchenko started his story with Meshkov misunderstanding the message from Fedyaev and Gern's letter. Then, after describing his life in the barracks, he gratefully remembered the daughters of General Isaiev, told about his illness, Alexandriysky's sympathetic treatment, and finally outlined his travel across the steppe and desert, his first and second voyage, and the winter at Kosaral. He also commented on Butakov whom he had taken a great liking to and respected profoundly.

"He produced a good impression on me too," Gern remarked, offering Shevchenko a cigarette. Lighting it from Gern's cigar, the poet asked:

"Tell me what is going on in the world. Levitsky told me that Paris and Hungary had been put on their knees, and this morning I heard from the Poles that Western Europe regards Russia as a world gendarme. An accurate definition, I must say. But what goes on in our country now? In St. Petersburg? In Ukraine? In the Caucasus? And, the main thing, what's up in our fiction?"

"Unfortunately, there is not much good news. You must have heard already about Belinsky's death, haven't you?"

"What! Belinsky dead? What an irreparable loss!" Shevchenko exclaimed with sincere grief. "When did it happen?"

"He died on the twenty-sixth of May last year in St. Petersburg. There is only one consolation in his death — it saved him from becoming a political convict for his letter to Gogol."

"What letter? I don't know absolutely anything about it. Please tell me everything, just everything."

"It was a letter written in response to Gogol's latest book *Selected Excerpts from the Correspondence with Friends.*'

"A disgusting and dishonorable book!" Shevchenko remarked. "Excuse me for interrupting you. So what did Belinsky write on this account?"

"It was not a letter but more of a destructive condemnation pronounced against Gogol for betraying the glorious traditions of our progressive literature and public thought, and for trying to justify obscurantism, serfdom, embezzlement of public funds, theft and bribery. Every single word of Belinsky's lashed out and burned like a fire."

"But... could it really have been published?"

"Of course not! Belinsky wrote it abroad in Salzburg where the doctors had sent him for treatment. The letter is being passed from hand to hand in thousands of copies now. Belinsky called for the immediate emancipation of the serfs, for universal education, and wrote about the constitution and a republican social system. It's not a letter, but a *Marseilaise* rousing for an armed uprising to gain freedom, a hymn of the future revolution!"

"My God! I wish I could read it! Isn't there anyone in Orenburg who has a copy of it?"

"You could find one probably. But for a political exile as you are it would be extremely dangerous having it on you and even mentioning in conversations ever hearing about it or having read it. Haven't you heard what happened to Petrashevsky and his circle?"

"Absolutely nothing. My dear Karl Ivanovich, you are forgetting where I have been. I'm over two years behind life."

"You are right. Well, Petrashevsky was arrested this spring, along with everybody who had ever visited him."

"What for? What were they accused of?"

"Nobody knows anything so far. All sorts of contradictory rumors are making their rounds. But, incidentally, everyone says that the letter was read aloud at his home and circulated in handwritten copies. The trial has not been held yet. All of them are confined in the Peter and Paul Fortress. More and more searches and arrests are being authorized in St. Petersburg all the time. People are getting panicky, what with the extremely difficult and bad times. France and Hungary have been crushed, but an uprising against the Austrian yoke is about to break out in Italy. Our muzhiks are rebelling. In the Caucasus there is a war against the highlanders. All this taken together has frightened our government so much it is tightening the noose around the neck of our hapless Russia remorselessly, and I don't see a gleam of hope for the future."

Shevchenko had a feeling as if a draft had chilled him. Could he count on being freed under such circumstances? It was not news of this kind he had expected from Gern! He recalled how Mombelli had invited him to Petrashevsky's Fridays and told him that the soirees drew progressive people who openly exchanged thoughts about the books they read, delivered lectures, and argued about the future of Russia. Was Mombelli apprehended too?

"Karl Ivanovich, tell me who, apart from Petrashevsky, was arrested?" Shevchenko asked after a lengthy pause.

Gern threw the cigar into the ashtray, but then he picked it up again and pulled on it deeply. The conversation had visibly agitated him.

"I don't remember much. Among the arrested was the young writer Dostoyevsky, Maikov, Mombelli, Speshnev. Also, the poet Pleshcheiev. Maybe I'll recall somebody else later on."

Shevchenko dropped his head sadly: he had known Pleshcheiev as well.

"I beg of you: don't breathe a single word on this subject even in my home" Gern said. Apart from friends, I am always visited by all sorts of people in my line of duty. And I have enemies overt and covert enough and to spare."

"It's like the times of the 'Holy Inquisition,' when parents were afraid of their children, husbands of the wives, children of parents and all of them of the neighbors, acquaintances, relatives and friends."

"It is," Gern agreed. "By the way, I had a talk about you with Butakov. There is an unoccupied outhouse in my yard, with two little rooms, a kitchen and entrance hall. The building is of wood — dry and warm. Alexei Ivanovich told me that you needed a studio and some living quarters. So settle here. In the loft there are some pieces of furniture, though they're not new. I'll have my batman clean the rooms and stoke the stove for you every day. Breakfasts and dinners you will have together with us. My wife will be very glad to have you around."

"Thank you very much, but I have already put up at Lazarevsky and Levitsky's home. They'll be offended mortally if I leave them. But the idea about the studio is fine, although Butakov wanted me to work at the headquarters."

"There isn't a spare cranny there now. So don't hurry to turn down my offer, and mind the proverb: 'He that will not when

373

he may, when he will he shall have nay,'" Gern said with a mild laugh.

"All right, I'll remember that one," Shevchenko replied with a laugh as well. "You know," he added ironically, "for all the dark and gloomy horizons, I still see a bit of blue sky in the hope of being promoted to a noncom."

He gave Gern such a slyly cunning wink it made the host burst into a roar of laughter.

Much as Gern tried to talk him into staying longer, Shevchenko took his leave and hurried to his friends.

Walking down the streets of Orenburg, Shevchenko was beset with joyless thoughts. What he had learned from Gern overwhelmed him, and sadness crept into his heart again.

Suddenly he recalled that Maksheiev had also been acquainted with Petrashevsky and taken part in the circle's heated arguments about the destiny of Russia and the peoples of the East. Would the bloody paw of the Third Department snatch him from life here in Orenburg as well? Or would his moving from the capital into the provinces save him from arrest and penal servitude after all? The authorities must have attached no mean importance to the case of Petrashevsky since even Gern, usually a levelheaded man, had told about it with such agitation. Shevchenko had to write to Lazarevsky who had been transferred to St. Petersburg and promoted to a considerable office, and he also had to warn Maksheiev.

His thoughts whirled wildly through his head. First of all he had to calm down and steady his nerves. That was the first thing he usually did when his heart was upset. He turned into a barren and solitary boulevard, sat down on a bench, and sat there with closed eyes for a long time.

The sharp pain from the blow of fate that had struck his heart cruelly at first had already abated. The rudeness, dirt and misery of a soldier's life now seemed to him not a nightmare, but a disgusting, albeit common detail. That was not the main thing. The main thing was that now he knew as never before that not only progressive individuals who understood the essence of social relations, but even common and politically inexperienced people could well distinguish a criminal and villain from a martyr. The people did not hold in contempt a fighter, neither when he was a political convict shackled with jingling fetters, nor when he was forced into the army as a soldier. The people knew…

"Yes, that's exactly how it is!" Shevchenko said aloud and rose from the bench.

Pospelov and Levitsky were waiting for Shevchenko for dinner. They had only eaten half of the meal when bells jingled outdoors and Fedir Lazarevsky jumped from a *tarantass*.

"Fedir's come!" Levitsky rushed outdoors to him. "Fedir, Fedir, Taras Grigorievich has returned!" he shouted.

"Really?! Well, that's a surprise and joy!" Lazarevsky ran up to Shevchenko and enclosed him in an emotional embrace. "At long last! Have you come for good or only for a while?"

"I don't know. I'll be living here some time, and then we'll see."

"You've grown stronger," Shevchenko said with warmth in his voice, as Lazarevsky was taking off his dusty cloak and woolen cloth overcoat.

"I'm as dirty as a cat that's been roving around lofts and roofs," he said to Shevchenko, glancing quizzically at Pospelov who had tactfully stepped aside.

Shevchenko introduced them to each other, then Lazarevsky left to wash himself, came back dressed in a house jacket shortly after, and joined them at the table.

By and by the conversation revolved around topics of common interest. Everyone was happy at this unexpected and desired meeting. And Shevchenko cheered up.

Next morning at nine o'clock, promptly on the hour, Shevchenko arrived at the headquarters to report to Butakov.

"I thought I'd find you a room for a studio here at the headquarters, but it did not come out," Butakov said right away. "All the rooms are occupied, and it would be impossible for you to work in the general office: everyone would be looking into your album, you'd be made to wear a uniform and jump to attention every time an officer entered the room. I've rented an outhouse at the Gerns for you."

"Thank you, but Ksenofont Yegorovich and I have already put up at my friends Levitsky and Lazarevsky."

"Oh? Wonderful then. Have your living quarters wherever you wish, but take the outhouse for the studio. With your friends there is a homey comfort, whereas in the studio you'll have quiet and everything else you need for work. Finish your drawings, adding the final touches to them. We'll have them glued on Whatman paper, make a gorgeous album, and send it as a present to the czar on his saint's day on the sixth of December, so work energetically and fast."

"Aye-aye!" Shevchenko replied in marine fashion and snapped to attention.

"I, too, am in a hurry to finish my charts — geographic, hydrographic, topographic and nautical. I also want to make a weather and physiographic map, but I'm afraid I won't have the time for them. Then there is the report to prepare for the Geographic Society and the full description of the Aral Sea for the war ministry. So I'll be laying my shoulder to the wheel pretty hard. In case of any unforeseen difficulties, see me here or, still better, at my home. I advise you not to make your civvies an eyesore for the superiors. Here is my address" — he gave him a slip of paper — "and drop in whenever you can. I've become used to all the expedition members during these two years and, to tell you the truth, took a liking to you. Give me your address as well because it's a long way to the Gerns'."

Shevchenko's heart missed a beat.

"Permit me, dear Alexei Ivanovich, on behalf of my compatriots and of myself and Pospelov, to invite you to our place. I and Ksenofont, and all the crew... we took a liking to you as to someone dear, and the voice of the people is the voice of God."

Butakov blushed, giving an embarrassed smile, thanked him for the invitation in a simple and warm way, and then switched to his usual businesslike tone of voice:

"So that you finish everything in time I'll have an artist from the exiled Poles sent to you for help. He will come tomorrow to the Gerns. Well, good luck."

When Shevchenko was already opening the door, Butakov suddenly stopped him.

"Wait a minute, Taras Grigorievich. You might not know, but during the spring last year an inquiry about your behavior, current views and health arrived from St. Petersburg. Governor Obruchev and General Fedyaev asked Meshkov and the local doctors about you. I do not know the reason for the inquiry, but I am sure that someone is interceding for you. Meshkov gave you a wonderful reference which was signed by the local authorities and sent to St. Petersburg. There is no response to it so far. But the important thing is that according to the conclusion of the medical commission, you suffer from a heart disease and have thus been transferred to noncombatant service."

"What does that mean?" Shevchenko asked.

"If you were to meet with usual army circumstances or a campaign, you will be relieved of drill or combat. They might make you work in an office, a hospital, or as a mess attendant. And since you are an exile and already work in the capacity of artist, your illness is yet another serious reason for your being pardoned."

"Well, I'll have to thank fate for this turn, too," the poet responded with a sad smile.

15. AN ARTIST FROM THE CAPITAL

Sophia Ivanovna Gern loved company. Apart from her exiled Polish compatriots, the Gerns entertained a lot of acquaintances — from old retired generals to young ensigns just out of military school.

She also liked to have herself considered a connoisseur of art, although she actually understood little about it, and all her raptures or carelessly mocking opinions about a book, a play or the performance of an actor were appropriated from the thoughts of others. She praised what everyone else praised and evaded any conversation about something new until she heard the judgment of a real connoisseur. These innocent ruses helped her gain the fame of a cultured woman with a refined taste and artistic flair.

Whenever she met a real actor, artist or some famous violinist or pianist, she liked to play the part of a patron and really helped the touring performer sell tickets for the concerts or collect money for a sick actor.

On learning that Shevchenko would be living in her outhouse, she made the batman Guriy bring from the loft an old but decent enough settee, two soft armchairs, a number of chairs, and a large table on which Shevchenko could put his drawings and draft boards. She herself hung clean white curtains on the window, placed an ashtray and decanter on the table, and lined the shelves with some tableware so that the poet could have something to brew himself tea in or prepare a light repast.

Shevchenko thanked the Gerns heartily for their care, and immediately started unpacking his treasures.

The Gerns had their afternoon meal at four o'clock. On the first day Shevchenko was carried away by his work so much he forgot about meal time, and Karl Ivanovich himself had to come and invite him to the table.

"How did you exist in that primeval Kosaral?" Sophia Ivanovna asked during the meal. "I can imagine it on a ship, but how was it in the winter quarters?"

"Sometimes I had my meals at the fort with our infantrymen, but mostly we ate in our earth house, because we 'mariners' were serviced by the ship's cook on land as well. Frequently I visited my acquaintances at Raïm or dropped in to the local sutler. He was a shrewd character keeping a store and something like a canteen where his customers were given more to drinking than to eating, although I could always get some hot food there."

"But I don't think the sutler treated you gratis? You had to have money, didn't you?"

Shevchenko involuntarily drew a sigh, recalling how difficult it had been to come by that accursed money.

"Occasionally I painted portraits," he replied after a pause. "But the people there were not rich, and so there was not much money they could offer. I charged ten rubles a portrait."

"Ten rubles? Incredible! Did you hear, Karl? Ten rubles a portrait! And in oils, I suppose?"

"Of course not. In water colors, but sometimes with a mixture of white lead and India ink on colored paper. It came out not too bad, you know."

"But it was for a song anyway," Sophia Ivanovna kept repeating. "Oh well, we will find you customers here. And not from the poor category. I will take care of that myself."

"But don't you tell anybody that Taras Grigorievich charged so little," Gern remarked, knowing too well the garrulity of his Zosia. "This case needs a different approach: say, a famous painter from St. Petersburg has shown up in town. He graduated from the Academy of Fine Arts where he studied under the glorious Brüllow, he has painted portraits of Prince and Princess Repnin, Princess Keikuatova and many others. So here is an occasion to have yourself painted on canvas."

"Why are you lecturing me? I know how to go about it!" Sophia Ivanovna said angrily. "You can rely on me Taras Grigorievich: I will find customers for you, but for the present would you please give me your plate. This cold boiled pork has come out fine, I believe."

The days of a new life ensued. In the morning, after a hastily drunk cup of tea, Shevchenko hurried to his studio, and almost simultaneously with him came his assistant; Bronislaw Zaleski, or simply Bronek, was Werner's friend, a fact which drew the two men close together right from their first meeting.

Zaleski was five years Shevchenko's junior. The son of a physician from Vilnius, he graduated from a Gymnasium, enrolled in the University of Dorpat and during his second year of studies became an active member of a clandestine students' society. The society was exposed; Zaleski was arrested and exiled to Chernihiv. Two years later he was granted permission to finish his studies at the University of Kharkiv, after which he returned to Vilnius where he entered the civil service. Some time later he was arrested again and forced into the army as a private in a line battalion of the Orenburg Military District.

He had never been an artist, but he loved painting and had studied drawing since his school days. Persistent that he was in this pursuit, he became a wonderful copyist, excelling in drawing intricate ornaments, masks and human heads. He had a keen grasp of outlines and drew highlights so softly and evenly as if he were using not a pencil but India ink and brush; but no composition or color scheme turned out well in whatever he drew. Zaleski simply made a clean breast of it to Shevchenko. From the outset Shevchenko employed his skills in working graphic details, and took upon himself the more complex work necessitating creative flight. His vivid visual memory retained all the highlights he had to add to his sketches and the distinctive features of the local color schemes, and now he colored every drawing, inundating it with dazzling light, a secret he had learned during his studies at the Academy of Arts, for which his fellow students called him a "Russian Rembrandt."

Most of the time they worked in silence. Shevchenko hummed some barely audible song, but sometimes they threw aside their pencils and brushes from exhaustion and suddenly plunged into a long, sincere conversation, in which each found a response to his own feelings and a tender sadness of recollection and painful regret for his ruined life and bold hopes.

During the first days Shevchenko mostly asked Bronek about life at Orenburg, the horrible cholera that had almost devastated the town, and about other exiles.

"Bronek, do you have anything new and significant to read?" he asked Zaleski on the fourth day of their acquaintance. "I was cut off from the developments in fiction for almost three years, and so I lag behind them like a resurrected corpse."

"I don't have anything at the present moment," he said, blushing as if he were to blame for not having a book. "But I'll be visiting the library today. What is it that you want to read?"

"What library are you talking about?" Shevchenko asked in surprise. "Is there really such a thing as a soldiers' library in this place?"

"There is one for the officers at the headquarters, but soldiers also get something from it occasionally. But I visit the local public library. It's got all the best journals and almost all the books that are published in St. Petersburg, Moscow and elsewhere. There are even some of our Warsaw publications."

"How did you manage to subscribe to it? For us soldiers it's strictly off limits. Why, you must have been asked for your passport for this purpose."

"It's prohibited for sure. The librarian is an exile just like us, but only a civilian. I visit him after closing hours. He quarters at the library and has never refused to put aside a good and new book for me. Let's visit him this evening. By the way, he's read your *Kobzar*, so you'll have anything you wish."

"My greatest thanks!" Shevchenko said, overjoyed. "Now let's pick up the laboring oar quick: we've got mountains of work to do!"

When dusk descended, Bronek prepared to leave while Shevchenko usually went to the Gerns for the evening meal or walked to his friends, where Axinia always left the best morsel of food for him. That evening, however, he finished his meal quickly and then hurried to Cathedral Square where Bronek was waiting for him.

The librarian opened the door at once, and drew back in confusion on seeing Shevchenko standing behind Bronek.

"Don't be afraid," Bronek said, smiling. "This is my and

Werner's Friend Taras Shevchenko, the famous Little-Russian poet. Just like me he cannot visit you in the daytime. So greet him and give him the best book you have."

The librarian asked them politely inside, offered Shevchenko a chair, and asked what he would like to read.

"I am three years behind the events in fiction," the poet explained. "Let me have the best from what has appeared within this time. I have to catch up with life."

The librarian started putting on the table book after book. The sheer amount of them made Shevchenko confused; in the end, he chose a set of the *Otechestvenniye zapiski* for 1847 and *White Nights* by Dostoyevsky for the simple reason that he had heard this new name for the first time among the others whom the gendarmes arrested along with Petrashevsky and Mombelli.

In the meantime, Zaleski had also chosen some books for himself, and after thanking the pleasing librarian, they left.

In the evenings, Shevchenko and Pospelov stayed at home. Pospelov played chess with Levitsky or told about his voyages around the world. He was overjoyed to see new books which were read and discussed by all of the friends throughout the subsequent evenings. Gern dropped in on them, too. Then Butakov started frequenting their home, since he had no acquaintances in Orenburg at all. He felt like a stranger in this town, and only in the friendly circle of his former assistants did his soul really feel at home.

Shevchenko took to reading greedily: apart from poetry, novels and stories, he carefully studied the scholarly articles and critiques, followed the developments in international politics, and did not skip a single section of the thick literary monthlies. He almost learned by heart the review on Humboldt's *Cosmos*, read with interest about the inventors who had so far failed in developing an electric lamp, and even asked the librarian for a textbook on physics, considering that he also had to have an idea about this science since it was studied at secondary schools.

During his first days in Orenburg Shevchenko sent a letter

to Lizohub, asking him to write in great detail about life in Ukraine, their common friends, and the fate of the members of the Brotherhood of Cyril and Methodius. At that time Lazarevsky gave him the letter from Varvara Repnina which he received for Shevchenko in 1848 when the poet was away with the expedition. In it, the princess implored Lazarevsky that he inform her of Shevchenko's whereabouts and his life.

The message moved the poet deeply. That same day he wrote her a long letter, thanked her for not forgetting him, and added such lines: "Not so much time has passed, but what a lot has changed within me at least. You would not recognize in me now the former foolishly passionate and exalted poet! Now, I am all too prudent. I am now the veritable opposite of the former Shevchenko."

Yes, severe life had taught him quite a few things, and now he knew much better what he had to desire for his home and.

"I'll send her a self-portrait. Tomorrow I'll finish it and send it off. Let her see what's become of me," he said to himself, and put the letter into the drawer of his desk.

Sophia Ivanovna kept her word. A week had not passed since their first conversation when the batman Guriy came running to Shevchenko: "Taras Grigorievich, the lady wants to see you. She said you take along the paints and something to paint on."

Shevchenko wiped his hands, showed Bronek what he had still to do, and went to see the Gerns.

"Oh, here you are," Sophia Ivanovna said on meeting him. "Let me introduce: Nikolai Grigorievich Isaiev, and this is a good acquaintance of ours, the artist Taras Grigorievich Shevchenko."

"Are you a relative of the late General Isaiev?" Shevchenko asked as he shook hands with the ensign.

"No, just a namesake," the officer replied laconically. "Excuse me for interrupting your urgent work, but I would like to ask you paint my portrait."

"With pleasure. In oils or water colors?"

"In water colors so far and after New Year — I am expecting

a promotion for the New Year — I will ask you to make a full-length portrait."

"Would an album-size portrait be all right with you?"

"Of course."

"May I ask you to follow me to my studio?"

The officer was not too keen to yield to the suggestion.

"No, it's inconvenient for me. It would be better for me to sit for the portrait here, if Sophia Ivanovna has nothing against it, of course."

The hostess did not object, but only suggested they go to her boudoir lest any unexpected guests disturb the artist.

"Wonderful!" Isaiev said, getting on his feet, and went ahead as a person who knew every corner of the house.

He sat down on a low armchair upholstered with rose plush and edged by dark-green tassels.

"How much for the watercolor?" the ensign asked carelessly while Shevchenko was lowering the curtains to the middle of the side window so as not to spoil the lighting.

"Thirty rubles," Shevchenko said decisively.

"Hum, a bit expensive," Isaiev said with a slightly wry face. "All right, I agree, although you could have reduced the price a bit, because I have a lot of acquaintances, and quite a few of them, especially the ladies, would like to have their youth and beauty retained on canvas."

Shevchenko did not say anything in reply, opened his paint box, poured himself a glass of water, and started to work.

The officer was young, handsome and smart looking. He made it a point to emphasize that he was a person from the capital, a reveler, fence, and lady killer; he asked casually to have his military bearing accentuated, along with the distinctive mark of a man's profession leaves on him, which makes the viewer always discern an actor, military man or priest regardless of the clothes they were in a painting.

As Shevchenko retouched a highlight of the sitter's eyelashes and turned round at the hostess's voice, his brush unexpectedly grazed against the bridge of the nose on the portrait. The brush left a barely visible line, which made Isaiev's face rougher than it actually was. Shevchenko reached for the brush and wanted to undo the damage, but Sophia Ivanovna's exclamation stopped him.

"Oh, it's just wonderful! Take a look, *cher* Nicholas. What a severe warrior you are here, a hero!"

"It happened accidentally. It's just a slip of the brush," Shevchenko began to explain.

But Isaiev saw the change, and said, "Yes, wonderful! Don't touch it! That's just what I was telling you about. A wonderful talented work! Everyone wants to have his ... how should I put it ... inner spirit captured on canvas. As a patriot, officer, and mainstay of our most illustrious monarch, it is only natural for me to wish all this to be reflected in my features."

"All right, let it be," Shevchenko responded calmly. Suddenly he also wanted to leave and even intensify this repugnant "essence" which Isaiev had to vividly spoken about.

He worked for another three hours, and then put the brushes aside.

"That's enough for today. I'm tired. What about seeing me tomorrow at the same time?"

"All right, if you want it that way," the ensign agreed.

On the third day the portrait was finished. Isaiev went into raptures about it and gave Shevchenko the thirty rules at once, without any attempt at haggling. Three days later a liveried lackey delivered Shevchenko a perfumed letter on expensive lilac-colored paper with a golden coat of arms stamped on it. The message was from Baroness Blaramberg, the wife of the Quartermaster General of the Orenburg Military District.

The baroness invited Shevchenko to pay her a call the next day at one o'clock: she wished to have her portrait painted.

Baroness Blaramberg met him affably, invited him into her boudoir, and started asking him in great detail when he had graduated from the Academy, which of his canvases had been entered in exhibitions, and whose portraits he had done. She mentioned casually that she was acquainted with old Venetsianov and Shchedrin, knew Tropinin, "a born artist just like you," she added, and commented enthusiastically about the Italian landscapes of Shchedrin. Overall, it proved that she loved and knew art, and Shevchenko suddenly thought that it would be a pleasure to be talking with her twice a week about everything that was so dear to him as an artist.

She commissioned as half-length portrait. Then she went over to what must have been the most important thing for her: in what dress?

Her chambermaid brought in a heap of gowns and dresses of various color, design and purpose. Shevchenko inspected each dress and put it on the baroness' shoulder to see how it reflected on her face. What they liked most was a black velvet gown with a large décolleté and a riding habit of ordinary blue. The baroness, however, wavered indecisively.

"But in a riding habit you have to sit outdoors, on a porch somewhere, a verandah or in a park lane, while now it is November. I will simply freeze. It fits me so nicely, though ..."

"So we'll postpone my work till next spring, or you will sit in black: and in spring, if you find my work good enough, I will make your portrait outdoors, in a riding habit on horseback like Brüllow painted the Shishmariov sisters or his *Woman on Horseback* and other ladies."

"A wonderful idea!" the baroness exclaimed for joy. "I agree."

Shevchenko gave a smile. He had never painted such beautiful and graceful animals as horses which could really give an artist many moments of pleasure in his work. In high spirits at the prospect of such a new and distinctive challenge, he came to an agreement on the fee as well as on the days and hours of the sittings, and took his leave.

However much Butakov hurried to have all the work finished, he realized that the materials of his expeditions would reach the capital only by the New Year. He could not deliver a carelessly done or unfinished work — that would be tantamount to him abusing the scientific value of an effort that had taken him two years to accomplish. So he worked almost twenty hours a day and hurried on Shevchenko and Zaleski all the time.

At last, on the twelfth of December, the members of the expedition delivered the material to the military governor Obruchev.

Along with the album, Butakov handed in an extensive economic and scientific account of the expedition, as well as large geographical, topographical, geological, hydrological and navigation charts of the sea, its islands and coasts. A number of soldiers, accompanied by Werner and Shevchenko, carried the chests with the collections that were ready to be sent off to St. Petersburg.

In Obruchev's large study there was, apart from Gern, an aide on duty. Two orderlies stood at the door.

After everything had been laid out on a long conference table, Butakov, Pospelov, Werner and Shevchenko — all of them in dress uniform — stood to one side and looked impatiently at the little door near the desk, over which loomed a one and a half life-size portrait of the czar. The aide had disappeared behind that door to report to the governor that the members of the expedition were waiting for him.

"Why isn't Maksheiev with us? He's here in Orenburg, after all?" Shevchenko inquired quietly.

"I saw him and invited him to join us. But he said that ho took part in the work of the expedition only occasionally, so he thought it inconvenient to come," Butakov replied.

At that moment the door curtain moved, and a shortish lean general wearing a worn uniform without any decorations quickly entered the study. Butakov stepped forth and reported:

"In compliance with the instructions of your Excellency, the members of the descriptive Aral Sea expedition have come with the finished charts, landscapes, sketches, accounts, and all the other materials, as well as with the scientific collections."

"At ease!" the general ordered and shook Butakov's hand amicably.

"Alexei Ivanovich, I am very glad you managed to finish your productive expedition in time and so brilliantly. It is a great contribution to Russian science."

Butakov bowed, and then turned to his fellow travelers in order to introduce them officially, but the general came up to them himself.

"Good day, gentlemen. It gives me pleasure to greet and congratulate you on the great and useful job you have done. Alexei Ivanovich, please introduce them to me."

"Ensign Pospelov Ksenofont Yegorovich, navigator with the Baltic Navy," Butakov said, introducing the young mariner.

The general strongly shook Pospelov's hand in a simple and cordial way.

"Thomas Antonovich Werner, noncommissioned officer with the First Battalion of the Orenburg Special Line Corps," Butakov continued. "A geologist on our expedition, mineralogist, botanist, ichthyologist, entomologist and the like."

In disregard of every military regulation, the general strongly shook Werner's hand as well.

"And who did these wonderful landscapes?" the general asked, approaching the table on which were laid out the charts, draughts, albums, and several pictures which were not included in the album because of their larger size.

"Let me introduce your Excellency to the creator of this beauty, our talented artist Taras Grigorievich Shevchenko, Private with the Fifth Battalion, former student of the Russian Imperial Academy of Fine Arts and former instructor in drawing at the St. Vladimir University of Kiev," Butakov said, slightly faltering toward the end of the introduction.

Shevchenko stood stiffly in front of the general and, as regulations demanded, "devoured" the brass with his eyes, but the general extended his hand and said politely:

"I am very glad to meet you! Yes, we have few talented

representatives of the arts in Orenburg. But I was told that you are also a well-known poet. Show me what you have done, please."

Shevchenko came up to the table, and opening the album, started first showing the steppe landscapes and new forts along the expedition's trek, explaining in brief from what direction they had been painted and where the main ramparts and trenches were located, but then he got carried away and told the general about the nature of the steppe, the Aral Sea, its coastal cliffs and coastline, islands, sandbanks, reefs, sudden gales arid squalls. He did not notice how he had been talking like that for over half an hour.

Then Obruchev asked Butakov and his fellow travelers at length about various details of the expedition, and said at last:

"I must express to you, Alexei Ivanovich, and all the other members of your expedition, my gratitude for the excellent work, and consider it my duty to ask the emperor and the war ministry to have you decorated and promoted accordingly. And, also to have your fate alleviated," he added, turning to Shevchenko and Werner.

16. THE POLISH CIRCLE

"Today, though, I won't leave you alone," Zaleski said. "In the evening I'll take you to our circle. You know yourself that there are quite a few of us Polish exiles here. Not all of them, however, are in the army: some were deported to this place to live under police surveillance. I was asked to bring you long ago, but for this dratted work I had no time to breathe. They are good people; you won't regret coming."

"All right, let's go then," Shevchenko agreed.

The first acquaintance with the Polish circle produced a tremendous impression on Shevchenko. It was like a breath of fresh air for him. Throughout the whole morning of the next day following the meeting he recalled what they had talked about and regretted that he had failed to ask them much more than he did and had not made their acquaintance earlier. When dusk fell, he picked up the book he had read and hurried to the library for another helping of "mental pabulum."

At his request, the librarian had kept for him all the latest articles by Belinsky, Dostoyevsky's *Netochka Nezvanova*, Goncharov's novel *An Ordinary Story*, and Turgenev's plays. Loaded with these treasures, Shevchenko returned home. Pospelov took to reading one of the books right away, and Shevchenko became absorbed in another the moment he settled in an armchair.

In the morning of the next day, Shevchenko dressed in his velvet jacket and went to see the baroness.

He visited her three times a week now and worked on her portrait with true passion. Whereas he did Isaiev's portrait with a sense of inner opposition and prejudice, this painting aroused in him the real artist.

The baroness sensed this as well. At times, after having sat motionlessly, she came up to his easel and regarded her likeness with a thoughtful and serious look, after which she returned to the sofa wordlessly and took on the necessary posture. But once she remarked:

"Yes, not many of the artists I have known try to grasp what the sitter is thinking about…"

Five days after the charts and the album were delivered to the governor, Gern visited Shevchenko's studio, where the poet was writing poetry most of the time or reading prohibited books and painting landscapes in oil from his Aral sketches.

"General Obruchev requests that you report at his home after midday. It looks like he wants to commission his portrait."

"So I'll have to wear a soldier's uniform?" Shevchenko asked, slightly dismayed.

"On the first occasion — yes. Then we'll see. Obruchev is not of the haughty type. By the way, he has already forwarded an inquiry to the Third Department, reminding them about his reference on you sent two years ago and asking whether you could be permitted to draw and paint. In the military line, Obruchev recommended you to a non-com rank."

Shevchenko kept silent. Gern picked up his cap and, smoothing down his hair, said in a weary voice:

"Oh, those promotion lists for the New Year will be the end of me! Every day we compile new lists, from which some names are stricken off and others added. And behind each name there's a covert struggle going on. I have not a moment's peace either throughout the day or night."

Shevchenko diligently polished his boots, cleaned his uniform, shaved, and left for the governor's palace. He entered through the back door, from which came the smells of the kitchen and cheap tobacco. In the kitchen there sat, apart from the cook, an elderly noncom with two medals and a St. George Cross on his chest.

"Good day!" Shevchenko greeted him, and stopped in indecision.

"What do you want?" the noncom asked gravely. 'Report to his Excellency that Taras Shevchenko has arrived!"

"Of all the things to ask me!" the noncom muttered, annoyed. "If you've got a complaint, approach your company commander. That's if you've still got some common sense to get away for your foolishness," he added gravely, and turned away to indicate that the conversation was over.

"His Excellency ordered me to report after midday today."

"So he ordered you, did he?" the noncom turned round, surprised. "What are you then? A tailor?"

"No, an artist. Report just that to his Excellency."

The noncom shrugged his shoulders, undecided what to do, curled his lower lip, got to his feet, and disappeared behind the door. Several minutes later he was back and beckoned to Shevchenko.

"Go to the general. Why didn't you tell me right away that you're an artist," he said, seeing Shevchenko through the corridor and rooms of the palace.

"That's the door," the noncom said under his breath, and tiptoed away.

Shevchenko knocked on the door quietly.

"Come in!" a voice came from behind the door.

"Oh, it's you, Shevchenko." Obruchev gave a friendly smile when the poet had crossed the threshold. "Good day, good day! I wanted to ask you to paint a portrait of my wife, and then of me, if everything goes all right. Please be seated," he said, motioning to an armchair near his desk and then pulled a long silken cord behind his back.

Somewhere far away a bell rang with a barely audible jingle. A lackey appeared in the door noiselessly.

"Call the lady," the general said, and turned to Shevchenko again. "I will introduce you to my wife now, and you will then agree on the sittings and on everything else."

Shevchenko made a bow silently.

"Well, we've sent off your wonderful album to His Imperial Highness, and, I hope, your fate will be worked out for the better. We, for our part, will see to it that you get on your feet. Why did you have to get mixed up in this foolish clandestine brotherhood?"

The general's wife entered the room, her silken dress rustling softly; she did not look at the soldier sitting in the armchair.

"Did you call me, Voldemar?" she asked in French.

"I did, my dear," the general replied. "Here is the St. Petersburg artist whose album we sent to the emperor the other day. I have invited Mr. Shevchenko to paint your portrait."

"Oh, was it you who painted Baroness Blaramberg? I saw her portrait. It is very life-like, even a bit embellished," she said after Shevchenko had bowed silently. "So do you agree to paint me?"

"As you wish, your Excellency," Shevchenko replied, snapping to attention and even clicking his heels.

"My name is Mathilda Petrovna," she said graciously. "And what is yours?"

"Taras Shevchenko."

"Taras... and your patronymic?"

"Grigorievich," the poet said, bowing slightly, in an unmilitary fashion this time.

"Well then, Taras Grigorievich, let us not delay Vladimir Afanasyevich anymore: we have a lot of work to do now. Come to my chambers, and there we'll talk things over."

She took him to a little sitting room that was unusually cozy and well lit by three large windows. Mathilda Petrovna showed him her favored dress, in which she wanted to sit for the portrait. She chose a life-size portrait without wavering and wished to look "absolutely her living likeness" on the canvas. The only thing left for Shevchenko to do was to find the best illuminated place in the room, seat his sitter in an armchair, and make her adopt the best posture.

Not a single word was uttered about the price.

17. AT THE TURN OF TWO YEARS

When Shevchenko returned from the Obruchevs, a letter from Lizohub was waiting for him. It was like a waft of warmth from his homeland, conjuring up in his mind the fragrance of Kiev's autumnal orchards and the easy comfort of Sedniv. Lizohub congratulated him on his return to Orenburg, writing that this was probably the poet's first step on a new road and a sign of a change in his destiny; he also promised to send a parcel with warm clothes, books, and produce from his own farm.

The second page of the letter must have been written several days later, because it was a response to Shevchenko's questions contained in his second and last letter.

Lizohub wrote:

"You ask me, my friend, about the fate of those who were arrested along with you. I know a few things about the young people only, since they correspond with their old parents.

"The students Andruzky and Posiada were held behind prison bars for several days each and then taken to Kazan where they were permitted to enroll in the local university. When they graduated from it and were granted their diplomas, they were sent to work at their professions in one of the central provinces of Russia 'under police surveillance,' with the right to return to Ukraine. Hulak's friend, the student Tulub, was not taken to St. Petersburg, since nothing serious was found at his home during the search. He was given the opportunity to graduate from Kiev University and was then exiled to Zlatopol in Poltava Province to live 'under police surveillance.' With no Gymnasium there, he had to teach the children of the nobility at a district school.

"The traitor Petrov, the sonny of a gendarme officer, was accepted for a job with the Third Department and issued five hundred rubles in silver as a reward: he whom no university students would have tolerated in their midst for being a Judas, was granted, on the gendarmes' order, an officially registered diploma from Kiev University with the title of 'full-time student'; on receiving his five hundred pieces of silver, this blackguard did not go and hang himself like Judas Iscariot, but continues to live happily, and, perhaps, crawls like a poisoned vermin.

"We have not heard any hint of the Brotherhood members of the older generation. The only thing I know is that they have been exiled to live somewhere 'under police surveillance' and teach, without any right to visit Ukraine even on holidays."

"Satraps! Barbarians!" Shevchenko exclaimed, not able to restrain himself, and in response to Levitsky and Lazarevsky's quizzical look, added: "Andruzky squealed too much from fright. It was good that the others did not confirm his testimony. He drowned himself with his long tongue. As for Posiada... the only thing that worried him was the bitter lot of the peasantry and the abolition of serfdom; he hadn't the slightest idea about constitutions, republics or reforms. During the interrogations he replied briefly, did not squeal on anybody, and confronted with the gendarmes' pressure, he proved to be much cleverer than the scholar and smart professor Kostomarov... I pity Hulak. His is a keen mind and strong character — a real fighter, I'd say. The gendarmes sensed it, too, and threw him into the Schlüsselburg Fortress. I wonder whether the poor fellow is still alive."

Shevchenko heaved a sigh.

"How did you get the letter?" Pospelov asked. "Was it through the ordinary mail? You must write to your friend at once, so that he be more careful and avoid such subjects in his letters: he might get himself into trouble and ruin you completely."

"Don't you worry: Lizohub is a cautious person," Lazarevsky intervened. "The letter was brought by a landowner's wife whose son served here, and apart from her, nobody knows about its existence. She probably doesn't suspect what its contents are all about."

The next morning Shevchenko was again visited by Gern.

"Where is Zaleski?" he asked.

"Bronek doesn't work here anymore," the poet replied. "Do you need him?"

"No, on the contrary. It's good that we are alone here. I want to tell you about a very strange matter which you alone can explain."

"I'll try, if I can," Shevchenko said in surprise, pushing an armchair toward Gern. "What's happened? You look so agitated."

"Not so much excited as bewildered," Gern replied, sitting down in the armchair. "Close the door lest anyone eavesdrop on us."

Shevchenko looked into the adjoining room and kitchen to see whether Guriy was there, then he locked the front door and settled opposite Gern.

"Colonel Matveiev, as you know, is an utterly decent person, and I trust him like I would myself," Gern said. "Yesterday he had a meal at the restaurant and accidentally found himself beside the company of General Tolmachov, his aide Mansurov and some other people. Matveiev is not particularly fond of them since they are from the company of the former governor Perovsky. He was surprised to see our Maksheiev in their midst.

They were all pretty drunk, and suddenly Maksheiev started slandering Butakov."

"That's incredible!" Shevchenko exclaimed.

"Matveiev heard him saying that Butakov starved the crew and made a fortune on it, and that all the longitudes and latitudes he established were wrong, because his chronometers stopped functioning after they had dropped to the ground one day, no one knew when they started going again, and that's why his chart was inaccurate, and something else of the sort... Butakov was supposed to have mixed up all the local names of the islands and coasts, then he stopped going ashore altogether and charted the coastline from the schooner 'by eye,' and only off the Khiva shore did he go ashore alone at night in disregard of the prohibition of the war minister and the minister for foreign affairs who had strictly forbidden to approach Khiva; what he had been doing in hostile territory at night God alone knew. So something has to be done with Butakov at once: either take measures against Maksheiev for the slander, or, on the contrary, brand Butakov with suspicion. I asked Matveiev to keep silent for the time being, and came here for your advice."

"My God!" Shevchenko exclaimed. "What abominable slander!"

"Don't take it so close to heart, Taras Grigorievich," Gern calmed him. "You were there and saw everything with your own eyes. Although you are not a sailor or topographer, you've learned to understand such things throughout the year and a half you have been on the expedition. Let us consider everything point by point. Obruchev entrusts such matters to me, so sooner or later we'll be in need of your cooperation. Well then, let's begin without any delay."

"All right, ask your questions!" Shevchenko moved closer to Gern, after having regained self-control. Still, his jaw muscles moved on his face, betraying his agitation.

"Is it true that you were hungry while at sea?"

"Yes, such things did happen; especially during the second

navigation, when Maksheiev wasn't with us anymore. The foodstuffs for the expedition, however, were not procured by Butakov but by the Orenburg officials in charge of provisions. Some of the stocks arrived from other towns to the order of the Orenburg Military District. Medical attendant Istomin kept the records all the time and checked on the accounts. I helped him occasionally, and by the invoices and way-bills I know the true situation of things. Probably, both the groats and the flour and all the other foodstuffs were good at first, but the groats grew moldy in the moist Orenburg stores, and then, moist as the groats were, they traveled under tarps for some two months in what amounted to tropical heat. The rusks were moldy as well. Istomin saw personally to it that every rusk was roasted, and none of our men got poisoned or was taken ill. The groats for the porridge were also roasted. Maggots appeared in the salted beef then, but the meat was so salty it didn't rot. It was boiled thoroughly before consumption. Indeed, it wasn't tasty, but there was nothing to be done — everyone realized that in a desert you had to be glad having what you had to eat. Nobody complained: on the contrary, we tried to help by catching fish and shooting whatever game we could."

"Where is Istomin now?"

"He stayed behind at Raïm as a medical attendant at a military hospital."

"Could he confirm all that?"

"Of course, under oath, just like Werner, Pospelov and I."

"And what happened to the chronometers?"

"One of them really fell to the ground and stopped for several minutes, but Butakov kept regulating it for about three days with the help of astronomical observations, and this year before the navigation he again regulated all the chronometers for three days in the estuary of the Syr Darya. If they had been incorrect, why then did Maksheiev, who was worn out by sea sickness, simply copy and include in his records Butakov's data, without going ashore himself? This, too, can be confirmed by Pospelov,

Werner, and me, and even by boatswain Parfenov who's been at sea for thirty years and learned his trade almost as well as a naval officer."

"Had there been any surveys 'by eye'?"

"By the ministry's instructions, Butakov was prohibited from setting foot on the Khivan lands, so whether he liked it or not the southern coastline had to be surveyed 'by eye' from the *Constantine*. During fine weather and dead calms we established our position by compass and used instruments, the names of which I forgot. Pospelov will tell you what they are called."

"I don't want to take Pospelov in on that matter yet."

"Neither do I. Just visit us today in the evening and ask Pospelov out of seeming curiosity to explain to you how a coastline is surveyed from a ship. He'll tell you. If it had not been for that ministry order and instruction, Butakov would have gone ashore a hundred times and made a survey of all Khiva instrumentally. He just didn't want to irritate Nesselrode and Chernishov. He is no coward, and the risk of being captured and sold into slavery would not have stopped him."

"So why then did he have to go ashore to the Khivans?"

"Not to the Khivans, but secretly from them in order to sound the depths of all the five estuary arms in the Amu Darya delta. Last year he and Pospelov waded across these arms the whole night through, and this year he did it with Rybin at the risk of their lives. The boats followed them at some distance in case anything happened, and we on the schooner didn't shut our eyes till dawn, listening alertly to every rustle in the reeds. The sailors just prayed for their Alexei Ivanovich."

"One more question. What about those local place names?"

"Butakov wrote them down from the words of the Kirghiz guide we took along on our second voyage. On the old chart from the time of Perovsky's rule Butakov saw that all the names were really mixed up."

"All right," Gern said, getting to his feet. "Everything seems to be clear. I'll drop in on you in the evening and have a talk with

Pospelov. Tomorrow I'll have to be at the headquarters. Oh my God, how sick I am of it all. There is work up to my neck, and I have to do all of it myself."

"How come? You've got so many assistants: five ensigns, clerks, orderlies…"

"I cannot entrust such matters to the clerks, and the ensigns are outright blockheads who don't know anything. Isaiev tops them all! He cannot write a simple report, without making twenty grammatical errors, and the simplest of thoughts he muddles up so much you have to rewrite every one of his 'works.'"

"Not the man to invent gunpowder, is he?" Shevchenko laughed, seeing Gern off.

In the evening Gern dropped in as if by accident and met with a bustling Lazarevsky preparing to leave for a business trip. So as not to interfere with his preparations, Gern took Pospelov to a corner for a chat. He did not stay long. Now he was well prepared to provide a precise answer to Matveiev on all points. Shevchenko saw him off into the street and asked him, worried:

"What will become of Maksheiev now?"

"If he continues carrying on like that, we'll call him to account."

In the morning a little covered wagon rolled up. Lazarevsky bid everyone farewell and disappeared into the depths of the wagon. Under the horses' yokes the noisy Russian jingle bells, the companions of all the travelers of the past centuries, went off in a monotonous song. Levitsky left for his office, while Shevchenko retired to his room to get ready his painting gear before going to Mathilda Petrovna.

"Some Kirghiz is asking you," Axinia suddenly interrupted his preparations, "He says that he came from Orsk."

"From Orsk? But there are no Kirghiz at Orsk anymore," Shevchenko said, getting up with a surprised look. "Must be some *akyn*. Is he old, lean, bearded?"

"Oh no. He's young, younger than our gentleman, and good looking."

Shevchenko went out into the kitchen.

"Jaisak!" he cried out joyously.

"Taras *Aga*, my dear man! Oh, how glad I am to have found you. A *jatak* passed on to me the note from you, but I've lost it somewhere. I've been looking for you throughout Orsk all day yesterday. I've been at the fortress, asked the big chiefs. I saw Golden Mustache, and asked him. He said that he didn't know where you lived."

"Come in, come in!" Shevchenko put an arm around his shoulders. "Axinia, treat my guest to whatever you have. How did you get here? How's Kuljan, how do you live, and where do you wander? Where are you wintering now?" he bombarded the young Kazakh with questions.

"I live well. Kuljan asked me to thank you for our happiness. We had two *baigas:* one at Irghiz Kala and the other at the Syr Darya. Akbozad and Karkerat came first again. Djantemir tells me, 'You're my son now, so you and I have one household, one flock, one herd.' Once a caravan arrived and asked for food. Djantemir took money from them, and gave the Bukharans my sheep instead. I said, 'But they are my sheep.' To which he replied, 'Since you are Kuljan's husband, we make one family.' The same happened when a Russian caravan arrived. And here Meshka *Mayir* and a general came to Raïm, and said, 'A caravan is coming to Jaman Kala, so it needs sheep, *airan,* kumiss, but there are no Kirghiz around.' The caravan had angry and hungry men who did not want to trade anything; they went to another caravanserai, but Jaman Kala needed the wares badly. Without a caravan there is no life in the steppe. Meshka told Djantemir, 'If you please, you can go back to Jaman Kala and live there on the Or River. But we'll take one part of the steppe for ourselves and you can have the other, if you want.' Djantemir did not return to Jaman Kala: he is better off on the Syr Darya, with a lot more sheep and camels than he had before. So I went to Meshka *Mayir,* and said, 'Take me — I have over a thousand sheep, fifty camels, and a herd of horses. I was joined by Taijan and another two families who also have sheep. The only thing we have to do is shoot the wolves every year. 'Come to us,' the *mayır* told me, 'and we'll shoot the wolves for you.' He keeps your pennants for the chase next year. I took my *apa*, the camels, flock and herd, and left. Then I bought a new door and windows for Djantemir's house and live there now."

"And Rahim?" Shevchenko asked.

"Rahim left with us. Djantemir wanted to kill him at first, cursed him, gave him a terrible whipping, but in the end he let him have five hundred sheep and almost burst from rage. We saw how the Russians mow hay for the winter and we do the same, so that our flock won't perish during *jut* and we turn into beggars like my *ata*. Soon I'll have a son. Taras *Aga*, come and live with us. You won't have to do 'left-right', and you'll feel fine with my people."

Jaisak's naïve suggestion moved Shevchenko. In the meantime, Axinia had served them a heap of hot Siberian meat dumplings, Ukrainian sausage, and tea. Shevchenko produced a bottle of wine, and filled two glasses.

"The Prophet forbade us to drink this," Jaisak said, pushing the glass aside.

"But that's not vodka. It's grape juice, sweet and fragrant. You don't have to drink it; just taste it. It's a sin to kill, steal, do people injustice, but to taste the juice of grapes which grow on this earth — I don't see a sin in that. It isn't strong at all; even our women drink it. You must drink it, so that Kuljan, and your son, and Taijan, and all your *aul* — that all of you be happy."

Jaisak dropped his head; then he took the glass abruptly.

"I agree, if it's for you, Taras *Aga*, so that you be free and wander to your dear steppe," he said, and not knowing of the Russian custom to clink glasses when drinking a toast, downed the drink in one gulp.

However much Shevchenko tried to persuade him to follow up the drink with another one, Jaisak refused, and said, clacking his tongue:

"It tastes good and smells wonderfully. Much better than our kumiss. But the Prophet forbade us, and we have to obey the Prophet."

"How's your eagle?" the poet asked.

"He's a fine hunter: killed me three wolves."

"And what about fox?"

"That's just why I came here — to sell furs of fox and wolves."

Jaisak got up quickly, went into the kitchen, and was back a minute later, carrying a carpet bag stuffed tightly with furs.

He took out two large silver-fox furs and gave them to Shevchenko: "That's a present for you. When you get married, give them to your bride. Yesterday I took them to a merchant. He offered me ten and two rubles a piece. I wanted to ask your advice: is it a good price or not?"

"In the store they sell them for fifty. Ask for twenty — twenty-five rubles."

"The storekeeper won't give me that much. They must be sold to women, but I don't know anyone around here. Meshka *Mayir* is going back to Jaman Kala tomorrow, and takes me along. What am I to do, Taras *Aga*?"

Shevchenko looked at the clock.

"Jaisak, I have to go now. I am painting the portrait of the wife of the biggest chief in Orenburg, and I am late already. Stay here or go with me and I will show you the house of a much respected lady whose portrait I painted, too. You'll go in and show her the furs yourself. Tell her that you were sent by the artist who painted her portrait, and ask thirty rubles for the bigger furs and twenty-five for the smaller. This is a town. I myself cannot go around and offer them for sale; I'd get into big trouble, if I did it."

"All right, I'll sell them myself."

Jaisak gathered up his furs and they walked quickly to the house of Baroness Blaramberg. On approaching gate, Shevchenko showed Jaisak where to enter, and went on his way.

Mathilda Petrovna was already waiting for him. Shevchenko

apologized for being late and told her about the golden eagle and the silver-fox furs which had helped a young *jigit* marry the girl he loved.

Shevchenko's story about Djantemir, Kuljan and Jaisak was very much to the liking of the governor's wife. In its funny places she laughed sincerely. During these moments Shevchenko captured at last that sparkle of life in her face that lent its chilly and aloof expression a sudden flash of inspiration, through which a little part of her soul could be glimpsed.

The work on the portrait became easy and joyous, and progressed at an unusually rapid pace when suddenly it was interrupted by the appearance of the smart looking noncom who had reported to the general of Shevchenko's arrival the first time.

"Excuse me, your Excellency," he said, clicking his heels and stiffening in front of Mathilda Petrovna. "There is a Kirghiz who keeps insisting that he be let in. He says he's come to see the painter to offer silver-fox furs for sale."

"Impossible!" Shevchenko got frightened and put his palette aside. "Excuse me, Mathilda Petrovna, the man does not understand what is allowed and what is not. I saw him to the house of the baroness, and didn't even tell him where I was going. By what miracle did he find me here?"

He wanted to leave together with the noncom, but Mathilda Petrovna stopped him.

"Don't chase him away, Taras Grigorievich! You excited my curiosity about that Asian Romeo and his Juliet so much that … Call him in. I want to have a look at him … and well… at his silver-fox furs, too."

"But I told you already: I need Taras *Aga* who is painting the chief's wife as if she were alive," Jaisak indignantly pressed home his demand to Obruchev's cook and batman. "Call me Taras *Aga*, please."

Presently Shevchenko and the noncom entered the kitchen.

"Why did you come here, Jaisak?" Shevchenko said reproachfully. "I told you to show the furs to the other lady and then go to my quarters..."

"But I have to go back to Jaman Kala with Meshka *Mayir* tomorrow! That general's woman took two furs, but I still got a lot of them. They all must be sold," Jaisak said.

"All right, then! I didn't call you to this place, but since you've come, the lady wishes to see you. Let's go! Where are your furs?"

Jaisak took off his sheepskin coat, fur cap and felt boots, and with fur socks on his feet, followed Shevchenko.

"Good day, woman of the biggest chief in Orenburg," Jaisak said, greeting her with a bow.

"Good day, my dear," she replied, regarding the young Kazakh with curiosity. "Show mo your fox furs."

Jaisak sat down on the carpet, crossing his feet in Oriental fashion, and started taking the furs out of his carpet bag one by one.

"Oh, they smell horribly!" she could not hold herself in check.

"The smell will disappear in a couple of days. The furs must have been kept in a trunk together with sheep skins," Shevchenko explained.

"How much do you ask for them?" she said at last.

"Thirty rubles, and if you take two, it will be twenty-five a piece," Shevchenko replied for Jaisak.

Mathilda Petrovna fingered the fur reflectively, and then reached for the bell.

"Ask the master," she said to the lackey.

Obruchev entered almost the next moment.

"Look, Voldemar, what furs I have been brought. This is a hunter who kills his game with a golden eagle," she explained pointing at Jaisak who had got to his feet the moment the general came in. "He asks thirty rubles for one fur. Shouldn't we take two of them?"

"Of course, if you like them. You cannot go around in sable every day, and the ermines don't go together with your black dresses."

Shevchenko stood off to one side stiff at attention, although he was dressed in a frock coat.

"Oh, good morning, Shevchenko," the general said, noticing the poet.

"Good morning, your Excellency," Shevchenko responded promptly, worried how the general would react at the sight of the civvies, although Mathilda Petrovna herself had told him to come in civilian clothes "so as to feel closer to art."

"Well, how does your work progress?" Obruchev asked, forgetting Jaisak and his furs for a moment.

"Little by little, your Excellency. I managed to convey the likeness at once, but the portrait lacked... well, how should I put it... it lacked some life perhaps. It was only today that I suddenly captured it, and I think the portrait has come to live under my brush."

The general went up to the easel and looked at the unfinished portrait for a long time.

"Yes, something has changed in it indeed. Look, Mathilda, it seems the sun has splashed its ray on it. Well, carry on. I won't be distracting you anymore. So are you taking the furs?" he said, turning round at the door. "Yes? Good, I'll have the money brought to you at once."

"I'll take two of the largest furs," Mathilda Petrovna said, watching Jaisak with curiosity all the time.

He picked out a pair of the best furs. She took the money from the lackey, silently counted off not five but six red ten-ruble bills, and then turned to Shevchenko: "Will you go on painting?"

"Yes, if you are not tired yet," Shevchenko said, picking up the palette and taking Jaisak by the elbow.

"Wait for me outdoors. I'll be busy for some time, or you can go to my quarters. I'll be back soon, and in the evening we'll think things over."

When Jaisak left, Shevchenko started working quickly, putting dab after dab onto the canvas with a sense of joy and self-confidence.

Mathilda Petrovna sat with a thoughtful expression on her face, occasionally smiling faintly and a shade sadly at her thoughts, as if she were bidding farewell to the half-forgotten, naïve dreams of her youth which had unexpectedly surfaced from the bottom of her heart. No longer was she a reserved lady of fifty, which made her look like a school marm or like a dried-up flower. Today her soul opened to the eyes of the artist for the first time, although she did not say a single word to him; her soul was so lonely in the huge, luxuriously furnished and empty parlors and halls of this palace. Jaisak's youth and the story about his love had roused her. And although a faint odor of the sheepskin still hung in the air, the image of the young herder whose eyes beamed happiness, a confidence in life, and an unconquerable power of youth, had produced a deep impression on her. It made her feel bitter; it pained her at the thought that she had not experienced such great, unselfish and pure love in her life.

From the Obruchevs Shevchenko hurried to his quarters where Jaisak was waiting for him.

"Meshkov will leave no sooner than by midday," Shevchenko told Jaisak. "By that time we'll have made a visit to Gern. Maybe Sophia Ivanovna will buy a fur for herself or for her sister."

They soon went to bed in order to be up early next morning.

"Are you really in such a hurry to get back to Kuljan?" Shevchenko asked, as they walked to the town's outskirts in the morning. "You miss her, don't you?"

"No," Jaisak shook his head. "On the day when you celebrate the birth of your God, a large caravan is to arrive at Jaman Kala from Moscow. It will be heading for Margelan and Bukhara. I am going to Bukhara. Two of my brothers — Kasim and Tyulenbai — are there. I promised *ata* I'd buy them out of slavery when I grew rich. That's what my *ata* willed before he died. They must be free."

Jaisak's words made Shevchenko start, and he did not utter a single word during the rest of their way.

Sophia Ivanovna bought one fur from Jaisak, and Gern gave them the address of her sister; but it was late already, Jaisak quickly said goodbye to Shevchenko, and trotted off to the fortress lest he miss Meshkov. Shevchenko remained in his studio and plunged deep in thought.

Jaisak's words had settled on the poet's heart in a heavy black cloud. He had graduated from an Academy of Fine Arts, stood on his own feet, achieved fame, traveled throughout Ukraine, published his album of engravings *Picturesque Ukraine,* and made his way in life, while his brothers and sisters vegetated as serfs. What had he done to save them? Now he reproached himself for every goblet of champagne he had drunk, for every party, at which he had dressed in aristocratic clothes, wooed women, commanded the attention of friends, and recited his poems about the bitter lot of serfs, without using the occasional money he had made to free his kith from serfdom.

It is for them that fate had punished me so severely, he thought with despair.

Leaden drops of tears rolled from his eyes.

Throughout the whole day Shevchenko was in a taciturn and gloomy mood. He sat in loneliness in his studio till dusk fell, chewed on the dry bread he had bought in the morning, and went to sleep on the narrow army cot, because he could not return to the quarters he shared with his friends who would immediately start asking him questions and make his misery the more unbearable.

Once Baroness Blaramberg took Shevchenko under her wing, he received several more commissions to paint portraits, which kept him busy from the earliest hours of the morning, since the December days were the shortest in the year.

On the thirty-first of December a courier carrying an official letter with five seals of red wax resembling blood blotches mercilessly whipped his tired horses through the Sakmar Gate and burst into Orenburg — and the next moment the headquarters clerks started writing long lists of those who had been decorated with orders, promoted, or assigned to higher offices. No one in Orenburg, except for Obruchev, Gern and the clerks, knew what joy or disappointment the morning of New Year held in store.

Shevchenko sat in his studio, chewing on his pen and thinking about what the next year would bring him, when Gern suddenly entered. He greeted the poet, looked into all corners, and sat down opposite him.

"What, you're about the same affair again?" Shevchenko asked, raising his blue eyes to Gern.

"No, I just wanted to tell you that your album will be presented to the czar only after Butakov finishes writing and presents his *Description of the Aral Sea* first. Not the scientific one with all the data and figures he prepares for the Geographical Society, nor the hydrographic description he forwarded to his ministry of the navy, but an abbreviated one written in a simple language, which will be shown to the czar together with your album. That is why your future will be decided upon not now, but later on, after Butakov leaves for the capital."

Shevchenko discerned something ominous in Gern's voice, and asked anxiously:

"What's happened, Karl Ivanovich?"

"So far we've received only the response to our plea of two years ago, in which we asked the authorities to permit you to paint and alleviate your lot because of your illness."

Shevchenko grew pale, got on his feet, and leaning on the table with his palms, bent toward Gern: "And what happened?"

"It was only now that Count Orlov presented our plea to the czar, and, the way he wrote it, "the most august permission did not follow."

"Which means that I have again been prohibited from taking up either brush or pencil, doesn't it?" Shevchenko asked in a dull voice.

"It means that you'll have to be careful now. Nobody will hide away the Aral drawings you did for the needs of the state, but accepting commissions for portraits openly and painting them here in the studio is out of the question; you'll have to be extremely careful with the people who'll be asking you to do their portraits, and accept orders only from the absolutely honest and decent under the condition that nobody else will catch you at the work. But don't lose heart," Gern took him by the hand, "everything will pass and change for the better."

"Yes, of course, everything will pass," Shevchenko replied dejectedly.

"Obruchev asks you to hope for better times and not be sad. Continue painting Mathilda Petrovna's portrait, and we'll warn her to have the sittings arranged in another room and during the hours when there are no officers in the palace. So cheer up, old chap! He'll see your album — and everything will be all right! Now listen to the news: Butakov has been awarded the Order of St. Vladimir, and Serhiy Levitsky has been transferred to St. Petersburg to a much higher office. Colonel Matveiev got a St. Anna Order, and from tomorrow on Obruchev is a General of the Infantry."

"What about Ensign Isaiev? When I was painting his portrait, he told me he was expecting a promotion."

"Such a straitlaced fool expecting a promotion? Let him be content with his rank for several years more until he becomes a bit brighter, if that's still possible at all. But putting it frankly, if a head is empty, reason will hardly grow in it."

Shevchenko regained his self-control and even laughed at what he heard, but when Gern left, he again dropped his head in grief.

The New Year was celebrated at home. Up till midnight Shevchenko did not tell anyone the news he had heard, but when the cuckoo called midnight and Butakov as the senior, both in age and rank, raised the goblet and congratulated everyone on the New Year, Shevchenko congratulated Butakov on receiving his decoration and Serhiy Levitsky on his promotion and transfer to the capital.

The news made everyone merry and joyous, and only moments later did the friends notice that Shevchenko did not share their merriment.

"And what does the New Year promise you?" Butakov asked, worried.

"I, too, received a present from the Holsteinian Prince."

Then he told them about the reply of Count Orlov. Everyone fell silent. The expression of joy on Levitsky's face faded, and suddenly he felt miserable wretched and ashamed for his luck at a time when dark clouds obscured Shevchenko's prospects. Butakov's brow furrowed. He realized like no one else that if the czar had not forgotten Shevchenko's poetry, no drawing, no album whatsoever would win Shevchenko his freedom. But he did not utter a word nor show in any way how his heart sank at the presentiment of evil times to come.

On New Year's Day Butakov and Pospelov went visiting their friends and acquaintances. Levitsky left, too; Shevchenko stayed at home and wrote Varvara Repnina a letter that was full of despair. He begged her to intercede for him and save the artist and poet in him. The letter came out tragically worded, but Shevchenko did not attempt to change its tenor; then he wrote a letter to Zhukovsky who had helped him so much in gaining his freedom.

Even now Shevchenko did not realize that the entire royal family considered him their personal enemy. He complained bitterly to Zhukovsky that Brüllow could, but did not wish to, come to his rescue, and implored Zhukovsky to help him obtain at least the permission to draw and to paint.

Levitsky was busy with the preparations for his departure, while Butakov was finishing his *Description of the Aral Sea*. The sailors, too, were in a hurry to return to the Baltic Sea, and Shevchenko's quarters were a beehive of a pre-departure bustle.

In the middle of January, a letter from Mikhailo Lazarevsky addressed to his brother Fedir arrived from St.Petersburg. Fedir was out of town on business. Since his friends had no secrets from each other, they decided to open the letter and read it over tea in the evening.

After the customary New Year's greetings and inquiries about his brother's health, Lazarevsky described the execution of the members of Petrashevsky's secret circle:

"It was something unbearably horrible. From dawn people in their hundreds moved to the square where this disgusting and gory show was to take place. In the crowd, the mothers, brothers and parents of the doomed were pointed out. Some of them could not stand on their feet and were supported by strangers who themselves trembled from agitation.

"At last their horrible cortege appeared under a strong escort. They were driven in open carts in twos and threes without any caps and dressed in light summer coats in which they had been arrested in the spring, although there was a fierce Epiphany frost outdoors. Blue from the cold and with prison pallor on their faces, the resembled corpses.

"I wanted to run away from the scene, but my feet seemed to be rooted to the ground, as my keen attention greedily captured and seared in my mind all the stages of this frightening ceremony.

"The verdict was read for an endlessly long time. In the crowd dozens of pallid lips repeated the names and the horrible words "To death.' Then each of the sentenced men was made to get on his knees, and the executioner wearing a blood red shirt, black velveteen trousers and lacquered boots, broke over the heads of the doomed a sword that had been filed down beforehand. In this symbolic way, they were deprived of their honor, nobility status, titles, all human rights, diplomas, decorations as well as military and civilian ranks; then the priest came up and gave them the last blessing. At long last shrouds — long, coarse shirts with sleeves reaching to the ground — were pulled over their heads.

"Behind me I heard a woman crying out in despair, and that cry, piercing and filled with unspeakable horror, still rings in my ears. I could not bear it any longer and ran away from the scaffold and the crowd, in which some people experienced a cruel nervous shock, while others prepared themselves to watch the death throes of the country's best men with an openly keen interest, like they would watch a dangerous performance of acrobats under the cupola of a circus.

"Toward the evening I was visited by my compatriots who told me that the doomed were pardoned and their death sentence commuted to long years of penal servitude in Eastern Siberia."

The letter had several more lines addressed to Shevchenko, but it fell out of his hands and remained lying unread to the end on the table. Everyone was silent. Czarism was looking into their eyes with the cruel, dull stare of an executioner, which suddenly made everyone feel chilly, although the room was well heated.

"Burn it." Pospelov was the first to come to his senses.

Nobody stirred. He brought the letter up to a candle and held it to the flame until it licked his finger.

18. ON THE OUTSKIRTS OF ORENBURG

A sense of dreary loneliness assailed the poet after the departure of Butakov, Pospelov and Levitsky. He moved over into his studio at the Gerns' where it was always tidy and warm.

The poignant yearning for a home overwhelmed him with unusual force.

"I'm a tramp, a derisible tramp," his lips whispered.

As long as he could remember he had lived at other people's homes — at first when he had been a serf, a mute creature who had to follow his master wherever his lordly whims took him. Then he lived in the workshop of Shiryaev, a well-known St. Petersburg contractor who painted the palaces of the nobility as well as the theaters and best buildings in the capital. After the occasional nights at the home of the artist Soshenko, he settled in the huge and luxuriously furnished studio of Brüllow where he lived several years. Then...

Could he really remember all the crofts and manors he had visited in Ukraine, when though a famous poet, he nonetheless remained homeless and a semi-sponger.

It was only in Kiev that he had lived not as a guest but rented with Sazhin a tiny apartment on Khreshchatik Lane in a house which did not differ much from a village cottage.

And again he took to wandering, and was invited to stay at sumptuous manors with snow-white palaces built either in the subtly austere Empire style of Czar Alexander's era or in the excessively embellished Ukrainian baroque. And everywhere he was but a guest, everywhere a stranger and wanderer. In the end, there was the Third Department, prison, the Orsk Fortress, barracks, the schooner *Constantine,* and the Kosaral earth house which, too, was not called his but Maksheiev's.

When would this endless tramping cease? Where was the haven where he could drop his life's heavy anchor and find a family, a wife, and children? Would he ever find it at all? He was tired of his perpetual wandering, and his soul had grown chilly amongst strangers, even though they were kind people. Even the best of friends can never become the dearest person a man could wish for. His tired heart and lonely soul longed for dear and human warmth.

Thomas Werner and Bronek Zaleski were the first to notice how profoundly sad the poet became after the departure of his friends, and started inviting him more cordially to their homes, surrounding him with heartfelt attention bordering on piety. They saw in him not only a talented poet and artist, not only was he their friend in need, but a public figure who desired the freedom of the people of Russia and Ukraine and, along with them, of Poland as well.

Shevchenko was gratified by the attention he was accorded: it warmed him after the humiliations and offenses of the past year, and he permitted them to console him like an orphaned child picked up by strangers on the cruel pathways of war.

A period of financial difficulties set in for the poet. The fees he had received from Isaiev, the baroness and the others had dwindled away before the New Year. Now he was without a bean in the world.

On Obruchev's advice, Butakov did not detail Shevchenko to the line battalion stationed in Orenburg, because the commander of the 23rd Infantry Corps, General Tolmachov, a great stickler for form and precise compliance with the letter of the law, would have immediately restricted him to barracks and then sent him to one of the remotest forts of the Orenburg line. For that, however, Shevchenko was deprived of his soldier's rations and uniform. Now he had to earn his own livelihood.

Gern did not charge him anything for his quarters and food and invited him for breakfast and midday meals every day, but by some barely noticeable signs, Shevchenko sensed that his presence either stood in the way or got on the nerves of Sophia Ivanovna, and so he came only when Karl Ivanovich was at home. Gern's duties however, made him unexpectedly and frequently leave home, and that was why Shevchenko remained without a meal time and again, and had to be content with black bread throughout the whole day.

Now he did not dare take any commissions for paintings anymore. He had painted a number of good landscapes after his Aral sketches, but did not risk signing them and kept them in Lazarevsky's room, sadly reflecting that even the best of canvases, without the artist's signature, lost half its value. One such landscape he sent to Lizohub with the request to add the signature in cinnabar and sell it for at least fifty rubles; he was inexplicably happy and grateful to him when the wished for money arrived with the return mail.

In early March he received a letter from Repnina. As always, it was full of sympathy for the poor exile.

"It is only now that I really appreciate at last the great talent of our Gogol and his *Dead Souls*. You are right, Taras Grigorievich: it is one of our best hooks. I did not understand him before," she wrote as an aside.

Shevchenko was sincerely happy at this acknowledgment. He always admired Gogol, and hurried to write a long letter to Repnina in response.

This time he had to resort to guile: he knew Repnina to be deeply religious. She was an exalted, mystically inclined woman, and offending her feelings would mean losing her friendship and respect, which he valued highly. Therefore he omitted any mention in the letter about Gogol's latest book in which, influenced by a religious psychosis, he rendered void his great writings and justified such things as serfdom, the execution of the Decembrists, the shackles to which Patreshevsky's group was condemned, the terrible caning in the army, the flogging, and all the other horrors of Czar Nicholas' regime.

Repnina was a reliable friend to be sure. She had not been afraid to write to Orlov, pleading that Shevchenko be pardoned or at least permitted to paint, for which she received a stern reply with an outright threat of arrest and trial if she did not stop interceding for the exiled poet. Repnina realized that the times had passed when when the wives of Volkonsky and Trubetskoi could go to Eastern Siberia to ease the penal servitude of their husbands who had taken part in the uprising against czardom in December 1825. Nonetheless, she did not succumb to fear, and continued corresponding with the poet, employing a number of rather naïve ruses for this purpose: lest the letters attract the gendarmes' attention, she asked her friend Glafira Psyol to write the address in her hand, the letters were mailed not from Yahotin but from some neighboring township, and addressed to the Headquarters of the Orenburg Military District for the attention of Captain Karl Gern. All this entailed a considerable risk, which made Shevchenko value all the higher every word she wrote.

Lazarevsky's second portrait, which Shevchenko had started working on, was gathering dust, as were the portraits of Karl Ivanovich and Sophia Ivanovna. Gern was always busy and his wife sat rarely and unwillingly for her portrait, while Shevchenko wanted very much to thank the Gerns by painting their portraits, for all the good things they had done for him.

Now he devoted all his time and effort to self-portraits, painting himself dressed in uniform, frock coat, or black cap. One of these self-portraits he sent to Lizohub, and another to Repnina.

His friends tried to persuade him to paint himself not in a usual room, but fettered in shackles behind prison bars. He did not agree with such a symbolic representation of himself, but he did take to the brush again. The self-portrait he did came out quite well. His Polish friends asked him to give them the portrait as a memento. Although he had not a single copper about him at that time, false shame did not permit him to admit his wretched poverty. Thinking tensely how to make a little money at least from the sale of his self-portrait, he told them that he had promised to show it to his acquaintances first and took it to his quarters which he now shared with Lazarevsky back home after his three-week absence.

Shevchenko showed him the self-portrait.

"It's wonderful! The likeness is remarkable," Lazarevsky repeated again and again, alternately looking at the portrait at close distance and from afar. "Where did you paint it?"

"At the home of my Polish friends," Shevchenko explained. "Take it, for God's sake! I want it to be yours, because it might be begged out of me by others and I need money badly now."

The offer made Lazarevsky confused.

"I think it's impossible, old chap. Your portrait is a valuable work of art and very dear to me, but now, with Serhiy in St. Petersburg, I'm in financial straits. He earned much more than I did, you know. So I've got nothing to pay you with, 'pon my word."

Shevchenko raised his foot and showed him a tattered boot.

"See what footwear I have. Give me your old boots, and that's all I ask of you."

Lazarevsky felt the blood rush hotly to his cheeks and his

heart contracted into a lump. He rushed over to his wardrobe, took out a pair of boots that were almost new, and gave them to the poet.

"What did you wear during the frosts? You had a pair of felt boots, didn't you?"

"I had, but I wore holes in them by February. It doesn't matter much now, though: there'll be spring soon, and anyway. ." and Shevchenko told his friend what a bad turn his personal affairs had taken.

"Butakov and Obruchev wanted to do me a good turn by reminding Orlov about me, but it came to evil. Now my Aral album won't help me either, perhaps," he said with a sigh.

Lazarevsky's heart contracted again. Gern had once told him about the hopelessness of Shevchenko's situation. Lazarevsky kept silent lest he make Shevchenko's wound fester the more. The next day he wrote his brother Mikhailo a letter and asked him to help the poet immediately. The letter did not remain without a prompt answer: his friends in the capital clubbed together and sent him a hundred rubles.

Three weeks passed.

It was Maundy Thursday, a sunny day in April. The large bells in the belfries leisurely called to one another in a sad way befitting the mood of the lent, while the rooks cried noisily and fought for the possession of their nests of the previous year in the grove beyond the Ural River and in the willows and birch trees growing throughout the town. The birch trees had turned a brown-lilac, all of them knotted with swollen buds. A sickly green grass had burst forth along the fences on the streets and dingy boulevards which, as usual, were deserted, dull and littered. The smells of pastries and roasted pork wafted from the homes.

Shevchenko had his midday meal at the Gerns' and went out on the porch together with Karl Ivanovich. Gern stopped on the steps as he girded on his sword belt, and was carried away by the sight of a wedge of cranes drifting past in the sky.

"It's off to the headquarters again for me," he said with disappointment. "How I wish I could snatch but one day off to go hunting! There's waterfowl galore in every lake and puddle throughout the steppe, and here I've got so much work to do I burn the midnight oil. By the way, we received the mail today. If there's a letter for you, I'll drop in for a minute and treat you to a holiday gift. Will you be in?"

"I intended to take a stroll along the Ural, but for the sake of a letter I'm prepared to stay put until dusk," Shevchenko said, walking off slowly to his studio in the outhouse.

In the corner stood the easel with Gern's portrait, the face was already painted, but the hands, arms, shoulders and uniform only sketched in vague outline. Shevchenko picked up the brushes reluctantly and started touching up the golden pads of the epaulettes, then the thick cords of the aiguilettes, glancing through the window now and again.

Carried away by the work, ho did not notice how two hours had elapsed. As he tore himself away from the portrait, he caught a fleeting glimpse of Isaiev passing from the wicket gate to the main building.

So Gern's back home and I missed him, Shevchenko thought. Isaiev must have brought some papers from the headquarters for him to sign.

Throwing his threadbare coat over his shoulders, Shevchenko trotted across the yard to the back entrance and went into the kitchen where Guriy was taking ruddy Easter cakes smelling delectably of saffron and lemon peel, out of the oven. Shevchenko cleaned his dirty boots on the door mat and made for the door of the inner corridor, when Guriy suddenly blocked his way.

"The captain's out," he said. "He hasn't returned yet."

"I'll see the lady, then."

"You can't; she's sleeping."

"What do you mean, 'she's sleeping?' I just saw Ensign Isaiev going in."

Instead of an answer, Guriy took hold of both door jambs more firmly.

"Why, have you gone mad?" Shevchenko said indignantly. "If she's got guests, I can see her just as well."

"That's the reason why you can't, because the ensign's in there right now," Guriy snapped back, and looked straight in Shevchenko's eyes. "Taras Grigorievich, are you a little child, or what? How can you see her, if she's entertaining her lover?"

Shevchenko looked at Guriy with wide-open eyes.

"Being married to such a fine man, that disgusting skirt had to take up with an outright louse," Guriy went on. "Today's Maundy Thursday, and here she... Another woman would've been blessing God for such a husband as our captain... But no, she mixes with those Poles and then with the officers... and here I'm made to be covering up all that filth. Ugh!"

"What filth are you talking about?" Shevchenko asked in a feeble whisper.

Guriy carried on, now and then glancing at the door leading into the corridor with hatred:

"That louse comes here to foul up the nest of an honest man, and then he gets drunk and brags, 'No woman can withstand my advances.' His batman frequently brings her messages from the ensign. 'He'd better keep his mouth shut,' the batman told me, 'because this affair might end up with trouble.' Indeed, we common folk would have fought it out between us, given the woman a good drubbing — and that would be the end of it. But the lords take to pistols and swords right away. In such cases, trouble is just around the corner! That Isaiev louse keeps blabbering God knows what in all the restaurants and in the officers' club."

Guriy heaved a sigh and carefully pushed Shevchenko away from the door.

"Go now, Taras Grigorievich. It'll be better that way."

Shevchenko went out into the yard, then he made for the street and walked wherever his feet carried him.

In the end he came to the house where Lazarevsky lived. Lazarevsky was at home. His room smelled of freshly baked Easter cakes. A red-faced Axinia put the samovar on the table.

Shevchenko took his coat off, only now noticing that he had left his cap at the Gems'.

"All right, let's get down to supper," Lazarevsky said. "By the way, here's twenty rubles for you. That's the remainder of my traveling allowances which go as payment for your portrait."

"Thank you," the poet said, strongly shaking Lazarevsky's hand, and added unexpectedly, "Don't worry, brother. They're all alike: angels to the eyes, but actually such…"

Utterly surprised, Lazarevsky started asking what had happened, but Shevchenko kept silent.

"Move to my place again," Lazarevsky pleaded. "I feel so lonely now that Serhiy and Mikhailo are gone. You're the only person I can speak to in Ukrainian. Indeed, move in again! For me you're not only a favorite poet now, but someone as dear as my homeland."

"All right!" Shevchenko agreed at last. "Besides, I have to finish your portrait. I'll bring the paints tomorrow, and on Saturday I'll move in."

"Wonderful! We'll be still working tomorrow, but we agreed to appear at work by turns, since everyone needs to buy something or visit the barber's. I'll be home at two o'clock, and we'll have a meal together."

Mumbling another "All right," the poet drank his tea and started undressing.

In the morning, Lazarevsky went to his office, without waking up the poet. Shevchenko woke up late, had a shave, and hurried off to get his paints at his studio at the Gerns' home. No sooner had he entered the studio than Gern knocked on the door.

"Here is an Easter letter for you, my friend," Gern said, giving him the letter. "That's point one. Secondly, I've decided to have a rest today and sit for my portrait for a while. I wanted to go hunting, but I'm so tired I can't go anywhere. Still, you must have taken offense at Zosia and me, seeing as you haven't finished our portraits yet," he added, walking up to the easel. "Oh, I see you've done something in my absence. Permit me to make one little remark, though: this cord of the aiguillette is always shorter than the other one. Here, take a look!"

Gern took off his greatcoat, and sat down in his usual place.

"What a pity!" Shevchenko said with a sigh. "It'll have to be changed."

He moved the easel closer to the window, carefully scratched off the dried-up paint, and took up his brush.

"Aren't the headquarters really at work today?" he asked at length.

"They are, but the clerks have gone to church, and I said I was going hunting so they'd give me some peace. And all of Orenburg is outdoors now anyway, shooting wild ducks."

The conversation lapsed. Suddenly Shevchenko glimpsed Isaiev sneaking across the yard.

Shevchenko stalled, and the brush fell out of his hand.

"What's the matter?" Gern asked, alarmed.

"No-thing," Shevchenko said, and bent down for the brush.

"Did you see somebody passing by there?"

"Y-yes, possibly."

"Well, that's the end of my rest. Somebody must have come for me," Gern said, got to his feet, reached for his greatcoat, and made to leave.

"Wait a minute!" Shevchenko rushed after him, and took him by the sleeve. "Be prepared for the worst..."

"What do you mean?" Gern asked, not understanding the warning. He looked Shevchenko in the eyes, grew pale, and rushed to the back door.

Shevchenko ran after him. Gern burst into the kitchen, from there he reached the corridor, dining room, looked into the empty sitting room and study. Then he kicked open the locked door of the bedroom and disappeared inside.

A minute or two passed.

The door was flung open.

Shevchenko barely managed to draw back when Isaiev came tumbling into the dining room, hitting his head against a sideboard.

Without thinking what he was doing, Shevchenko rushed to his studio, frantically picked up his paints and brushes, and hurried to Lazarevsky's quarters.

19. THE "SHOWDOWN"

Isaiev burst like a madman into the office of Cavalry Captain Mansurov, and without greeting him, banged his fist on the desk.

"I'll make him fight a duel. A lot of blood is going to flow! Serge, you must be my second!"

"First of all, be as kind as to greet me, and then tell me who you intend fighting?"

"Gern! He offended me terribly! Disgraced me, as a matter of fact! Dishonored me before the soldiers! Put your coat on, and deliver my challenge!"

"Come, come! Is the reason of the trouble a woman again? What a lewd buck you are indeed!" Mansurov said, shaking his head. "Tell me everything from beginning to end."

"It all started with Zosia Gern. Drat it, but she's an extraordinarily delicious dish! Fell head over heels in love with me, and that German swine… became jealous like a simple muzhik. All right, he could have challenged me like a decent man, but he… burst into the bedroom just at the most critical moment…"

"Ha-ha-ha!!!" Mansurov roared with laughter. "Wait a minute, but you've got a bloodied ear! Could that homebred Othello have bitten your ear?"

"He didn't, but he yanked me out of her bed, almost tearing my ear off. I must fight him! At once!"

Mansurov burst into a roar of laughter again, wiped the tears of mirth out of his eyes, and shook his head disapprovingly.

"What a fool you are! Gern is the best marksman in the Orenburg area, and back in St. Petersburg he won three prizes for marksmanship. He'll pick you off like a wild duck. It won't be a duel but suicide for you."

Isaiev piped down right away.

"But I'm an officer. I must fight him or else be dismissed from the ranks. What will I be living on then?" he asked piteously.

"You're a dunce and blockhead — that's what you are, and not an officer!" Mansurov continued. "Aren't there enough serf lasses, town girls or modistes for you around here? But no he had to have a lady. With ladies it's much more complicated: gentlemen don't like sharing their wives with anybody else, you know."

"You'd better stop philosophizing, and tell me what I'm to do now. His batman and that *khokhol* painter, who did my portrait, saw everything."

"I can just imagine! Must have been a unique scene!"

Another fit of roaring laughter gripped Mansurov, then the expression of mirth faded from his face abruptly, he rose from his chair, and started buttoning up his uniform.

"What I hear is really bad! Shevchenko is received at the best homes and might broadcast the scandal throughout Orenburg. And you, too, have been blabbering God knows what. In such a case, a duel is unavoidable. It all happened because of Obruchev and those damned liberal nobles! They make too much of that *khokhol*, recommend one another for promotions and decorations, leaving the loyal servants of the czar in the cold. You, too, hoped to get a second star on your shoulder straps, didn't you?"

"You bet! I had to become a second lieutenant and command half a company," Isaiev took up the cue angrily. "But don't evade the point, Serge, and tell me what to do."

"On the other hand, that *khokhol* isn't such a fool as to chatter more than is good for him. I think he'll keep his mouth shut. And if you yourself bridle your tongue, everything will be kept in the dark. Gern wouldn't like to be called a cuckold."

"Yes, but I've been offended."

"It's unclear yet who's been offended more. But to take revenge for the scratched ear — that's very much to the point. It calls for some good thinking on how to go about it. You're not the only one who's out for his blood."

Isaiev's eyes flared up with rage, he craned his thin neck and was all attention. Mansurov lit up a pipe, and carried on, winking cunningly now and again:

"Who compiles the lists of those to be recommended for decorations? Gern as the aide responsible for special missions. Obruchev approves them. Their entire cohort received orders and other decorations for the New Year. The same thing will occur on Easter Day, and next winter again, and so on. It'll be so always and everywhere until we unseat them. We've been considering that many a time with Tolmachov. He hates Gern and Obruchev and all that liberal bunch of theirs, as exemplified by that lout Matveiev. And he hates them more than you do. Let's go to Tolmachov. Maybe we'll come up with something together."

"But I don't want Tolmachov knowing anything about the scandal."

"First of all, Tolmachov is one of us, and besides, we don't have to tell him everything. A hint would be enough."

Isaiev wavered, but the thought that Gern might challenge him to a duel put a stop to his wavering, and both men went to the fortress where Tolmachov had his quarters.

The general was at home. On learning that they had come not on a visit but on some business, he invited them to his study and locked its door, ready to hear them out. Isaiev briefly set forth his unpleasant case in a tone emphasizing the highest trust in the general.

"Why the hell did you have to fall for that Polish skirt?" the general said angrily. "Of all the impregnable fortresses to take, when its gates are held open wide for every passerby. But for an officer of the general headquarters to take a common soldier in on the secrets of his bedroom and compromise a brother officer — that's something I don't understand altogether. It's what you get for that foolish liberalism. Ever since our dear Perovsky left us, life's been a torture for decent people here. Unfortunately, Obruchev is extremely careful and it's difficult to find a weak spot in him: he doesn't accept bribes, has no interest in women, neither does he indulge in drinking. He's prosecuted quartermasters and suppliers for the slightest offense and complied with laws and orders. The headquarters under him is more like a school for the daughters of the nobility; he corrupts the soldiers with his lenient ways and is friends with the mariners, especially with that... What's his name?"

"With Butakov!" Mansurov prompted, anxious to please. "Yes, yes! Our mariners, as you know have been traipsing around the world, and they picked up a rebellious spirit in Europe. That Butakov alone has it up to his gills! He doesn't send a sailor, but gets into the water himself to sound the depth. As to the unjust ways of decorating and promoting people, we've become used to that. Obruchev decorates anyone he likes. That's what he's governor for. Now if we could remove him... Then ranks, crosses and stars would come spilling on our chests and shoulder straps. By the way, the poor devil Perovsky writes to tell me that he is not his own self anymore, because he's missing the Yayïk Cossacks. Even our sovereign recently noticed how gloomy and sad Perovsky was. 'What's the matter with you, Perovsky?' he asked him once. Our Vasiliy Alexeyevich told him straight off that he was missing his Ural life. The sovereign smiled and said that the matter could be settled, which means that if Obruchev were to slip on something, our dear Perovsky would be back with us again. But so far we have to suffer and wait..."

"Everything you say is correct, your Excellency. But advise our young friend what he is to do. He won't unseat Obruchev, but Gern must be punished for the scratched ear. A duel with such a dangerous adversary as Gern must be avoided."

The general kept silent for a minute, then admitted outright: "This story is an incredible nonsense not worth a copper.

The best thing would be to close your eyes on it and forget it. But — " He stopped abruptly, and added as an afterthought: "This matter can gain all of us something and Gern might be given a rap over the knuckles at the same time. Gern must have read the sovereign's resolution on Shevchenko's case many a time and reported it to Obruchev no less frequently. Gern and Obruchev were the first to flout the czar's will by assigning Shevchenko to the Aral expedition as an artist. Even now they flout it systematically, openly and brazenly. If the sovereign were to learn how his orders are complied with in Orenburg, the skin would be flying off Gern and Obruchev's backs in strips and pieces. Truth is, Shevchenko would suffer, too, regrettably, for he's a talented artist. But for us he's no more than a soldier who must do his soldier's duty, instead of loafing about the Orenburg parlors. And when Nikolai Grigorievich" — the general turned to Isaiev — "submits a report to Obruchev on Gern, and on Obruchev, too, by the way, the general will have to reprimand his subordinate in the strictest terms. In this way we'll make them remember Easter Day as the blackest event they ever experienced in their lifetime. And if Nikolai Grigorievich sends a similar report to Count Orlov, I can wager a hundred thousand rubles that the general's monograms will be stripped off his epaulettes, and eventually he'll lose his office of military governor. Then we'll have Perovsky back again."

"But what about Gern?" Isaiev cut in, unable to restrain his vengefulness.

"For Gern a duel will be the farthest thing on his mind then! He, too, will lose his aide's aiguilettes and his officer's uniform perhaps. That seafaring 'scientist' Butakov will also get his share of punishment, and no albums of colored charts will save him from falling into disgrace."

"Wonderful!"

"Accept our warmest gratitude for the advice!" Mansurov and Isaiev said, passionately shaking the general's hand. Tolmachov smiled contentedly into his mustache.

"I congratulate you, gentlemen, on a great victory," he replied cheerfully. "At last we have found a weak point in the liberals. Now they're in our hands."

"A thousand times *merci*." Isaiev said, clicking his heels. "So the only thing left is to write the report."

"And as quickly as possible, so it will be submitted tomorrow morning," Tolmachov added. "Its effect will be stunning."

To write a usual brief report had always been a difficult task for Isaiev. He was constantly at odds with his grammar, the simplest thought did not materialize on paper, hard as he tried, but instantly became as heavy as blocks of granite, and words and phrases were repeated innumerably on the same page.

But now he had to write not a brief report, but an entire serious delation to be read by Obruchev and the chief of the gendarmes, and probably even by the czar himself. The ensign broke into a sweat, and no sooner had he collected his petty thoughts than the clock struck three and the headquarters became deserted. The first to disappear were the officers, then the clerks closed up their desks and melted away imperceptibly like ice in the sun, while Isaiev was still sitting over his delation, helplessly gnawing at his pen and tearing up what he had written again and again.

"Your Excellency, the officers left for dinner a long time ago. It's impossible to do everything. You'd better go and have a rest," the clerk on duty addressed him. "Besides, the floor must be mopped and the office cleaned up for the holidays."

Isaiev started like a crook who had been caught red-handed, swept his writing off the desk with a jerky hand, and looked at the clerk.

"Indeed, it's time to go home," he said, regaining his self-control, shoved the paper into his pocket, and sadly trudged off to Mansurov again with a sense of stark fear: he might come across Gern on the street.

Mansurov read what Isaiev had written, and threw the paper onto his desk.

"What a fool you are — a straight-laced fool!" he blurted out. "Whoever writes delations like that? 'I have the honor to report to your Excellency that the artist Shevchenko, who painted my portrait and the portrait of your Excellency's wife as well as the portrait of Baroness Blaramberg and of many others, is an exiled soldier, and according to the orders of His Majesty the Emperor, he has to be in the barracks and not writing and painting.' He knows that well enough himself! In the word *honor*, the last vowel is an *o*, not an *e*, *portrait* is written with an *ai*, not an *ei*. Oh, you wretched scholar!"

"But I was in a hurry, and so excited. Correct spelling just wasn't on my mind. It's already five o'clock now, everyone's gone home long ago," Isaiev tried to justify himself. "Be a friend, Serge, and help me! The pen's slipping out of my fingers at the thought that the sovereign might read my report."

"All right! The hell with you! I'll help, not so much for your sake as because of Obruchev sitting on our necks. I'll never be a lieutenant-colonel to the end of my days under his rule," Mansurov snapped out with determination.

He wrote for over an hour, now crossing out entire phrases, then adding something to what he had written. In the end, he leaned back in the armchair with an air of satisfaction, and started reading his delation* aloud:

"On an impulse of fervent loyalty to my sovereign and country, I, Ensign Isaiev Nikolai Grigorievich, consider it my duty and a matter of honor and conscientiousness to bring to the notice of your Excellency that your aide Gern Karl Ivanovich, Captain-Lieutenant of the Navy Butakov Alexei Ivanovich, and other authorities of the Orenburg County have, probably by ignorance, outrageously trampled upon and gone against the will of our most August Monarch, expressed in the resolution on Private Shevchenko ratified with the hand of His Imperial Highness to

---

* The original of the delation has not come down to us, so the author takes the liberty of reproducing its probable substance. — *Zinaïda Tulub*

the effect that the said artist and writer be made a soldier and dispatched under the strictest surveillance of the authorities, with the prohibition to write and to paint, to the Orenburg Territory to do military service there and, in accordance with the instructions of the Third Department of the Personal Office of His Imperial Highness, the said Shevchenko was to be posted to one of the farthest forts of the Orenburg line.

"At the present time, however, Shevchenko is registered as an artist on the descriptive expedition of the Aral Sea which finished its work long ago, resides in Orenburg at the home of the aforementioned Gern Karl Ivanovich, an aide responsible for special missions of your Excellency, goes about town in civilian clothes, is received in the highest society without formality, and paints the portraits of highly respected persons, including the governor's wife, thereby earning his living, which I have the honor to bring to the notice of your Excellency in order that respective measures be taken and all those guilty in this violation of the monarchic will be properly punished."

Mansurov finished reading this vile sample of his writing, having savored every single word of it, then he clacked his tongue contentedly, and motioned Isaiev to an armchair near the desk.

"Sit down and write two copies of it. One goes to Obruchev, and the other to St. Petersburg to the Third Department and Count Orlov. Copy it carefully, and mind you don't make any mistakes," he added, putting two pages of the best paper in front of Isaiev.

Isaiev was busy almost till midnight, copying the delation. In the morning he did not go to the headquarters, but sent his batman to the post office to mail two registered letters. During the midday meal he emptied a bottle of vodka and retired to bed at once.

Gern was not on speaking terms with his wife and did not notice her presence. He had slept the night on the sofa in his study and woke up with a headache, but after a cup of strong coffee he forced himself to get dressed and looking as smart as ever, he appeared at the headquarters promptly on the hour.

His morning passed in looking through the classified special delivery mail, then he busied himself writing a report to Obruchev, went through the list of participants in the holiday parade for a long time before he secured Tolmachov's final approval, and only by midday did he get down to routine matters and the usual everyday mail. The sizable pile of letters, complaints, and packages gradually melted in front of him. He opened the letters quickly, read them through, made the necessary notes on each, put some aside to be reported to Obruchev separately, and then picked up the next package.

The last in the pile was a letter postmarked *Local Mail*. He tore it open, pulled out the stiff sheets of paper neatly folded in four, and started reading. The blood rushed to his head.

"What a villain! What filthy vermin!" he whispered.

Yes, Isaiev had written it. It was really his crabbed handwriting, but the sinister logic and malice of the delation was not his. Somebody else had composed it with the spiteful mentality of a gendarme. Isaiev could have never hit upon the idea himself, and the proof of it was the fact that he was the first to have his portrait painted by Shevchenko which he passed over in silence in the delation. He was simply used as a tool. The venomous delation was directed not so much against Shevchenko as against Obruchev, Gern and Butakov.

"What baseness," Gern said through set teeth. "But what scoundrel stands behind it? Could it be the doing of Perovsky's people?"

Gern went up the inner spiral stairway to the first floor to see Obruchev in his private apartments.

"Now, here you are at last, my dear fellow!" the general greeted him. "Would you please inquire whether the invitations for the post-Lent banquet have been sent out to everyone?"

"Yes, sir!" Gern replied mechanically. "But permit me first of all to present this sample of unparalleled villainy," Gern added, putting Isaiev's delation on the desk.

Obruchev shot a surprised glance at Gern, put on his glasses and started reading. With every line he read his face turned alternately pale, brick-red, covered with blotches and profuse beads of sweat.

"What a scoundrel! Oh my God, what an out-and-out blackguard!" the general muttered again and again. "What a dirty, base soul. But I cannot leave the delation without considering it."

"No, you cannot," Gern confirmed. "The question has been put all too dangerously and basely."

"You believe so, too? So what do you think must be done then?"

"First of all, a search must be made at Shevchenko's quarters, but he must be warned to destroy or hide his manuscripts, if he has any correspondence and drawings. If the search does not produce anything and Isaiev hasn't written to the Third Department, the matter might be hushed up somehow. But the tenor of the delation is too brazen and malicious. It is fraught with serious consequences. So maybe... It's a pity the post office is closed, for I could have found out... The matter must he postponed for consideration after the holidays."

"Yes, yes, of course," Obruchev said, agitated. "Please make the proper arrangements, dear Karl Ivanovich. One more thing: send that villain an invitation to the banquet. Of all the things I had to live to see! I'd have spit at him, and here I must shake his hand and invite him."

And suddenly, his voice breaking into a thin falsetto, he cried out:

"Oh no, I won't endure it! In this case you have to be a rock, without pity or respect for anyone or anything decent! Poor wretch Shevchenko! What a bitter fate for such a talent."

"Calm down, for God's sake! If the search does not produce anything, it will neutralize the delation by half."

"Yes, yes! You are right! Act and do it in a hurry. Call other officers for help."

"No, I'll do it myself," Gern said with determination and quickly left the study. Back in his office, he locked the mail in a drawer and made for the door.

"Get me a horse!" he called to the orderly on duty.

A saddled horse stood always at the ready in the headquarters stable for urgent occasions. The orderly arrived at a run, leading the horse, and Gern galloped off to his home.

A padlock hung on the door of the outhouse.

"Where's Shevchenko?" Gern asked Guriy.

"I don't know. He hasn't returned since he left yesterday," Guriy replied, looking at "his captain" with alarm and pity. "You should eat something, your Excellency. Otherwise you'll get weak and catch some illness in no time. I'll have a meal served at once."

It was only now Gern felt how hungry he really was. He took off his greatcoat, greedily gulped down the thoughtfully served cutlet and a cup of strong coffee with cream, and made to leave immediately.

"If Taras Grigorievich shows up, tell him not to go anywhere, and serve his meal at his studio. Tell him I need him on urgent and extraordinarily important business. I'll be back soon," he added and mounted his horse.

At the headquarters Gern wrote a letter to the gendarmerie colonel, requesting that the order of a search at the quarters of Private Shevchenko be issued to clear up whether the latter was writing poetry and painting in defiance of the "Most August" will, and then ho called the clerk on duty.

"When are you relieved, dear chap?" Gern asked him.

"At nine in the evening, your Excellency."

"Well, after you are relieved deliver this letter to the gendarmerie colonel and make him sign for it," Gern ordered, went outdoors, called a coach, and made off to Lazarevsky's.

The venom of Isaiev's delation did not go to Obruchov's entire system at once.

At first he flung snatches of abuse and contempt against the scandalmonger Isaiev, pitying Shevchenko in the process, but when Gern had left and he read through the delation a second time, he realized with full clarity that the edge of the delation's message was directed not against the artist, but against himself.

"Oh, what an abhorrent snake!" he cried out shrilly. Slightly opening the door of the large banquet hall, where, under the management of Mathilda Petrovna, four lackeys were laying the huge tables for the banquet to break the fast, he called her in a voice he himself did not recognize:

"Mathilda, come here! Quickly!"

"What is the matter?" she asked on entering. "Why are you shouting like that! People might think God knows what "

"It's horrible! Simply incredible!" Obruchev exclaimed, not listening to her. "That scoundrel Isaiev informed on us that we permitted Shevchenko to write and to paint in defiance of the emperor's will. Do you understand what that smacks of? Even your portrait was dragged into the delation!"

"What delation?" she asked, surprised. "And what has my portrait to do with it?"

"I told Butakov that Shevchenko was forbidden to write and to paint, but the captain insisted and kept persuading me: 'For the needs of the state and for science even convicts, let alone exiles, can be used.' So I went and took pity on the poor wretch, and now it spells my destruction! You know how rancorous our sovereign is! It's just enough for a report to reach Orlov — and that will be the end of my career! Everything will go to rack and ruin. And there is no one to stand up for me!" Obruchev cried hysterically, clutching his head.

"God forbid, Voldemar!" Mathilda Petrovna tried to calm him down. "Everything will work itself out somehow."

But it only made Obruchev the more agitated.

"I have no protectors among the higher-ups!" he shouted. "I am a little man who's paved his own way in life! I'm not an aristocrat with influential aunts or noble relatives! That's what being kind and pitying people can lead to! Enough of that. I'll bring him back to the barracks! Into prison with him! I've got children, a family! I just can't play with their future!"

"Hush! Hush! For God's sake, hush!" Mathilda Petrovna implored him.

She gave him tincture of valerian to drink, offered him smelling salts, but Obruchev would not calm down for a long time and kept repeating with a ring of despair in his voice:

"In our day it's impossible to be a human being! You have to be a rock! An animal! An executioner! Oh my God, whatever will happen to me now? What will happen?"

By midday all the offices were closed, and the clerks had left. Lazarevsky, too, hurried to his quarters. After the midday meal Shevchenko took to painting again. The work progressed easily and quickly — he sensed with joy that the portrait was coming out well, not only because it represented the sitter's likeness so well; it was painted with feeling and emanated the warmth of his relationship with his young friend.

After working for over an hour, he made a last daub, and put the palette on the windowsill.

"Enough," he said to Lazarevsky. "Otherwise I might spoil it unexpectedly. In the twilight of your life you'll look at the portrait, recall our friendship and say a kindly word about your Kobzar."

Lazarevsky silently put his arm around Shevchenko's shoulder.

The friends started to prepare for matins and the solemn breaking of the fast. Lazarevsky was invited to the Obruchevs, and Shevchenko to Madame Kutina, the landlady. A look in the mirror prompted him to visit the barber's in the neighborhood. Lazarevsky was changing when a coach stopped at the porch and Gern entered his room almost at a run.

"Where is Shevchenko?" he asked, without greeting.

"He's preparing to go on a visit and went to the barber's around the corner," Lazarevsky replied sensing something ominous.

"For God's sake, call him quickly and tell him to go to my home on the double. He's been denounced to Obruchev, and there'll be a search at his studio today. Burn everything that might bring him any harm: destroy all traces of poetry, drawings, letters, and hide the most valuable things in a reliable place. And I beg of you to make it really fast: every minute is precious."

"Be seated please, and I'll call him right away," Lazarevsky said, going off into a hustle.

But Gern was in a hurry himself and, after saying goodbye, he added to the confused young man:

"Tell him to use my coach. Every minute is precious."

Lazarevsky ran off to the barber's, looked inside, but Shevchenko was already gone. He returned home at a trot, entered the kitchen and called Shevchenko who was pressing the trousers of his new frock coat just then.

"We've got to go to your studio: it'll be searched tonight. You've been denounced to Obruchev."

"The vermin's seeking revenge," the poet remarked with a smile, and went outdoors.

Shevchenko and Lazarevsky reached his studio by coach in fifteen minutes. He dumped a suitcase of various papers onto the table, and asked ironically:

"Well, what do we burn of this lot?"

In the meantime, Guriy had brought firewood and kindled the stove, Lazarevsky started looking through the mail.

"I don't know myself. Gern mentioned drawings and manuscripts. Well, and what about the rest?"

"Burn Varvara Repnina's letters. Orlov threatened her with arrest for corresponding with me," Shevchenko said with determination and tossed a bundle of her letters he cherished so much into the stove.

Following Repnina's letters, the portraits of Gern and his wife were consigned to the flames, as were dozens of sketches of the Aral Sea and its coastal cliffs, and Lizohub's letters.

"Maybe we should leave something?" Lazarevsky asked once again.

To which Shevchenko replied one and the same thing: "Burn!"

"Listen, Taras," Lazarevsky stopped him at last. 'If we burn everything, they'll realize that you've been warned of the search and the suspicion will fall on Karl Ivanovich. He's the only person who could have known about the search at all. Something has to be left behind as bait for the gendarmes."

"You're right," Shevchenko agreed. "Enough of the burning. Let's go to your quarters now. We'll have to destroy something there, too."

They checked once more to see whether any rough copy of a poem or a drawing was left, and were about to leave when Shevchenko decided to stay at the last moment.

"Go home yourself. Hide your portrait, and everything you've got in your writing desk throw into the flames to the last scrap. Here, take my bootleg books. Keep them as the apple of your eye until better times. I have to meet my 'guests' openly. Besides. I'll have to clean up: look what a mess we left. It's the eve of Easter Day, after all, and every home has been cleaned for the occasion."

Lazarevsky did not argue. Shevchenko saw him to the coach, embraced him strongly, and the coach rolled away.

At the Sakmar Gate a coach with the chief of police, the parade-ground aide Martinov, and a gendarme colonel came driving on their way.

They're after Taras, Lazarevsky thought and a chill ran down his spine.

Shevchenko put the suitcase under the table, arranged his personal belongings in order, glad to have left his oil paints at Lazarevsky's quarters, swept up the floor, quickly pulled on a new shirt, dressed in his holiday frock coat, put on a tie and cuff links as if he were really prepared to go to a party, and that moment he heard the coach rolling up, heavy footfalls, and the jangle of spurs. Someone pulled the unlocked door open, thumped in the little entrance hall with heavy boots and the gendarme colonel entered the room, followed by the chief of police and the parade-ground aide. Two policemen took up position at either side of the door.

"You're under arrest!" the colonel said rudely to Shevchenko, and ordered the policemen: "Search the quarters!"

One of them rushed to the other room, where a candle was also burning, and started rummaging in the bed. The other lit a candle and went into the kitchen, while the colonel and the chief of police dumped onto the table the contents of the suitcase which held only one quarter of what had been in it before, and started reading the letters that had been left as bait for the searchers. They leafed through the books and old newspapers in search or marginal marks. Martinov did not take any part in the search. Wearing a full dress uniform he sat in an armchair by the window. His face had an expression of contemptuous boredom, as he lazily pulled on a cigarette and glanced quizzically at Shevchenko.

The poet stood silently near the table; he was outwardly calm, though his face was a little paler than usual and his blue eyes seemed to have turned completely black. He had expected an ordinary search of the type practiced in the barracks in the presence of the battalion officers of the day and two noncoms, but the appearance of a gendarme colonel overwhelmed him and told him everything. Here was a much more complicated case. It was not simply the consequence of a delation written by a vengeful ensign whose information could be easily turned against him, since he had been the first to have his portrait painted and recommended others to avail themselves of the artist's services. Either something had happened with the Polish circle or Isaiev had sent his delation to the capital. That would bring Shevchenko back to Orsk to the barracks and drill.

His thoughts thrashed like mice in a trap, as in his mind he chose the proper replied to the possible interrogation. The desire to evade a new blow of fate and not tumble into the trou-de-loup along his path to freedom grew with mounting force from the bottom of his heart.

The searched lasted a long time. It became unbearably hot in the room. A cloud of cigarette smoke hung under the ceiling. The stove gave off a stifling heat that made the corpulent colonel busy wiping the sweat off his clean-shaved head with a handkerchief. He unbuttoned the collar of his uniform, and then Martinov went over to the window and flung it open.

The room was invaded by the fragrant cool of the spring night, mixed with the fragrance of resinous aspen buds and blooming bide cherry. A young nightingale was timidly trying to burst into song under a pitch-black sky studded with flickering stars.

And suddenly this fragrance-laden, fresh silence was rent by the boisterous, dissonant toll of Easter bells. Shevchenko straightened up, while the colonel rose to his feet.

"We've been here too long. Griniuk! Sevastianov! Put all the papers into a sack. We'll look into them back at the station," he added, selecting two or three letters from the bundle and shoving them into his pocket. "Don't be late for the banquet, gentlemen. They say the Obruchevs are serving some special pâté of duck liver."

Then he stepped up to Martinov and threw out his arms to embrace and kiss him by Greek Orthodox custom

"Christ has risen. Accept my best wishes!"

The gesture made Martinov recoil, and he looked in Shevchenko's direction.

"*Aprés! Et pas ici*,*" the muttered through set teeth and withdrew to the window, through which he flicked his glowing cigarette butt into the night.

The chief of police and the colonel were hurriedly buttoning up their greatcoats when a weird sound made them turn round abruptly: Shevchenko was gazing into the night and shaking all over in a fit of angry and wild laughter.

February 1959 — October 1962

---

* *Aprés! Et pas ici.* — Later! And not here. (Fr.)

GLOSSARY OF KAZAKH WORDS USED IN THE BOOK

A

Aga, lit. elder brother; form of respectable address to an elderly person

Agach, tree

Airan, a drink prepared from fermented milk

Ait (n.), religious festival; (exel.) Sick him!

Ak, white

Akyn, folk singer, poet-improviser

A man (interj.), Help! Have mercy!

Amengerka, wife or bride-to-be which after the death of her husband or fiancé passes on to his brothers or next of kin as inheritance *Apa*, mother

Aral, island.

Aral Teniz (sea with islands), Aral Sea

Argamak, thoroughbred horse

Askar, soldier (infantryman)

Ata, father

Aul, village or nomad camp

Aulia, saint, holy man

Axakal, white-bearded, old man. The Muslims are permitted to wear beards from 60 year's on; those with black beards are called *karasakals*, with white beards, *axakals*

Azan, call for prayer cried out by a muezzin from the minaret of a mosque

B

Bai, rich landowner who, apart from servants, herds and cattle, had at times his own armed guard or retinue

Baibishe, senior wife in a polygamous marriage

Baiga, horse race

Baigash, beggar

Batyr, a brave, hero

Barimta, armed raid on a cattle herd or *aul* for plunder

Bishbarmak, cooked mutton

C

Chapan, a man's or woman's ankle-length coat like garment with long sleeves, mostly of wool, sometimes of silk 'or velvet

D

Djelomiyka (jolim ul), light summer yurt

J

Jailiaou, summer alpine pasture

Jamba, bar of silver or gold used as a target in archery competitions during a *toi*

Jalak, a hopelessly poor nomad who owned no cattle

Jigit, a young man, brave warrior

Joktau, funeral lament, dirge

Jut, glazed frost

K

Kade, a bridegroom's wedding present for his bride

Kal bopali, words used to call tamed eagles

Kamcha, whip

Kara, black

Karligach, swallow

Kerege, lattice framework of a yurt, over which thick felt *(koshma)* is stretched

Ketmen, a kind of hoe

Kistau, winter pasture

Kshi apa, the youngest mother; the children of the elder wives called thus the youngest wife of their father

Kulash, a unit of length of about one and a half meters (the distance between the fingertips of a man's outspread hands)

Kyit, a present which the bride's parents gave to their future son-in-law and his parents on the day of engagement

M

Malakliai, man's cap of fur or felt

Manty, largo steamed dumplings with mutton filling

N

Nuker, member of the retinue of a *bai*, khan, sultan, or any other dignitary

S

Saba, kumiss-skin

Saukele, tall fur cap of a bride, embroidered with silver or gold thread

Shakpar, war club with a thick, sometimes spiked, end

Shangarak, top hole in a yurt, which serves as a vent for the fire and is covered, if necessary with a *tunduk*

Soyil, a sword with a long shaft instead of a hilt

Suuk Tiube, (lit. cold hill), a hill between the present cities of Alma-Ata and Frunze

T

Tamga, the coat of arms of a kin

Toi, a three-day family holiday held on the occasion of a significant event (the birth of a child, a wedding, and the like)

Tomaga, head cap for a golden eagle or falcon, embroidered with gold thread or beads and owl feather

Tugir, a tripod perch for a golden eagle in a yurt

Tunduk, a piece of felt to cover the top hole in a yurt

Tyulengut, bodyguard of a khan or rich *bai*. The *tyulenguts* were mostly descendants of slaves, or the poorest members of a kin

Y

Yassak, a tax the authorities of czarist Russia levied on the Kazakh people

Z

Zakat, an annual alms tax that each Muslim is expected to pay to be used for charitable or religious purposes

Dear Reader,

Thank you for purchasing this book.

We at Glagoslav Publications are glad to welcome you, and hope that you find our books a source of knowledge and inspiration.

We want to show the beauty and depth of the Slavic region to everyone looking to expand their horizons and learn something new about different cultures, different people, and we believe that with this book we have managed to do just that.

Now that you've got to know us, we want to get to know you. We value communication with our readers and want to hear from you!

We offer several options:

- Join our Book Club on Goodreads, Library Thing and Shelfari, and receive special offers and information about our giveaways;

- Share your opinion about our books on Amazon, Barnes & Noble, Waterstones and other bookstores;

- Join us on Facebook and Twitter for updates on our publications and news about our authors;

- Visit our site www.glagoslav.com to check out our Catalogue and subscribe to our Newsletter.

Glagoslav Publications is getting ready to release a new collection and planning some interesting surprises — stay with us to find out!

Glagoslav Publications
Office 36, 88-90 Hatton Garden
EC1N 8PN London, UK
Tel: + 44 (0) 20 32 86 99 82
Email: contact@glagoslav.com

Glagoslav Publications Catalogue

- *The Time of Women* by Elena Chizhova
- *Sin* by Zakhar Prilepin
- *Hardly Ever Otherwise* by Maria Matios
- *The Lost Button* by Irene Rozdobudko
- *Khatyn* by Ales Adamovich
- *Christened with Crosses* by Eduard Kochergin
- *The Vital Needs of the Dead* by Igor Sakhnovsky
- *A Poet and Bin Laden* by Hamid Ismailov
- *Kobzar* by Taras Shevchenko
- *White Shanghai* by Elvira Baryakina
- *The Stone Bridge* by Alexander Terekhov
- *King Stakh's Wild Hunt* by Uladzimir Karatkevich
- *Depeche Mode* by Serhii Zhadan
- *Saraband Sarah's Band* by Larysa Denysenko
- *Herstories*, An Anthology of New Ukrainian Women Prose Writers
- *The Hawks of Peace* by Dmitry Rogozin
  by Leonid Andreev
- *The Battle of the Sexes Russian Style* by Nadezhda Ptushkina
- *A Book Without Photographs* by Sergey Shargunov
- *Sankya* by Zakhar Prilepin
- *Wolf Messing - The True Story of Russia's Greatest Psychic* by Tatiana Lungin
- *Good Stalin* by Victor Erofeyev
- *Solar Plexus* by Rustam Ibragimbekov
- *Don't Call me a Victim!* by Dina Yafasova
- *A History of Belarus* by Lubov Bazan
- *Children's Fashion of the Russian Empire* by Alexander Vasiliev
- *Empire of Corruption - The Russian National Pastime* by Vladimir Soloviev
- *Heroes of the 90s - People and Money. The Modern History of Russian Capitalism*
- *Boris Yeltsin - The Decade that Shook the World* by Boris Minaev
- *A Man Of Change - A study of the political life of Boris Yeltsin*
- *Gnedich* by Maria Rybakova

More coming soon…

www.ingramcontent.com/pod-product-compliance
Lightning Source LLC
Chambersburg PA
CBHW020859080526
44589CB00011B/361